Anton Chekhov
Through the Eyes of Russian Thinkers

Anton Chekhov Through the Eyes of Russian Thinkers

Vasilii Rozanov, Dmitrii Merezhkovskii and Lev Shestov

Edited by
Olga Tabachnikova

Translated by
Olga Tabachnikova and Adam Ure

Translation Editor:
Adam Ure

ANTHEM PRESS
LONDON · NEW YORK · DELHI

Anthem Press
An imprint of Wimbledon Publishing Company
www.anthempress.com

This edition first published in UK and USA 2012
by ANTHEM PRESS
75-76 Blackfriars Road, London SE1 8HA, UK
or PO Box 9779, London SW19 7ZG, UK
and
244 Madison Ave. #116, New York, NY 10016, USA

First published in hardback by Anthem Press in 2010

© 2012 Olga Tabachnikova editorial matter and selection;
individual chapters © individual contributors

The moral right of the authors has been asserted.

All rights reserved. Without limiting the rights under copyright reserved above,
no part of this publication may be reproduced, stored or introduced into
a retrieval system, or transmitted, in any form or by any means
(electronic, mechanical, photocopying, recording or otherwise),
without the prior written permission of both the copyright
owner and the above publisher of this book.

British Library Cataloguing in Publication Data
A catalogue record for this book is available from the British Library.

Library of Congress Cataloging in Publication Data
A catalog record for this book has been requested.

ISBN-13: 978 0 85728 574 4 (Pbk)
ISBN-10: 0 85728 574 2 (Pbk)

This title is also available as an eBook.

This book is dedicated to the memory of two of its contributors:
Aleksandr Pavlovich Chudakov (1938–2005)
and Anna Lisa Crone (1946–2009)

CONTENTS

Acknowledgments	ix
Introduction	xi
List of Names	xxxi
List of Russian Cultural Concepts	xlix
Three Brief Biographies – Rozanov, Merezhkovskii and Shestov	liii

Part One: Vasilii Rozanov   1

1. Rozanov on Chekhov: 'Overcoming Literature' and Extending Horizons   3
  Vladimir B. Kataev

2. Kind and Quiet: Vasilii Rozanov's Reading of Chekhov   13
  Aleksandr Medvedev

3. Contemporaneity, Competition and Combat. Facts and Fictions about Everybody and Passiveness, Orientalism and Anaesthesia in Rozanov's View on Chekhov   37
  Rainer Grübel

4. 'Tree of Life' and 'Dead Waters': Why was Rozanov Afraid of Chekhov?   63
  Michal Oklot

Part Two: Dmitrii Merezhkovskii   91

5. Chekhov and Merezhkovskii: Two Types of Artistic-Philosophical Consciousness   93
  Aleksandr Chudakov

6. Negating His Own Negation: Merezhkovskii's
   Understanding of Chekhov's Role in Russian Culture   113
   Anna Lisa Crone

7. An Illuminating Misinterpretation? On Merezhkovskii's
   Literary Criticism of Chekhov   129
   Karoline Thaidigsmann

8. Can Merezhkovskii See the Spirit in the Prose of Flesh? 141
   Vladimir Golstein

Part Three: Lev Shestov   167
9. Lev Shestov on Chekhov   169
   Andrei Stepanov

10. Between Tragedy and Aesthetics: Shestov's
    Reading of Chekhov – a Gaze Directed Within   175
    Olga Tabachnikova

11. Shestov–Chekhov, Chekhov–Shestov   199
    Savely Senderovich

12. Philosophy's Enemies: Chekhov and Shestov   219
    Svetlana Evdokimova

    Notes on Contributors   247

ACKNOWLEDGMENTS

It has been a long journey – from conceiving the idea of this book to its completion. Various people have been indispensable in bringing this project to fruition. My first word of gratitude goes to the translation editor and a fellow translator of this volume, Adam Ure, whose prompt, efficient and enthusiastic participation transformed raw material into a final typescript. I would also like to thank Rosie Davies and Claire Arianwen Jewkes, who assisted with proofreading in the initial stages. I would hardly have gathered such a splendid team of authors without helpful advice from various Chekhov scholars worldwide – Harai Golomb, Gordon McVay, Emma Polotskaia and others. Marietta Chudakova kindly permitted us to publish a translation into English of her late husband's article. Radislav Lapushin helped in more than one way – with unceasing encouragement, professional advice and by putting final editorial touches to the chapter of his former supervisor – Anna Lisa Crone – who did not live to see the book published. As will be clear to any experienced reader, without the two contributions by these distinguished scholars, Chudakov and Crone, to whose memory this volume is dedicated, the collection would have been much diminished. Finally, I wish to thank all the contributors to this book for their exciting, thought-provoking chapters, as well as friendly co-operation and patience. I hope they will enjoy the final result of our team effort as much as I do.

As the editor, I hereby gratefully acknowledge the Early Career Fellowship Grant from the Leverhulme Trust, UK, which enabled me to bring this research project to completion.

On a different note, I also wish to thank my father, Mark Tabachnikov, for being a constant source of inspiration – with regard to Chekhov, and for that matter – to most things in life. Very few of us can boast of having had a spiritual kin, a perfect interlocutor. I can. So: to my father who is like no one else…

INTRODUCTION

'Introduction is too strict a frame for being able to contain a substantial literary material'
            Lev Shestov, *Dostoevsky and Nietzsche*

'Save me God from dryness, whereas a warm word [...] will not spoil the publication. [...] Lord, stir me away from commonplaces'
          Anton Chekhov, *from private correspondence*

'Nothing in the twentieth century could foreshadow the emergence of a poet like Brodsky' is perhaps the strangest statement by the great Czeslaw Milosz. Instead, everything in the twentieth century could be seen as having foreshadowed Brodsky's coming. It was inevitable as a most natural existential and linguistic response to the alienating absurdity and sophisticated cruelty of that century. By the same token, everything in the nineteenth century Russia could be seen as having foreshadowed the coming of Anton Chekhov. He was, if you like, a historical necessity. In the disenchanted generation, suspended between 'extreme materialism and most passionate idealistic strivings of the spirit',[1] at the time when populism and utilitarianism, although on their last legs, still dominated both life and art, someone who could walk the border without taking sides, who could 'rise above' and find a different route, was desperately needed. As Chekhov himself said about the traveller Przhevalskii: 'In our ill age, when European societies are swamped with laziness, boredom and faithlessness, when in a strange combination a dislike for life coexists with a fear of death, [...] we need devotees like we need the sun'.[2] Chekhov was one of these devotees.

 It was a time when 'Nietzsche exclaim[ed] "God is dead" – a sentence which means that no spiritual unity remains alive in society, so that men will be entitled from now on to try everything. [...] Christianity [was] no longer a universal evidence, [...] terrible wars [were] at hand, Freud [was] born... – and, simultaneously, some rather obscure symbolist poets decide[d] to break up prosody'.[3] Disintegration is always difficult, time going out-of-joint leaves invalids behind; the era of the social, of the collective, of the general, the time of meaningfulness had ended. The new era – of individualism, of meaninglessness, 'of psychology' – was dawning. Someone had to provide continuity. Chekhov bridged the gap, stepping decisively on the new ground, while remaining steeped in the old values.

On the other hand, he was simply an individual of complete inner freedom – of independence to such a degree that occurs very rarely, and regardless of the epoch. He was least of all concerned with whatever historical mission he might fulfil. He would be very surprised to find out that more than a century later the world is braced to celebrate 150 years of his birth, that his plays are still staged all around the globe, giving way in popularity only to Shakespeare. At the same time, Chekhov still remains one of the most elusive, un-deciphered, and even misinterpreted writers. Attempts to pin him down end up, more often than not, with attempts to inscribe him to the respective agendas of those who write about him.

This book has been conceived in the context of this perpetual challenge. For it seems that the key to Chekhov's pluralistic world is in a multiplicity of voices, in a polyphony of interpretations; especially if one uses, as it were, a double mirror which reflects a reflection: evaluating with our modern eyes the treatment of the writer by his distinguished readers, such as those listed in the title. Vasilii Rozanov, Dmitrii Merezhkovskii and Lev Shestov were Chekhov's contemporaries, who outlived him by a number of years, having plunged deeper than he into the new cultural phase which received the name of the Russian Silver Age. But before we discuss the actors, we shall describe the stage. That is to say, we shall linger more over the chronological background that unites the three Russian thinkers in question.

It was the last wave of cultural heat before the frost of *bezvremen'e* which descended soon onto post-revolutionary Russia. If one accepts Yuri Lotman's characterizations of Turgenev's oeuvre as demythologizing and subversive, as a meeting place of the meaningful with meaningless,[4] one can see how this might have laid the foundations of the line developed by Chekhov – where the meaningless takes the upper hand and encroaches ruthlessly upon the domain of the meaningful. No longer does the Antichrist or Saviour come from outside – 'hell is within us' becomes the dominant sentiment. And if the Silver Age can be regarded as a bridging phase between old and new, between the nineteenth century – the 'century of seeing, not glimpsing; of responsibility, not the incoherence of guilt', when the 'scale of reality was quantitatively human' – and the twentieth, when owing to its supersonic speeds it became 'difficult to comprehend wounded honour, the grid of class barriers, someone's brooding over a ruined estate, the contemplation of a single tree, or ambivalence at prayer',[5] then Chekhov can be viewed equally – as a bridging writer.

It was a strange fusion of opposing strivings, with a distinct expectation of major (and imminent) changes. The mystical mood and renewed religious search co-existed (and often in a dialectic relationship) with the opposite enthusiasm – for Darwinism and Marxism, with the general socialist-utopian ideas derived from a simplistic view of art and utilitarian denial of aesthetics. Akhmatova's apt description of the Silver Age and the everyday reality of the Russian artistic intelligentsia as 'a terrible celebration of dead foliage' (*strashnyi prazdnik mertvoi listvy*) betrays that elusive mood of the last carnivalesque and lawless freedom, in anticipation of a catastrophe, and her famous 'We are all revellers here, fornicatresses' (*Vse my brazhniki zdes', bludnitsy*) only seals this in a tangibly personal way.

Chekhov felt what was coming; perhaps not in historical, but more in metaphysical terms. In Bitov's words, 'he felt with his skin, like that Japanese fish which predicts earthquakes, what the twentieth century will bring to Russia'.[6] He did a lot to resist the perverse elements of the New Age, to prevent their deadly triumph, but quietly, from within, rather than in Tolstoyan, more theatrical and patriarchal manner. The topic of Chekhov's relationship with the Silver Age still remains complex and largely under-researched.[7] Contemporary critical literature on him was as rich and plentiful during the Silver Age as during his lifetime, and by and large as distorting (despite the fact that the new – Modernist – generation propagated more sophisticated views on literature than their simplistic predecessors). Starting with the gloomy predictions of Aleksandr Skabichevskii of 1886, of Chekhov's doomed fate (a young talent who will die forsaken in a ditch) and Nikolai Mikhailovskii's lamentation (1890) which followed an earlier article by Roman Disterlo, a critic in *Nedelia*, about the writer's lack of ideals, the label of a passive, morose and subdued singer of the weak and hopeless, the image of a tubercular Muse, of the 'voice of twilight Russia' became a routine part of critical writings on Chekhov. His questions without answers disturbed his contemporaries, who were used to clarity of direction, or in any case were used to craving it. Thus the urge to 'finish Chekhov's narrative' was invariably pressing. Some, like Aikhenval'd, Al' bov or Eikhenbaum, saw Chekhov as searching for ideals, longing for the sublime, for the general idea, and perceived his message as supremely compassionate; others, like Mikhailovskii, Liatskii or Volzhskii, on the other hand, denied him any ideals whatsoever, and talked of his cynicism, cold-bloodiness and indifference. Interestingly, every camp would ultimately appropriate Chekhov. Moreover, the whole of Russia would increasingly appropriate him.

Indeed, as M. A. Murinia observes, quoting Vasilii Rozanov,[8] having Chekhov's portraits in every household of the Russian intelligentsia was a symbol of a particular mentality, of a kinship of the soul, and thus became an intrinsic sign of the epoch. Not knowing his work was considered disgraceful in the public opinion. Chekhov's text expanded its boundaries, bursting into the empirical reality. A publication of his letters in 1912–16 was a revelation which significantly contributed to the rethinking of his legacy. 'A poet of all of us' (A. V. Amfiteatrov); 'In Chekhov Russia fell in love with itself' (V. Rozanov) are just a few expressions of that time which demonstrate the all-pervasive and mythological character of this appropriation. Like Ernest Hemingway later for the Russian intelligentsia of the 1960s, or better yet, as Vladimir Vysotskii for the whole country in the Brezhnev period, Chekhov became an irreplaceable part of national life, destiny, culture (whether literary or not), of the early twentieth century. Yet he remained a mirror in which all those writing about him would find mainly their own reflections – their own speculations, often contradictory with respect to other criticism.[9] And the uneven, polemical, even passionate attitude towards the late writer continued. As Andrei Bitov aptly remarked, Chekhov was apparently surrounded by jealousy.[10] The situation did not change much after his death.

In this respect, Russian thinkers played the same role as literary critics or creative writers. In fact they united all these apostasies in a typically Russian synthesis of literature and philosophy. However, with all the artistic-literary flavour of their philosophizing, their agendas were still tailored more towards conceptual thinking, towards abstract categories. Chekhov, on the other hand, was extremely concrete. Yet, they seem to have been magnetically attracted to him, each in their own way, and managed to discover Chekhov as a thinker.

'All definite knowledge [...] belongs to science; all dogma as to what surpasses definite knowledge belongs to theology. But between theology and science there is No Man's Land, exposed to attack from both sides; this No Man's Land is philosophy [...] The conceptions of life and the world which we call "philosophical" are a product of two factors: one, inherited religious and ethical conceptions; the other, the sort of investigation which may be called "scientific"'.[11] Chekhov believed in science, and behind his poetic sensibility one feels also the shrewd eyes of a scientist which look soberly at the world; yet these 'inherited religious and ethical conceptions' are as strong in his works as is his sceptical scientific outlook. Was it this painful combination that attracted philosophers to wrestle with the writer? Did they feel the sense of his unlicensed authority that implied some superior knowledge of the universe? He did, after all, strip the eternal categories, such as religion, politics and sex, from their 'intrinsic properties', showing the relativity and neutrality of all concepts in their dependence on very concrete circumstances and agents.[12]

Stuck on that No Man's Land, compressed between faith and reason, the rational and irrational, philosophy, in the end, is cautious; perhaps because, unlike natural science, it is 'restricted' by the vague vastness of its subject, having to reason about everything. That is why it often ends up vacuous, enslaved by dogma. Chekhov stayed away from conceptions, and, in a doctor's fashion, focused on the individual. He was also fearless, or better to say courageous, perhaps knowing instinctively what Mikhail Bulgakov expressed decades later through his literary embodiment of Christ: 'Cowardice is the worst of vices'.[13] Yet, when you skim through Chekhov's pages with the eyes of a philosopher, you can find anything you like – be it from an ontological, eschatological or epistemological perspective, whatsoever… Only instead of Dostoevskii's ideas-people, Chekhov's idea is 'hidden in such a clear exposition that it may not be taken as an idea, until you have grown up sufficiently to discern it'.[14] The protagonists of this collection grew up sufficiently to distinguish Chekhov's ideas, to penetrate his subtle world – as evasive as a 'fleeting vein' which deceives the needle. All three of them are united by their prominence as Silver Age philosophers; all three had written articles on the writer. Moreover, together they represent a collection which is culturally, philosophically and aesthetically diverse, and it is this diversity, within the above thematic unity, which makes studying these philosophers' views on the writer more novel than analyzing Chekhov in more homogeneous contexts – that of the Symbolists or of the realist critics contemporary to him.

Each one of them was enwrapped in his own idiosyncrasy. Rozanov's tangibly physical feeling for life, his moral ambiguity and longing for warmth, Merezhkovskii's cautious grandeur of utopian theories, his purity of heart combined with human coldness and Shestov's Quixotic struggle against necessity and his fighting against reason with its own weapon – all this serves as a litmus paper which, when dipped into Chekhov's world, reveals the truth about them, and him, and us – when we put our hands into this solution, trying to make sense of it – as well as about the times – of then and now. Hence the never-ending value of every new attempt to look back, which attains a stereoscopic vision, the kind of optics that only passing time can provide. 'A face does not see a face to which it is pressed up close – the large can only be seen from a distance' (*litsom k litsu litsa ne uvidat' – bol'shoe viditsa na rasstoianii*).[15] Hence also the value of this book.

Speaking more broadly, the three thinkers whose perspectives on Chekhov constitute the focus of the present collection represent the new aesthetic-philosophical reality rooted in the 1880s – the time of Chekhov's fledging into a prominent writer. Thus the study of the above thinkers' perception of Chekhov comes down to studying the ways in which the end of a cultural era relates to its beginnings. This is a broad field which is still covered only patchily, and invites newcomers and new perspectives. The question of Chekhov and philosophy is also very much in its infancy.[16] This collection humbly hopes to have made the next step in this direction. However, as was mentioned, pure and scientific philosophy is not a Russian trait. Only in symbiosis with literature does it begin to thrive and bear fruit. By the same token, as they were part of the Russian religious-philosophical renaissance, the common ground of our three thinkers is that they combine in their works both philosophical and artistic approaches. This combination of the aesthetic/artistic and the philosophical/ethical, which is explicitly an integral part of their outlook, and implicitly of Chekhov's, will be a focal point of the pages ahead. Yet, the point of view for analyzing their accounts on the writer will be literary, and faithful to Chekhov's poetics.

***

An eternal return to Chekhov from ever-changing viewpoints up until our Age is clearly not accidental. Amongst the principal reasons for this may be Chekhov's ability to have touched the most vital chord of human existence – what can be called an ideological drive, which seems to be even stronger in humans than their primary sexual drive. The importance of a faith, of an ideology for a personality, looms large from very early on. As a French poet Yves Bonnefoy wistfully asked, is it not the case that 'our task of speaking beings, of beings who elevated themselves from simple matter, thanks to words', is 'to create a different world, of values and meaning?'.[17] Surprisingly, whether this drive is of a religious or anti-religious nature matters little; rather, as in the Russian proverb: 'a sacred place cannot stay empty'. Thus during the course of history, especially modern history, people have become captives and hostages of ideologies, with terrible global as well as local consequences. Even in art this striving is all-pervasive, almost contagious. Hence the words of Anatolii Nayman[18] about the new (Silver Age) 'art–cum–religious–rite' which, as he points out, 'could "come to terms" with nineteenth century art–cum–analysis, art–cum–ideas, art–cum–sermon, if only because all of these are "more than mere art".'[19] Hence also Brodskii's striving, following Akhmatova, to fulfil the 'grandeur of the preconceived idea' (*velichie zamysla*). Yet, as the poet Sergei Gandlevskii penetratingly observed, 'creativity and creativity alone is too absorbed with itself to keep in mind at the same time a need for breaking records or for matching up with high paragons'. Furthermore, Gandlevskii quotes Chesterton's observation that cultural endeavours with a view to immortality, as a rule, are doomed for oblivion, while works written almost in a non-serious manner, as if for the day, often happen to live forever.[20]

In other words, ambitions, of which ideologies are a special case, are restraining, they may give a powerful engine, but they seem to remove wings, so that a free, unbound flight becomes impossible. Chekhov, in his 'shy lack of concern over […] the ultimate aims of mankind and [his] own salvation',[21] in his lack of ambition, was free. Many, like Boris Pasternak or Andrei Bitov, have noticed this freedom, this great humility, this lack of being a captive of ideologies, and it is above all Chekhov's inner freedom which prompted them to compare him with Pushkin. The comparison underlined not only their organic and multifaceted belonging to European civilization, but also Chekhov's role in Russian literature (and culture in general) at the turn of the nineteenth century – which happened to be almost as magnanimous and revolutionizing as Pushkin's for the turn of the eighteenth. Indeed, in his concealed subversiveness, intrinsically free from the power of stereotypes, Chekhov revived Russian prose by injecting poetry back into it, and renovating its dominant form by a dramatic shift from the long novel to the short story. He equally revolutionized theatre by turning the external pressure of a melodramatic plot into the internal intensity of human psychology. With his open lyricism he, as it were, moved the loop of a spiral up from the long-since condemned and rejected formula of 'Art for Art's sake', only to bring it to new heights, by 'thinning reality', as Andrei Belyi remarked.[22] Chekhov transgressed into the transcendental without leaving the realms of this world. He thought his task was simply to show how people live. In fact he told us how they are unable to live.[23] His shining, penetrating irony not only echoes Pushkin's cheerful, provocative gaiety, but also mixes a smile with sadness in a very modern way. Yurii Levitanskii's '*Ironicheskii chelovek*'[24] can be viewed as a concise portrait of the hero of our time (at least a Russian hero), and this hero remarkably resembles Chekhov. Strangely, a post-totalitarian Russian person, tired, as one has been, of hypocrisy and lies, can recognize oneself in Chekhov – who was tired already then of the lies and hypocrisy inherent in civilization. Yet in Chekhov there is a harmony of form that opposes the disintegrating world, and a liberating freedom of a personality which is not partisan, but prefers his own, even if lonely, way to the seeming comfort of illusory groupings.

What is interesting about this is the fact that the process of rejecting existing ideologies, any attempts to break away from their enslavement, normally leads to the construction of new, no less vile, and restraining ideologies, as the end of the nineteenth century (Nietzsche, Marx), and the whole of the twentieth (communism, fascism) have shown. Thus Chekhov's line of remaining outside ideologies, following instead every concrete human being, without passing judgments, rather capturing the main metaphysical features of the object, in an almost unconscious camera-like fashion, almost despite himself, is highly important. The latter characteristic is indigenous of a true poet, as Brodskii aptly noted.[25] Importantly, while framing reality in such a way, Chekhov never descends into cynicism, to the freezing faithlessness. Most of us who read, write and think, are, as it were, 'literary people'. In the sense that mentally we create a parallel, alternative narrative of our life, in the style of

Pushkin: '*t'my nizkikh istin mne dorozhe nas vozvyshaiushchii obman*' ('To the multitude of low truths I prefer an illusion that elevates us'). Chekhov is different. Utterly sober, stripping off rather than dressing up, he nevertheless does not take us down, he lifts us up instead, but without the illusion! How? Maybe the chapters ahead hold an answer, or at least a key, to this and other Chekhov's enigmas ...

***

The contributions to the book have been made by Chekhov specialists from around the globe. The pluralistic approach undertaken here ensures not only diversity and richness of opinions, but also the undercurrent dialogues which exist between chapters. This may lead sometimes to the repetition of key quotations, but not to a repetition of ideas. Most contributions have been newly commissioned, and several are reprints, published earlier only in Russian.[26] Broad thematic coverage, original perspectives and the critical evaluation of the existing assessments of Chekhov and his Silver Age reception also characterise the book. The appropriate choice of names of philosophers, whose treatment of Chekhov is analyzed here, is reinforced by the fact that a discussion of one often invokes a discussion of the others too. There is a further dialectic here, for individual opinions, as well as cultural paradigms – moral, philosophical and aesthetic – in the public and artistic consciousness, are viewed dynamically, as a function of time.

***

Vasilii Rozanov (1856–1919)

The volume begins with the section on Vasilii Rozanov – perhaps the most idiosyncratic of the three thinkers in question. A philosopher with outstanding literary talent and insight, the first to criticize Decadent literature, obsessed by the questions of sexual love, tormented by religious search, notorious for his anti-Semitism, Rozanov was close to the subjective foundation of philosophy and the aesthetics of Symbolism, and saw the meaning and value of literature in penetrating (and portraying) the individual world of a writer.

Rozanov's treatment of Chekhov is characteristically ambiguous. The chapters of the section demonstrate this ambiguity in evolution, and allow a glimpse into the tangled inner world of the philosopher through his uneven, at times tormenting, attitude to the writer. As a human being, was he afraid of Chekhov, or was he jealous (or both); did he bear a grudge or conceal fondness? As a thinker, how did he inscribe Chekhov into the world of his own philosophical, religious and aesthetic concerns? How did his vision of the writer change with time and why? These are just a few of the variety of questions with which the contributions to this section deal.

The section opens up with Vladimir **Kataev's** chapter, who points to various fundamental similarities in Chekhov's and Rozanov's worlds. In an engaging manner, Kataev makes some general observations of the Rozanov–Chekhov relationship, and of the significance of both authors for the cultural developments of the twentieth century. Rozanov and Chekhov simultaneously, possibly independently, represented the defining turn for the paths which literature and philosophy took in the last century. The foundations of this turn were laid in Russian thought and aesthetics in the 1880s. Both addressed the problem of understanding which later became central for Chekhov. Moreover, Chekhov essentially inscribed Rozanov as a character into his texts. Despite their belonging to different branches of Russian culture, there are famous antinomies which characterize both, as well as their biographical proximity and their efforts to expand the horizons of literature, burst out of existing canons and established traditions. By reminding us that neither Chekhov, nor Rozanov could possibly be fair in their mutual assessment, as this requires a different vision available only through historical time, Kataev rounds off sharp angles and explains what exactly could have been the subject for mutual appreciation, but was instead misinterpreted by both Chekhov and Rozanov.

Aleksandr **Medvedev** picks up all the threads when he comprehensively examines Rozanov's treatment of Chekhov within the historiosophical and religious/spiritual discourses, analyzing all five essays which Rozanov wrote on the writer. Medvedev points to a teleological crisis placed by Rozanov at the root of the passivity and lack of will power of Russian, as opposed to European, civilization. By associating Russian literature with the New, and European with the Old Testament, Rozanov explains the difference between Russian and European consciousness. He exposes the formal character of Russian faith which, according to him, leads to the anti-historical character of Russian mentality and life, depicted with great precision in Chekhov's artistic world. Rozanov's understanding of Russian (as opposed to European) literature is connected to the medieval Christian paradigm, highly ethical and moral, with a sacred role assigned to art and artists. In this vein, new cultural waves for him exemplify a crisis of this worldview, bringing the selfishness of Decadence and the destruction of the personality. It is this conception of literature, Medvedev concludes, that determines Rozanov's reading of Chekhov. Medvedev demonstrates how ultimately Rozanov's perception of Chekhov is carried out in the framework and spirit of Russian religious tradition, where the concepts of mercy and quietness, together with *strannichestvo* and suffering, play a central and vital role.

The essay by Reiner **Gruebel** provides a refreshing methodological contrast to both Kataev's and Medvedev's contributions by its existential approach. Drawing extensively on personal accounts, memoirs, letters and notebooks, Gruebel recreates vividly the portraits of two real personalities – Rozanov and Chekhov – and tries to untangle their (far from straightforward) relationship, especially, if not predominantly, in terms of Rozanov's attitude to Chekhov. This existential reconstruction (which refuses to take things at face value), when combined with an analysis of Rozanov's published texts concerning Chekhov, sheds new light on Rozanov's treatment of Chekhov's work by providing a helpful background of personal subjectivity, inseparable both from Rozanov's attempts at an objective reading of Chekhov and from his philosophy. Gruebel examines Rozanov's publications on Chekhov in chronological order, taking into account their genres, topics and political-ideological contexts. He concludes by explaining the multiplicity of Rozanov's attitudes to Chekhov, not only by Rozanov's and Chekhov's evolutions in a variety of contexts, but also by Rozanov's fourfold attitude – of a philosopher, historian, journalist and artist.

Michal **Oklot** begins by continuing the existential line developed by Gruebel, but in contrast to the latter places his investigation into a philosophical framework. In fact, his starting point is precisely the same as Gruebel's – recounting Rozanov's complex attitude to Chekhov as seen through the philosopher's own reflections on the correspondence and friendship which were never really actualized. However, giving the same factual material, Oklot poses different questions than Gruebel and takes a different approach. More precisely, he rejects a comprehensive cataloguing method of commenting on all Rozanov's remarks on Chekhov. Instead he opts for Kataev's organizing principle of distinguishing conceptual, poetic and biographical affinities between the two figures (and draws on Kataev's research presented in the earlier chapter of the volume), but changes the angle by posing a question, often underestimated by critics: 'Why was Rozanov afraid of Chekhov? What was it that repulsed him about the writer?' In his attempts to explore this issue, Oklot makes the important point that 'Chekhov's interests were dangerously close to Rozanov's philosophical territory'. Oklot then places the discussion in the framework of Rozanov's understanding of literature, adding also eschatological and epistemological dimensions. Indeed, just like in Evdokimova's chapter on Shestov and Chekhov, which comes later in the collection, the issue of Chekhov's (and this time of Rozanov's) attitude to the problem of cognition is of the essence in Oklot's comparative analysis of the two figures. At the end of his multifaceted exploration, with interesting references in particular to Gogol´, Leont´ev and Dostoevskii, Oklot arrives at stating Rozanov's ultimate acknowledgement of Chekhov's 'victory' when the writer's 'crude materialism' was 'empirically confirmed' for the dying philosopher.

Dmitrii Merezhkovskii (1865–1941)

The hero of the next section of the volume is Dmitrii Merezhkovskii, whose criticism on Chekhov is characterized by an even greater ambiguity than Rozanov's. One of the oldest Symbolists and the author of what came to be regarded as the first aesthetic manifesto of Russian Decadence, Merezhkovskii himself became perhaps symbolic in Russian culture as a forceful expression of religious-mystical sensibility based on major antinomies, with his principle of oppositions, underlying all his literary-critical studies.

Expanding the boundaries of their mutual relationships and literary contexts, the Merezhkovskii–Chekhov theme opens up a much more general question of the changing aesthetic-philosophical paradigm of the time. This is elucidated brilliantly in the opening chapter of this section, by Aleksandr Chudakov. It is followed by a no less significant polemical essay by Anna Lisa Crone who takes issue with scholarly evaluations of Merezhkovskii's criticism on Chekhov, most of which are, in her view, biased towards Chekhov and thus unable to give a balanced analysis. Crone disavows these types of assessment giving a fair treatment of Merezhkovskii's works which illustrates how he, often inadvertently, brought to light the way in which Chekhov, effectively against his own intentions, promoted the very values of religion and spirituality that Merezhkovskii denies him having. This polemical dialogue between the two distinguished scholars to whose memory the present book is dedicated, perhaps constitutes the pinnacle of the whole volume, in every sense: semantic, aesthetic and ethical.

Thus Aleksandr **Chudakov** views both figures in the contexts of their intellectual and spiritual activity as archetypes of artistic-philosophical consciousness of the turn of the nineteenth century. Starting with Chekhov's response to Merezhkovskii's early criticism on him, Chudakov then proceeds to describe the evolution of their relationship in the framework of the socio-intellectual concerns of the epoch. As well as similarities in their artistic outlook, Chudakov explores their underlying fundamental differences which set them apart on opposing poles. The Chekhov–Merezhkovskii case study, he argues, exemplified the first phase of the shift between the new cultural-philosophical, as well as literary-stylistic paradigm which opposed the old paradigm of classical Russian literature. This phase, as Chudakov explains, went essentially unnoticed because of its old-fashioned, 'gentlemen-like' form (rather than publically scandalous). What interests him most, however, is 'not the general opposition between the two types of European cultural consciousness: romantic/positivist; ascending–rhetorical–explicit/descending–reserved–implicit, which Chekhov and Merezhkovskii come to represent, but their particular case as a concrete and early manifestation of these fundamental antinomies'.

Anna Lisa **Crone** on her part sets out to re-assess without prejudice Merezhkovskii's criticism on Chekhov for what it is, rather than, as has often been the case, in the context of their personal relations or the use of both as representative examples of two opposing intellectual types of *fin de siècle* Russia. With a detailed knowledge of Merezhkovskii's oeuvre and his religious and philosophical preoccupations, Crone examines his essays on Chekhov, starting with the more 'objective' and Chekhov-centred viewpoint, and then following Merezhkovskii to his next phase, when the framework of his literary criticism became more philosophical and metaphysical than aesthetic. However, rather than drawing from Merezhkovskii's own philosophy to explain his judgments on Chekhov, Crone makes a clear distinction between the critic's ideological-religious orientation and his ability to produce valuable literary-critical works. She focuses on Merezhkovskii's essay 'Chekhov and Gor´kii' to argue that against widely accepted views which consider this in tandem with the preceding essay of the volume 'The Coming Ham', it should be read as a piece of praise to Chekhov on Merezhkovskii's part. Using a sophisticated reasoning, which involves a double negation, Crone argues that 'Merezhkovskii shows Chekhov's religion of man exposed as bankrupt by Chekhov himself'. This allows Crone to view Merezhkovskii's criticism of Chekhov as entirely positive because of its revelation of these precious (spiritually constructive) hidden messages. Interestingly, the line which emerges from this interpretation of Merezhkovskii is strikingly close to that arising from Medvedev's interpretation of Rozanov's criticism on Chekhov: both critics assigned to Chekhov the role of a Christian martyr, even if this role is subconscious, akin to professing the Christian faith before the actual emergence of Christianity.

The line of this polemics is continued by Karoline **Thaidigsmann**, who demonstrates in her chapter, as a certain variation on Crone's stance, how Merezhkovskii in an unconscious and indirect fashion illuminates Chekhov's art and artistic *Weltanschauung*, even when misinterpreting the writer, and thereby contributing to the comprehension of Chekhov's work. She starts by showing how Merezhkovskii's early literary criticism on the writer significantly contributed to the understanding and esteem of Chekhov's art and literary talent. However, she argues that in Merezhkovskii's later essays, this sensibility for Chekhov's art was sacrificed to a large extent. Indeed, under the specific requirements of Merezhkovskii's religious philosophy, Chekhov and his literary works have been judged negatively. On the one hand, Merezhovskii's various statements on Chekov in the years between 1888 and 1914 reflect the critic's own spiritual evolution of the time, while on the other hand Merezhkovskii's essays shed an illuminating light on Chekhov's art, even when he sets himself apart from the author and harshly criticizes his view on reality. In these later writings, however, the illumination of Chekhov's work cannot be grasped any more on the level of explicit statements made by the critic, but has to be deciphered. It is this decoding that Thaidigsmann ultimately offers.

Vladimir **Golstein's** concluding chapter of this section contributes to the intensity of diverging views presented hitherto. He closes the circle by returning to what for Crone would be a Chekhov-biased stance, exposing Merezhkovskii's contradictions, especially in his treatment of the writer, and inscribing them into a broader context of the inner world of the Russian intelligentsia, thus divorcing the two figures into their very different niches of Russian culture. Golstein reveals the complexity of Merezhkovskii's engagement with Chekhov as a dynamic process of appreciation at one level, and insensitivity and a lack of penetration at another. He investigates Merezhkovskii's long preoccupation with the writer in two related contexts – the intellectual context of the time and the context of Merezhkovskii's own philosophy, considered in evolution. When exploring the nature and origins of Chekhov's opinions on Merezhkovskii, Golstein rejects the path previously taken by other scholars (for example, Elena Tolstaia) of trying to trace and decode Merezhkovskii's would-be appearances as a character of Chekhov's writings (notice that a similar phenomenon was described in the section on Rozanov). Instead, Golstein wants to analyze what Chekhov's comments on Merezhkovskii, which can be traced to the former's life and writings, reveal about Chekhov and his work. Golstein views a persistent misinterpretation of Chekhov as paradigmatic of Russian culture, implying that Chekhov's freedom inevitably clashes with tendentiousness of existing ideologies. In this framework, he concludes his essay by examining the famous problem of the poet and the mob in the context of Merezhkovskii's treatment of Chekhov. The concept of 'satiety' – i.e. self-satisfaction, self-righteousness and self-centeredness – extensively explored in Chekhov's works, is fundamental to Golstein's analysis. He asserts in this connection that those who are steeped in their satiety are symptomatically unable to discern Chekhov's message, and clearly puts Merezhkovskii in that camp, thus by and large making alliances with Chudakov's interpretation, and opposing Crone's.

Lev Shestov (1866–1938)

The concluding section is dedicated to a fascinating Russian Jewish religious thinker whose irrationalist and existential stance inspired poets more than philosophers, and who remains arguably unread to this day. Shestov assigned to Chekhov the utmost significance, but his controversial treatment of the writer (the text which Bunin, for example, placed amongst the best written on Chekhov, while Chukovskii 'read with indignation'), has not (yet?) received due appreciation, despite the fact that it continues to evoke polemics. This is perhaps a story of Shestov's life, not so much because of his focus on the tragic, but because of the inescapable solitude and uniqueness of his path that cannot par excellence have any following, or be generalized. It can leave deep marks in culture, though, which are then developed by others, even if without acknowledgement or realization of the borrowing. This section will analyze the Shestov–Chekhov connection from a variety of angles, including the hitherto unstudied influence of Shestov's philosophy on Chekhov's writings, an influence which arguably took place.

In his concise, but illuminating contribution which opens the section, Andrei **Stepanov** deliberately turns away from the standard route taken by scholars studying Shestov's treatment of Chekhov. This route usually focuses on Shestov's provocative labelling of Chekhov as 'the singer of hopelessness'. Not dismissing the overall importance of this idea, Stepanov however notes that the content of Shestov's article cannot be reduced to just this. Instead, Stepanov interprets Shestov's reading of Chekhov, which he justly calls paradoxical, by juxtaposing some of Shestov's philosophical dominants with Chekhov's artistic ones. Having explained the irrational nature of Shestov's philosophical thought, Stepanov illustrates how Shestov finds the main elements of his own philosophy in Chekhov's artistic world – in the writer's rejection of the rational and in his search for the miraculous, only in the aesthetic sphere. However, as Stepanov explains further, in Chekhov's world there is what is absent in Shestov's: a mutual reversal of rational and irrational. More generally, Chekhov's texts turn out to be broader than Shestov's interpretation. Still, this interpretation, which by Stepanov's admission is in many ways inadequate, touches upon some deep strata of Chekhov's world. Apart from the engagement of both figures with the epistemological problem there is a further proximity between them – in their very type of thinking which Stepanov identifies as 'discrete-paradoxical'. Despite Chekhov's extreme concreteness and Shestov's abstractness, both tend to illustrate not so much a rational *Weltanschauung*, but an irrational world outlook which admits a multiplicity of truths. Stepanov concludes his analysis by pointing to the deepest similarity between Shestov and Chekhov – in their 'desperate hope in the fulfilment of the impossible'.

Olga **Tabachnikova**'s (i.e. my own) contribution complements Stepanov's in taking what he puts aside as a commonly shared and not very productive approach to Shestov's treatment of Chekhov – to focus on Shestov's labelling the writer as a destroyer of human hopes – to be my point of departure. However, my subsequent premise is to demonstrate that in his evaluation of

Chekhov, Shestov in fact describes his own self and his own philosophical path. Thus instead of attacking the writer, it is Shestov's own mirror image against which he directs his bitter sarcasm in connection to Chekhov's focus on tragic and overstrained people, amongst whom Shestov places Chekhov as well. This is a rather typical Shestovian technique – of 'Shestovizing' the authors under his study, if necessary at the expense of falsifying the facts. In this instance it is Simon Karlinsky's thorough research which helps me to refute Shestov's vision of Chekhov as an overstrained and tragic person with a defining existential crisis, from which he emerged a new man with a steadfast focus on tragedy. However, Shestov's constructions touch upon an important nerve of Chekhov's world – the role of culture and cultural habits in human existence, and the flimsy nature of this role. I discern in this a direct link to Freud and dedicate the next part of my chapter to a detailed discussion of this link, as well as of the relevance to it of positivist philosophy, commonly supposed to be hostile to Shestov's thought. The third part of my contribution aims at exploring Chekhov's alleged hatred (so precious to Shestov) of ideologies and ideals. I conclude by a discussion on the psychological dynamics of tragic Chekhov's heroes who, according to Shestov, have nothing to lose and who are thus forced to create from the void. Ultimately I find the roots of the distortion by Shestov of the writer's image in his own aesthetic myopia of the philosopher.

Savelii **Senderovich**, who continues the section with his substantial essay, approaches the theme of Shestov and Chekhov from a refreshingly new angle, not only giving an assessment of Shestov's reading of Chekhov, but also uncovering how his philosophical ideas resonated in Chekhov's artistic world. Such an impact is invariably difficult to prove with certainty, and all one can do is to offer a grounded elaboration of a conjecture. Senderovich gives a persuasive argument to support his conclusions, but the final judgment will have to rest with the reader. He begins by highlighting the importance of Shestov's thought for twentieth century literature, which went practically unacknowledged. Senderovich points out that under Nietzsche's influence, Shestov chose tragedy as an existential category, and realized that any authentic consciousness lives on a tragic territory not amenable to rational constructions. The same conclusions, Senderovich argues, were independently reached by Chekhov in his own artistic way. Notwithstanding various excesses and the simplifications of Shestov's treatment of Chekhov, Senderovich at the same time stresses the importance and value of Shestov's existential approach to the writer, and singles out Shestov's pioneering achievements on this route. As a meeting point of Chekhov with Shestov's motifs, Senderovich distinguishes Chekhov's last play *The Cherry Orchard*. Senderovich provides a detailed analysis of the way in which, as he argues, Chekhov appropriated Shestov's ideas. The reason for this he sees not only in the philosophical kinship of both figures, but also in Chekhov sharing with Shestov a whole field of meanings. Senderovich defines this field as a certain existential sociology 'where social problems are violently interwoven with the roots of individual existence, while the uniqueness of the individual manifests itself as a social farce'.

No less substantial is Svetlana **Evdokimova**'s chapter which concludes the section and the volume. Effectively taking issue with the premise held by Senderovich – of Shestov's indirect influence on Chekhov – Evdokimova states unequivocally that 'there is no question about any kind of mutual "influence," conscious or subconscious either' and sets to focus instead on 'that which unites the writer and the philosopher with various philosophical movements of their time'. The common ground between the writer and philosopher she finds in the distinctly 'un-philosophical' stance of both, in their recoil from ideologies, movements, and from systems of beliefs. Having elucidated various idiosyncratic elements in Shestov's reading of Chekhov, she stresses Shestov's achievement in having correctly sensed and identified in the writer a new outlook which remained unread by Chekhov's contemporaries and which would later be associated with existentialism and phenomenology. Evdokimova demonstrates a variety of ways in which Chekhov was for Shestov a 'brother in arms' – in particular in both men's disdain of authorities, clichés, and the enslaving power of civilization's excesses. As one of the central problems for both Chekhov and Shestov, Evdokimova identifies (in a similar way to Stepanov) the attitude of both towards knowledge. She develops this line further to the interesting conclusion, that for Chekhov the tragedy of mankind is in never really having tasted from the tree of knowledge, whereas for Shestov it is in the opposite – in the human preference of the tree of knowledge to the tree of life. Evdokimova's subsequent argument shows that 'ultimately, Chekhov's struggle with philosophy and his mockery of philosophers were even more radical than Shestov's'. She concludes by elucidating Chekhov's new vision of art which accommodates the new age and 'emerges from the modern man's state of disbelief and his confrontation with the absurd'. This illuminating portrayal of Chekhov in the context of his time shows a definite kinship between Evdokimova's contribution and other chapters of the collection.

* * *

As the reader will see, being faced with a multiplicity of views on Chekhov and his treatment by these three Russian thinkers creates an effect of looking through a kaleidoscope, full of moving mosaics which, when rearranged in a different pattern, show an entirely new picture. Indeed, every thinker under study has his own vision of the writer, which is by itself a dynamic entity. And Chekhov, with his non-tendentiousness and elusiveness, often serves as a testing ground that reveals the hidden tendencies of his assessors. On top of that each of the contributors to this volume has his or her own vision of the figures in question, thus multiplying yet further the points of view. The resulting richness ought to give a truly multifaceted interpretation of Chekhov and the Silver Age philosophers studied here. The schematic and bookish names on the cover should start filling up with life. If this happens, our goal is achieved. In that we have animated those plain shadows from our distant literary history, we have set in motion the dust of time – a process akin, if you like, to what a writer does when he makes words turn into life, into a real living experience. That is what art is about – whether as a means of cognition or as a source of joy. That is what Chekhov would share – shying away from all labels, from any philosophy of life apart from life itself, he escapes final interpretation – as he must have done once again in our book. And thus, perhaps, his goal is also achieved. As long as art has a goal; for art is, as Brodskii put it, 'a means of conveyance, a landscape flashing in a window – rather than the conveyance's destination'.[27] Which echoes with Pushkin's: 'His song is free like the wind, but like the wind fruitless' (*'kak veter, pesn' ego svobodna, zato kak veter i besplodna'*). In this vein it only remains for us to hope that, apart from providing new illuminating perspectives on the exciting topic of the Silver Age philosophical perception of Chekhov, this book will also be a pleasure to read to all those for whom Russian culture remains as attractive as it is enigmatic; and for whom literature has no goal …

Olga Tabachnikova

Notes

1. This is characterization of the time given by Dmitrii Merezhkovskii in his seminal work of 1893 *On the Causes of the Decline and on the New Trends in Contemporary Russian Literature*.
2. Anton Chekhov, Obituary to the traveller N. M. Przheval'skii, *Polnoe Sobranie Sochinenii i Pisem v 30 tomakh* (Moscow: Nauka, 1974–82), vol. 16, p. 236.
3. Yves Bonnefoy, 'On Some Problems in the Translation of Poetry', *New York Review of Books*, 7 February 1974, p. 376.
4. Yuri Lotman, 'Siuzhetnoe prostranstvo russkogo romana XIX stoletiia' in *Izbrannye statii* (Tallinn: 'Aleksandra', 1993), vol. III, pp. 104–06.
5. Joseph Brodsky, 'Foreword' to *An Age Ago, A Selection of Nineteenth-Century Russian Poetry*, selected and translated by Alan Myers (New York: Farrar-Straus-Giroux, 1988), pp. xi–xix (pp. xii–xiv).
6. Andrei Bitov, '*Moi dedushka Chekhov i pradedushka Pushkin*', *Chetyrezhdy Chekhov*, ed. Igor' Kokh (St Petersburg: Emergency Exit, 2004), p. 11.
7. The only existing books exploring Chekhov's relationship with the Silver Age are in Russian: *A. P. Chekhov: Pro et Contra. Tvorchestvo A. P. Chekhova v russkoi mysli kontsa XIX – nachala XX v. (1887–1914)*, Anthology, eds. I. N. Sukhikh and A. D. Stepanov

(St Petersburg: *Izdatel' stvo Russkogo Khristianskogo gumanitarnogo Instituta*, 2002) and *Chekhoviana. Chekhov i 'serebrianyi vek'*, ed. M. O. Goriacheva and others (Moscow: Nauka, 1996).

8. See M. A. Murinia, 'Chekhoviana nachala XX veka (Struktura i osobennosti)' in *Chekhoviana. Chekhov i 'serebrianyi vek'*, ed. M. O. Goriacheva and others (Moscow: Nauka, 1996), p. 16.

9. It is Andrei Stepanov who aptly calls Chekhov a perfect mirror that reflected the opinions of those looking in it: see Andrei Stepanov, 'Anton Chekhov kak zerkalo russkoi kritiki' in *A. P. Chekhov: Pro et Contra. Tvorchestvo A. P. Chekhova v russkoi mysli kontsa XIX – nachala XX v. (1887–1914)*, Anthology, ed. I. N. Sukhih, A. D. Stepanov (St Petersburg: *Izdatel' stvo Russkogo Khristianskogo gumanitarnogo Instituta*, 2002), 976–1007, p. 976.

10. Andrei Bitov, 'Moi dedushka Chekhov i pradedushka Pushkin', *Chetyrezhdy Chekhov*, ed. Igor´ Kokh (St Petersburg: Emergency Exit, 2004), p. 15.

11. Bertrand Russell, *History of Western Philosophy and its Connection with Political and Social Circumstances from the Earliest Times to the Present Day* (London: George Allen & Unwin Ltd, 1961), p. 13.

12. This idea is developed by Simon Karlinsky in his Introduction to *Anton Chekhov's Life and Thought. Selected Letters and Commentary* (Berkeley, Los Angeles and London: University of California Press, 1975), pp. 1–32.

13. See the concluding chapters of Bulgakov's novel *Master i Margarita* (1929-1940), where this idea is repeatedly put forward.

14. Andrei Bitov, 'Moi dedushka Chekhov i pradedushka Pushkin', *Chetyrezhdy Chekhov*, ed. Igor´ Kokh (St Petersburg: Emergency Exit, 2004), p. 9.

15. Famous lines from Sergei Esenin's poem of 1924 'Pis´mo k zhenshchine' ('Letter to a lady').

16. There are two books – one trilingual, the other one Russian – which deal specifically with the issue of Chekhov and philosophy: *Anton P. Čechov – Philosophische und Religiöse Dimensionen im Leben und im Werk*. Proceedings of the 12th International Chekhov Symposium, Badenweiler, 20–24 October, 1994, eds. Vladimir B. Kataev, Rolf-Dieter Kluge and Regine Nohejl (Munich: Verlag Otto Sagner, 1997) and *Filosofiia A. P. Chekhova*, ed. A. S. Sobennikov (Irkutsk: IGU, 2007).

17. Yves Bonnefoy, 'A l'impossible tenu: la liberté de Dieu et celle de l'écrivain dans la pensée de Chestov', *Cahiers de l'émigration russe 3* (Paris: Institut d'Etudes Slaves, 1996), special issue 'Léon Chestov. Un philosophe pas comme les autres?', p. 16, translation is mine.

18. Anatolii Naiman (Anatoly Nayman) – a Russian poet, who used to be Anna Akhmatova's literary secretary, and later wrote his reminiscences of her (see the next endnote).

19. Anatoly Nayman, *Remembering Anna Akhmatova*, transl. by Wendy Rosslyn (London: Peter Halban, 1991), p. 37.

20. Sergei Gandlevskii, 'Olimpiiskaia igra', in *Iosif Brodskii: tvorchestvo, lichnost, sud´ba. Trudy triokh konferentsii* (St Petersburg: Zhurnal Zvezda, 1998), p. 117.

21. Boris Pasternak, *Doctor Zhivago*, the phrase is translated by Simon Karlinsky (see his Introduction to *Anton Chekhov's Life and Thought. Selected Letters and Commentary* (Berkeley, Los Angeles and London: University of California Press, 1975), pp. 31–2).

22. Andrei Belyi, 'Chekhov. "Vishnevyi sad"' ['Chekhov. "Cherry Orchard"'] in *A. P. Chekhov: Pro et Contra. Tvorchestvo A. P. Chekhova v russkoi mysli kontsa XIX – nachala XX v. (1887–1914)*, Anthology, eds. I. N. Sukhikh and A. D. Stepanov (St Petersburg: Izdatel'stvo Russkogo Khristianskogo gumanitarnogo Instituta, 2002), p. 838.

23. Andrei Ar´ev, '*Nasha malen´kaia zhizn´*': Introduction to Sergei Dovlatov, *Sobranie sochinenii v 3 tomakh* (St Petersburg: Limbus Press, 1993), p. 7.

24 Yuri Davydovich Levitanskii (1922–96) – a prominent Russian poet. His famous poem '*Ironicheskii chelovek*' ('Ironic person', published in 1977) describes a man unassuming and heroic.
25 The precise quotation reads: 'A good poem, in a sense, is like a photograph that puts its objects' metaphysical features into sharp focus. Accordingly, a good poet is one who does this sort of thing in a camera-like fashion: quite unwittingly, almost in spite of himself' (Joseph Brodsky, from the Foreword to *An Age Ago. A Selection of Nineteenth-Century Russian Poetry*, selected and transl. Alan Myers (New York: Farrar-Straus-Giroux, 1988), p. xvi).
26 These are: Aleksandr Chudakov's 'Chekhov i Merezhkovskii: dva tipa khudozhestvenno-filosofskogo soznaniia' (pp. 50–67), Vladimir Kataev's 'Chekhov i Rozanov' (pp. 68–74) and Andrei Stepanov's 'Lev Shestov o Chekhove' (pp. 75–9) in *Chekhoviana. Chekhov i 'serebrianyi vek'*, ed. M. O. Goriacheva and others (Moscow: Nauka, 1996), as well as Savelii Senderovich's 'A.P. Chekhov and L.I. Shestov and Notes on the Existential Sociology' (an amended form of an article published previously in *Voprosy Literatury*, 2007, No. 6, pp. 163–78).
27 Joseph Brodsky, 'Footnote to a Poem', transl. by Barry Rubin, in *Less than one. Selected Essays* (England: Penguin Books, 1987), p. 202.

LIST OF NAMES

Adamovich, Georgii Viktorovich (1892–1972) – Russian poet, translator and literary critic. He emigrated from Soviet Russia in 1924 and lived in Berlin and later in Paris; actively participated in the cultural life of Russian emigration.

Aikhenval´d, Iulii Isaevich (1872–1928) – Russian literary critic, also known as a philosopher and translator. His stance could be labeled idealistic and irrationalist, and he is often referred to as an impressionist. In emigration since 1922. Died tragically as a result of an accident (fell under a tram in Berlin).

Akhmatova, Anna (Anna Andreevna **Gorenko**, 1889–1966) – classical Russian poet.

Aksakov, Sergei Timofeevich (1791–1859) – Russian literary figure of the nineteenth century remembered for his partly autobiographical tales of a landlord's family life, hunting, fishing, and butterfly collecting.

Aksakov, Konstantin Sergeevich (1817–1860) – Russian historian, pamphleteer, poet and philosopher, one of the earliest exponents of Slavophile ideas.

Al´bov, Veniamin Pavlovich (1871 – ?) – teacher from Simferopol. His biographical data could not be retrieved (see further on this in *A. P. Chekhov: Pro et Contra. Tvorchestvo A. P. Chekhova v russkoi mysli kontsa XIX – nachala XX v. (1887–1914)* (*A. P. Chekhov: Pro et Contra. Chekhov's creativity in Russian thought of the late XIX – early XX centuries (1887-1914)*), Anthology, ed. I. N. Sukhih, A. D. Stepanov (St Petersburg: *Izdatel´ stvo Russkogo Khristianskogo gumanitarnogo Instituta*, 2002), p. 1024).

Amfiteatrov, Aleksandr Valentinovich (1862–1938) – Russian writer, literary and theatre critic, and publicist.

Annenskii, Innokentii Fedorovich (1855–1909) – outstanding Russian poet, critic and translator. Influenced by the French Symbolists, he in turn was one of the key exponents of the first wave of Russian Symbolism.

Antonii Surozhskii (Andrei Borisovich **Blum**, in English known as **Bloom**, 1914–2003), metropolitan – leading Russian orthodox theologian and preacher of the twentieth century. From 1950 he was the head of the Assumption Church of the Patriarch parish in London.

Arsen'ev, Nikolai Sergeevich (1888–1977) – leading Russian religious philosopher, in emigration since 1920; participated in the Ecumenical movement.

Artsybashev, Mikhail Petrovich (1878–1927) – Russian writer. A proponent of Russian naturalism, Artsybashev scandalized his readers with his 1907 novel *Sanin* and its depictions of the hedonistic lifestyle of its eponymous hero; opposed Bolshevik rule, emigrated in 1923.

Averintsev, Sergei Sergeevich (1937–2004) – outstanding Russian philologist, cultural historian, medievalist.

Bakhtin, Mikhail Mikhailovich (1895–1975) – outstanding Russian philosopher, literary scholar and art theoretician.

Bal'mont, Konstantin Dmitrievich (1867–1942) – Russian Symbolist poet and translator; one of the major exponents of Russian Symbolism; died in emigration.

Belinskii, Vissarion Grigor'evich (1811–1848) – Russian literary critic and philosopher, of Westernizing tendency; one of the most influential in Russian letters, oriented towards social justice and personal freedom.

Belyi, Andrei (Boris Nikolaevich **Bugaev**, 1880–1934) – Russian poet-Symbolist, novelist, essayist, philosopher and literary theorist; one of the founders of the Symbolist movement in Russia.

Berdiaev, Nikolai Aleksandrovich (1874–1948) – Russian religious philosopher, one of the most prominent Russian thinkers of the Silver Age, personal friend of Lev Shestov; was forced into exile from Soviet Russia in 1922, and spent the first years of emigration in Berlin, but then moved to Paris.

Bitov, Andrei Georgievich (born in 1937 in Leningrad) – prominent contemporary Russian writer; under the Soviet regime was ideologically oriented towards liberal and dissident values; since 1991 – President of the Russian Pen-Club.

LIST OF NAMES   xxxiii

Bitsilli, Petr Mikhailovich (1879–1953) – leading cultural historian, classical philologist, specialist in the European Middle Ages and the Renaissance; in emigration since 1920.

Blok, Aleksandr Aleksandrovich (1880–1921) – outstanding Russian poet; one of the leaders of the Symbolist movement. Highly respected by his peers and greatly admired by subsequent generations of Russian poets.

Boborykin, Petr Dmitrievich (1836–1921) – prolific Russian novelist, playwright, feuilletonist, journalist, literary and theatrical historian, author of more than 100 volumes. His immoderate productivity was mocked by his contemporaries who associated his name with bad writing on topical issues.

Breshko-Breshkovskii, Nikolai Nikolaevich (1874–1943) – Russian writer, journalist, art critic; in emigration since 1920.

Brezhnev, Leonid Il′ich (1907–1982) – Soviet leader: General Secretary of the Central Committee of the Communist Party of the Soviet Union from 1966.

Briusov, Valerii Iakovlevich (1873–1924) – prominent Russian Symbolist poet, writer of prose, dramatist, literary critic, translator and historian; one of the prominent exponents of Russian Symbolism. After the 1917 Revolution remained in Russia and supported the Bolsheviks.

Brodsky, Joseph (Iosif Aleksandrovich **Brodskii**, 1940–1996) – outstanding Russian poet, now classic, Nobel Prize winner for literature of 1987; was prosecuted in the Soviet Union and eventually forced into exile; since 1972 lived in the United States, was a university Professor of Russian literature, and a poet-laureate (1991–1992).

Bulgakov, Mikhail Afanasievich (1891–1940) – outstanding Russian prose writer and playwright.

Bulgakov, Sergei Nikolaevich (Sergii) (1871–1944) – Russian religious philosopher, theologian and economist, a prominent cultural figure of the Silver Age. The son of a priest, he started out his career as a political economist and was carried away with Marxist ideas. However, he proceeded to abandon them, turning instead to idealism and religious philosophy and becoming a priest (ordained in 1918). Bulgakov turned to Christian idealism under the influence of thinkers such as F. M. Dostoevskii and V. S. Solov′ev;

proclaimed a 'new religious consciousness' and a renewal of the Orthodox Church. In later years he made important though controversial contributions to the development of Russian Sophiology and is a representative of an Orthodox philosophy on sophiological foundation. Bulgakov was exiled from Soviet Russia in 1922 and eventually settled in Paris.

Bunin, Ivan Alekseevich (1870–1953) – outstanding Russian writer and poet, representative of Modernism, the first Russian recipient of the Nobel Prize for Literature (in 1933). Fled Russia after the Bolshevik Revolution (in 1920) and was respected as the doyen of the Russian classical tradition in Emigration.

Burenin, Viktor Petrovich (1841–1926) – Russian pamphleteer, poet and literary critic, member of *The New Times* editorial board.

Chaadaev, Petr Iakovlevich (1794–1856) – famous Russian philosopher, founder of the Westernisers school of thought ('Philosophical Letters', 1936); provided a critique of Russia from the Catholic and European cultural stance.

Chekhov, Aleksandr Pavlovich (1855–1913) – Russian writer and journalist, elder brother of Anton Pavlovich.

Chernyshevskii, Nikolai Gavrilovich (1828–1889) – Russian social and literary critic, publicist and utopian philosopher, guiding spirit of nihilism and a major representative of positivist materialism in Russian philosophy of the nineteenth century; activist of the revolutionary-democratic movement, author of the famous novel 'What is to be Done?' (1863).

Chukovskii, Kornei Ivanovich (Nikolai Vasil´evich **Korneichukov**, 1882–1969) – famous Russian poet, literary critic and translator; although Chukovskii has written brilliant works of literary criticism, he is known above all for his poems and stories for children (a common route for many talented writers during Soviet times was to channel their creative ability to a politically safe field of writing for children).

Danilevskii, Nikolai Iakovlevich (1822–1885) – Russian economist, naturalist, ethnologist, philosopher, historian, and ideologue of the pan-Slavism and Slavophile movement. He expounded a view of world history as circular and was the first writer to present an account of history as a series of distinct civilizations.

D'Annunzio, Gabriele (1863–1938) – Italian poet, dramatist, novelist, journalist, and adventurist.

LIST OF NAMES   xxxv

Derzhavin, Gavriil (Gavrila) Romanovich (1743–1816) – classical Russian poet, representative of Classicism; elevated to a high position of state under Empress Catherine the Great, he dedicated many of his well-known odes to her.

Diagilev, Sergei Pavlovich (1872–1929) – the world-famous Russian impresario and art critic, one of the most influential figures in the Russian avant-garde in the field of Russian theatre of the epoch of Russian Modernism, publisher and patron of arts. Famous for founding the *Ballets Russes* in Paris (1909–1929) and launching the careers of many famous choreographers and dancers including Nijinsky, he collaborated with most of the leading Russian and European artists of his time, including Stravinskii, Debussy, and Ravel. He also had a close association with leading Russian writers and artists such as Aleksandre Benois, Leon Bakst, and Dmitrii Filosofov. Diagilev was also one of the founders of the association *Mir iskusstva* ('The World of Art') and the editor of the journal of the same name (1899–1904), and special assistant to the Director of the Imperial Theatres.

Dimitrii Rostovskii (in real life: Daniil Savvich **Tuptalo**, 1651–1709), metropolitan – leading Russian orthodox theologian, writer and preacher of the 17th century, author of hagiography collections (1689–1705) which became popular in Russia; author of sermons, religious plays and poems; canonized in 1757.

Dobroliubov, Nikolai Aleksandrovich (1836–1861) – Russian literary critic, essayist and revolutionary publicist. The son of a priest, he embraced Western ideas of progress, and from 1856 worked as senior critic for the influential liberal journal *The Contemporary* (*Sovremennik*). An associate of materialist philosopher Nikolai Chernyshevskii.

Dolinin, Arkadii Semenovich (1883–1968) – Russian literary scholar and critic, author of books on the works of F. M. Dostoevskii: *In creative laboratory of Dostoevskii* (1947), *Latest novels by Dostoevskii* (1963), *Dostoevskii and others* (1989).

Doroshevich, Vlas Mikhailovich (1865–1922) – Russian journalist, publicist, theatre critic, editor of a leading Russian liberal newspaper *Russkoe slovo*, author of the book of notes on Sakhalin (1903).

Dostoevskii, Fedor Mikhailovich (1821–1881) – classical Russian novelist. Renowned for his insightful psychological depiction of characters and the treatment of philosophical-ethical topics in his works. His experience as a forced labour worker in Siberia (1850–1854) led him to a Christian philosophy of life.

Eikhenbaum, Boris Mikhailovich (1886–1959) – prominent Russian literary critic; never emigrated and was victimised during Stalinist campaign 'against cosmopolitanism' carried out in the late 1940s; has written substantial works on literary theory and history.

Engel′gardt, Nikolai Aleksandrovich (1867–1942) – Russian writer, journalist, literary critic, historian of literature.

Epifanii Premudryi (The Most Wise) (?–1420) – Russian writer and author of famous hagiographies, *The Life of St. Stefan of Perm* (later 1390s) and *The Life of St. Sergii of Radonezh* (1416–1417), whose ornamental writing style, considered by some philologists as an expression of the apophatic theology of the monastic and spiritual movement Hesychasm (the teaching about the Divine Light and Heavenly Uncreated Energies), influenced modern writers from Nikolai Gogol′ to Alexei Remizov and Boris Pil′niak.

Erofeev, Venedikt Vasil′evich (1938–1990) – outstanding Russian prose writer, author of such works as *Moskva-Petushki (Moscow-Petushki*, also translated as *Moscow to the End of the Line, Moscow Stations and Moscow Circles)* and *Vasilii Rozanov glazami ekstsentrika (Vasilii Rozanov through the Eyes of an Eccentric)*.

Erofeev, Viktor Vladimirovich (born in 1947 in Moscow) – contemporary Russian prose writer of liberal orientation, and a host of the cultural television programme '*Apokrif*' ('Apocrypha'); spent part of his childhood in France, because his father was a Soviet diplomat; was involved in dissident activity during Soviet times; also writes literary-critical works.

Esenin, Sergei Aleksandrovich (1895–1925) – outstanding Russian poet of the twentieth century.

Fedotov, Georgii Petrovich (1886–1951) – leading Russian religious philosopher, medievalist, cultural historian, publicist; in emigration since 1925.

Fet, Afanasii Afanas′evich (1820–1892) – outstanding Russian lyric poet. His passionate style had considerable influence over later Russian poets, in particular Aleksandr Blok.

Filosofov, Dmitrii Vladimirovich (1872–1940) – Russian critic and essayist. Son of the famous public figure Anna Filosofova, enjoyed a scandalously intimate relationship with both Dmitrii Merezhkovskii and his wife Gippius. Collaborated with the *World of Art* group, was instrumental in founding the Petersburg Religious-Philosophical Society.

Florovskii, Georgii Vasil'evich (also known as Georges **Florovsky**, 1893–1979) – highly significant theologian, scholar of Orthodoxy, and Orthodox priest. Fled the Russian Empire after the Bolshevik Revolution and taught at prominent western institutions. His work was controversial for its use of Patristics to re-evaluate Russian religious culture and its rejection of many of the traditions of speculative religious philosophy in Russia.

Fofanov, Konstantin Mikhailovich (1862–1911) – Russian poet. One of the fathers of Russian Modernism, fallen somewhat into semi-obscurity owing to the greater prominence of his contemporaries Fet and Nekrasov.

Frank, Semen Liudvigovich (1877–1950) – prominent Russian religious philosopher. Born into a Jewish family, he converted to Orthodoxy in 1912. Influenced at various points by Nietzsche, Frank rejected positivism, and looked to the founding of a spiritual and cultural elite to guide society.

Gandlevskii, Sergei Markovich (born in 1952 in Moscow) – contemporary Russian poet, writer and literary critic.

Garshin, Vsevolod Mikhailovich (1855–1888) – prominent Russian author of short stories. He published approximately 20 stories, which included allegories, fairytales, and war stories. The most well-known of them are 'The Red Flower' (1883) and 'Four Days' (1877). A victim of severe bouts of mental illness, he committed suicide at the age of 33, by throwing himself down a stairwell.

Georgii Pobedonosets (St George the Victorious) (AD Third Century–303(304)) – a Saint-soldier specially honoured in Russia, Great Martyr, beheaded during the rule of the Emperor Diocletian. Depicted on the Moscow coat of arms as a horseman, trampling with his lance on a snake.

Gershenzon, Mikhail Osipovich (1869–1925) – prominent Russian literary historian and critic, philosopher, publicist and translator; an initiator of the famous publication '*Vekhi*' ('Landmarks') in 1909 where a group of prominent Russian philosophers analyzed the political and spiritual situation in Russia and criticized the radical Russian intelligentsia; publisher of the collections of works by I. V. Kireevskii (1911) and P. Ya. Chaadaev (1913–1914); throughout his life was also faithful to his Jewish roots by actively participating in Jewish cultural life.

Gertsen/Herzen, Aleksandr Ivanovich (1812–1870) – influential Russian writer, philosopher and social critic. Influenced heavily by Western ideas of progress and rationalism, Gertsen opposed Tsarist autocracy, advocated social reform in Russia and supported revolutionary movements across Europe. At one point associated with revolutionary Mikhail Bakunin, he died in exile in France, and said to be the 'father of Russian socialism'.

Gippius, Zinaida Nikolaevna (1869–1945) – Russian Symbolist poet, writer and literary critic; also published under the pseudonym Anton Krainii. She emigrated from Soviet Russia and settled in France (with her husband, Russian thinker Dmitrii Merezhkovskii) in 1920. Gippius was a prominent figure within the Silver Age of Russian culture both before and after her emigration; firmly opposed Bolshevism and acutely suffered the loss of the Motherland.

Gogol´, Nikolai Vasil´evich (1809–1852) – Classical Russian prose writer and dramatist of the period of Romanticism, master of the short story, known for his striking style, biting satire, and penchant for the farcical and grotesque. In his later years became gripped by a series of religious crises, burnt much of his unpublished manuscripts, and died in torment. His life and work has become one of the most important literary legends of Russian 20th century literature.

Gol´cev, Viktor Aleksandrovich (1850–1906) – prominent Russian journalist, in 1885–1906 the Chief Editor of the journal *Russian Thought*.

Gollerbach, Erikh Fedorovich (1895–1942) – Russian (Soviet) literary and art critic, poet, literary historian and bibliophile, author of memoirs about Rozanov. In 1915–1918 he was engaged in the correspondence with Rozanov, whom he considered to be his literary and philosophical teacher.

Goncharov, Ivan Aleksandrovich (1812–1891) – classical Russian writer.

Gor´kii, Maksim (Aleksei Maksimovich **Peshkov**, 1868–1936) – prominent Russian/Soviet prose writer and dramatist. Orphaned early and having experienced a difficult childhood, Gor´kii (his chosen pseudonym meaning 'bitter' in Russian) was driven by a fierce sense of social justice, and used his writings to criticize the Tsarist regime. Associated with the Social-Democratic movement and the Bolsheviks, he later had a fractious relationship with the Soviet leadership. After several spells overseas, he finally settled in Moscow where he died in suspicious circumstances. He is seen as the initiator of Soviet literature, and his work – as dedicated to the Socialist revolutionary movement.

Gorodetskii, Sergei Mitrofanovich (1884–1967) – Russian poet. Initially associated with the Symbolists, later became known as a leading member of the Acmeist school.

Griboedov, Aleksandr Sergeevich (1795–1829) – classical Russian writer.

Grigor'ev, Apollon Aleksandrovich (1822–1864) – Russian critic, memoirist, and translator. Wielded considerable influence on the native-soil movement (*pochvennichestvo*) in Russia, importing Herder's ideas on the organic development of civilizations; had significant influence over the ideas of the Dostoevskii brothers, Konstantin Leont'ev and Vasilii Rozanov, as well as over the traditions of organic criticism in Russia.

Grigorii Palama (Gregory Palamas) (1296–1359), Saint – prominent Byzantium theologian, church patriarch, systematiser of the mystical teaching of Hesychasm.

Grigorovich, Dmitrii Vasil'evich (1822–1899) – prominent writer of liberal orientation, writing in the spirit of the *Natural School*, contributor to the progressive journal *Sovremennik*. His most important works are the tales *The Village* (1846) and *Anton Goremyka* (1847). A friend of most of the prominent figures in nineteenth-century Russian literature, he was also known as the person who introduced Dostoevskii to Nekrasov in 1845.

Gromov, Mikhail Petrovich (1927–1990) – Russian literary scholar, Chekhov specialist: *Book on Chekhov* (1989), *Chekhov* (1993).

Il'in, Ivan Aleksandrovich (1883–1954) – Russian religious philosopher, who wrote on the role of the state and the philosophy of law. A conservative and monarchist by persuasion, he was deported by the Bolsheviks and lived in Germany and Switzerland; had great influence on 20th century Russian thought, literature and culture.

Ioann Groznyi (Ivan the Terrible) (1530–1584) – Russian Tsar (from 1547) whose reign is connected on the one hand with turning Russia into great power (inclusion of Kazan and Astrakhan khanates and Western Siberia) and on the other hand with an extremely despotic rule (*oprichnina* – special administrative elite, its territory and army; mass executions and murders; defeat of Novgorod).

Ioann Lestvichnik (Saint John Climacus, also known as **John of the Ladder**), Saint (AD 525 – c. 606) – leading Byzantium theologian, the head of a monastery on Sinai (hegumen), the author of the famous 'Ladder of Paradise' – guidance of monastic life.

Iushkevich, Semen Solomonovich (1868–1927) – Russian (Jewish) writer, literary historian, dramatist, and journalist.

Ivanov, Viacheslav Ivanovich (1866–1949) – prominent Russian Symbolist poet, literary critic, translator and philosopher; had a higher doctorate in philology; was one of the ideologists and cultural pillars of the Silver Age; spent the last years of his life in Italy.

Ivanov-Razumnik (Razumnik Vasil´evich **Ivanov**, 1878–1946) – Russian literary critic, pamphleteer and historian whose works are steeped in philosophical and sociological ideas; defined his credo as 'immanent subjectivism'; in 1919–1924 was one of the founders of *Vol´naia Filosofskaia Assotsiatsiia* (*Free Philosophical Association*) in Petrograd.

Katkov, Mikhail Nikiforovich (1818–1887) – Russian conservative journalist, influential during the reign of Alexander III.

Kireevskii, Ivan Vasil´evich (1806–1856) – prominent Russian philosopher. One of the intellectual founders of the Slavophile movement, opposed the Westernizing ideas of his rivals such as Gertsen.

Knipper, Ol´ga Leonardovna (1868–1959) – Russian stage actress, the wife of Anton Chekhov.

Kondakov, Nikodim Pavlovich (1844–1925) – leading Russian art scholar, academician, historian of the Byzantium and ancient Russian art; in emigration since 1920.

Korolenko, Vladimir Galaktionovich (1853–1921) – prominent Russian writer, journalist and publicist.

Kozhanchikov, Dmitrii Efimovich (died in 1877) – St Petersburg merchant, publisher and bookseller.

Kuprin, Aleksandr Ivanovich (1870–1938) – outstanding Russian prose writer, respected for his short stories which were highly admired by contemporaries such as Chekhov and Bunin.

LIST OF NAMES   xli

Lebedev, Mikhail Ivanovich (1811–1837) – Russian landscape painter.

Lenin, Vladimir Il'ich (Vladimir Il'ich **Ul'anov**, 1870–1924) – Russian Marxist revolutionary, politician, the orchestrator of the October revolution of 1917 and the first leader of the Soviet state.

Leont'ev, Konstantin Nikolaevich (1831–1891) – Russian conservative writer, philosopher, journalist, and literary critic (who was also at different times of his life a surgeon and diplomat), whose political and aesthetic ideas influenced Vasilii Rozanov. In many ways highly conservative and reactionary, drawn to Byzantine culture as the basis for Russia's spiritual development; was also attracted by Apollon Grigor'ev's theories of the organic growth of civilizations. His historisophical critique of the decline stage of Western civilization marked by egalitarian and utilitarian liberalism anticipated later 20th century catastrophist ideas of, among others, Oswald Spengler and Stanisław Ignacy Witkiewicz. In last years of his life, he was engaged in the correspondence with Rozanov, who considered him as one of his most important spiritual and literary teachers (next to the philosopher and literary critic N. N. Strakhov (1828–1896) and F. M. Dostoevskii (1821–1881)). In his later life became a monk.

Lermontov, Mikhail Iur'evich (1814–1841) – classical Russian poet, prose writer, and dramatist. The major exponent of Russian Romanticism, Lermontov was highly influential in the development of Russian poetry and the Russian novel. His experience as an army officer in the Caucasus influenced much of his work; died in a duel.

Leskov, Nikolai Semenovich (1831–1895) – classical Russian prose writer and journalist. Although neglected under the Soviet regime, he is now established as one of the great writers of 19th century Russian classicism.

Levitan, Isaak Il'ich (1860–1900) – leading Russian landscape painter, friend of A. P. Chekhov.

Levitanskii, Yuri Davydovich (1922–1996) – a prominent Russian poet.

Liatskii, Evgenii Aleksandrovich (1868–1942) – Russian literary critic and historian; writer, folklore scholar and ethnographer; aesthetically conservative.

Lotman, Iurii Mikhailovich (1922–1993) – outstanding Russian literary scholar, theoretician of literature, cultural historian, representative of the semiotic school.

Maikov, Apollon Nikolaevich (1821–1897) – prominent Russian poet; associated with Nekrasov and Turgenev.

Marcus Aurelius (Marcus Aurelius Antoninus Augustus, AD 121–180) – Roman Emperor and philosopher, representative of stoicism.

Marlinskii, Aleksandr (Aleksandr Bestuzhev-Marlinskii, 1797–1837) – Russian romantic writer and critic.

Mei, Lev Aleksandrovich (1822–1862) – Russian poet.

Men′shikov, Mikhail Osipovich (1859–1918) – conservative journalist, contributor to *Novoe Vremia*.

Mikhailovskii, Nikolai Konstantinovich (1842–1904) – prominent Russian literary critic, journalist, philosopher and sociologist; exponent of positivism and influential liberal-democratic publicist, he belonged to the populist movement, which saw its aim in getting close to the people, in particular in educating and emancipating peasantry; regarded as having continued civic traditions of such socially-oriented literary critics as N. G. Chernyshevskii and N. A. Dobroliubov. As a leader of the populist criticism, Mikhailovskii represented sociological method which criticised Chekhov for his lack of 'general idea', ideals and indifference towards social problems.

Mill, John Stuart (1806–1873) – English liberal philosopher and political theorist.

Milosz, Czeslaw (1911–2004) – outstanding Polish poet, translator and essay writer; spent a long time in emigration, predominantly in France and United States. Towards the end of his life Milosz returned to Poland. In 1980 won a Nobel Prize for literature.

Minskii, Nikolai Maksimovich (Nikolai Maksimovich **Vilenkin**, 1856–1937) – Russian poet, dramatist, philosopher and critic. One of the leading members of the Russian Symbolist movement, helped to found the Petersburg Religious-Philosophical Meetings.

Miroliubov, Viktor Sergeevich (pseudonym **Mirov**, 1860–1939) – Russian opera singer, journalist and publisher; friend of Chekhov; headed the magazine *Magazine for Everybody* (*Zhurnal dlia vsekh*) in 1898-1906. Initially associated with progressive democratic writers, he later developed mystical-religious inclinations which led to his departure from erstwhile allies such as Gor′kii.

Nadson, Semen Iakovlevich (1862–1887) – influential Russian poet. Although eclectic in style, in many ways he paved the way from the Russian classic style of the nineteenth century to the Russian Symbolist movement.

Nayman (Naiman), Anatolii Genrikhovich (born in 1936 in Leningrad) – Russian poet and writer; in his youth – Anna Akhmatova's literary secretary.

Nekrasov, Nikolai Alekseevich (1821–1878) – prominent Russian poet, critic and publisher, whose social conscience and concern for Russia's poor was highly influential on liberal and revolutionary writers and thinkers in Russia. As owner of the prominent liberal journal *The Contemporary* (*Sovremennik*) he was associated with Dobroliubov and Chernyshevskii.

Nikitenko, Aleksandr Vasil′evich (1804–1877) – Russian censor and historian of literature.

Pasternak, Boris Leonidovich (1890–1960) – classical Russian poet.

Pertsov, Petr Petrovich (1886–1947) – critic and editor of some of Rozanov's books.

Petr I, Velikii (Peter the Great) (1672–1725) – Russian Emperor, whose reign is connected with large-scale state reforms and creation of the Russian Empire.

Pilsudski, Jozef (1867–1935) – Polish politician and military leader. Led Poland to independence after World War I, later commanded Polish forces in the Polish-Soviet War.

Pisarev, Dmitrii Ivanovich (1840–1868) – influential Russian critic, radical social thinker, and proponent of 'rational egoism' and nihilism.

Pisemskii, Aleksei Feofilaktovich (1821–1881) – Russian novelist, dramatist, critic, and journalist.

Platonov, Andrei Pavlovich (1899–1951) – outstanding Russian modernist prose writer, poet and journalist. He created a unique existentialist and theological Soviet prose, which he developed through the deconstruction of the socialist realist aesthetics and ideology. His most famous novels include *The Foundation Pit* and *Chevengur*.

Plekhanov, Georgii Valentinovich (1857–1918) – Russian critic, revolutionary and Marxist theoretician.

Pleshcheev, Aleksei Nikolaevich (1825–1893) – Russian radical poet, highly respected by progressive thinkers and writers; the 'literary godfather' of writers such as Chekhov, Garshin and Nadson.

Pleve, Viacheslav Konstantinovich (1846–1904) – Russian Minister of Internal Affairs and head of the Tsarist police force. Murdered by extremist revolutionaries.

Polonskii, Iakov Petrovich (1819–1898) – Russian poet and writer of prose. Formed a 'poetic triumvirate' with Fet and Maikov.

Prishvin, Mikhail Mikhailovich (1873–1954) – prominent Russian/Soviet writer and diarist. As a schoolboy he was taught by Vasilii Rozanov, who expelled Prishvin over his bad behaviour.

Protopopov, Mikhail Alekseevich (1848–1915) – Russian literary critic. Associated with the Russian Populist movement, he privileged literature's social function over its aesthetic qualities.

Przheval'skii, Nikolai Mikhailovich (1839–1888) – outstanding Russian traveller and explorer; carried out various expeditions into Central Asia and made a number of scientific discoveries.

Pushkin, Aleksandr Sergeevich (1799–1837) – classical Russian poet, prose writer, dramatist, publicist, literary critic, founder of the new Russian literature and Russian literary language.

Remizov, Alexei Mikhailovich (1877–1957) – prominent Russian modernist writer, 'ornamentalist' (both in prose and graphic art), painter. He was one of Rozanov's faithful followers, as he used to say. In 1922, he published a book on Rozanov, *Kukha*, consisting of their correspondence and commentaries. His works include *The Pond* and *The Clock, Limonar, The Fire of Things, The Whirlwind Russia*.

Rossolimo, Grigorii Ivanovich (1860–1928) – Russian neurologist, professor of the Moscow University.

Savrasov, Aleksei Kondrat′evich (1830–1897) – outstanding Russian landscape painter, one of the founders of the partnership of the Itinerants (a late nineteenth century Russian school of realist painters); teacher of I. Levitan.

Schopenhauer Arthur (1788–1860) – German philosopher, representative of philosophical pessimism.

Sedakova, Olga Aleksandrovna (born in 1949 in Moscow) – prominent Russian poet.

Sergii Radonezhskii, Saint (1314–1392) – Russian Orthodox Saint, regarded as a great devotee of the Russian land, founder and hegumen of the Trinity lavra of St Sergius near Moscow (1345). His pupils founded more than 40 cloisters across Russia; canonized in 1452.

Shchedrin, Silvestr Feodosovich (1791–1830) – Russian landscape painter.

Shcheglov, Ivan (pen name of Ivan Leont′evich **Leont′ev**, 1856–1911) – writer, playwright, theatre critic whose writing career flourished in the 1880s; author of *The Dacha Husband* (1896), also collaborated with Chekhov on a farce entitled *The Power of Hypnotism*.

Shmelev, Ivan Sergeevich (1873–1950) – Russian writer. From a devoutly Orthodox family, he stood firmly in the traditions of Russian nineteenth-century classicism; emigrated in 1922.

Shperk, Fedor Eduardovich (1872–1897) – Russian poet, critic, writer, philosopher, friend of Rozanov.

Shternberg, Vasilii Ivanovich (1818–1845) – Russian landscape and genre painter.

Sienkiewicz, Henryk (1846–1916) – Polish writer.

Siluan (Silouan) Afonskii (1866–1938), saint – leading Russian devotee of the twentieth century; active on Mt Athos since 1892, canonized in 1988.

Skabichevskii, Aleksandr Mikhailovich (1838–1910) – literary critic-positivist and literary historian, close in orientation to the populist N. K. Mikhailovskii; criticised Chekhov for his lack of 'uniting ideological element' and 'fleeting impressions'.

Skitalets (Stepan Gavrilovich **Petrov**, 1869–1941) – Russian writer.

Sofrinii (Sakharov) (1896–1993), archimandrite – outstanding Russian orthodox theologian and devotee of the 20th century; was active on Mt Athos (1925–1947), where he was a pupil of the elder Silouan of Athos (Staretz Silouan); in 1959 in the county of Essex in England he organised Sviato-Ioanno-Predtechenskii monastery (Tolleshunt Knights, Maldon); author of the book *Staretz Silouan* (Paris, 1952); publications in English: *The Undistorted Image: Staretz Silouan* (1958); *Monk of Mt Athos* (1973) and *Wisdom from Mt. Athos* (1975).

Soldatenkov, Koz´ma Terent´evich (1818–1901) – Moscow textile factory owner, famous publisher, Maecenas, leading collector of books and Russian paintings. His collections became part of the Tretiakovskaia Gallery, Russian Museum and Russian State Library.

Sologub, Fedor Kuz´mich (Fedor Kuz´mich **Teternikov**, 1863–1927) – prominent Russian poet and prose writer. A major figure in the Symbolist movement, he started his career as a provincial school teacher.

Solov´ev, Vladimir Sergeevich (1853–1900) – highly influential Russian religious philosopher, poet, essayist and literary critic. He reportedly coined the phrase 'the Silver Age', and his philosophy and poetry were highly significant for the Russian religious renaissance at the start of the twentieth century. Much of his work investigates the concepts of sophiology, all-unity (*vseedinstvo*) and catholicity (*sobornost´*); in his later years he was drawn towards Ecumenism. He greatly influenced and inspired Russian Symbolist movement in arts including poets Andrei Belyi and Alexander Blok, and a philosopher Pavel Florenskii.

Spasovich, Vladimir Danilovich (1829–1906) – Polish critic, essayist and lawyer.

Spengler, Oswald Arnold Gottfried (1880–1936) – German historian and philosopher.

Stanislavskii, Konstantin Sergeevich (1863–1938) – prominent Russian theatre director and actor.

Stepniak-Kravchinskii, Sergei Mikhailovich (1851–1895) – Russian populist-revolutionary, writer; founded the 'Trust of Free Russian Press' in London (1891).

Strakhov, Nikolai Nikolaevich (1828–1896) – Russian conservative philosopher and literary critic, influenced by the ideas of the native-soil movement (*pochvennichestvo*). A one-time collaborator of Fedor Dostoevskii and Apollon Grigor´ev, he later became a close friend of Lev Tolstoi. He was a literary patron to, and one of the greatest philosophical influences over, Vasilii Rozanov.

Stravinskii, Igor Fedorovich (1872–1971) – famous Russian composer, pianist and conductor, one of the principal figures of musical avant-garde.

Suvorin, Aleksei Sergeevich (1834–1912) – prominent Russian journalist and publishing magnate, literary critic and memoirist, dramatist and theatre manager, he was also the owner and Editor-in-Chief of the influential conservative Petersburg newspaper *The New Times* (*Novoe Vremia*), founder of the magazine *Istoricheskii Vestnik*, employer of Rozanov and close friend and publisher of Anton Chekhov.

Suvorina, Anna Ivanovna (1858–1936) – second wife of Aleksei Suvorin.

Tikhonov, Vladimir Alekseevich (1857–1914) – Russian writer. An army officer and actor, he later worked for Suvorin's *The New Times*.

Tiutchev, Fedor Ivanovich (1803–1873) – classical Russian poet.

Tolstoi, Lev Nikolaevich (1828–1910) – classical Russian writer, philosopher and religious activist. One of the most important novelists of Russian and world literature, he was also highly influential throughout the world for his philosophy of love.

Trotskii, Lev Davidovich (Lev Davidovich **Bronshtein**, 1879–1940) – Russian politician, revolutionary and literary critic. One of the leading Bolsheviks, Trotskii also played a prominent role in early Soviet literary criticism. Despite his later removal from the political scene, his scathing attacks on many idealist writers such as Merezhkovskii and Rozanov laid the foundations for the Soviet Union's continuing condemnation of many such writers.

Turgenev, Ivan Sergeevich (1818–1883) – classical Russian prose writer of liberal orientation. A master of the novel and short stories, he interwove the depictions of beautiful scenery with psychology of love, and described with great precision and penetration the life of Russian gentry contemporary to him; was firmly opposed to serfdom and protested against it by artistic means.

Turkov, Andrei Mikhailovich (born in 1924 in Mytishchi, near Moscow) – Russian critic and literary scholar.

Tychinkin, Konstantin Semenovich (dates unknown) – tutor of Suvorin's children; editing Director of *Novoe Vremia* and later director of its printing house.

Uspenskii, Gleb Ivanovich (1843–1902) – Russian writer, associated with Nekrasov and the revolutionary intelligentsia.

Veinberg, Petr Isaevich (1830–1908) – Russian poet and translator; was more appreciated for his popular translations of Western writers such as Byron and Goethe than for his own work.

Volynskii (Flekser), Akim L'vovich (1863–1926) – Russian journalist, literary and ballet critic, art historian and philosopher, he was a representative of philosophical idealism, editor of the journal *Severnyi vestnik*. Volynskii was amongst the first of those who developed religious-philosophical aesthetics of Symbolism. While associated with the Symbolists and Decadents who grouped around the Merezhkovskiis, he won some degree of infamy through his scandalous attacks on the radical writers of the nineteenth century such as Chernyshevskii and Dobroliubov.

Volzhskii A. (Aleksandr Sergeevich **Glinka**, 1878–1940) – Russian literary critic and historian, representative of neo-idealism.

Vorob'ev, Maksim Nikoforovich (1787–1855) – Russian landscape painter.

Vysotskii, Vladimir Semenovich (1938–1980) – outstanding Russian poet, songwriter and actor; cult figure in Russia of his times and beyond.

Witkiewicz, Stanisław Ignacy (1885–1939) – Polish novelist, playwright, painter, photographer and philosopher.

Zaitsev, Boris Konstantinovich (1881–1972) – Russian prose writer and translator. Helped to bridge the Realist and Modernist movements in Russian literature, was deeply shocked by the Russian Revolution of 1917 and moved towards Orthodoxy; emigrated in 1923.

LIST OF RUSSIAN CULTURAL CONCEPTS

Bezvremen´e (literally: without time, in the absence of time; figuratively: best captured by Shakespearean 'the time is out of joint') – gloomy historical period when genuine cultural life freezes and goes 'underground' due to extreme political oppression.

Black Hundreds (*Chernaia Sotnia*) – Extremist Russian nationalist movement.

Fasting – ritual abstention from food and drink; in Russian orthodoxy the number of fasting days reaches 200.

'Gore' Griboedovskoe – comedy in verse *Gore ot uma* ('Woe from Wit') (1828) by A. S. Griboedov (1795–1829), which became his most famous work.

Iaroslavna – the heroine of the literary jewel of ancient Russian literature 'The Lay of Igor's Warfare' (end of the 12th century), which describes the military campaign of her husband Igor Sviatoslavich, the prince of Novgorod-Severskii against Polovtsians (1185); she is the first female character of the ancient Russian literature.

Lampadnyi stakanchik (lampion) – luminaire which is made out of a little glass with oil and wick, lit up in front of icons as a sign of prayer.

'*Mertvyi dom*' – F. M. Dostoevskii's novel *Notes from the House of the Dead* (1862).

Mitia Karamazov – hero of F. M. Dostoevskii's novel *The Brothers Karamazov* (1880).

Ivan Karamazov – hero of F. M. Dostoevskii's novel *The Brothers Karamazov* (1880), famous in particular for his idea commonly phrased as 'if there is no God then everything is permitted'.

1 ANTON CHEKHOV THROUGH THE EYES OF RUSSIAN THINKERS

'Nedoby(t)chik' – a man who cannot provide for his family.

Old Believers (*Staroobriadtsy*) – religious group which separated in 1666–1667 from the official Russian Orthodox Church in protest against the Church reforms introduced by Patriarch Nikon, and continued the liturgical practices which the Russian Orthodox Church abandoned.

Palekh – a village of Palekh region of Ivanovskaia province (*oblast'*), one of the centres of artistic trade, famous for its lacquer miniature in the 'palekh' style. From the eighteenth century it has been a centre of icon-painting in the traditions of Russian painting of the fifteenth to seventeenth centuries.

Platon Karataev – hero of L. N. Tolstoi's novel *War and Peace* (1869), who embodies national ideals of the Russian nation – 'all Russian, kind and round'.

Pochvennichestvo – a nationalist trend in Russian social thought of the 1860s, its main premise was the idea of 'national soil' ('*pochva*') as the foundation of Russian social and spiritual history. Main editions: *Vremia* ('Time', 1861–1863) and *Epokha* ('The Epoch', 1864–1865). F. M. Dostoevskii was one of its most famous representatives.

Riurik, Sineus, Truvor – according to the legends in Russian chronicles, these are the three brothers Varangians who were summoned by the Slavs in order to put a stop to the local internecine feuds in Novgorod, and who founded the Russian state.

Silver Age – early twentieth century blooming period of Russian culture (literature, philosophy, music, theatre and visual arts) dominated by Modernism which came to replace the utilitarian and positivist attitudes of the previous generation; the name was given by analogy with the Golden Age of Russian poetry of Pushkin's era (early nineteenth century). The period was also marked by a flurry of outstanding theoretical work.

***Slavianofily* (Slavophiles)** – representatives of one of the movements of Russian social and philosophical thought of 1840–1850 (A. S. Khomiakov, I. V. and P. V. Kireevskiis, I. S. and K. S. Aksakovs, Yu. F. Samarin) who, in their polemics with the 'Westernisers' oriented towards the Western European way of development, promoted an original, Russian orthodox way of historical development for Russia.

Sobornost´ – a term of Christian theology signifying the communal nature of the Church; in the nineteenth century Russia was understood as a principle also defining the foundation of Russian social life as having roots in the peasant community.

'Sredi doliny rovnyia' ('Amidst the plain valley') – famous song, written to the 1810 poem of Aleksei Fedorovich Merzliakov (1778–1830).

Staroobriadchestvo – the movement of **Old Believers** (see the entry above).

Strannichestvo – Russian concept of pilgrimage with the aim of god-seeking, of distancing oneself from earthly matters and sharing saintly spirit; or simply hitting the road out of spiritual and intellectual anxiety in search for the sacred meaning of life.

Zastupnitsa (**Heavenly Mediatress**) – in Russian orthodoxy this refers to the Virgin Mary and expresses the idea of merciful interceding (*zastupat'sa*) for a sinner before God.

THREE BRIEF BIOGRAPHIES

Vasilii Rozanov

Vasilii Vasilievich Rozanov was born on 20 April (2 May) 1856 in Vetluga, Kostroma province, to the family of a forester. His parents died early. He survived thanks to the care of his elder brother Nikolai, to be educated in a gymnasium in Nizhnii Novgorod. In 1882 Rozanov graduated from Moscow University where he studied philology. He then worked as a teacher in various gymnasiums in Russian provincial towns.

His first published work was a treatise *On Understanding*, printed in Moscow in 1886. However, Rozanov's interests gradually drifted from the philosophical to the religious, as can be seen from the articles he wrote in the 1890s. They paved Rozanov's path to conservative journalism, and he soon left school teaching, which he profoundly disliked, and moved to St Petersburg. After an initial period as a civil servant (which he also could not tolerate), from 1899 Rozanov took up an editorial post on Aleksei Suvorin's newspaper *Novoe vremia*.

In the early 1900s Rozanov gained a reputation as a talented conservative journalist. He published widely, but became best known at the time for his studies of F. M. Dostoevskii (most notably for his work on the 'Legend of the Grand Inquisitor', part of Dostoevskii's novel *The Brothers Karamazov*).

Rozanov's first marriage – to Dostoevskii's former lover Apollinaria Suslova, who was 17 years older than Rozanov – had proved disastrous and disintegrated in 1886, with Suslova refusing a divorce. Rozanov thus had to live with his second wife, Varvara Dmitrievna Butiagina (whom he wedded secretly and by whom he had children) in a 'state of sin' in the eyes of the Church as lawful marriage was impossible without Suslova granting him a divorce. This intensified his contemplation of Christianity, especially Russian orthodoxy, in relation to the concepts of family, love and sex. This led Rozanov to criticism of the 'historical Church' which evolved into his wrestling against Christianity in general. He criticised the 'Religion of Golgotha' for the sake of the 'Religion of Bethlehem'. The metaphysics of sex became one of the central philosophical themes for Rozanov. In his original vision, Rozanov regarded human nature in the unity of body and spirit, intrinsically linked to the Divine Logos, but not through universal reason. For him this link was provided instead by physical love which Rozanov deemed highly spiritual. This view went against traditional Russian puritan attitudes, with their modest concealment of sexual matters in literary discourse, and tortured ambivalence on the part of Russian classics, such as Tolstoi and Dostoevskii, with respect to physical love as steeped in sin and shame.

In 1900 Rozanov founded the Religious-Philosophical Society together with co-members Dmitrii Merezhkovskii, Nikolai Minskii and Zinaida Gippius. Later, however, Rozanov was excluded from it as a result of his ambivalent position with respect to the Beilis affair: a fabricated trial case against a Ukrainian Jew Menahem Mendel Beilis, accused of ritual murder of a Christian boy. The case against Beilis was lost, and the affair was regarded by progressive Russian liberals as an insult to the Russian nation, and by the wider world as a manifestation of the anti-Semitic policies of the Russian state. More generally, Rozanov displayed deep ambivalence with regard to the Jewish question, combining openly anti-Semitic with almost Philo-Semitic positions, as manifested in his contradictory publications.

Notwithstanding his numerous writings on social and cultural issues, politics and education, Rozanov remains best known for his literary-philosophical works which constitute a substantial part of his legacy. Despite his disdain for the Decadent movement and criticism of Russian Symbolists whom he reproached for their rift with Russia's classical tradition, Rozanov's ultimate special genre of inner dialogues and profoundly subjective reminiscences uses poetic craft very akin to that of his literary opponents.

In the period leading to his death on 5 February 1919 in Sergiev Posad near Moscow, where he moved with his family from Petrograd in 1917, Rozanov existed in a state of destitution and hunger. His last thoughts were focused intensely on the fate of Russian literature. On his deathbed Rozanov dictated to his younger daughter his bequest to Russian writers to prevent the eternal frost which he believed was dawning over literature and culture worldwide.

Rozanov's original and paradoxical writings have enjoyed a second birth with their republication in Russia in the post-Soviet period almost a century after their first appearance. Their thematic division correlates with the original chronology, mirroring the evolution of his ideas. Thus Rozanov's metaphysics of sex is reflected in his book *In the World of the Obscure and Unresolved* (1901) and in the collection of articles *The Family Question in Russia* (1903). His views on Christianity in relation to the themes of sex, family and religion were reflected in the books *Near the Church Walls* (1906) as well as *Dark Face* and *People of the Moonlight* published in 1911. Rozanov's *Solitaria* (1912) and *Fallen Leaves* (1913) marked a new genre of introspection and reminiscences concluded with his last book *The Apocalypse of Our Time*, published amidst the crisis of 1917–18.

Dmitrii Merezhkovskii

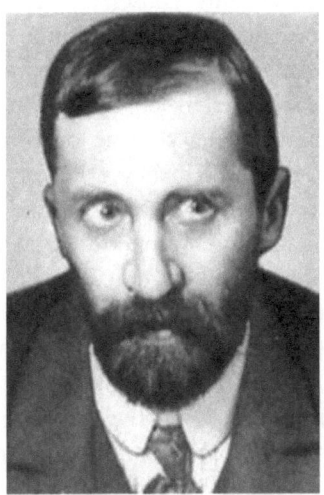

Dmitrii Sergeevich Merezhkovskii was born on 2 (14) August 1865 in St Petersburg to a noble family. In 1875 he entered a Petersburg gymnasium, where, despite its oppressive atmosphere, he began writing poetry, which by the early

1880s was already being published. In 1883 Merezhkovskii embarked upon his studies of history and philology at Petersburg University. His dissertation (which Merezhkovskii defended in 1888) was dedicated to Montaigne; the same year his first collection of poetry was published. It contained some civic and populist themes which he later abandoned. By the end of the 1880s Merezhkovskii had begun contributing to the journal *Severnyi Vestnik* which brought together the first Russian Symbolists, in particular Zinaida Gippius, whom Merezhkovskii married in 1889. According to Gippius, they never parted even for a day during their 52-year-long union which was marked by a profound spiritual and intellectual kinship, despite apparently having suffered an ailment of emotional under-fulfilment.

In 1893 Merezhkovskii's book *On the Causes of the Decline and on the New Trends in Contemporary Russian Literature* was published, perceived by his contemporaries as the first aesthetic manifesto of the Russian Decadence movement. In it Merezhkovskii set out to oppose democratic social orientation, philosophical materialism and the realism of Russian literature. Instead, he saw a future in a 'new ideal art' which would reflect the sort of religious-mystical sensibility inherent, to him, in classical Russian literature. Symbolism, which he now championed, was for Merezhkovskii more than an artistic school, it embodied the whole sensibility underpinned by a 'new religious consciousness' and an understanding of the universe through religious faith. Merezhkovskii saw his civic and artistic duty in saving Russian spirituality from degradation by developing this new religious consciousness. Within this framework Merezhkovskii reacted to the first Russian revolution of 1905, warning against the encroaching forces of philistinism, faithlessness and mediocrity. In the wake of the revolution the Merezhkovskiis left Russia for Paris where they stayed from 1906 until 1908. That city later became for the couple a refuge from the Bolshevik revolution of 1917, which they decisively rejected. This ultimate emigration – in 1919 – was a never-healing wound for both. Until the end of their lives the Merezhkovskiis continued to fight against Bolshevism and to grieve their lost Russia; to the extent that Dmitrii Merezhkovskii ended up supporting Mussolini and Hitler, seeing fascism as a force capable of defeating Bolshevism. This alienated many of his former followers and admirers, and when the philosopher died in Paris in 1941, nobody came to his funeral.

Merezhkovskii was prolific in his creative output both in pre-revolutionary Russia and in exile. In Petersburg he founded (in 1900) the Religious-Philosophical Society together with Vasilii Rozanov, Nikolai Minskii and Zinaida Gippius. He also created a mystical-idealistic journal *Novyi Put'* (1903–04) and collaborated extensively in the Symbolist periodicals. Merezhkovskii's legacy includes extensive studies of Russian classical writers whom he perceived in a religious-mystical light. He also penned historical novels and plays, religious-philosophical essays, poetry, biographies of leading Church reformers, as well as political articles. While in St Petersburg, Merezhkovskii and Gippius hosted the most famous literary salon frequented by the artistic Russian elite of the time – Symbolist poets and religious philosophers.

In Paris the Merezhkovskiis founded a philosophical-literary gathering '*Zelenaia Lampa*' which largely continued their previous philosophical theme, but was also illuminated by the new missionary endeavour – to fight against Bolshevism. Despite his difficult character (he was perceived by many as excessively dry, arrogant and rational), Merezhkovskii's cultural importance and influence and his role in the Silver Age of Russian culture are undeniable. He was nominated for the Nobel Prize in literature on several occasions, with Ivan Bunin dislodging him to take the prize in 1933. His wife Zinaida Gippius outlived him by four years, and wrote the (unfinished) book of memoirs entitled *Dmitrii Merezhkovskii*.

Merezhkovskii's main religious-philosophical ideas (the dialectics of paganism and Christianity; of 'flesh' and 'spirit'; the idea of the Third Testament) were reflected in his novel trilogy *Christ and Antichrist* comprising *The Death of the Gods: Julian the Apostate* (1895–96); *The Resurrection of the Gods: Leonardo da Vinci* (1901) and *Antichrist: Peter and Alexis* (1905), as well as in his literary-critical and philosophical study *L. Tolstoi and Dostoevskii* (1900–1902).

Lev Shestov

Lev Shestov (Lev Isaakovich, born Yehuda Leib Shvartsman) was born in Kiev on 31 January (12 February) 1866 to a big Russian-Jewish family of seven children. His father was a successful 'self-made' merchant and religious scholar. Lev was growing up a sensitive and idealistic boy, enthused by Russian literature. After his study in Kiev gymnasium, he entered Moscow University (1884) to study mathematics, but then transferred to Law. His dissertation, on the conditions of the Russian working class and the new Factory Legislation, was found too left-wing and remained undefended. However his interests soon departed from socialism, and he became engrossed in existential problems of the tragic human predicament – a theme which ultimately underpins Shestov's entire philosophy.

Upon graduation, while working for his father's business, he started to publish work in local Kiev journals – articles of literary criticism saturated with philosophy. In 1895 Shestov suffered a nervous crisis and went for treatment abroad. It is there that he met and married in 1897 a Russian Orthodox woman, Anna Berezovskaia. They subsequently had two daughters, Tatiana and Natalia, but the marriage was kept secret from Shestov's strict Jewish parents until his father's death in 1914.

At the turn of the century Shestov started publishing large works in book form on literary and philosophical issues, interpreting Russian classical writers in a Nietzschean key and providing a revision and thorough critique of Western speculative philosophy and autonomous ethics. His passionate interrogations of various thinkers, writers and philosophers, Russian and Western-European alike, revealed the gap between human psyche and its literary expressions, between what is said and is meant (or rather – what is concealed). Philosophically Shestov's credo was shaped as anti-rationalist and existentialist with his interpretation of the Fall as a tragic and fateful spurning of the tree of life for the fruits of the tree of knowledge which bring nothing but suffering and death.

Up until the First World War Shestov mostly stayed in Europe with his family, but spent the turbulent years between 1914 and 1920 back in Russia. Then in January 1920 he fled from the Bolshevik regime and soon settled with his family in Paris. With his beautiful literary style and original ideas Shestov rapidly made a name for himself in pre-revolutionary Russia and proceeded to become part of French intellectual life. He influenced a number of prominent French intellectuals, such as Albert Camus, Jules de Gaultier and Georges Bataille, and introduced Husserl's phenomenology to the French; furthermore, Shestov can be considered as a precursor of Sartrean existentialism. Among his intellectual friendships he counted Edmund Husserl, Martin Buber, Lucien Levy Bruhl and many others. He also stayed in touch with the life of the Russian émigré community and cherished his life-long friendships with fellow Russians, most notably Nikolai Berdiaev. Lev Shestov died in Paris on 20 November 1938. Although supra-national and supra-temporal in his philosophical interests, Shestov remains very much a part and product of Russian culture, and one of the most fascinating thinkers of the Russian Silver Age.

Shestov's main publications include his early books on literary-philosophical topics, such as *The Good in the Teaching of Tolstoi and Nietzsche* (1900), *Dostoevskii and Nietzsche: Philosophy of Tragedy* (1903) and *Apotheosis of Groundlessness: an Attempt of Adogmatic Thinking* (1905), which was written in aphoristic form and received as highly subversive both in style and content. Amongst his later and more philosophically oriented writings one could single out *Sola Fide* (unfinished; written in 1913–14, but published only posthumously in 1957 in French and in 1964 in Russian); *Potestas Clavium* (1923); *In Job's Balances* (1929), *Kierkegaard and the Existential Philosophy* (1936 in French, 1939 in Russian) and his seminal work *Anthens and Jersulalem* (1938 in French, 1951 in Russian).

Part One
VASILII ROZANOV

1

ROZANOV ON CHEKHOV: 'OVERCOMING LITERATURE' AND EXTENDING HORIZONS[1]

Vladimir B. Kataev

I

Among the notes found in Chekhov's archive, the following passage can be found:

> While we in our intelligentsia circles pick over old material and, according to the old Russian custom, denounce each other, life, which we do not know and do not notice, boils all over us. Great events will catch us unprepared like sleeping beauties. You will see that the merchant Sidorov and a school teacher from the provincial town of Elets, who see and know more than we do, will push us right to the back because they will have accomplished more than all of us put together.[2]

This note dates back to the late 1880s or early 1890s, when Chekhov worked on '*Rasskaz neizvestnogo cheloveka*' ('An Anonymous Story', 1893), and the mention of a teacher from Elets does not appear here by accident. It is not just the belief in Russia as full of provincial towns. Chekhov might have had in mind the example of the philosophical work *On Understanding* (*O ponimanii*) which appeared shortly before this note (1886),[3] the first publication by Vasilii Rozanov, who became a teacher in Elets in 1887.

This is the first similarity between these two contemporaries: a profound and simultaneous interest in the problem of understanding. In Rozanov's work, understanding is a measure of the usefulness of a branch of science or philosophy. He thus regards understanding as the ultimate goal of scientific and philosophical cognition. One of Rozanov's students in Elets was a boy named Kurymushka – the future writer Mikhail Prishvin – who gave his own response to the book when he learned of its existence: 'How good it would be to have such a book on understanding'. The boy would be able to avoid suffering from the 'illness of a lack of understanding' on the part of others.[4] Thus a philosophical level of understanding was translated to the level of everyday consciousness. In the same way, the problem of understanding, applied to the level of consciousness and the behaviour of an ordinary, 'average' person, assumed an important place in the works by Anton Chekhov from the mid 1880s onwards.

In 'Toska' ('Misery', 1886), no one can understand the true reason for the angst of the drayman Iona, including himself. In '*Pripadok*' ('A Nervous Breakdown', 1888), the student Vasil´ev is driven to a nervous breakdown by the incomprehensible and alien outside world. To the hero of the story '*Strakh*' ('Terror', 1892), life seems frightening because it is incomprehensible. All these stories and novellas by Chekhov, where the hero is an ordinary person and does not have the strength to find his way through life, are united by the central theme of non-understanding (an inability or unwillingness to understand another person). Chekhov's subsequent work, *Ivanov* (1887), is also a play about non-understanding. It is built entirely on the meeting of two opposing viewpoints: Ivanov's viewpoint is: 'I do not understand what is happening to me', but the other protagonists believe: 'We understand him only too well'. It is this opposing encounter which leads the hero to commit suicide. In Chekhov's later works, the opposition between understanding and non-understanding moved from the surface of plotlines to the depths, but was still preserved up to his very last works. In Chekhov's world, both non-understanding and misunderstanding are the principal reasons for human tragedy.

However, one cannot really speak of the direct influence of Rozanov's book *On Understanding* in the forming of Chekhov's fundamental theme of understanding. Rather, their simultaneous focus on the problem of understanding, albeit from different starting points, was a mark of the time that shaped them both. To the end of his life, Rozanov maintained a feeling of resentment towards his contemporaries for having underestimated his first book.[5] Maybe it was Chekhov's consistent emphasis on the theme of understanding which led to the subject of research in Rozanov's first philosophical work. It was in the 1880s that the foundations were laid and routes designated for the subsequent turning point in both Russian thought and Russian aesthetics. In their own ways, Chekhov and Rozanov both expressed this turning point, which determined the development of literature and philosophy in the twentieth century.

Another example of the resonance between Rozanov and Chekhov is much more personal. It is connected with one of Chekhov's masterpieces, the story 'The Man in a Case' (*Chelovek v futliare*, 1898). Iurii Sobolev once pointed out that a 'living model' for the character of Belikov could have been Mikhail Men′shikov, a hydrographer and well-known publicist from *The Week* (*Nedelia*). Chekhov wrote of him in his diary: 'In dry weather he wears galoshes and carries an umbrella against sunstroke, he is afraid to wash with cold water, etc.'[6] However, the commentator of the academic collection of Chekhov's works doubted this: 'Men′shikov's resemblance to the story's protagonist is too superficial, he participated in a number of sea expeditions, published various literary articles – in a word, he cannot be related to the Man in a Case'.[7] Dmitrii Galkovskii (who in *Infinite Dead End* (*Beskonechnyi tupik*, 1988) attempts to write in Rozanov's style, repeating his invectives against Russian literature) suggests a completely improbable scheme: he declares that the Man in a Case is Chekhov himself. He then characterizes Men′shikov as having nothing in common with the 'cowardly, boring and accurate idiot Belikov',[8] who, as he implies, was simply defamed by the writer.

However, those who deny that Men′shikov could be a prototype (clearly not the only one) of the hero of 'The Man in a Case' are in the wrong, as the following episode, which involves Rozanov, suggests.

The only surviving letter from Chekhov to Rozanov, of 30 March 1899, states: 'Last time we [Chekhov and Gor′kii] talked about your feuilleton in *The New Times* [*Novoe Vremia*] concerning physical love and marriage (in relation to Men′shikov's articles). This essay is superb and, by the way, the references to the Old Testament are remarkably poetic and expressive'.[9] Chekhov spoke with Gor′kii about Rozanov's article *Krotkii demonizm* ('Petty Demonism'), published in the collection *Religion and Culture* (*Religiia i kul′tura*, 1899). In it, Rozanov acutely criticised Men′shikov's article 'On Superstitions and the Truth of Love' (*O sueveriiakh i pravde liubvi*). He wrote: 'Men′shikov is against "marriage", against "love" and all these "physical" nightmares – just like a 16-year-old girl, but with the experience of an 11-year-old [...]. He explores the fact of so-called physical love, but, no matter how attentively we read these articles [...] we did not discover any motif in them, except that "love is a sin"'.[10] Rozanov decisively argues against Men′shikov, summons him to understand 'sensual and physical love' as 'a happy duty and simultaneously as an inexpressible happiness of being, filled with mysterious meaning and religious height'. He supports his opinion by references to the Old Testament, the Book of Ruth and the Book of Tobit. The Bible and Gospels, according to Rozanov, borrowed 'precisely the sensual love, the "little flame" of love, but fully surrounded it by poetry. And having borrowed it, they explained its meaning by the words, "this is a great mystery"'.[11]

Here are the famous lines from Chekhov's 'Man in a Case': 'The only things that were clear to his mind were government circulars and newspaper articles in which something was forbidden. When some proclamation prohibited the boys from going out in the streets after nine o'clock in the evening, or some article declared carnal love unlawful, it was to his mind clear and definite; it was forbidden, and that was enough. For him there was always a doubtful element, something vague and not fully expressed, in any sanction or permission'.[12] This is how Chekhov characterizes the Man in a Case, inserting directly into his text a phrase from Rozanov's polemic with Men´shikov. Also, in another story from 'Little Trilogy' (*Malenkaia trilogiia*), 'About Love'(*O liubvi*), the same citation is given from Paul's message to the Ephesians: 'This is a great mystery'. (Chekhov praises Rozanov's article in his letter to him of 1899, after 'The Little Trilogy' had already been published. But he refers not to the latest of Rozanov's collection, but instead to his feuilleton in *The New Times*, which points to the fact that he very well remembered the first publication of 'Petty Demonism' in edition 7807 of *The New Times*, 19 November 1897 – on the eve of Chekhov's work on the stories which comprised 'The Little to Trilogy'). Chekhov indirectly condemned Rozanov's ideological opponent. One could say that Rozanov, via his formulae, entered into one of the most famous Chekhov's texts.

This example adds to our knowledge of Chekhov's creative work, demonstrating how the material for his characters had been accumulated gradually, and from a great variety of sources. While resonating with Rozanov's text, Chekhov gave his own assessment of the topic 'regarding physical love and marriage' in his 'Little Trilogy', to which Rozanov dedicated so many of his writings at the turn of the nineteenth century. Chekhov's answer can be formulated by the words of Alekhin, one of those who discuss the question 'about love': 'So far only one incontestable truth has been uttered about love: "This is a great mystery". Everything else that has been written or said about love is not a conclusion, but only a statement of questions which remain unanswered. The explanation which would seem to fit one case does not apply in a dozen others, and the very best thing, to my mind, would be to explain every case individually, without attempting to generalize. We ought, as the doctors say, to individualize each case'.[13] Chekhov's response to the huge problem posed by Rozanov was methodological and concerned the way art can treat this theme, as well as much else.

II

However, the problem of the connections between Rozanov and Chekhov is not exhausted by these episodes.

When looking at them from the end of the twentieth century, their destinies become more visible, as well as the measures to be applied when comparing these two figures. Their common features, as well as their sharp differences, are partly visible, but also require further study.

What unites these two contemporaries biographically? They were almost the same age, but had such different lives.

Both came to Russian literature after everybody else – and both came from outside, from a province, in order to take their place at the centre of Russian thought and Russian aesthetics. Both went through Moscow University and were lectured by Buslaev and Zakhar'in. Both had to find their way with respect to the heritage of the same ideological fathers, men of the sixties and seventies. For almost ten years, both were simultaneously attracted and repelled by Tolstoi's 'The Kreutzer Sonata' (*Kreitserova Sonata*, 1889), by Tolstoi's preaching. Both came of age largely under the influence of a newspaper: it formed their style, architectonics and genre.

Aleksei Suvorin played a leading role in both men's biography. It is interesting to note that what attracted them both to Suvorin was also what made Chekhov ultimately part ways with him, while Rozanov remained loyal to his patron.

'Everywhere is a desert to the lonely man' was inscribed on Chekhov's ring, while Rozanov's 'ring of solitude' was 'put on from birth'.[14] This is only a fraction of the biographical similarity. What about their outlooks on life and their attitudes to creativity? Of course, Chekhov and Rozanov represent different, often opposing, branches of Russian thought and aesthetics, and continue different traditions in Russian literature. This is quite obvious and does not require explanation. However, there are a number of features in their literary positions and their works which can be legitimately juxtaposed.

Thus, a comparative analysis of Chekhov's *Notebooks* and Rozanov's *Fallen Leaves* (*Opavshie list'ia*, 1913, 1915) merits study. *Fallen Leaves*, like the *Notebooks*, was written almost in passing, without a general plan and without deliberate intention. As Siniavskii comments, 'Strictly speaking, this is a book from the rubbish bin. It does not have a unifying idea, or a preconceived plot, or even a purpose. Yet this is a book about himself to a larger extent than any other book close to the writer's body and soul'.[15] Almost everything in this description of Rozanov's *Fallen Leaves* can be applied to Chekhov's *Notebooks*. However, these books are organized by different authorial identities.

It is conventional and tempting to identify Chekhov's 'I' in his *Notebooks*: they have been long since treated as Chekhov's thoughts (and passed into common use as aphorisms), while they are nothing other than a stockpile for the future monologues and dialogues of his characters. We learn about the authorial 'I' only from later texts, where these notes are included in other systems and constructions. The craft is the same in the *Notebooks* and in *Fallen Leaves*, but there is no intimacy in the *Notebooks*. In *Fallen Leaves* there is the 'I' of the writer, while in the *Notebooks* – the 'I' of a character. Both the harmonized prose of Chekhov and the deliberately untidy prose of Rozanov are the result of high art, of thoroughly considered constructions.

Chekhov's famous antinomies were recollected by Bunin: a writer must be poor, almost destitute, as this is a necessary condition for creativity, but at the same time he must be incredibly wealthy to be able to see the world, without which no creativity is possible; or, the belief in personal immortality is absurd and superstitious; where on the next day he promises to prove that personal immortality exists as easily as two times two is four. Bunin was left puzzled after such conversations: what did Chekhov really think about immortality, poverty and wealth?[16] But did not Rozanov lead his readers into a dead end in the same way; either 'red' or 'black', first in his various articles and books, and later on even on the same page? In this new writer's position, Rozanov continued what Chekhov had already started.

Another similarity can be observed in the phenomenon of 'going beyond the bounds of literature'. 'Rozanov perceives himself as the last *realist*. This is as if Chekhov had turned a microscope inwards on himself and thus, once again in the personality of Rozanov, killed literature'.[17] Chekhov amazed his contemporaries by the fact that he could turn everything into a plotline for a story: a glass, an ashtray or a monk. For Rozanov anything – tears, pain, rubbish, spitting – became material for literature without a plotline, without a framing novella and without comic colouring, as Shklovskii noted.[18] Both the novelty of Chekhov's plotlines, and the lack of them in *Fallen Leaves*, seemed to contemporaries as 'going beyond the bounds of literature', although in reality it was an extending of the traditional boundaries of literature.

III

What Rozanov and Chekhov wrote and said about one another is interesting, but ultimately is unjust and short-sighted. The scales in these statements are not yet settled, and a different lens was required, a lens which only subsequent history could produce.

In his two articles on Chekhov of 1910,[19] Rozanov, with all his goodwill, with almost loving intonations, creates an image of Chekhov evidently prompted by Suvorin, who also loved Chekhov, but who understood and accepted him completely, and was jealous of Chekhov for having broken away from *The New Times*. 'Chekhov will not be forgotten', 'he became the most loved writer of our lack of will, our lack of heroism, our routine', but 'his talent has always been and remains second-rate', Chekhov did not have a hint of the creative powers of Gogol', Tolstoi or Dostoevskii, and comparisons of Chekhov with Shakespeare are simply tasteless. Therefore all that happened to 'our Antosha Chekhonte' in the twentieth century, finding in him universality, worldwide appeal, acknowledging him as one of the spiritual teachers and greatest artists, all this would seem to Rozanov incredibly unexpected. On the other hand, it is precisely Rozanov who first pointed out the philosophical dimension of Chekhov's oeuvre.[20]

On the other hand, Chekhov – who viewed the religious-philosophical gatherings of the beginning of the century as meetings of 'angry gymnasium students', and who saw in Rozanov's publications in *The New Times* the at times uncivilised brutality of a Russian policeman,[21] (and at times some highly native elements, such as Old Testament poetry, or the breadth, wit and talent of Rozanov's essay on Nekrasov) – could not appreciate the two-faced nature, the ambivalence of Rozanov's writings, or the daring nature which for Rozanov constituted both a principle and a device. On the other hand, this was deployed by Rozanov when in his fifties, i.e. after Chekhov's death.

The posthumous destiny of these two writers turned out to be very different. Grossman says of Chekhov in his *Life and Fate* (*Zhizn' i sud'ba*, 1960), through the lips of his hero Mad'iarov, that Chekhov is allowed in our country because he has not been understood (neither by the authorities nor readers).[22] Can one say that Rozanov was forbidden because he was understood correctly? This is unlikely, as Rozanov's grandiosity and the guarantee that he will forever remain in Russian literature is not in his separate themes, no matter how original or prophetic these might be, but in his method, his principle, the structure of his thought, and his unique Rozanovian logic. Maybe it is a cause for joy rather than regret that 'all life long and afterwards' he has been 'not famous, but simply not unknown'?[23] The thought of becoming fashionable, becoming an icon, or a model for the many tiny Rozanovs of modernity, is something that he himself would have viewed as the gloomiest possible fate.

Rozanov, that is to say the type of Russian man embodied by him, has on numerous occasions been turned into Chekhov's literary hero. Some of his features are recognizable in the protagonist of the story 'On the Way' (*Na puti*, 1886): he intended to follow through every idea uncompromisingly, an aim which would possess him completely. Thus, when Rozanov concluded that in the split between God and sex, Christ is to blame, he started to attack Christ and Christianity. But then he threw himself in the same dedicated way to follow the ideas of Christ. Or, similar to Iakov Terekhov, the hero of Chekhov's story 'The Murder' (*Ubiistvo*, 1895), who strove to believe in his own way and searched for his faith all his life, Rozanov dedicated himself forever to the search for his inner, personal God, different from other gods.

Long before his death, Rozanov carried the Apocalypse within himself, prophetically feeling its approach. However, as a Russian inhabitant, as a living person, he was overthrown by the Apocalypse that overcame Russia, and was surprised by the unexpected emergence of the phenomenon which had been for him, as thinker and writer, so obvious for so long. One wonders what Chekhov's reaction would have been to the Apocalypse?

Next to Rozanov's heat and coldness, and his intense religious reflection, is it not Chekhov's decision to remain outside religion, or his acknowledgement that he did not know the true God, that to which the Angel of Apocalypse referred with disdain as neither hot, nor cold, but warm? No. Because when Chekhov said 'between "there is God" and "there is no God" there lays a vast gulf which a true wizard overcomes with difficulty', he spoke of his firm choice, of his everlasting search for faith. This constitutes another meeting point with Rozanov.

Rozanov's trilogy is related to that line in world literature which runs from *Tristram Shandy*,[24] through *Evgenii Onegin*,[25] to *Ulysses*.[26] It remains one of the most original works of Russian and world literature of the twentieth century. Russian literature did not follow Rozanov's route: the plot in prose did not die, the novel is still alive, and dramatic form followed Chekhov. Literature has overcome the Apocalypse, but constantly looks back to it.

Translated by Olga Tabachnikova

Notes

1 This is a slightly amended version of the chapter '*Chekhov i Rozanov*' from *Chekhoviana. Chekhov i 'Serebrianyi vek'*, ed. by M. O. Goriacheva and others (Moscow: Nauka, 1996).
2 A. P. Chekhov, *Polnoe sobranie sochinenii i pisem v tridtsati tomakh* (Moscow: Nauka, 1974–82), vol. 17, p. 195.
3 V. Rozanov, *O ponimanii. Opyt issledovaniia prirody, granits i vnutrennego stroeniia nauki kak tsel'nogo znaniia* (Moscow, 1886).
4 M. M. Prishvin, *Kashcheeva tsep'*, in *Sobranie sochinenii v 8 tomakh*, 8 vols. (Moscow: Khudozhestvennaia literatura, 1982–6), p. 68.
5 See V. Rozanov, *Literaturnye izgnanniki*, 2 vols. (St Petersburg, 1913), vol. 1, pp. :127–8.
6 Iu. Sobolev, *Chekhov. Stat'i. Materialy. Biografiia* (Moscow, 1930), p. 163.
7 See Chekhov, *Polnoe sobranie sochinenii*, vol. 10, p. 372.
8 D. Galkovskii, '*Beskonechnyi tupik. Fragmenty iz knigi*', in *Nezavisimaia Gazeta* (18 April 1991), p. 5.
9 Chekhov, *Polnoe sobranie sochinenii*, vol. 8, pp.140–1.
10 V. Rozanov, *Religiia. Filosofiia. Kul'tura* (Moscow: Respublika, 1992), p. 154.
11 Ibid., 158–9.
12 Anton Chekhov, 'The Man in a Case', in *The Wife and Other Stories*, trans. Constance Garnett (Icon: San Diego, 2006), p. 171.
13 Anton Chekhov, 'About Love' in *The Wife and Other Stories*, p. 197.
14 This refers to Rozanov's quotes, and to the fact that when in his twenties Pavel (Anton Chekhov's father) had a signet ring made on which it was inscribed: 'Everywhere is a desert to the lonely man'. See Donald Rayfield, *Anton Chekhov* (New York: Henry Holt and Company, 1997).
15 A. Siniavskii, "*Opavshie List'ia*" *V. V. Rozanova* (Paris: Sintaxis, 1982), p. 112.
16 See I. A. Bunin, 'From an Unfinished Book on Chekhov', in *Literaturnoe nasledstvo* (68), pp. 666, 670, 674.

17 A. Siniavskii, p. 134.
18 See V. B. Shklovskii, 'Rozanov', in *Gamburgkskii schet* (Moscow: *Sovetskii pisatel'*, 1990), p. 125.
19 V. Varvarin (V. V. Rozanov), '*Nash "Antosha Chekhonte"* ', in *Russkoe Slovo*, No. 13 (17 January 1910). The same in V. V. Rozanov, *Mysli o literature* (Moscow: Sovremennik, 1989), and *Sochineniia* (Moscow: *Sovetskaia Rossiia*, 1990), as well as V. Rozanov, 'A. P. Chekhov', in *Chekhovskii Iubileinyi sbornik* (Moscow, 1910). See also, V. Rozanov, '*Literaturnye novinki (o p'iese Chekhova Vishnevyi sad)*, in *Novoe Vremia*, No. 10161 (16 June 1904); V. Rozanov, '*Pisatel'-khudozhnik i partiia*', in *Novoe Vremia*, No. 10196 (21 July 1904); V. V. Rozanov, '*Mimoletnoe. 1915 god*', in *Nachala*, (1992), pp. 16–1, 24, 27.
20 'But Chekhov wrote a lot of philosophy. [...] Chekhov is a thinker; he is a lyricist', in V. V. Rozanov, '*Pisatel'-khudozhnik i partiia*'.
21 See Chekhov, *Polnoe sobranie sochinenii*, vol. 10, p. 141.
22 Vasilii Grossman, *Zhizn' i sud'ba* (Moscow: Knizhnaia Palata, 1990).
23 Venedikt Erofeev, '*Vasilii Rozanov glazami ekstsentrika*', in *Laterna Magica: literaturno-khdozhestvennyi, istoriko-kul'turnyi almanakh*, ed. by V. P. Erokhin (Moscow: Prometei, 1990), p. 106.
24 *Tristram Shandy* (shorthand for *The Life and Opinions of Tristram Shandy, Gentleman*, 1759) is a novel by Laurence Sterne.
25 *Evgenii Onegin* (1825–32) is a novel in verse by Aleksandr Pushkin.
26 *Ulysses* (1922) is a novel by James Joyce.

2

KIND AND QUIET: VASILII ROZANOV'S READING OF CHEKHOV

Aleksandr Medvedev

Apart from numerous references in other places, Rozanov devoted five essays to Chekhov.[1] In his first essay, written not long before Chekhov's death in 1904, Rozanov, while considering Russia's fate, gives a historic-cultural reading of *The Cherry Orchard*. In this, Chekhov's last play, Rozanov sees a reflection of the crisis among the Russian people, of not being able to set targets and aspirations in their personal lives: 'Do you not understand, for what purpose serve love, thoughts, home life, morals, money – for all these people? You cannot take these things with you.'[2] This crisis leads to the passivity and lack of will in Chekhov's heroes: 'Lopakhin also saves money, reads Buckle just like Epikhodov (an excellent character, especially upon the stage), Liubov' Andreevna is attached to her Parisian gigolo,[3] and Trofimov studies at the university. Each of them is not defined by his role. On stage, however, the figure of the student Trofimov is sympathetic, although idle and passive.[4] He is unable to finish his course, and at the end cannot even find his own boots (which Varia eventually finds for him).'[5] This crisis of values is witnessed not only in the passive, but in the more active characters: 'The only aspiration anyone shows is when Lopakhin tries to get hold of money: but it is totally incomprehensible why he needs it: money for money's sake? But Pliushkin already knew this, and he is a new person for a new Russia, although very energetic and clever, however energetic and clever in a stupid way, for he is directionless to the highest degree; vacuous. If there is nothing *definite* to spend it on, effectually, spiritually, then there is no need at all to save it.'[6] This loss of a worldview, ideals and values, according to Rozanov, leads to the destruction of life: 'Cherries flower, and people wither away. Everyone departs, nothing remains in its place, tomorrow everything will be worse than today, and even today everything is miserable'.[7]

Rozanov contrasts the passivity and inactive nature of Russian life as depicted by Chekhov, with European civilization ('homeliness, life, economy'), a product of significant events such as the Middle Ages, the Renaissance and the Reformation which turned life completely 'upside down'. Such events have given a meaning and value to the basis of European life. Rozanov finds in the Reformation the reason for cultural flourishing in Switzerland (Calvin, Zwingli, Rousseau) and Germany (Humboldt, Ritter, Lessing, Goethe): 'the basis of German civilization was laid by the colossal movement of the Reformation; and just like the burning ash of the volcano allows remarkable grapes and fruits to grow, so on this ground, heated by a great movement, have grown flourishing cities, science and philosophy, an astonishing preponderance for labour'.[8] In the spirit of Chaadaev, Rozanov, unable to find in Russia's past historical cataclysms, national shakings or religious movements, points to the contrasting passivity of Russian civilization: 'We have not experienced great animations, great inspirations [...] The Russian field from the time of "Riurik, Sineus and Truvor" still exists as a field, as virginal steppe; no one has "tilled" Russia's soil'.[9] Rozanov believes that only the Old Believers (*staroobriadtsy*) in Russia managed to develop their culture and home life, a fact proved by their contributions to mercantile culture (Soldatenkov or Kozhanchikov): 'The Old Believers knew their Calvins and Zwinglis, maybe "dark", hardly literate, and their home life, community, their huts, and agriculture, all came together under them, around Bern or Geneva. In this way, the "colour of their skin" (home, life, economy) is light, because their nerves were at one time deeply shaken in the European way'.[10]

Rozanov associates Chekhov in this historical discourse with a demand for the positive ideal. Rozanov considers *The Cherry Orchard* 'a beautiful, but powerless work of art': 'a sad spectacle; but there are also so many similar works in Russian literature, of immeasurable brilliance, strength and beauty. They struck (beginning from *'Gore' Griboedovskoe* [Griboedov's comedy in verse *Woe from Wit*]) at the Russian impressionability; and the Russian soul rushes off out of *shame* (an eternal motif), but there is nowhere to rush to, there is no sun. Only the Slavophiles tried to show "the sun" (there were no attempts among others), but this turned out more or less to be like "the moon made in Hamburg", i.e. something unreal'.[11] The lack of an ideal in Chekhov permits Rozanov to see the culmination of the Gogolesque tendency in Russian literature.[12] He is placed alongside writers who display a 'profound lyricism from boredom, idleness from melancholy (Lermontov, Gogol´, Turgenev)', and Gogolesque 'satires, torments'; 'but all this is anger at the pale colour of the skin, when the question is really about nerves'.[13] Rozanov sees one of the reasons for Chekhov's popularity among Russian society in his depiction of Russian passivity and idleness: 'he became the favoured author of our lack of will, our lack of heroism, our adoration of the routine, our love of the "average" [...] They will never forget Chekhov... We see in him the infinite, the infinity of our Russia. Is this good? It is average. Is it bad? No, average. Oh Lord! Pull slowly, you nag, right unto the deep grave!"[14]

The crisis of a lack of aims, the lack of an ideal in Chekhov, according to Rozanov, leads to pessimism and entropy: 'His sad thought and his tone is only half alive. It flickers, twinkles, warms up, but never burns. And looking at this "flickering", looking at it for a long time, one is suddenly filled with a mystical horror: "It will suddenly go out". And you shout: "Burn everything, better to burn everything than this terrible darkness and cold where everything is suddenly extinguished!"'[15] The absence of energy in Chekhov leads Rozanov to recall the love of being, the love of life in Dostoevskii, which he hears in the words of Mitia Karamazov: 'In a thousand torments – *I am*. I writhe – and still *I am*'.[16]

In sum, Rozanov places Chekhov alongside those writers who, being dependent on civilization and not opposing it in anyway, merely depicted it (Hugo, Dickens, Thackeray, Scott, Goncharov and Turgenev); he contrasts these with the type headed by Tolstoi (Dostoevskii, Goethe, Byron, Schiller and Heine), who fought against civilization and therefore displayed its 'central nerve'.[17]

Rozanov develops his historical-cultural reading of *The Cherry Orchard* in an article from 1909, which examines the issue of spiritual and axiological foundation of Chekhov's work in the spirit of Weber's 1905 work *The Protestant Ethic and the Spirit of Catholicism*. Protestantism (the 'sober and labour-loving "German God"') has developed a cult of labour, whereas Catholicism and Orthodox ('"the most important Russian God", compassionate to everything weak and lazy') have given rise to a cult of sloth. He writes: 'The countries of beautiful Madonnas and mournful Mothers of God have given us to a type of life which is collapsing and falling apart, poetic idleness, a lack of moral responsibility, a life full of vice and prayer'.[18] In the heroes of Chekhov's plays, in particular in the lazy Petia Trofimov, who never finished his studies, Rozanov sees the historic-cultural expression of this 'organic connection' of Orthodoxy with idleness: 'he is so lazy and incapable of anything that he cannot even find his own rubber boots, and the lady of the manor has to find them for him and throw them into the entrance hall. In *The Cherry Orchard*, everything is falling on its side. Here not just eight out of ten are lazy, but all ten are lazy, old, wretched and not needed by anyone!'[19]

Rozanov states that this is a sinful situation, blanketed in the play with 'smoky poetry, attractiveness': 'All *The Cherry Orchard* is poetic; and this student – is very kind. Why? What is this? Some kind of initial Korea, "a country of morning quiet and peace"?[20] Or a second Spain, before she was invaded by the French or the English: a country of beautiful, poor, and poetic wanderers'.[21]

It is clear that Korea and Spain are here poetically connected with the key concepts of Orthodox culture, kindness, quiet, suffering, and poverty. ('Wealth is sinful. Poverty is the ideal'.[22]) Russian literature with its evangelical values, according to Rozanov, 'warms up and irons out Russian vices, Russian weaknesses, Russian inadequacies'.[23]

Rozanov expounds on the problem of the Christian basis of Russian life in an essay written to mark the 50th anniversary of Chekhov's birth. He turns here mainly to the stories 'Women' ('*Baby*', 1891) and 'The Peasants' (*Muzhiki*, 1897), and examines them through the prism of his overriding concern, the state of the Russian family: 'The story "Women" should be fully incorporated into "the History of the Russian Family", "the History of Russian Family Life"'.[24] Rozanov believes that Chekhov wrote family tragedies, because of the status of contemporary 'evangelical' civilization. Based on the antithesis of the Old and New Testaments,[25] Rozanov exalts European consciousness with its values of personal freedom and human rights, to the Old Testament's commandment 'an eye for eye' (Leviticus 24:20), and Russian consciousness, where the value of the individual person is absent, to the formal and passive 'commandment of Evangelical forgiveness': 'You may break people's arms and legs, but no one will pull out the pillow from under your head because of this, no one will rip the hair from your head. (1) "We are commanded to forgive", (2) "In each person there is a Divine spark, even among those who break people's arms and legs", (3) "In fact everything is in the past, arms and legs are broken, you cannot reverse anything, so why mess up anyone's hair?", (4) and the fundamental point, "What does this have to do with us? [...] Everything is as it should be", "everything is done in a Christian way". "In a Christian way": (1) A person sinned – a person cannot live without this, Christ came to earth for the remission of such sins; and therefore (2) "One must make penitence after a sin" and "return to the good path". This is what Christ says in the parable of the Prodigal Son, and anyway it goes without saying'.[26]

In Chekhov's 'Women' and 'The Peasants', the heroes live by the traditional values of Russian Orthodoxy: a ritualized faith, external piety (observation of religious holidays, rites, strict fasting, reverence for icons, unquestioning faith in the 'letter' of the Scriptures), a faith in God's merciful forgiveness of sins, reverence for the intermission of the Mother of God, a fear of God (a fear of death, expectation of Judgement Day, punishment of the sinful in eternal fire), a striving for the 'Kingdom of God', the commandment of not fighting evil with force, and the acknowledgement of woman as Satan's handmaiden (the archetypal temptress Eve). But this Orthodox metaphysics does not only fail to ease the difficult lives of Chekhov's heroes, but also serves as a cover for cruel relations towards one's fellow man. Our sympathy for the failure (*nedobychik*) Nikolai Chikel'deev only arises after his death.[27] The commandment forbidding fighting evil with force, taken as a tolerance of violence, becomes justification for a husband to beat his wife.[28] The defenceless child Kuz´ka ends up in the hands of the despotic hypocrite Matvei Savich, who ruined his mother.[29]

Rozanov contends that in Chekhov's stories, an abstract Christianity consciousness, which lacks the value of individual personality (for Rozanov the archetype of this impersonal Christian consciousness is Tolstoi's Platon Karataev), in real life leads to a cruel attitude to actual people: 'Everything is rounded off in something good and kind. Our Rus´ is kind in its roundedness. For how rounded was Platon Karataev (in *War and Peace*). He lived such a long time and never got angry. He was shot in the end, but even then he remained "rounded" [...] Here the "roundedness" of Platon Karataev breaks down: no one wants a "failure" (*nedobytchik*), no one feels anything towards a "failure" (*nedobytchik*) – and not out of rage, but out of *tiredness* [...] Well, where are the "ten commandments" of morality, where can we place here the Sermon on the Mount from the Gospels? "Blessed are those who ravenously seek the truth..."'.[30] Rozanov explains the formality and passivity of the commandments of the New Testament as manifested in the Russian consciousness as emerging from the lack of the Gospels' social function, and the social indifference of an abstract Christ: 'The Gospel does not care about society, but "saves only the soul" [...] We would like to have some land. But the Teacher said nothing about the earth or about bread. He pointed to Heaven and said, "That is what you need to aim for"'.[31]

According to Rozanov, the formal nature of Russian faith leads to an anti-historical aspect of Russian consciousness and life, which Chekhov epitomizes in his characters: 'The wind howls in the field. History has come from nowhere [...] It does not give us a true history, so we shall live by little histories. "Little manufactured histories". [...] This is Chekhov'.[32] This anti-historical aspect leads to the death of civilization. Relying on Suvorin's recollections that Chekhov had a strange love for cemeteries,[33] Rozanov interprets Chekhov as a someone who is interested in 'the death of the human, death of the individual [...] of civilization, of society, of phases in culture and history'.[34]

This anti-historical dimension is revealed in Chekhov's artistic space, which Rozanov presents as a characteristic Russian landscape (marshland, prison, cemetery, school, church): 'A sky without stars, without strength, wind without indignation, bad weather, rain, cold, murky, a day which is little different from the night, a night which is little different from the day, short grass, little trees, marshland – lots of marshland; and further, on the distant horizon, the jagged fencing around the "castle prison", and further – a cemetery, and closer to us a school, and to the side – a white church with a bell and a cross, – this is Chekhov's setting, where he grew up and fell ill, and imprinted everything in his mind'.[35] In this description of the typical Chekhovian space, Rozanov employs negative phrases (without, not), which reinforce the idea of the entropy, poverty and weakness of Russian life, and its anti-historical side. Rozanov also sees such an idea in Chekhov's descriptions of fields and the steppe: 'The Russian field from "Riurik, Sineus and Truvor" has always lived like a field, likewise the primordial steppe; as if no one in Russia ever "tilled the soil"'.[36] In order to demonstrate that this is not a problem which Rozanov has created himself, but is actually the essence of Chekhov's work, Rozanov notes Chekhov's references in his stories to the time of Riurik. In 'The Wife' (*Zhena*, 1892), Riurik becomes the symbol of Russian anti-historicism: 'And the tree is the same as it was under Riurik, it has not changed, the same Pechenegs and Cumans. We only know that we burn, hunger, and struggle against nature in every possible way'.[37] In 'The Student' ('Student', 1894), Ivan Velikopol´skii thinks about 'how exactly the same wind blew under Riurik, and under Ivan the Terrible, and under Peter, and under these there was exactly the same cruel poverty, hunger, exactly the same thatched roofs with holes, ignorance, sadness, exactly the emptiness around, darkness, the feeling of oppression – all these horrors were then, are now and will be in the future, out of the fact that even if one thousand years pass, life will not become any better'.[38]

In order to understand Rozanov's next essays on Chekhov it is necessary to examine Rozanov's conceptualization of the Russian writer and Russian literature as a whole. In the phenomenon of the Russian writer, Rozanov sees the manifestation of the Orthodox cult of the holy, the sacred as the highest form of art.[39] Rozanov notes that traditional religious concepts were being applied to modern Russian literature. The understanding of the writer in Russian nineteenth-century consciousness was defined through a medieval Christian paradigm – through such concepts as a focus on high aesthetics, the unity of the word and personal life, sacrificial servitude, and the posthumous 'canonization' of the writer. Rozanov notes this in particular in the 'reverence' for Pushkin. It is these traits which for Rozanov distinguish Russian literature from its European counterpart.[40]

Rozanov insists that Christianity sources (the medieval concept of self-denial), the nourishing spiritual of Russian classicism, had dried up by the end of the nineteenth century: The 'happy period' of Russian nineteenth-century literature, for which Russia had waited 'for eight hundred years', was approaching its end.[41] Rozanov saw the destruction of the person as a fundamental Christian value in the 'dark *egoism*' of Decadentism: 'The spiritual "human" has died and only the physiological human remains'.[42] Rozanov interprets Chekhov's work within the context of this culmination of 'the happy period' of Russian nineteenth-century writing, the 'extinguishing' of nourishing Russian literature of the medieval tradition: 'Literature in the sense of rational-artistic progress, in the sense of individual creation' will end with Chekov's 'artistic and realist miniatures'.[43]

Rozanov's interpretation of Chekhov is defined by this conception of literature. On one hand, Rozanov sees Chekhov's positivism and atheism, the fact that he lacks anything 'metaphysical, mystical and religious', as flaw, but also as a characteristic of his time, and one of the reasons for Chekhov's popularity among the Russian intelligentsia.[44] On the other hand, in the Rozanovian interpretation of Chekhov one notes key Christian concepts, and the traditional basis of Russian religious consciousness, which link Chekhov to the Christian traditions and ideals of ancient Rus´.

The image of the suffering Chekhov appears in Rozanov's essay marking the writer's death (1904). In this work, Rozanov examines Chekhov's relationship with liberal journalism. Relying on Doroshevich's memoirs of Chekhov, printed in *The Russian Word* (*Russkoe Slovo*) in 1904, Rozanov sees Chekhov's book on Sakhalin as a forced submission to the liberal demands of Skabichevskii and Mikhailovskii, who accused the writer of a lack of ideas and principles.[45] Following on from Doroshevich, Rozanov considers *Sakhalin Island* a victim of this polarized nature of Russian criticism: 'Criticism has tied the artist's wings. It has deprived Russia of works, perhaps equal to *The House of the Dead*. The artist-belletrist gave it up for statistics'.[46] The polarized nature of Russian literature, according to Rozanov, deprives Chekhov the thinker of the lyricism of the nightingale's freedom, which Chekhov, as is known, valued more than anything:[47] 'Either sing your own song freely – though no one will hear you; or you will be heard, but sing our song'.[48] In this description of the battle against the liberals, whom Rozanov labels 'the prophets and lawmakers' of contemporary literature, Chekhov's image takes on as a Christ-like character, that of a martyr who is sacrificed to an impersonal 'party' of conservative Pharisees and liberal Sadducees: 'The party's sin lies in the fact that they did not live themselves, and yet demanded someone else's life for themselves. And so out of the drops of Chekhov's blood, more than one drops on the shining clothes of his gravediggers'.[49]

Such Christological concepts are key in Rozanov's essay 'Our "Antosha Chekhonte"' (*Hash 'Antosha Chekhonte'*, 1910), and 'The Letters of A. P. Chekhov' (*Pis'ma A. P. Chekhova*, 1916). Rozanov sees in the image of Chekhov the desacralization of the Russian classical writer 'with a grand programme'. Chekhov comes down to the reader from the holy Mount Olympus of Russian classicism: 'Among the bearded, moulded by Mother Nature as deeply mighty, and deeply original figures of Turgenev, Tolstoi, Pleshcheev, Mei, Nekrasov, Dobroliubov – the figure, or rather the little figure of Chekhov appears insignificant, ordinary'.[50] Chekhov's proximity to the reader is opened up by his distancing from the reader 'the Assyrian gods' of literature – Turgenev, Goncharov and Pisemskii ('what do they have in general with us?'), the too genial Tolstoi and Dostoevskii ('the reader feels them outside "himself", not with "himself"'), the party-minded polarized Gor´kii and Korolenko: 'Only Chekhov, Chekhov alone, was "with everyone" and "like everyone" – but in an idealized form'.[51] Rozanov recalls his 'enormous and exclusive popularity' as the popularity of a writer who expresses the views of the Russian intelligentsia: '*"A man of his time"*'.[52]

The religious basis of this form of democratic activity, Chekhov's proximity to the simple person, is a form of kenosis – the descent of Christ to the people.[53] Chekhov epitomizes in his own personality and demonstrates in his work the kenotic motifs of Russian religiosity – mercy towards the sinner, pity, simplicity, and diminishment:[54] 'He was too much "our brother", the same as "we sinners", – weak, insignificant and at the same time not bad people [...] "The public", dull and lacking in pretention, fell in love with "Antosha Chekhonte", its own "Chekhonte", – this person with a pince-nez, a completely ordinary person. Like a virtuoso, like a genius, Chekhov expounded the ordinary depiction of ordinary people. "Without a hero" – this is the title one can give to all his works, and about him we can say not without sadness: "Without heroism". In fact, we shall never again come across such an absence of the storm. And it is characteristic that the very amount of Chekov's short stories is small. What a contrast with the multi-volumed works of Dostoevskii and Goncharov; what a contrast with the eternally heroic Lermontov who burst into heavens'.[55] This Chekhovian ordinariness is where lies 'simplicity' – the most important concept of Russian culture. The Russian cult of simplicity is linked to the kenotic humbleness of Christ.[56]

Rozanov sees Chekhov's closeness to the reader in his depiction of the fate of the typical Russian person, a depiction which is steeped in the kenotic motifs of simplicity, kindness and pity: 'This is our own person, when during our student years we rushed about our lessons, or an acquaintance, who did not finish his courses, when entering the medical faculty, would have become a lawyer, but he did not become a lawyer, and now he lives "just so", in a word, the face and figure "of an ordinary Russian person from the educated classes", who are all kind and who are all pitiful, who cannot help with anything and who are in need of assistance [...] In Chekhov Russia fell in love with herself. No one expressed its collective type like him, not only in his works, but, in the end, in his face, his figure, his manners and, it seems, the image of life and behaviour. "Everything ended up like for all Russians: he studied alone, and started to do something else; of course, he did not live long. Who among us lives long?"'.[57] Bitsilli would later write about this pity as a core aspect of Chekhovian pathos: 'Everything that he saw, that he understood, arouses his pity. Pity is Chekhov's core sentiment. It is all-encompassing and knows no exceptions. He felt pity for those in need, those in trouble, those who are incapable of love and who long for "heroes", he felt pity for the steppe, for its grass withered by the sun, pity for the solitary poplar on the hill. To regret and to forgive – this is the only thing man should live by'.[58]

Emerging from the anthropological nature of Russian literature, from the philosophy of the person which lies at its core, Rozanov turns his attention first to the personality of the writer. He is not simply concerned with the artistic merits of Chekhov's prose, but is also concerned with Chekhov's creation of characters with beautiful personalities, so that in Rozanov's interpretation of Chekhov, one notes both the importance of the portrait and the iconographic quality of the prose.[59] Carefully examining Chekhov's portrait, Rozanov physiologically reads his soul, examines Chekhov as a post-classical Russian writer 'without a grand programme', for whom a closeness to the reader is characteristic, as well as dialogue, silence, observation, a refusal to teach: 'Chekhov's portrait, as he "looks at you" through his pince-nez with its little chord – this is more of a portrait of a reader than a writer. It is taken, it is "captured" as if in a conversation with you – or rather in a conversation with a whole group of people like "you", the reader [...] In this portrait and in all his portraits he is depicted as if he is listening, and not even talking; listening – "to what everyone is saying", and this person is clever, observant, but slightly weak-willed and even slightly indifferent [...] He is too private a person or too weak – perhaps partly out of laziness, partly out of a lack of concern – and therefore does not delve deeply into the main issue with the thought: "Well, all problems will pass, and people will nevertheless remain"'.[60] In Chekhov's portrait Rozanov also discerns the meaningful simplicity of gestures: 'One leg is placed on the other, the head is supported by a hand, his hair is neither short nor long, not particularly smooth but not too curly, probably light brown – but this *pince-nez*, so common among everybody – and finally the expression of his face is more boring than sad – of course intelligent, but without any of the universal problems, without "spiritual interests", "universal grief", or "political indignation"'.[61]

For Rozanov, the writer's personality is the result of his moral creativity and his spiritual journey, and he uses Chekhov's portrait to present a deep, spiritual image of Chekhov: 'On the small plaque of rosewood or blessed cypress, from the kindly countries of the East, with a thin needle is engraved the image of a quiet, graceful person, "just like all of us", but different from "everyone" with the nobleness of the drawing, all its lines. In Chekhov Russia fell in love with itself'.[62] Key in this description are the kenotic concepts of kindness, quietude, humbleness, simplicity and humility, which act as 'icons' in the image of the quiet and observant Chekhov ('always so quiet and noiseless').[63] The English critic John Middleton Murry referred to this spiritual purity as being the essence of Chekhov; Murry talks of the purity of Chekhov's soul, his spiritual beauty, the source of his 'greatness as an artist and his significance for us today'.[64]

It is no accident that the icon appears as a core detail in Rozanov's spiritual portrait of Chekhov. It is well known that Chekhov's father did not only direct a church choir in which his sons sung, but was also an icon painter. On his mother's side, Chekhov was related to the icon painters of Palekh.[65] Rozanov recalls the image of the cypress depicted in Chekhov's 'The Steppe' (*Step'*). The old believer Pantelei Kholodov eats with a cypress spoon with a cross and drinks from *lampadnyi stakanchik* (lampion).[66] When talking to Pantelei, Egorushka learns the values of traditional Russian piety; the old man reminds him that he was named after the great martyr Georgii Pobedonosets, Pantelei wishes to die in peace, his heart desires a killed adder ('a quiet beast, innocent [...] It loves humans'), reveres the Mother of God as our Intercessor (*Zastupnitsa*) ('Save and Bless us, Queen of Heaven'), and believes in the mercy of God: 'We prayed, we prayed, cried, cried, and God heard us. He had pity, this means'.[67] The simple, peaceful and wise Father Khristofor Siriiskii gives off a smell 'of cypress and dried cornflower'.[68] Just like his name, deriving from the Greek for 'Christ-bearer', he carries Christ in his heart. His face shines with a 'good, kind-mannered smile': 'with wonder he looked upon God's world, and smiled so widely that it seemed that his smile touched the brim of his top hat'.[69] Returning from Mass, he 'emits radiance' ('smiling and shining'), praises the sick Egorushka and with mercy cares for him.[70] In this way, we see how details in Chekhov (the cypress, a key component of Russian spirituality) is used by Rozanov to open up Chekhov's Christian spirituality.[71]

Rozanov does not evoke 'quietness' and 'kindness' as key concepts of the Chekhovian image from within, from his own subjectivity.[72] These crucial aspects of Russian religiosity are rigid constants in Chekhov's artistic world, they are his key symbols which open up the full depth of ancient Russian traditions. Kenotic mercy, pity for sinners, native to Russian religious consciousness, can be seen in the old nanny Marina and Sonia from *Uncle Vania* (*Diadia Vania*, 1897). Sonia calls for her father to show kindness: 'Sonia (*on her knees, turning to her father nervously, through her tears*): You must be kind, father! Uncle Vania and I are so unhappy! (*Holding back her despair.*) You must be kind!'[73] In the famous final monologue, under Telegin's quiet melody, confessing her faith in God's unending mercy, Sonia announces her sympathy, her pity for the 'kind', 'poor' Uncle Vania: 'Beyond the grave we shall say that we suffered, that we wept, that our life was bitter, and God will have pity on us, and we are with you, uncle, kind uncle, we shall see that bright, beautiful and splendid life, we shall rejoice and look back on our sorrow here with pity, with a tender smile, and we shall rest [...] We shall hear angels, we shall see Heaven shining like diamonds, we shall see that all this earthly evil, all our suffering shall sink away in the compassion which will fill the entire world, and our life will become quiet, tender, sweet, like an embrace. I believe, I believe… (*She wipes away his tears with a handkerchief.*)'[74] The singing of angels, the sight of the starry sky, kindness and quiet, remind one of Christmas Night, where the angels praise God: 'Glory to God in the highest, and on Earth peace, goodwill toward men' (Luke 2:14). The connection with Christmas is not accidental if we recall the prophecy of Christmas Night in the Wisdom of Solomon, which speaks of *quietness*: 'For while all things were in quiet silence, and that night was in the midst of her swift course, Thine Almighty word leaped down from heaven out of thy royal throne, as a fierce man of war into the midst of a land of destruction' (Wisdom of Solomon 18:14–5).[75] Such adoration shows that the most important aspect of the Incarnation of God is His endless mercy: 'In your wretched cave, you came to us graciously (you suffered with us), wrapped in swaddling'.[76] Chekhov gives Sonia the final monologue, and underlines the crucial Orthodox emphasis on mercy.[77]

In the story 'In the Ravine' ('*V ovrage*', 1900), quietness becomes the image of the presence of God and His grace and consolation which, notwithstanding the 'feeling of inconsolable despair', is felt by Lipa and her mother Praskov´ia: 'And no matter how great is evil, still the night was calm and beautiful, and still in God's world there is and will be truth and justice, just as calm and beautiful, and everything on earth only awaits to be made one with truth, just as moonlight merges with the night. And both, huddling close to one another, fell asleep comforted'.[78] This night is reminiscent of the practice of hesychasm, the mysticism of silence and light.

Kindness and quietness are the essential characteristics of Chekhov's righteous man. The unknown old man brings some comfort to Lipa, who is carrying home her dead son: 'The old man picked up an ember, blew on it – only his eyes and nose were lit up, then, when they had found the yoke, he went with the light to Lipa and looked at her, and his face expressed compassion and tenderness. "You are a mother," he said. "Every mother grieves for her child."'[79] The old man displays the same compassion ('Believe my word, my dear'), as was shown him by a passing gentleman. 'He looked at me with pity, and tears filled his eyes'.[80] Lipa understands the kindness and quiet shown by the wanderers she meets as an expression of their holiness: 'You looked at me just now, and my heart softened. And the boy is quiet. And I thought: you must be holy men'.[81] Kindness and quietness marks the kind faces of the Christ-like men of Chekhov's works, such as the novice Ieronim and his friend, Father Nikolai from the story 'The Night Before Easter' (*Sviatoiu noch´iu*, 1886).[82] Quietness is expressed by the righteous man's meekness, humility and passivity. Ieronim's quietness shows through his 'quiet' words. ' "Forgive me, for the sake of Christ," answered Ieronim quietly; "Christ has risen! Is there no one else?" asked the quiet voice'; this is also shown in his modest behaviour: ' "I shall come to him quietly, so that the others do not see" '.[83] Nikolai's quiet is expressed in his humility, love and kindness: 'Nikolai always spoke quietly, tenderly, as if he noticed that whoever slept or prayed, went past, like a midge or a mosquito. His face was kind, compassionate'.[84] Nikolai's spiritual image, his 'soft and delicate' nature, is composed from the motifs of mercy, pity, goodness and tenderness: 'A good soul! Lord, how kind and gracious! Many a mother is not as kind to her child as Nikolai was to me [...] He would embrace me, stroke my head, speak to me in caressing words as if to a small child'.[85] This love is understood in a purely Russian manner, as maternal love, full of compassion and mercy.[86] The reader sees these virtues in Ieronim and Nikolai, and is reminded of the image of Saint Sergei Radonezhskii, who is remembered in various epithets, as being 'kind', 'quiet', and 'soft of heart'.[87]

For Rozanov, the image of the 'sad' Chekhov corresponds to his spiritual landscape: 'It is very appropriate to Chekhov, to his sadness, his longing; to the sterility of his subjects, of the faces, the situations which fill his kind, gentle works. They are all like the steppe with bells. But "amidst the plain valley" ('*Sredi doliny rovnyia*'), as the song goes'.[88] Rozanov expounds on the landscapes in Chekhov's works, the bleak, horizontal depictions of the Russian land, as an artistic expression of his longing for the ideal and for God: 'In Chekhov, everything crawls along the ground. Like life, like nature, like everything'.[89] This spiritual horizon can be seen in 'The Steppe', where the description of the 'wide, endless plain' is stepped with motifs of peace, longing, boredom, incompleteness and the anti-historical nature of life:

> The dew evaporated, the air was still, and the dew evaporated, the air grew stagnant, and the disillusioned steppe took on its jaded July aspect. The grass drooped, everything living was hushed. The sun-baked hills, brownish-green, lilac in the distance, with their quiet shadowy tones, the plain with the misty distance and, arched above them, the sky, which seems terribly deep and transparent in the steppes, where there are no woods or high hills, seemed now endless, petrified with dreariness... How stifling and oppressive! The chaise races along, while Egorushka sees always the same thing – the sky, the plain, the hills ... The music in the grass was hushed, the petrels had flown away, the partridges were out of sight. Rooks hover idly over the withered grass; they are all alike and made the steppe even more monotonous. A hawk flew just above the ground, with an even sweep of its wings, suddenly halted in the air as though pondering on the dreariness of life, then flutters its wings and flew like an arrow over the steppe, and there was no telling why it flew off and what it wanted.[90]

But behind the poverty and boredom of Chekhov's 'average, plain Russia',[91] Rozanov sees a spiritual landscape, imbued with the kenotic ideals of kindness, quiet, and poverty: 'Rus´ is quiet. Rus´ is smooth. It smells of bog, of must, but "everything is kind". Why is it kind? To whom is it kind? It is kind to whoever says this, to whoever sees this, yes, it is kind to us all'.[92] 'But the Russian person, the Russian landscape, Russian fate – these are always kind. I want to make a rebuke: Chekhov makes people content with the little things'.[93] The prototype of this Chekhovian landscape is Tiutchev's 'These Poor Hamlets' (*Eti bednye selen'ia*, 1855),[94] which expressed the essence of the Russian landscape. Tiutchev saw in the Russian land the poverty and the simplicity of the kenotic submissiveness of Christ.[95] Tiutchev's love for 'submissive nakedness' can be heard in Vershinin's words about the 'modest birches', which sound like a confession from Chekhov himself: 'The beautiful, modest birches, I love them more than any other tree. It is good to live here'.[96]

Rozanov sees the artistic parallel of Chekhov's kenotic landscapes in Levitan. Rozanov notes that Levitan expressed the very 'psyche' of Russian being, which lies in the flat plains and in the ordinary, rather than in towering hills or mountains.[97] In his 'ordinary' landscapes, Levitan overcame the classic and romantic expression of nature: 'Everything is modest, humble [...] Nowhere does Levitan ever take "a particularly beautiful Russian landscape" (and there *is* such a thing) [...] He without exception takes a poor village, a tree; and his forests – are always poor, not very distinguished'.[98] Quoting Tiutchev's 'These Poor Hamlets', Rozanov sees in the sad, aching beauty of Levitan's landscapes the kenotic essence of the poor and squalid Russian countryside. Levitan could be described with Rozanov's description of A. Volynskii: he 'bowed down before Russian humility, before Russian quietness, before the Russian aversion to argument, **before Russian submissiveness [...] as if before all the greatest traits of humanity**'.[99]

For Rozanov, Chekhov's image of the kenotic landscape is also expressed through the representation of the wandering man. Rozanov cites 'idealism', the intelligentsia's striving somewhere into the distance, as one of the reasons for Chekhov's popularity: 'In all his letters there is some reflection of an unnecessary dream; a dream which, in truth, will come to nothing, but which is a dream nonetheless. Our impotent and weakened society once more can refer: "I dream just like Chekhov", like his "three sisters" or his "uncle Vania", and all these dull but kind characters'.[100] Behind this Chekhovian dreaminess lies the motif of Christian pilgrims and wanderers (*strannichestvo*): 'He had no nest, he was a wanderer [...] You amused yourself at our expense when everyone's situation was very difficult. But in your music there always sounded a chord, by which we knew that "there is another world". **And the essence of your song lies in the fact that it sung about one thing, here "about this", and** the dreams evoked something completely different, "about that".[101] In this image of the wandering Chekhov, one sees the characteristics of the Christian wanderer–pilgrim:[102] 'The foxes have holes, and the birds of the air have nests; but the Son of man hath not where to lay his head' (Matthew 8:20). Rozanov was not alone in sensing Chekhov's preponderance to wander and observe. Bunin quoted Chekhov shortly after his death: 'Recently people have started to think aloud: "To become a wanderer, a pilgrim, to wander around holy places, visit monasteries in forests, by a lake, to sit on a summer evening on a bench by the gates of a monastery"'.[103] The image of Chekhov, in the context of this kenotic wandering and pilgrimage, shows the writer as a kind of 'thoughtful artist', a 'traveller–observer':[104] 'With this wasting consumption in his chest, the unsuccessful doctor, in need of money, not great and not sharp, but "just so", Chekhov lived a short life, but saw everything, noting everything, not fighting with anything, and in no way developing the storm within him or without him. "Storms are on the ocean; what storms are there in Rus´? There creeps a little wind". And the endless plains of Rus´, with her quiet rivers, her faded plants, he looked on everything with a tender and sad gaze, the gaze of a man who arrives at his lodgings for the night and wonders whether it will be warm, whether he will have to suffer the cold once more'.[105] The Chekhovian landscape and the image of Chekhov himself forms in Rozanov's interpretation a single whole, seeped in the motifs of pilgrimage (*strannichestvo*), kindness, quiet, poverty and suffering.

Perceiving Chekhov within the historio-sophic discourse, Rozanov sees in his oeuvre the reflection of the historic-cultural teleological crisis, the crisis of ideals in Russian consciousness, which leads to an entropic 'fading' of Russian civilization. A charter-based, impersonal and asocial character of the Russian faith also facilitates an entropic anti-historical nature of Russian life. In this connection Rozanov raises the problem of spiritual and value-based foundations of Chekhov's oeuvre.

For Rozanov, Chekhov represents a concluding stage of classical Russian literature at the turn of the centuries, caused by the 'fading' of a thousand years' old Christian tradition which was spiritually feeding this literature. On the one hand, Rozanov regards Chekhov's positivism and atheism as his shortcomings, naming them amongst the reasons of Chekhov's popularity in society. On the other hand, in Rozanov's perception of Chekhov and his oeuvre, Russian orthodox kenotic concepts are visible. They help to inscribe the phenomenon of Chekhov into Russian religious tradition: suffering, compassion, quiet, humility, poverty, simplicity, understatement, endearment and pilgrimage. In his observations of the intelligentsia member and atheist Chekhov, Rozanov managed to see the authentic (in its spiritual purity), 'iconic' image of a 'dear' and 'quiet' Chekhov. This image for Rozanov is inseparable from the Russian horizontal landscape in Chekhov's texts, it is literally merged with the latter. The prototypes of Chekhov's landscape which express the longing for an ideal, for God are the 'humble' landscape of F. Tiutchev and kenotic, piercing beauty of the landscapes of Levitan. Thus Chekhov's problem of an ideal, his longing for God are resolved in Rozanov's interpretation by turning to the sources of Russian spirituality.

Through the historic-cultural prism of 'big time' (M. M. Bakhtin) Rozanov reveals a concealed dimension of Chekhov's oeuvre, opening up its authentic profound meanings which are visible within Chekhov's native kenotic tradition of Russian religiosity. The traditional content of Russian religious consciousness is not imposed by Rozanov on Chekhov's texts, instead it is inherent in Chekhov's consciousness. In these open spiritual constants which are the key symbols of Chekhov's artistic world, the profound reflection of the ancient Christian tradition is present in the folded form. This testifies to the continuous unity of the kenotic type of Russian spirituality.

Through his personal, live sensation, interpreting Chekhov's creativity from within Russian religious tradition from which it grew and on which it fed spiritually, Rozanov reaches congenial heights and finds the method which is authentic for understanding the writer. Chekhov is presented as a link in the 'unbreakable golden chain' of Russian religious tradition, the link which continued its 'light-pouring' (*svetolitie*), using the words of St Symeon the New Theologian, 'into the same image from glory to glory' (2 Corinthians 3:18). P. Bitsilli had all the reasons to say much later than Rozanov, when already in emigration, that 'non-religious' Chekhov, just as Pushkin, managed to express a 'humble and quiet poetry' of Russian orthodoxy, to give us the gifts of the spirit of 'meekness, mercy and compassion' which Chekhov is steeped in: '*The Captain's Daughter* is lit up with the same dim, warm and steady light of the "everyday" Russian orthodoxy which the best works of Chekhov exude. In a certain sense these two are the most "Russian" of all Russian writers'.[106]

Translated by Adam Ure

Notes

1. On relations between Chekhov and Rozanov see A. A. Medvedev, 'A. P. Chekhov', in *Rozanovskaia Entsiklopediia* (Moscow: Rossiiskaia politicheskaia entsiklopedia, 2008), pp. 1148–56.
2. V. V. Rozanov, *Literaturnye novinki*, in *V. V. Rozanov, Sobranie sochinenii. O pisatel'stve i pisateliakh* (Moscow: Respublika, 1995), p. 166.
3. Ranevskaia tears up the telegram from her lover, who has been living on her costs: 'Lord, Lord, have mercy on me, forgive me my sins! Do not punish me more! [*Takes the telegram from her pocket.*] I received this today from Paris… He asks for forgiveness,

he begs to return... [*Tears up the telegram*].' However, in the end she goes to him in Paris to live on the money sent by her grandmother in Iaroslav to save the estate. A. P. Chekhov, *Vishnevyi sad*, in *A. P. Chekhov, Polnoe sobranie sochinenii i pisem v tridtsati tomakh* (Moscow: Nauka, 1986), Works, vol. 3, p. 220. The passive Ranevskaia understands that her love is using her but cannot help herself: 'It is a stone around my neck, and it is taking me to the depths, but I love this stone and cannot live without it'. Ibid., p. 234.

4 In the words of Trofimov, who believes in progress and the necessity of labour, Rozanov hears the voice of the author himself and sees his 'sad view' of Russia: 'Here in Russia very few people work. The vast majority of the intelligentsia known to me do not search for anything and are not yet suited to labour. They call themselves intelligentsia, are rude to their servants, and address peasants like animals. They study poorly, do not read anything seriously, do not do anything, only talk about science, and understand little about art [...] There is only filth, vulgarity, barbarity ... I fear and dislike serious expressions, I fear serious conversations'. Ibid., p. 223. Here Trofimov is a typical superfluous man (*lishnii chelovek*) of the Russian nineteenth-century novel: a passive hero with a highly-developed self-consciousness.

5 Rozanov, *Literaturnye novinki*, op. cit., p. 167.
6 Ibid., pp. 166–7.
7 Ibid., p. 166.
8 Ibid., p. 168.
9 Ibid., p. 169. See Chaadaev's thoughts on the 'period of violent unrest', 'great events' in the west, which gave birth to 'great and fruitful ideas' and a basis for social life, and which were absent in Russia: 'We had none of that period of exuberant activity, of the fervent turmoil of the moral forces of nations [...] We live only in the narrowest of presents, without past and without future, in the midst of a flat calm'. P. Ia. Chaadaev, *Filosoficheskie pis'ma*, in *P. Ia. Chaadaev, Polnoe sobranie sochinenii i izbrannye pis'ma v dvukh tomakh* (Moscow: Nauka, 1991), vol. 1, pp. 324–5. Chaadaev opposes Russia's lack of 'traditional ideas about the human race', which the Europeans had developed in historical circumstances and which make up the substantive elements of the social world ('thoughts about debt, justice, morals, order'). The break with tradition, the refusal to follow the experience of the past leads the Russian into confusion, a lack of confidence, to a 'transparent sense of personality': 'he feels lost in the world'. European civilization for Chaadaev is the result of 'social ideas' of Catholicism ('the Kingdom of God on Earth'), which was distorted in Byzantine Orthodoxy. But unlike Rozanov, Chaadaev values the Reformation as a movement which destroys the unity of Europe which had been cemented by Catholicism: 'in all Protestant churches there is some strange longing for destruction'. See Ibid., pp. 325, 334, 413.
10 Rozanov, *Literaturnye novinki*, op. cit., p. 168.
11 Ibid., p. 169.
12 Chekhov recognized the vital need for an ideal, for example in 'A Boring Story' (*Skuchnaia istoriia*, 1889): 'in all the thoughts, feelings, and ideas I form about everything, there is no common bond to connect it all into one whole. Every feeling and every thought exists apart in me, and in all my criticisms of science, the theatre, literature, my pupils, and in all the pictures my imagination draws, even the most skilful analyst could not find what is called a general idea, or the god of a living man. And if there is not even that, then there is nothing'. A. P. Chekhov, *Skuchnaia istoriia*, in *A. P. Chekhov, Polnoe sobranie sochinenii i pisem v tridtsati tomakh* (Moscow: Nauka, 1985), Works, vol. 7, p. 307.

13 Rozanov, *Literaturnye novinki*, op. cit., p. 169.
14 V. V. Rozanov, 'A. P. Chekhov', in *V. V. Rozanov, Sobranie sochinenii. O pisatel´stve i pisateliakh* (Moscow: Respublika, 1995), p. 482.
15 V. V. Rozanov, 'Nash "Antosha Chekhonte"', in *V. V. Rozanov, Sobranie sochinenii. Legenda o Velikom Inkvizitore F. M. Dostoevskogo. Literaturnye ocherki. O pisatel´stve i pisateliakh* (Moscow: Respublika, 1996), p. 554.
16 Ibid.
17 V. V. Rozanov, *Na zakate dnei*, in *V. V. Rozanov, Sobranie sochinenii. O pisatel´stve i pisateliakh* (Moscow: Respublika, 1995), p. 228.
18 V. V. Rozanov, *Voprosy russkogo truda*, in *V. V. Rozanov, Sobranie sochinenii. Staraia i molodaia Rossiia* (Moscow: Respublika, 2004), pp. 102, 104.
19 Ibid., p. 102.
20 There is a connection between Rozanov's image here and Varia, Gaev and Ranevskaia, their spirit of eastern passive observation as they look out onto the orchard in the morning: 'Varia [*quietly*]: Ania is asleep. [*Quietly opens the window.*] The sun has already risen, it is not cold. Look, mother: what splendid trees! My Lord, the air! The starlings are singing! Gave [*opens the other window*]: The garden is all white [...] Liubov´ Andreevna [*looks out onto the orchard through the window*]: Oh, my childhood, my innocence! I used to sleep in this nursery, I used to look out onto the orchard, happiness would wake up with me each morning, and it was just as it is now, nothing has changed. [*Laughs from joy.*] It is all, all white! Oh, my orchard! After the dark, foul autumn and the cold winter you are young once more, full of happiness, the angels of heaven have not abandoned you [...] What a marvellous garden! A mass of white flowers, blue sky'. Chekhov, *Vishnevyi sad*, op. cit., pp. 209–10.
21 Rozanov, *Voprosy russkogo truda*, op. cit., p. 102.
22 Ibid., p. 106.
23 Ibid., p. 104.
24 Rozanov, 'A. P. Chekhov', op. cit., p. 478.
25 One of the central ideas of Rozanov's philosophy is the criticism of abstract Christianity, which is incompatible with lived life. Rozanov opposes the animosity of the New Testament to life and to genetic relations with the ontology of the Old Testament, which he represents by creating myths about sex, the family, childbirth and motherhood. Rozanov bases this key opposition between Old and New Testaments on Christ's teaching. See V. V. Rozanov, 'Po tikhim obiteliam', in *V. V. Rozanov, Sobranie sochinenii. V temnykh religioznykh luchakh* (Moscow: Respublika, 1994), p. 133. Also V. V. Rozanov, *Svecha v khrame*, in *V. V. Rozanov, Sobranie sochinenii. V temnykh religioznykh luchakh* (Moscow: Respublika, 1994), p. 348.
26 Rozanov, 'A. P. Chekhov', op. cit., pp. 478–9.
27 A. P. Chekhov, *Muzhyki*, in *A. P. Chekhov, Polnoe sobranie sochinenii i pisem v tridtsati tomakh* (Moscow: Nauka, 1985), Works, vol. 9, p. 311.
28 Ibid., p. 285.
29 A. P. Chekhov, *Baby*, in *A. P. Chekhov, Polnoe sobranie sochinenii i pisem v tridtsati tomakh* (Moscow: Nauka, 1985), Works, vol. 7, p. 354.
30 Rozanov, 'A. P. Chekhov', op. cit., pp. 480–1.
31 Ibid., pp. 479, 481.
32 Ibid., pp. 475–6.
33 'He had a strange love of visiting cemeteries, to read the writings on the headstones or to walk silently among the graves. [...] We went abroad together twice. Both times

we saw Italy. He was little interested in art, statues, paintings, churches... Cemeteries abroad interested him most'. A. S. Suvorin, *Malen'kie pis'ma*, in *Novoe vremia* (St Petersburg, 1904), 4 *iiulia*, p. 4. Chekhov's interest in cemeteries was linked to the tormenting question of the immortality of the soul, which he wrote about in 'The Steppe': 'In a solitary grave there is something melancholy, pensive and to the highest degree poetic; one feels its silence, and in this silence can be felt the presence of the soul of the unknown man who lies beneath the cross. Is that soul at peace on the steppe? Does it grieve in the moonlight? [...] There is not a passerby who would not remember that lonely soul and who would not keep on looking back at that grave until it was left far behind and hidden in the mist'. A. P. Chekhov, *Step'*, A. P. Chekhov, *Polnoe sobranie sochinenii i pisem v tridtsati tomakh* (Moscow: Nauka, 1985), Works, vol. 7, p. 52.
34 Rozanov, 'A. P. Chekhov', op. cit., p. 477.
35 Ibid., p. 476.
36 Rozanov, *Literaturnye novinki*, op. cit., p. 169.
37 A. P. Chekhov, *Zhena*, in *A. P. Chekhov, Polnoe sobranie sochinenii i pisem v tridtsati tomakh* (Moscow: Nauka, 1985), Works, vol. 7, p. 493.
38 A. P. Chekhov, *Student*, in *A. P. Chekhov, Polnoe sobranie sochinenii i pisem v tridtsati tomakh* (Moscow: Nauka, 1985), Works, vol. 9, p. 306.
39 In Russia, literature is not an end in itself, but a tool to attain spiritual and moral completion. Sakharov notes that the ability to live properly, to strive for this spiritual perfection, is the highest form of art. See Sofrinii (Sakharov), arkhim., *Pis'ma blizkim liudiam* (Moscow: Otchii dom, 1997), pp. 52–4. See A. A. Medvedev, *O khristianskoi paradigme v vospriiatii russkoi literatury Rozanovym*, in *Nasledie V. V. Rozanova i sovremennost': Materialy Mezhdunarodnoi nauchnoi konferentsii* (Moscow: Rossiiskaia politicheskaia entsiklopedia, 2009), pp. 40–50.
40 V. V. Rozanov, 'A. S. Pushkin', in *V. V. Rozanov, Sobranie sochinenii. O pisatel'stve i pisateliakh* (Moscow: Respublika, 1995), pp. 36–7. Lotman connects this theme with the fact that following the Petrine reforms and the state's control of the Church and the break with medieval traditions, secularized literature fills the empty place no longer occupied by spiritual authorities and becomes the main bearer of religious consciousness. Iu. M. Lotman, *Russkaia literatura poslepetrovskoi epokhi i khristianskaia traditsiia*, in *Iu. M. Lotman, O poetakh i poezii* (St Petersburg, 1996), p. 256. The presentation of the Word from teacher to student follows the Christian model of giving holy gifts. This is seen in Derzhavin's 'blessing' Pushkin, but also Chekhov's meeting with Leskov. The 'mystic', prophesying Chekhov's premature death, jokingly calls him to serve the people through literature, and compares himself to the Prophet Samuel and his blessing of David (Kings 16:13): 'I bless you with oil, like Samuel anointed David [...] Write!' A. P. Chekhov, *Pis'mo Al. P. Chekhovu mezhdu 15 i 28 oktiabria 1883 g*, in *A. P. Chekhov, Polnoe sobranie sochinenii i pisem v tridtsati tomakh* (Moscow: Nauka, 1985), Letters, vol. 1, p. 88.
41 V. V. Rozanov, *Dumy i vpechatleniia*, in *Novoe Vremia* (St Petersburg, 1900), 2 *aprelia*, p. 4.
42 V. V. Rozanov, *Dekadenty*, in *V. V. Rozanov, Sobranie sochinenii. Legenda o Velikom Inkvizitore F. M. Dostoevskogo* (Moscow: Respublika, 1996), pp. 412, 417, 419–20.
43 Rozanov, *Dumy i vpechatleniia*, op. cit., p. 4.
44 V. V. Rozanov, 'Pis'ma A. P. Chekhova', in *V. V. Rozanov, Sobranie sochinenii. V chadu voiny. Stat'u i ocherki 1916–18 gg.* (Moscow: Respublika, 2008), p. 210.
45 V. V. Rozanov, *Pisatel'-khudozhnik i partiia*, in *V. V. Rozanov, Sobranie sochinenii. O pisatel'stve i pisateliakh* (Moscow: Respublika, 1995), pp. 177–8.
46 Ibid., p. 177.

47 See Chekhov's famous note on internal freedom as the highest value: 'My holy of holies is the human body – health, mind, talent, inspiration, love and absolute freedom, freedom from force and lies'. In this way, Chekhov's internal freedom makes him a unique figure in Russian literature, on a par with Pushkin. Chekhov overcame Tolstoyanism, dethroned the Populists and the Decadents, and refused to fall under the spell of the radical intelligentsia, the modernists (Diagilev), the Religious-Philosophical Meetings and the 'self-satisfied' Merezhkovskii, and left the conservative Suvorin over the Dreyfus Case. Strada wrote about Chekhov's unique ability to preserve his spiritual freedom: 'Chekhov could be alone, he always had the strength to leave even the people close to him if the price of compromise was his moral freedom'. V. Strada, 'Anton Chekhov', in *Istoriia russkoi literatury: XX vek: Serebrianyi vek Pod red. Zh. Niva, I. Sermana, V. Ctrady, E. Etkinda* (Moscow: Progress – Litera, 1995), p. 65.

48 Rozanov, *Pisatel'-khudozhnik i partiia*, op. cit., p. 180.

49 Ibid., 180–2. Rozanov continues this theme in his *Opavshelistika*, and writes that Chekhov through his independence stands apart from the stereotypical Russian writer, the liberal and democrat. V. V. Rozanov, *Sobranie sochinenii. Sakharna* (Moscow: Respublika, 2001), p. 243. In 1915, reading 'The Story of an Unknown Man', Rozanov notes that Chekhov, along with such writers as Stepniak-Kravchinskii, Breshko-Breshkovskii, stupefies young people with an adulation of the revolution. V. V. Rozanov, *Sobranie sochinenii. Mimoletnoe* (Moscow: Respublika, 1994), pp. 194–5.

50 Rozanov, *Nash 'Antosha Chekhonte'*, op. cit., p. 550.

51 Rozanov, *Pis'ma A. P. Chekhova*, op. cit., p. 208.

52 Ibid.

53 Kenosis (in Greek κένωσις, meaning 'emptying', 'emptiness') is a key concept in Orthodoxy, focusing on Christ's willingness to accept humiliation and become man. The word kenosis comes from Paul: 'Who, being in the form of God, thought it not robbery to be equal with God: But made himself of no reputation, and took upon him the form of a servant, and was made in the likeness of men: And being found in fashion as a man, he humbled himself, and became obedient unto death, even the death of the cross' (Philippians 2:6–8). Kenosis becomes the central part of the Paul's writing, who sees Christ's endless love for the sinner. The love of the Russian soul for the Gospel's depiction of the humiliation of Christ is noted by Fedotov, who notes a specific Russian kenosis, different from Byzantine spirituality. See G. P. Fedotov, '*Russkaia religioznost'*', in G. P. Fedotov, *Sobranie sochinenii v dvenadtsati tomakh* (Moscow: Martis, 2001), vol. 10, pp. 95, 125, 329. The kenotic understanding of Christianity means sacrificial love ($αγάπη$), the willing descent of God to the sinner, and this overcomes the fear ($φόβος$) of God and the Law. Ibid., p. 207.

54 Mercy (in Greek έλεος) is one of the most important attributes of God, which implies His sympathy and compassion. Mercy is one of the main attributes of God (see Psalm 108:4) and of the Saviour ('You alone knowing, like a feeble human being, and mercifully (compassionately) taking his form'). See O. A. Sedakova, *Tserkovnoslaviano-russkie paronimi: Materialy k slovariu* (Moscow: Greko-latinskii cabinet Iu. A. Shichalina, 2005), p. 175. Mercy as an essential component of the Orthodox understanding of the Divine is depicted by God granting Grace as a *gift* which man has not earned, and to which man has no right: 'Not by works of righteousness which we have done, but according to his mercy he saved us, by the washing of regeneration, and renewing of the Holy Ghost' (Titus 3:5). In Russian kenosis mercy is seen in such key texts as the Jesus Prayer ('God be merciful to me a sinner', from Luke 18:13), and the anointing of the wounded robber. The image of mercy is the undeserved love and care for our neighbour.

55 Rozanov, *Nash 'Antosha Chekhonte'*, op. cit., pp. 550, 552.
56 The spiritual depth of 'simplicity' is revealed through its religious definition: 'Whole; open, straight, pure; insignificant, common; ordinary'. Sedakova, *Tserkovnoslaviano-russkie paronimi*, op. cit., pp. 287–8. In *War and Peace*, Tolstoi presents humble simplicity as a national ideal.
57 Rozanov, *Nash 'Antosha Chekhonte'*, op. cit., pp. 551, 553.
58 P. M. Bitsilli, 'Chekhov', in *Chisla* (Paris, 1930), No. 1, p. 167.
59 Rozanov believes that a person's face reveals the metaphysics of his personality, the secrets of his soul and his spiritual quality. See V. V. Rozanov, *O pisatel'stve i pisateliakh (Zametki i nabroski)*, in *V. V. Rozanov, Sobranie sochinenii. Legenda o Velikom Inkvizitore* (Moscow: Respublika 1996), p. 335.
60 Rozanov, *Pis'ma A. P. Chekhova*, op. cit., p. 208–9.
61 Rozanov, *Nash'Antosha Chekhonte'*, p. 551.
62 Ibid., p. 553.
63 Rozanov, 'A. P. Chekhov', op. cit., p. 480.
64 *Chekhov v Anglii*, in *Russkaia kultura bez granits* (Moscow, 1999), No. 1, p. 66.
65 'Pavel Egorovich painted icons. One of these has been preserved. It is the Mother of God with the Infant, painted with great care, patiently, clearly, exactly, as if from real life; it is the work of a man who did not doubt that the Mother of God exists physically, more of a photograph than an image, covered with faith and lyricism'. M. P. Gromov, *Kniga o Chekhove* (Moscow: Sovremennik, 1989), p. 33. In his letter to the famous Byzantine expert N. P. Kondakov, whom Chekhov knew well, he referred him to his book on icon painting *Sovremennoe polozhenie russkoi narodnoĭ ikonopisi* (St Petersburg, 1901). Chekhov believed that his time was witnessing the death of icon painting, where a national art was becoming a type of handicraft, a mass 'artificial production'. A. P. Chekhov, *Pis'mo N. P. Kondakovu ot 2 marta 1901 g.*, in *A. P. Chekhov, Polnoe sobranie sochinenii i pisem v tridtsati tomakh* (Moscow: Nauka, 1980), Letters, vol. 9, p. 23.
66 Chekhov, *Step'*, op. cit., p. 73.
67 Ibid., pp. 51–2, 69, 72.
68 Ibid., p. 97.
69 Ibid., p. 13.
70 Ibid., p. 97.
71 In Russia, the firm, aromatic wood of the cypress was used to make crucifixes, icons and beads. In Russian religious thinking, reverence for the cypress is linked to the fact that according to tradition, it was used in the cross on which Christ was crucified. *Bogosluzheniia Triodi Postnoi* (Moscow: Pravoslavnyi Sviato-Tikhonovskii Gumanitarnyi Universitet, 2005), p. 447.
72 Kenosis is closely associated with hesychasm, another key concept in Orthodox piety. Hesychasm (in Greek ησυχία – 'silence of the heart') is a core component of the ancient traditions of the mysticism and piety central to Eastern Christian monasticism. The foundation of hesychasm is the Jesus Prayer. One of the most important contributors to the theory of hesychasm was Gregory Palamas (died 1359), who wrote about the Taboric Light and the uncreated energies of God. The meanings of the Greek word *hesychia* (inner quiet, silence, rest) merged with Orthodox concepts of quiet (the Russian word for which is '*tikhii*', phonetically closer to the Greek). See *Grigorii D'iachenko, sviashch., Polnyi tserkovno-slavianskii slovar'* (Moscow: Izdatel'skii otdel Moskovskogo Patriarkhata, 1993), p. 722. In Orthodox traditions, quietness is an essential characteristic of Christ *Pravoslavnyi molivoslov i psaltyr'* (Moscow: Izdanie Moskovskoi Patriarkhii, 1993), p. 30.

73 A. P. Chekhov, *Diadia Vania*, in *A. P. Chekhov, Polnoe sobranie sochinenii i pisem v tridtsati tomakh* (Moscow: Nauka, 1986), Works, vol. 13, p. 103.
74 Ibid., p. 115–6.
75 Dimitrii Rostovskii, mitrop., *Skazanie o Rozhdestve Gospoda Boga i Spasa nashego Iisusa Khrista*, in *Zhitia sviatykh, na russkom iazyke izlozhennie po rukovodstvu Chet'ikh-Minei sv. Dimitria Rostovskogo: v 12 kn. (15 t.)* (Moscow, 1906, 1992), December, pp. 20, 72.
76 Sedakova, *Tserkovnoslaviano-russkie paronimi*, op. cit., p. 175.
77 Compunction (κατανύξις) or joyful sorrow (χαρμολύπη, χαροποιός), the penitential lamentation before God, saves man from the conceit which might come from joyful prayer. Engaging in 'blessed gladdening sorrow of holy compunction' which can raise man 'high above the things of this world' and present him 'pure to Christ'; 'joy and grief should contain joy and gladness interwoven in them, like honey in the comb'; 'God comforts the broken-hearted'. Ioann Lestvichnik, prep., *Lestvitsa* (Moscow: Moskovskoe podvor'e Sviato-Troitskoi Sergievoi Lavry, 2004), pp. 106, 112–3. N. S. Arsen'ev, who calls compunction one of the central phenomena of Russian religiosity, describes this as the meeting of the heart with God's grace. N. S. Arsen'ev, *Iz russkoi kul'turnoi i tvorcheskoi tradizii* (Frankfurt-am-Maine: Posev, 1959), p. 241.
78 A. P. Chekhov, *V ovrage*, in *A. P. Chekhov, Polnoe sobranie sochinenii i pisem v tridtsati tomakh* (Moscow: Nauka, 1985), Works, vol. 10, pp. 165–6.
79 Ibid., p. 174.
80 Ibid., p. 175.
81 Ibid., p. 174.
82 Chekhov's monks express the author's own inclination for the monastic life, to which he confessed more than once: 'If monasteries accepted non-religious people and if you did not have to pray there, I would become a monk'. A. P. Chekhov, *Pis'mo A. S. Suvorinu ot 1 dekabria 1895 g.*, in *A. P. Chekhov, Polnoe sobranie sochinenii i pisem v tridtsati tomakh* (Moscow: Nauka, 1978), Letters, vol. 6, pp. 104–5.
83 A. P. Chekhov, *Sviatoiu noch'iu*, in *A. P. Chekhov, Polnoe sobranie sochinenii i pisem v tridtsati tomakh* (Moscow: Nauka, 1984), Works, vol. 5, pp. 94, 98, 102.
84 Ibid., p. 99.
85 Ibid., pp. 96, 98.
86 Averintsev uses the Greek term 'ευσπλαγχνία' (merciful, sympathetic), which also refers to the blessed womb and the love a mother has towards her children. Averintsev argues that this specific type of love is shown also by God and Christ towards man. See S. S. Averintsev, 'ΕΥΣΠΛΑΓΧΝΙΑ', in *Alfa i Omega* (Moscow, 1995), No. 1, pp. 19–20. This also explains the specific reverence in Russia for the Virgin Mary, which is different from the cult built around Mary in Western medieval times. This is a particularly Russian understanding of love as compassion, which exists also between man and wife, such as Iaroslavna shows for her husband in *The Tale of Igor's Campaign* (*Slovo o polke Igoreve*). See S. S. Averintsev, *Kreshchenie Rusi i put' russkoi kul'tury*, in *Russkoe zarubezh'e v god tysiacheletia Kreshchenia Rusi: Sbornik* (Moscow: Stolitsa, 1991), p. 59.
87 *Slovo pokhval'noe prepodobnomu ottsu nashemu Sergiiu sozdano bilo uchenikom ego, sviashchennikom Epifaniem*, in *Biblioteka literatury Drevnei Rusi* (St Petersburg: Nauka, 1999), vol. 6, pp. 398, 395.
88 Rozanov, *Pisatel'-khudozhnik i partiia*, op. cit., p. 183.
89 Rozanov, *Nash 'Antosha Chekhonte'*, op. cit., p. 552.
90 Chekhov, *Step'*, op. cit., p. 16–7.
91 Rozanov, *Nash 'Antosha Chekhonte'*, op. cit., p. 554.
92 Rozanov, 'A. P. Chekhov', op. cit., p. 482.

93 Rozanov, *Pis'ma A. P. Chekhova*, op. cit., p. 211.
94 Averintsev examines Tiutchev's description of the essence of the Russian landscape, using key concepts of Russian piety as kenosis, silence, and apophasis. S. S. Averintsev, *Obraz Iisusa Khrista v pravoslavnoi traditsii*, in *S. S. Averintsev, Sobranie sochinenii. Sviaz' vremen* (Kiev: Dukh i Litera, 2005), p. 164. Christ's silence demonstrates the secret of apophasis and his kenotic love. Ibid., p. 161.
95 The Latin word '*humilitas*' comes from the word '*humus*', meaning fruitful earth. The earth is the symbol of kenosis, Christ's humiliation as he willingly comes down to earth and is made man. Antonii Surozhskii, mitrop., *Shkola molitvy* (Klin: Khristianskaia zhizn'*, 2004), p. 90.
96 A. P. Chekhov, *Tri sestry*, in *A. P. Chekhov, Polnoe sobranie sochinenii i pisem v tridtsati tomakh* (Moscow: Nauka, 1986), Works, vol. 13, p. 128.
97 V. V. Rozanov, '*Levitan i Gershenzon*', in *V. V. Rozanov, Sobranie sochinenii. V chadu voiny* (Moscow: *Respublika*; St Petersburg: Rostok, 2008), p. 34.
98 Ibid., p. 33–4. Rozanov's understanding corresponds to Levitan's own artistic credo as laid out in his essay on Savrasov's death (*Po povodu smerti Savrasova*, 1897). Levitan argues that Savrasov avoided in his work the pseudo-classical and romantic description of nature, as shown by Vorob'ev, Shternberg, Lebedev and Shchedrin, who 'sought motifs for their paintings outside Russia, their native country, and mainly treated the landscape as a beautiful combination of lines and subjects [...] Savrasov radically avoided this attitude towards the landscape, choosing not particularly beautiful places as the subject for his paintings, but, on the contrary, trying to find in its most simple and ordinary aspects those intimate, profoundly touching, often sad characteristics, which are felt so strongly in our native landscape and which irresistibly affect the soul. In Savrasov one noted a lyrical attitude towards the landscape and a limitless love to one's native earth'. Quoted in A. M. Turkov, *Levitan* (Moscow: Terra, 2001), p. 176.
99 V. V. Rozanov, 'A. L. Volynskii. "*F. M. Dostoevskii. Kriticheskie statii*"', in *V. V. Rozanov, Sobranie sochinenii. Staraia i molodaia Rossiia. Statii i ocherki 1909 g.* (Moscow: Respublika, 2004), p. 275.
100 Rozanov, *Pis'ma A. P. Chekhova*, op. cit., pp. 208, 210–1.
101 Rozanov, *Nash 'Antosha Chekhonte'*, op. cit., p. 553.
102 The concept of the wandering pilgrim also appears in that kenosis. The pilgrim's duty imitates the humiliation of Christ, 'who was glad to come down to earth as a wanderer [...] Wandering does not show a boldness of disposition, an unknowing wisdom, an undeclared knowledge, a concealed life, unseen intentions, hidden thoughts, a desire for humiliation, a desire for closeness, the way to the Divine, an abundance of love, the rejection of vanity, the silence of the deep [...] To be a pilgrim is a rejection of everything with the intention of making one's thought indivisible from God. The pilgrim loves and performs incessant lamentation. The pilgrim is the person who shuns all attachments, with relatives or strangers'. Ioann Lestvichnik, prep., *Lestvitsa*, op. cit., p. 33–4, 38.
103 I. A. Bunin, 'Chekhov', in *A. P. Chekhov v vospominaniiakh sovremennikov* (Moscow: *Khudozhestvennaia literatura*, 1960), p. 528.
104 The image of Chekhov as a 'wanderer–observer' is central in Dolinin's 1914 essay. Egorka, as he travels through the steppe, is seen as the symbol of Chekhov himself and all his future work: 'The wanderer–observer, incessantly feeling his own finiteness, can never join with anyone – this is how he was in life, in his relations with the people around him; this is how he was in his work – in his relations with his own

creations [...] He sought a 'general idea', 'the god of the living person'; he uncloaked all our private ideas, our temporary values. The reason for this is this; it is a flight from himself, the irresistible striving to go beyond the borders of our finiteness, to obtain a real all-encompassing synthesis'. A. S. Dolinin, 'O Chekhove (*Putnik-sozertsatel'*)', in *A. P. Chekhov: pro et contra: Tvorchestvo A. P. Chekhova v russkoi mysli kontsa XIX-nachala XX v. (1887–1914). Antologiia* (St Petersburg: *Russkii Khristianskii gumanitarnyi institut*, 2002), p. 935, 960.
105 Rozanov, 'A. P. Chekhov', op. cit., p. 481–2.
106 Bitsilli, 'Chekhov', p. 168.

3

CONTEMPORANEITY, COMPETITION AND COMBAT. FACTS AND FICTIONS ABOUT EVERYBODY AND PASSIVENESS, ORIENTALISM AND ANAESTHESIA IN ROZANOV'S VIEW ON CHEKHOV

Rainer Grübel

In essence, the question of Chekhov's reception by his contemporaries has not only not been resolved, it has not even been put correctly.

Avletina Kuzicheva, 1997[1]

I. Contemporaneity and Competition. General Aspects of Chekhov's Reception by Rozanov

I think if Anton Pavlovich Chekhov had said, 'The time has come, I need an apartment, a table, some rest and a wife', Suvorin would have replied: 'Have all this at your disposal in my home'.

Vasilii Rozanov, 1912[2]

Anton Chekhov had been dead for almost 12 years, when Vasilii Rozanov, reading the last volume of the writer's correspondence, wrote in the margin of a letter from Chekhov one of his famous thumbnail sketches. This miniature in prose lays bare his sorrow about the missed opportunity for a relationship with a great contemporary artist:

9. III. 1916
I lived all my life with people who were deeply irrelevant to me. And from those I was really interested in, I kept my distance.

(*on the copy of Chekhov's letter*)

[...] What would have been the result of a friendship with Chekhov? He clearly called me (in the letter), beckoned me.

I did not answer his very kind letter. This was even repellent. Why did I not reply?

Fate.

I felt that he was significant. And I did not like to come close to significant people.[3]

Rozanov tried to explain his behaviour toward the playwright and prose-writer Chekhov by saying that at the time he had read only his story 'The Duel' (*Duel'*), which left him with a negative picture of the author, the impression of a bragger and a chatterer. He found 'disgusting' (*otvratitel'no*) the scene with the woman bathing naked in front of men in a boat and turning on her back.[4] And he pretended that such admittedly wonderful pieces by Chekhov as Peasant Women (*Baby*) and The Darling (*Dushechka*) he read only later. We are not obliged to believe that the *Novoe Vremia* employee did not read the stories published by his newspaper's editing house. It seems that it was easier for him to remember the prosaist's texts on which he could comment negatively, than those about which he was enthusiastic. Chekhov's fame continued to be a problem for Rozanov until the end – his own books sold much less successfully!

In the above note Rozanov mentions a friendship which never existed. And he refers to a 'call' by Chekhov which, as far as we can judge, was never issued: the two writers never met. Rozanov himself wrote the first (undated) letter of their short correspondence. And this correspondence ended with the only known letter from Chekhov to Rozanov, written on 30 March 1899, which essentially was a refusal by Chekhov to satisfy Rozanov's request for some ancient Greek coins from the Crimean peninsula. Rozanov, a fanatical coin collector, turned to Chekhov for this purpose via Konstantin Tychinkin, *Novoe Vremia*'s director of the typography. Rozanov also apologized for asking such a delicate question via a third person. As an explanation for this ill-mannered deed Rozanov gave the reason, in itself dubious, that he had read a letter from Chekhov to Tychinkin, which astonished him by its 'simplicity of tone' (*prostota tona*).[5] Tychinkin, he says, convinced him to ask Chekhov for the coins, because of the latter's 'beautiful and soft character' (*prekrasnom i miagkom kharaktere*). In the second part of his letter Rozanov invited the writer to send him stories for the literary supplement to the *Torgovo-promyshlennaia gazeta* (the *Journal of Trade and Industry*), which he was asked to manage.

In his friendly but non-committal reply Chekhov wrote that Tychinkin had not yet informed him of Rozanov's request, and he therefore had no reason to look for ancient Greek coins, but that he could do so when he returned to

Yalta in the autumn.⁶ To the second question of Rozanov's letter the writer also gave an evasive answer, saying that he was busy preparing texts for the Marks publishing house, and that in Yalta he could not write 'at all' (*voobshche*). However, he said that he would like to reconsider the request after his journey to the north, when he would have written something. Showing his 'soft character' once more, Chekhov at the end of his letter praised Rozanov's article 'Gentle Demonism' on Men´shikov's essay 'On superstition and the right of love', and he added that Maksim Gor´kii, 'with whom I often talk about you',⁷ had praised Rozanov's article on matrimony and physical love. However, we should not forget that already in 1897 Chekhov's opinion of Rozanov was very critical. In one of his letters to Suvorin we read in a passage on Nikolai Engel´gardt (1867–1942), a new contributor to Suvorin's *Novoe Vremia*:

> This category [of people, to which Rozanov also belongs] has no definite world vision (*mirosozertsanie*), there is only a tremendous self-esteem, swollen up beyond all measure (*gromadnoe rasplyvsheesia samoliubie do-nel'zia*), and there is a morbid hostile attitude, deeply hidden under a hood, similar to a tombstone, which is covered with moss.⁸

In December 1901 in a letter to the publicist and former singer Viktor Miroliubov (1860–1936) about the establishment of the Religious–Philosophic Meetings, in which he collaborated with Rozanov, Chekhov gave an even worse appraisal of the journalist:

> I read in *Novoe Vremia* an article of the policeman (*gorodovoi*) Rozanov, from which I learned about your new activity. If only you knew, my dear fellow, how I was annoyed! It seems to me, that you should leave Petersburg. […] What do you, a good, straight person, have in common with Rozanov […]?"⁹

Chekhov's judgement about Rozanov was anything but consistent. In his letter of 30 December 1902 to Miroliubov he praised Rozanov's article on Nekrasov.¹⁰ 'For a very long time I have not read anything so talented, broad and kindhearted (*blagodushnogo*) and intelligent.'¹¹ Interestingly, Rozanov's view of Chekhov can in a sense be regarded as a mirror image of this ambivalence in Chekhov's view of Rozanov.

Rozanov did not reply to Chekhov's letter, which must have surely disappointed him. More precisely, he did not write a letter to Chekhov, but instead sent his own book *Literary Sketches*¹² (a book, by the way, which did not contain any article about the addressee, but extensive texts on Griboedov, Belinskii, Lermontov, Danilevskii, Katkov, Strachov, Leont´ev, Shperk, Dostoevskii and

Tolstoi) with a long dedication in it. He expressed his wish to send a copy of his book *Religion and Culture* to Chekhov's interlocutor Gor´kii, and finished with a statement, which was clearly about Chekhov rather than Gor´kii: 'May God give him success, *and it is necessary, to keep oneself in* check *(derzhat' sebia v rukakh)*. This is the great secret to live, to work and to have successes'.[13] To control yourself is the central maxim of stoicism, which Rozanov, as we shall see, thought was Chekhov's philosophy. And to have success was, as Rozanov must have assumed, Chekhov's aim as well as his own. For almost 20 years they competed to win the favour of the same public. Rozanov evidently does not seem to have been aware that this aim itself is in contradiction with stoicism.

The chronology of the lives of Vasilii Rozanov (1856–1919) and Anton Chekhov (1860–1904) marks them as contemporaries, born only four years apart. They were connected by a biographical, as well as psychological and economic bridge, in the figure of Aleksei Suvorin (1834–1912),[14] playwright, newspaper editor and Rozanov's employer, publisher and theatre manager who was able to support Chekhov.[15] Suvorin belonged to an older generation and supported both Rozanov and Chekhov as younger intellectuals and artists: he evidently had no doubt about their talent. The fact that both men had in common such a patron led to, in the eyes of Rozanov the critic, a rivalry between the prosaist, playwright and doctor Chekhov on the one hand, and the philosopher, journalist and prosaist Rozanov on the other.[16] Both were short of money for long periods of time, and both appreciated the recognition and the help of the economically and artistically successful, well-known self-made man.[17]

In 1916, when Chekhov had already been dead for 12 years, Rozanov called him 'the darling of Russian society' *(liubimets russkogo obshchestva)*.[18] However, despite his graphomania, Rozanov wrote only one article on Chekhov during the writer's lifetime. Even that was written only following a prompt from his employer, and it was published only a month before Chekhov's foreseeable and imminent death.

Suvorin's acquaintance with Chekhov began in 1886, ten years earlier than with Rozanov.[19] He started to print Chekhov's stories in his newspaper and wrote a positive theme, which Chekhov greatly appreciated.[20] Suvorin later invited Chekhov into his private theatre in St Petersburg, and published Chekhov's works in his own publishing house. In 1891 and 1894 Suvorin even offered to pay for Chekhov during their extensive travels together across Europe. Although their political views increasingly diverged – Suvorin became a conservative Slavophile and anti-Semite, and Chekhov was a liberal Westernizer – their friendship never ended.

Rozanov started to write for Suvorin's conservative *Novoe Vremia* only in 1895. It was then the biggest and most modern daily in Russia, for which the owner had taken the famous English *The Times* as a model. In 1899 Rozanov became a member of its editorial board, though without the obligation to be permanently present at the offices. Thus Suvorin's relations with the younger Chekhov had already been ongoing for ten years when he brought Rozanov to the newspaper.[21] Suvorin communicated with Chekhov mainly in letters, as the latter lived in Moscow or spent much time in Yalta owing to his illness, and the correspondence between them is some of Chekhov's most interesting. Rozanov and Suvorin often talked face to face, as they both lived in St Petersburg and frequently met in the editorial office of the newspaper or at the editor's home. They quite often wrote each other notes or extended letters, which Rozanov published after the death of the editor in 1912.[22]

When Rozanov wrote in his memoires of Suvorin (introducing their correspondence) that 'it was Chekhov who he [Suvorin] loved most of all in all the literary world, the old and the new',[23] it seems that he wrote with a touch of jealousy.[24] And in his reminiscences of how in 1904 the 74-year-old editor met the Chekhov's coffin (Chekhov died in Germany at the age of 44 and was brought to Russia by train), we hear the voice of a man who grew up without a father and who would have liked to have had a father-figure in the powerful editor:

> I remember him, how he met Chekhov's coffin in Petersburg.[25] With a stick in his hand (walking awfully quickly), shouting about the sluggishness of the pace of the procession, about the clumsy attempts to deliver the carriage to the platform. Looking at his face and listening to his abrupt words I saw exactly a father, to whom they bring the corpse of his child or the corpse of a promising young man, who passed away untimely. Suvorin saw nobody and nothing. He did not pay attention to anything, and expected only, expected, wanted, wanted ... the coffin!![26]

Already at the end of 1896, in a letter to Petr Pertsov (1886–1947), critic and later editor of some of his books, Rozanov explained why he did not like the writer Chekhov:

> Therefore I don't love Merezhk[ovskii], Chekhov (how do you know my attitude towards *him*? I have not written anything on this), Nietzsche: they sing of this 'outside place', and eat there a sausage and unpressed caviar, and they think, that this is all, what is necessary for a human being ...[27]

We can conclude that he also had other reasons not to write on Chekhov. A certain change of attitude towards the writer is present in a note of Valerii Briusov's dairy of 1902, which documents Rozanov's vision of Chekhov: 'Good is that writer, which you read and, while reading, you feel ashamed as if you were stripped; and this I felt, when I was reading Chekhov.'[28]

The feeling of competition and the impression that he himself had been unmasked in the prose and dramas of Chekhov might have been the motivation for Rozanov's having failed to do anything during Chekhov's lifetime to strengthen the opinion of the readers towards Chekhov in general and of his reader Suvorin in particular.[29] It is less evident, however, why Rozanov kept silent again about Chekhov during the last three years of his life, from 1917 up to 1919. It seems that Rozanov felt that Chekhov's life could not or should not be connected to the most important events in history, the end of the First World War or the two Russian Revolutions, which Rozanov himself had examined in *Apocalypse of our Time*[30] and *Black Fire*.[31] Rozanov, with his keen interest in Russian and world history, did not refer to Chekhov, but to Pushkin, Gogol' and Lermontov, and addressed Dostoevskii and Tolstoi, all of whom had the advantage of belonging to earlier generations.[32]

The five articles Rozanov wrote on Chekhov in the 12 years from 1904 to 1916[33] correspond on the one hand to changes in his views of Russian history and culture and their place in world history, and on the other hand with the different journals and newspapers where these articles were published. Rozanov was neither a man who stood up to his convictions in historical terms (in his role as a journalist), nor did he preserve them in different political and ideological contexts. Because he used to practice simultaneously in different contexts and genres several mutually-exclusive points of view, Stammler has labelled him a 'Proteus-like human being',[34] and I myself have called him a 'paraphrenic writer'.[35] We will therefore discuss in chronological order Rozanov's articles on Chekhov which appeared between 1904 (two), 1910 (also two) and 1916, and pay attention to the genres used, the topics referred to, and the contexts in which they were published.

II. Playwright Chekhov Speaks in *The Cherry Orchard* with the Voice of the Eternal Student Petr Trofimov (1904) and Represents a Poor Motionless and Passive Russia

It is better to study the alien good than your own 'nothing'.[36]
                                    Rozanov in 1916, having read Chekhov's letters

In June 1904, less than a month before the death of the already seriously ill Anton Chekhov, Rozanov's first article on Chekhov appeared in *Novoe Vremia* under the title *Literary Novelties* (*Literaturnye novinki*).[37] It was a typical review, referring to the recently published anthology of the association 'Knowledge' (*Znanie*), which had been inaugurated and was still directed by Maksim Gor'kii. Beside the stories of A. Kuprin ('A Peaceful Life', *Mirnoe zhitie*) and E. Chirikov ('On Guarantee', *Na porukakh*), S. Iushkevich's essay 'The Jews' (*Evrei*) and some poems by Skitalets (which Rozanov did not even mention), the collection also included Chekhov's last drama *The Cherry Orchard* (*Vishnevyi sad*, 1904).[38] Rozanov distinguished Chekhov's play as the best of all these works because of 'the skill of painting, the experience and the expounded thoughts'.[39]

Although the premiere of the play had already taken place in January 2004 in the Moscow Art Theatre in the presence of the author and with his wife Ol´ga Knipper playing the role of Liubov´ Ranevskaia, and Konstantin Stanislavskii (who also directed) playing Leonid Gaev, Rozanov's judgement concerned exclusively the text of the comedy. Nevertheless, he also had a possible (ideal) production in mind. He thus praised the 'beautiful framework of nature',[40] which in the first Act however can only be seen through the open windows of a room, but which is dominant in the second Act. However, Rozanov considered this landscape as the framework of 'Russian life' (*russkaia zhizn´*), which for him formed the centre of the whole play. And he criticized the fact that in this piece of art we do not come to know what love, thoughts, habits, and money mean for the protagonists, with the exception of the entrepreneur Lopakhin, who was interested exclusively in money. And even in his case, Rozanov argued, it is not clear what money really means to him. The reviewer thus asked with irritation, 'Money for money's sake?'[41] And he added that this concept was not even new, as it appeared earlier as Pliushkin's way of thinking in Gogol's *Dead Souls*.

Rozanov (mis)read the play as an allegory of Russian life in general, a new *Family-Chronicle* (*Semeinaia khronika*, 1856) in the manner of Sergei Aksakov, and took its characters only as elements of this allegory.[42] So he (mis)understood the eternal student Petr Trofimov, interpreting him not only as an 'innocent Adam'[43] (*nevinnyi Adam*),[44] but also as the voice of the author and as the moralizer of the play.[45] His long monologue in the second Act,[46] where Trofimov blames Russian intellectuals for their idleness and passivity, was taken by Rozanov as a Chekhovian reference to Russia's 'great hopelessness' (*velikaia beznadezhnost*)[47] at the turn of the century. By contrast, Rozanov himself appears convinced that the example of the Old Believers, who became successful traders, proves that Russia also has potential, and thus sees other options than those shown in the play.

In Rozanov's eyes, Russian literature was profoundly poetic and the roots of this poetry he saw in boredom, passivity and nostalgia. And for him, Chekhov took over this paralyzing heritage from Lermontov, Gogol´ and Turgenev. Its alternatives, he argued, were either poems full of expectations, as in Old Russian literature, or deeply personal works, rooted in the 'I' of the writer, and which, because of this individualism, could be representative for Russian society as a 'collective organism' (*organizm kollektivnyi*[48]) only in a problematic way. As a beautiful but limping and powerless artefact in the tradition of

Aleksandr Griboedov's *Woe from Wit* (*Gore ot uma*), Chekhov's play in Rozanov's view corresponded to a passive Russia which had not changed for centuries. Here he gave evidence of his critical and almost liberal view on Russia, which he acquired after the Russian defeat in the war against Japan, and which he maintained until the failure of the first Russian Revolution (1905) and the publication of Mikhail Gershenzon's famous anthology *Landmarks* (*Vekhi*) in 1909.[49] Having didactically criticized Chekhov's play, Rozanov at the time took Chekhov's side concerning the place of Jewish people in Russia. However, while Chekhov never accepted Suvorin's anti-Semitic inclinations, Rozanov changed his positive stance for an anti-Semitic one in the period from 1910 to 1917.

III. The Poet and Thinker Chekhov, Used as an Argument in the Cultural Combat on the Concept of Party Literature

Omnia in opinione sita.
All is situated in opinion.

Marc Aurel, *Meditations*, Book 2

[...] ne v mneniiach vsia sut', a v ikh prirode.
[...] the whole essence is not in opinions, but in their nature.

Chekhov in a letter to Suvorin, 23 October 1889[50]

Only five days after Chekhov's death, *Novoe Vremia* published Rozanov's extended article 'The writer as artist, and the party.'[51] Although Chekhov's name is not mentioned in the title, this article, written in the genre of a cultural and philosophical essay,[52] deals exclusively with the writer, his work and his relation to society and politics.

Rozanov starts his assessment of the work of the writer Chekhov with an axiological consideration of the ranking of Russian authors in Chekhov's time. Above Chekhov, Rozanov ranks only Tolstoi, and beside him Vladimir Korolenko (1853–1921). In Korolenko's case he mentions only *The Blind Musician* (*Slepoi muzykant*), a work of 1886. Comparing the time of Chekhov with the generations of Pushkin and Gogol', Lermontov and Dostoevskii, Rozanov concludes that Russian literature has experienced a general decline. He notices the same in foreign cultures, where the Italian Gabriele D'Annunzio and Polish Henryk Sienkiewicz are, in his eyes, examples of famous but insignificant contemporary writers. In his assessment, Rozanov completely ignores what was later to be called the Silver Age of Russian literature, with Vladimir Solov'ev, Bal'mont, Briusov, Gippius and Merezhkovskii as some of its early heroes.

According to Rozanov, this lack of significant contemporary writers (as well as politicians, strategists, religious leaders and so on) caused the authors of Chekhov obituaries to overestimate the late writer regarding him as a 'giant' (*gigantskaia figura*).[53] In contrast, Chekhov was for Rozanov just a noble, thoughtful man with a talent of the second order.[54] It is only through his 'mind' (*um*) and 'subtlety' (*tonkost'*),[55] that Chekhov exceeded the people of his time. Rozanov is also convinced that the author himself would have disliked this posthumous overestimation of his work. The critic even distorts a phrase of Pushkin about a 'mysterious law' (*tainstvennyi zakon*[56]) in order to support his claim that there is an evident discontinuity in history, which either throws up many figures of genius, or, as in Chekhov's time, none at all.

What is, in Rozanov's eyes, the reason for this lack of great men in Chekhov's time, which gave rise to such an 'ungrounded' labelling of the latter as a gigantic figure? It is, according to the critic, the fact that since the time of Belinskii and Chernyshevskii, Gertsen and Pisarev (and we could add Mikhailovskii and Plekhanov),[57] literature and its producers had been subordinate to politics. Although Rozanov admits that, once literature acquires a political dimension it becomes programmatic, he demands (this is a 'complicated matter')[58] from the writer, who becomes a member of a party movement, a vital mental and spiritual culture as compensation:

> If a party wants to appropriate a writer, it has to give him in return the gratification of that mental width and spiritual depth, and all sorts of ideological splendour, which the writer, especially a beginner, has the same right to wish for himself as the party, on its part, wishes his obedience, the 'exactness of fulfilment of its commands'.[59]

The critic insists on the individual philosophical orientation of Chekhov, which did not fit in either with the existing parties, or with their journals. Most of all he criticizes V.A. Gol´cev, who was from 1885 until his death in 1906 the head of the journal *Russian Thought* (*Russkaia mysl'*), because the latter suggested a creation of a special Chekhov room in the History museum of Moscow (since Chekhov was a contributor to his journal). Gol´cev's journal was surely less conservative than Suvorin's *Novoe Vremia*, where Rozanov was employed; it soon became the organ of the party of Constitutional Democrats (*Kadety*), which was founded in 1905.[60]

Rozanov's text presumably provoked Lenin's article 'Party organization and literature in accordance with party thought' which proved so disastrous for Soviet culture. In it Lenin stated:

> What is this principle of party literature? It is not simply that, for the socialist proletariat, literature cannot be a means of enriching individuals or

groups, but that it cannot be an individual undertaking at all, independent of the general proletarian cause. Down with non-party writers! Down with literary supermen! The literary business has to become *part* of the general proletarian business, a 'little wheel and little screw' of the single and united great Social Democratic mechanism, set in motion by all the conscious avant-garde of the working class. Literary business has to become an integral part of the organized, planned united Social Democratic Party work [*Lenin's italics*].[61]

Fifteen years later, this pamphlet would be used as the ideological foundation for the 'party principle' (*partiinost'*) in Socialist realism. Communist ideology became a compulsory and integral part of literary criticism and art. Indeed, what Rozanov claims in his article with respect to the position of an author in society and the author's relation to politics, in addition to what he writes about Chekhov as an artist, opposes Lenin's utilitarian attitude of writers as vehicles in ideological and social movements.

Rozanov views Chekhov as a poet and a thinker, who in such works as 'Ward Number Six' (*Palata No. 6*, 1892) proclaims his own stoic philosophy through the mouth of the medical doctor, a way of thinking which is neither in tune with the philosophical inclinations of Russian social movements of the second half of the nineteenth century, nor with Russian parties of the early twentieth century.[62] As different writers and scholars have shown, Chekhov indeed felt attracted by Marcus Aurelius, one of the most important Stoic philosophers.[63] In the Chekhov museum in Yalta we find a copy of a Russian translation of Aurelius's *Meditations*,[64] with marks and annotations left by Chekhov on the margins of the book.[65] Rozanov, far from a stoic himself, was the first to point to the stoic tradition in Chekhov's story and in the author's thought.[66] He did so either because of his own philosophical knowledge – he studied philosophy at Moscow University and his first book was the philosophical treatise *On Understanding* (*O ponimanii*, 1886),[67] or because Suvorin, who spent much time with Chekhov, told him about the fascination which the Roman philosopher exerted on the writer.[68]

However, it seems to be an error to suppose, as has been suggested, that Chekhov in his stories practiced an 'inseparable symbiotic connection' with the maxims of Marcus Aurelius.[69] Even if we put to one side the remarks in his notebooks and letters, in Chekhov's fiction the narrator sometimes refers explicitly to the Latin philosopher, for example 'A Boring Story' (*Skuchnaia istoriia*, 1889), 'Ward Number Six' and 'The Black Monk' (*Chernyi monakh*, 1894). Here, Chekhov's teller does not only quote Marcus Aurelius's sayings, but calls into question the Latin philosopher's thought. In 'A Boring Story', the main character (a professor of medicine who criticizes the younger generation for their ignorance of Marcus Aurelius, among others), does not display the appropriate inner calm when, effectively at his deathbed, he is confronted with the problem of (his) life's meaning.[70] The text neither presents the stoic quality of an equanimous habit, nor the restlessness of eternally questioning the meaning of life as its dominant ideology. 'Ward Number Six' juxtaposes the stoic disengagement from life and indifference to death with the reality of the miserable death of the hero, a doctor of medicine, who feels 'despair' and 'fear' instead of a stoic lack of concern.[71] It is here that Marcus Aurelius's famous aphorism (borrowed from Chrysippus): 'Hippocrates after curing many diseases caught a disease and died'[72] paradoxically does not permit the realization of the stoic virtue which it proclaims. The stoic way of thinking, its 'indifferent' (*ravnodushnyi*) quality dies with the doctor, now patient of his former hospital, and with it dies the idea that the author Chekhov was bound to this philosophy.[73] In this horrifying story, the author, as it were, loses control of his hero, and the moment of catharsis does not seem to be able to reconcile the terrible with the beautiful or secure hope of a world without suffering.[74] The book teaches that it is easy to preach stoic maxims but it is difficult to live by them.

In 'The Black Monk', a professor of philosophy dies with the illusion that he is a famous and important man. In this case, the stoic moment of *unassumingness* is presented merely as the background to his environment. Referring intertextually to the romantic motive of *The Double* and its transformation in Ivan Karamazov's meeting with the devil in Dostoevskii's later novel, the story sounds like a revocation of Tolstoi's didactic *ars moriendi* in *The Death of Ivan Il'ich*. Freise has exposed the art of verbal equivalence in this text,[75] but we doubt that symbolism is the right key to open it.[76] The most important equilibrium of the story is produced by the circumstance, that the alternative of the 'romantic' ('idealistic') and the stoic ('realistic') philosophical visions cannot be decided[77] In the complex construction of meaning in 'The Black Monk', Chekhov is surely nearer to Dostoevskii's dialogism than to Tolstoi's didactics.

Scholars also traced in 'Ward Number Six' a polemic with the philosophy of Marcus Aurelius and the reception of Schopenhauer,[78] who was influenced by Oriental philosophy. It would therefore be interesting to study the philosophical concepts in Chekhov's stories and plays in the context of philosophical Orientalism. In this sense they could be compared with and contrasted to the ideology of Lev Tolstoi, who was also an inquisitive reader of Schopenhauer.[79]

IV. The Praise of Chekhov's Art as an Adequate Expression for Russia's Love of Itself

> *I could love literature without taking it as an expression of Russia, because one can express also Russia's drunkenness and madness; and what can one love about this?*[80]

On the occasion of Chekhov's 50th birthday in 1910, Rozanov published two articles on the Russian writer. One of them appeared in January with the title 'Our Antosha Chekhonte' (*Nash Antosha Chekhonte*) under the pseudonym Varvarin in the newspaper *The Russian Word* (*Russkoe Slovo*),[81] which, since the first Russian revolution, was politically close to the Constitutional Democrats. The other, 'A. P. Chekhov', was included under Rozanov's own name in the *Chekhov Jubilee Anthology*.[82]

'Our Antosha Chekhonte' is Rozanov's most poetic and intimate essay on Chekhov, and his essay which assesses Chekhov's work most positively. It is addressed to the Russian author, who loves his people, referred to by the title's possessive pronoun. Here the essayist Rozanov demonstrates so much empathy towards his hero, as much as he would soon display towards his own persona as the hero of his books *Solitaria* (*Uedinennoe*, 1912) and *Fallen Leaves* (*Opavshie list'ia*, 1913, 1915). It is not surprising, therefore, that many sections of Rozanov's essay say as much about the author as they say about his subject matter.

Against the background of the serious and important figures of Turgenev, Tolstoi, Nekrasov, Dobroliubov and Chernyshevskii, graced with large beards, the modest figure of Chekhov appears in Rozanov's words, just as 'one of us'. Chekhov's portraits seem to present a person without the appeal of mind, without *Weltschmerz* or political indignation, according to Rozanov. This puts Chekhov, in Rozanov's view, in the artificial position of a second-rate author. Just like his characters, Chekhov seems to belong to the category of an average man, a man in the street, without genius, with little strength and, lacking a noble destiny. This picture corresponds not only to the (auto-) stereotype[83] of 'Russian weakness' (*russkoe bessilie*),[84] but also to the image of the every man.[85] Although it is a counter-type to the traditional hero with his 'exceptionalism', it is nevertheless again a type. And it is a type to which Rozanov gave shape in many of his narratives.

Rozanov contrasts this weak human being, its wisdom and its spirituality, against the wooden 'nothing man' (characterized by Rozanov's own term *nichto-chelovek*), a technician, who invented flying machines and the telegraph.[86] This opposition is Rozanov's version of the traditional Russian dichotomy of Slavophil and Westernizer.[87] It also forms a special type of Russian orientalism.[88] To study the works of Chekhov from this perspective would be most interesting. Chekhov's decision to take the side of the thinker and not of the maker explains, according to Rozanov, Chekhov's failure in medicine, and his success in literature.

Like a street lamp which illuminates everybody, in Rozanov's view, Chekhov watches everything that happens before him with indifference. This is the famous *impassibilité* (equanimity) of Flaubert's narrator toward the narrated persons[89] and events, and which Rozanov observes in the prose of Chekhov. Intriguingly, Chekhov's stance is opposed to the emotional engagement of the speaker in Rozanov's own prose. Chekhov puts this distance of the narrator in a form which Rozanov terms a 'miniature story' (*miniatiurnyi rasskaz*),[90] a form which would soon become Rozanov's own genre of choice. With regards to his own writing and his own view of writing as an organic process, Rozanov called these miniatures 'embryos'.[91] And here Rozanov is quite right, as he spots in Chekhov's prose the invention of the Russian short story.

Rozanov opposes Chekhov to the revolutionary democrat Mikhailovskii, a literary critic who propagated historical progress and judged Chekhov's works from the point of view of Russian populism. Thus Mikhailovskii complained about the lack of a clear worldview in Chekhov and his indifference towards narrated events.[92] Rozanov, however, praises Chekhov's narrative technique of discussing simple things without affectation:

> Chekhov has brought the ordinary expression of everyday life to virtuosity, he expressed it with real genius. 'Without a hero' – this could be the title of all his works, and speaking to yourself (*pro sebia*), one could add: without sadness, 'without heroism'. Indeed, such a lack of a steep wave, of a big swell as in the work of Chekhov we, as it seems, do not find anywhere else. And how characteristic it is that even the proportions of Chekhov's stories are small. What a contrast this constitutes to the multi-volume novels of Dostoevskii or Goncharov; what a contrast to the eternal heroic Lermontov, who breaks through into heaven …[93]

When Rozanov states that in Chekhov's texts, like in nature, nothing walks, but grows and spreads, he has his biological model of the world in mind, which coincides with Chekhov's own medical background and his view of the most ordinary as the most important. This was one of the special features of Rozanov's own literary vision, to see the ordinary as something amazing. In Rozanov's view the ordinary in Chekhov's literature borders on the beginning of something quite different. In this sense, it is not as removed from the adventurous in Gor'kii art as it might seem. However, in contrast to Gor'kii, Rozanov argues that Chekhov's time is the tired midday, when the ordinary is combined with the sour. The aim of this vision is not to admire the exceptional, but to be able to live with the mundane. And this is in Rozanov's eyes also the maxim of Chekhov's dramas. This model of the quiet but wonderful man in the work of the writer Rozanov derives – again we can relate to Russian orientalism – from an oriental background, 'out of the peaceful lands of the East' (*iz mirnykh stran Vostoka*).[94] As this model has noble elements, it can serve the critic as the ground on which Russia can begin to love itself. Rozanov is convinced that Chekhov has built in his texts a 'collective type' (*sobiratel'nyi tip*) in which every Russian can recognize himself.[95] This collective construction is not one of steadiness, of connection to the ground, but one of migration.[96] It lacks great thought and clear sound, but it has something within itself which until now did not exist anywhere else. To live with it appears unwise, and to live with something else would mean to achieve a happier but also more boring, state of mind. As a result, argues the critic, this viewpoint helps humanity to live in a ridiculous period of history.[97]

Rozanov knew that in this essay, he interpreted Chekhov as a poet who sings about life in this world in a way which transmits the feeling of living in quite a different world. He ended with the deliberation that Chekhov helps us to find the essence of existence and to view a human being as something in itself (*an und für sich*). It was the growing number of suicides in Russia that motivated Rozanov to add that nobody should throw away his life.[98] Gazing at the fading light, one can come to the knowledge, to the mystic horror, that it suddenly can be extinguished.

V. The Place and Function of Russian Culture in the World: Chekhov's Oeuvre as an Example of Compensation for the Ugliness of Russian Nature and the Russian People

> *The poor writers do not understand their fate: that 'there has come toothache', and the female reader puts away the 'likeable Chekhov'.*[99]

If one did not know that V. Varvarin was a pseudonym of Rozanov, one would never guess that 'A. P. Chekhov' was written by the same author as 'Our Antosha Chekhonte'. The former is as impressionistic as a critical essay. It places the playwright and prose writer in a global context and involves him in rather different universal geo-cultural considerations.

In this article, Rozanov considers his subject matter within the context of the opposition between on the one hand the beauty of nature with its mountains, lakes and rivers in Switzerland, the health, strength and activity of Swiss men (a product, according to Rozanov, of this nature), and on the other the cold sun, the dull stars and the morass of nature in Russia. It is these natural conditions which Rozanov deems responsible for the sickness, weakness and passivity of the Russian man. Rozanov would recall that in the little town of Belyi (Smolensk district), where he lived for two years as a teacher, the cemetery was the only place where you could go for a walk.[100]

Rozanov's organic worldview also explains his interpretation of the different attitudes to beauty in these cultures. Since in Switzerland, nature and people, a 'happy family' (*schastlivaia sem'ia*) are beautiful, there is no need to seek beauty and happiness in culture as a way of 'compensation'.[101] However, in Russia the ugliness of nature and the unhappiness of people call for such compensation. To exemplify his point, Rozanov discusses the Book of Job which, while narrating the case of a man who was as unhappy as the Russians, contains more life and soul than Job's life as such.[102] The same is true in Russian culture: we find in it more life and soul than in Russian reality. The writer of the essay argues: 'What is history for the Swiss people? What is poetry for the Swiss? What is music? Why have all these if they have beautiful lakes?'[103] Surely this was the first 'compensational' analysis of Chekhov's artistic work.[104]

Chekhov's work, like that of Turgenev, is in Rozanov's view motivated by this 'compensatory' duty. It is for this reason that Chekhov, when visiting Rome, went to a brothel rather than to the Colosseum. According to Rozanov, the doctor and writer expected to see more real life there than in the dead document of architecture. Rozanov combines this curiosity, which he regards as an interest in the death of civilization (embodied by a brothel), with Chekhov's general interest in death. He even fabricates a quotation: 'I love to watch how a human being dies. It is horrible, terrifying. But I long so much to watch it.'[105] And we cannot be sure that the quotation of Chekhov's conversation with an unnamed person, in which Chekhov allegedly confesses that he loves to walk among graves and to read the inscriptions on the gravestones, is not also an invention of the essayist.

While Rozanov begins with a general lamentation on Russian reality, he later reduces this to statements of Chekhov having lived in the 'most sorrowful time' (*samyi grustnyi period*) for Russia.[106] The period he has in mind is that of the lost war against Japan, which, after the Crimean war, became the second trauma of modern Russian history.

The essayist praises Chekhov's stories 'Peasant Women' (*Baby*, 1894) and Peasants (*Muzhiki*, 1897) as analytic sketches of life in Russia which should become the chronicles of Russian family life as well as of Russian everyday life. He claims to have read them 'with the dry professional eyes of a scholar' (*sukhim, delovym glazom issledovatelia*), and declares that Russians do not care about the Dreyfus case, while not trying to conceal his own growing anti-Semitism.[107] In the same context, he criticizes the indifference towards unethical attitudes with respect to women, which in his view are falsely legitimised by the Russian Orthodox propensity to forgiveness.[108] Rozanov's critique of moral indifference is part of his anticlerical and anti-Christian trait which was typical of him in this period. In the tradition of Comte's sociology, he argues that the reason for these phenomena lies in Russia's geographical proximity to the North Pole.

In 'Peasants', Rozanov recognizes more the hand of the medical doctor than that of the writer. He locates the central idea of the story in the statement 'he is not our bread-winner' (*On u nas ne dobytchik*), as it articulates society's indifference towards a disabled person.[109] In Rozanov's view, this characteristic can also be found in the ideology of Tolstoi's peasant – philosopher Platon Karataev in *War and Peace*.

Rozanov even mentions Chekhov's difficult financial situation as well as the absence of the sublime in his work. According to him, Chekhov doubted whether faithful love was possible in Russia, let alone eternal love. In his vague, indecisive tone, Chekhov was however (according to Rozanov) in tune with Russia. When Rozanov tries to find the reason why this author became so famous, he uses stereotypes of Russia and the Russians which are well-known from cultural history: 'He became the favourite writer of our lack of will, of our lack of heroism.'[110] Furthermore, it seems that Rozanov also blames Russian audiences for their mediocrity and lack of fairness, because they forgot Gor'kii, who, as well as being rough, unpleasant and short (*korotok*), was also sharp; but at the same time remembered the writer of mediocrity: Anton Chekhov.[111]

Rozanov's criticism of Chekhov's art was articulated more provocatively still in an undated conversation with Erikh Gollerbach, a friend of his late years and his first biographer.[112]

> 'Chekhov? Nothing special. I've had quite enough of him – up to here' [he pointed to his neck].[113] 'What is Chekhov? He looked at life; he simply wrote down what he saw. A very nice writer. He managed to please, and they began to read him. But he is cold and nothing special. I do understand his success, but I don't approve of it.'[114]

VI. Chekhov's Letters as Autobiography: 'Should We Create History?'

So in essence Chekhov depicts everywhere 'dead Russia', which under the whiff of his life-giving talent still flares up.[115]

The ambivalent picture of Chekhov that emerges from Rozanov may explain why it took the latter another six years before he devoted his next and final article to Chekhov. This time the subject was not so much the writer or his work as his life. On the completion of the six-volume edition of Chekhov's letters,[116] Rozanov refers to the first publication of Chekhov's correspondence as a 'mystic phonograph' which sounds from the author's grave.[117] Although Rozanov has much experience of editing correspondences,[118] he naïvely takes the letters of the doctor and writer as authentic articulations of his feelings and thoughts. This is the pseudo-objective ground on which he can consider these letters as 'the best possible' and 'exclusively legitimate' autobiography of the writer.[119]

Moreover, Rozanov is convinced that the appearance of these volumes will strengthen the public's love for Chekhov. According to the critic, the time of Turgenev, Goncharov and Pisemskii had passed with the end of 'slavery' in Russia, but yet Dostoevskii and Tolstoi differ too much from the average man, and their works therefore are unable to attract the wider public. Furthermore, the contemporary writers Korolenko and Gor´kii are too political to fascinate the masses. So Chekhov seems to be the only one who is accessible to all Russians, albeit 'in an idealized form'.[120]

In Rozanov's view, the photographic portrait of Chekhov shows him less as a writer and more as a person – and the kind of person who listens to everything that his *vis-à-vis* has to say. According to Rozanov, this habit of listening corresponds to the passive talent of writers in general – which of course corresponds to the passive Russian character. So in Rozanov's eyes, Chekhov's life is a metonymic picture of Russian life. It is also a picture of creativity which Rozanov in other contexts defined as the female capacity of conception.[121]

Again the critic explains Chekhov's kind of observation by his profession: doctors, he argues, are trained to observe only the body of a sick person and to disregard all metaphysics. This lack of metaphysical sensibility produces, according to Rozanov, a large hole which also manifests itself in the impossibility to understand death. This ignorance of death corresponds in the view of the critic to the helplessness of Russian society being faced with *Thanatos*.[122] A human being is not the master of his or her own life, as he or she is not the master of his or her own death.

For Rozanov, these associations between Chekhov's way of thinking and the Russian people explain the writer's popularity. Chekhov himself seems to be the embodiment of a beautiful, simple person with a dream which never comes true. In this vein, Rozanov makes a problematic simplification by identifying the author with his characters. Thus he regards the three sisters in the drama of the same name as speaking for Chekhov himself. Hence, the apogee of Chekhov's aesthetics is, according to Rozanov, the beauty of wishing. A typical stereotype of orientalism can be noted here once again.

For Rozanov as historian, Chekhov's letters have no subject, no content. He does not find any 'great deliberation' or any 'urgent problem' in the six volumes. Instead of these, Chekhov offers quietness in the small world.[123] However, in a manner which Rozanov interprets to be Chekhov's 'little egoism',[124] his calm world at the same time aspires to be the centre of the universe. In this way, Rozanov believes, the writer calmed Russian man during his timelessness (*bezvremen´e*), on a 'non-road' (*besputitsa*).[125] And although Rozanov does not assess this negatively, we cannot consider this benumbing as a positive judgement. In Rozanov's summary, Chekhov's letters present the picture of a medical doctor who practices anaesthesia.[126] As an ingredient of the *impassibilité* of Chekhov's narrative, this perspective could make the subject of further study. As an artistic attitude it should be related to the stoic ideal of indifference. Whether this is a special feature of the 'self-orientalization' in the art of a Russian writer is an interesting question.

The multiplicity of Rozanov's views on Chekhov has its roots not only in the historical development of Rozanov's worldview, and in the changing social and political context and convictions of the addressee (it is in most cases the reader of a newspaper who wants confirmation of his prejudices), but also in his fourfold guise as a philosopher who can identify stoicism, a historian who misses global concepts, a journalist who does not like the pictures of Russia and the Russians provided in Chekhov's texts, and of an artist who is enthusiastic about the art of telling stories and showing the simple cases of everybody (the *Jedermann*) and any time as the most intriguing subject matter in the world.

The conclusion that we do not make history may disappoint the historian; however, Rozanov as a human being seems to know that this is the case. Rozanov felt that his depiction of Chekhov could not be detached from his contemporary situation, from his feelings of competition and the verbal practice of cultural combat. But it seems that he found it easier to confess and communicate this complex attitude toward another human being, his literature and its reception, in a prosaic sketch rather than in a philosophical, historical or critical essay. For this reason, we end our examination of Rozanov's treatment of Chekhov with a sketch from Rozanov's 1915 book *Fleeting Things* (*Mimoletnoe*), the title of which reflects the fluidity of phenomena and visions. It talks about a non-meeting between Suvorin's second wife, Anna Ivanovna Suvorina, and the narrating I with Anton Chekhov, providing an inseparable mix of facts and fiction which is interesting, even beautiful. Its message is that although we do not make history, we sometimes seem to be able to prevent certain things from happening.

> I walked with [*Anton Chekhov's brother*] Aleksandr Pavlovich Chekhov (the 'Grey' in literature), when he told me in response to my persistent question about Chekhov [his brother], that the latter feels 'like this and like that', and that 'he came (to Petersburg) because of "that and that"'. We went down the staircase of the editorial office (he was a contributor to the chronicle of *The New Time*), when we met Anna Ivanovna (the wife of Suvorin), who came upstairs, dressed in sable.
>
> 'Aleksandr Pavlych! Is Anton Pavlych here ?!!!
>
> 'No'.

'Why "not"? I was told that he had arrived on the third.'

'No. It's possible, but I am not aware of it. No, this is probably an error...'

'What are you saying? What does it mean? Aleksandr Sergeevich (Suvorin) is looking for him and is expecting him...'

We said our Goodbyes and she left. She liked Chekhov as much as Suvorin himself liked him.

Both [she and Suvorin] were merry, simple, clear.

I said nothing to Aleksandr Pavlovich. What could I say? How? He lied – but already with a derivative lie which was based on that of his brother: what could he 'say', as his brother clearly said to him: 'Don't tell it'. And 'don't tell it', because Suvorin would have embraced him and taken him to his house, and what could he have said to his friends of the Gol'cev- and Korolenko-type, who whispered to him all the words, which 'posthumous', now, Merezhkovskii permitted himself about Suvorin ...[127]

Notes

1. Avletina Kuzicheva, '"Breaking the Rules": Chekhov and his Contemporaries', J. Douglas Clayton (ed.), *Chekhov Then and Now: The Reception of Chekhov in World Literature* (New York: Lang 1997) pp. 269–99.
2. Vasilii Rozanov, '*Iz pripominanii i myslei ob A. S. Suvorine*'", *Priznaki vremeni* (Moscow: Respublika 2006) p. 263.
3. Vasilii Rozanov, *Poslednie list'ia 1916 god* (Moscow: Izdatel'stvo Respublika 2000) 53.
4. Rozanov, *Poslednie list'ia*, p. 53. Nevertheless, Rozanov was famous because of his open and often provocative attitude *in eroticis*. Cf.: '"*Raspoiasannye pis'ma*" V. Rozanova', (*predislovie M. Pavlovoi*), *Literaturnoe obozrenie*, no. 11 (1991): pp. 67–71.
5. Vasilii Rozanov, *Mysli o literature* (Moscow: Sovremennik 1989) 508. Cf. Anton Chekhov, *Polnoe sobranie sochinenii i pisem v tridtsati tomakh. Pis'ma v dvenadtsati tomakh* (Moscow: Nauka 1980) 8: p. 621.
6. Chekhov, *Polnoe sobranie* (Moscow: Nauka 1980) 8: pp. 140–1.
7. Ibid.
8. Chekhov, *Polnoe sobranie* (Moscow: Nauka 1978) 6: p. 360.
9. Chekhov, *Polnoe sobranie* (Moscow: Nauka 1981) 10: pp. 141–2.
10. Vasilii Rozanov, '*25-letie konchiny Nekrasova*', *Novoe Vremia*, No. 9630, 24 December 1902.
11. Chekhov, *Polnoe sobranie* (Moscow: Nauka 1982) 11: p. 108. Already in a note of the late 1880s or the early 1890s Chekhov praised a teacher of the provincial town Elets, which as the merchant Michail Konstantinovich Sidorov (1823–87) belongs to people, who 'see and know more than we'. (Chekhov, Polnoe sobranie (Moscow: Nauka 1980) 17:195). Probably he had in mind Rozanov (A.A. Medvedev, Chekhov, *Rozanovskaia enciklopediia*. (Moskow: ROSSPEN 2008) 1149).
12. Vasilii Rozanov, *Literaturnye ocherki* (St Petersburg: Merkushev 1899).
13. Rozanov, *Mysli o literature*, p. 573. Rozanov's italics.

14 D. Rayfield, O.E. Makarova (ed.), *Dnevnik Alkesandra Sergeevicha Suvorina*. (Moskow: Nezavisimaia Gazeta, London: The Garnett Press 1999).
15 I.L. Shcheglov, 'Chekhov – *"suvorinskogo soderzhanka"* ', *Literaturnoe nasledstvo*. Vol. 68 (Moscow: Nauka 1960) p. 484. Cf.: 'All [...] from his money to his fame [...] he [Chekhov] owed the old man [Suvorin]'. *Pis'ma A. P. Chekhovu ego brata Al. Chekhova* (Moscow: Socekgiz, 1939) p. 273.
16 Rozanov's view of Chekhov is less obvious than his opinions on Dostoevskii, Gogol' or Pushkin. Nikoliukin, the editor of Rozanov's Russian collected writings did not include Chekhov in the list of 40 writers and philosophers in his Rozanov biography deals (Aleksandr Nikoliukin, *Golgofa Vasiliia Rozanova* (Moscow: *Russkii put'* 1998) p. 502.
17 Cf. the eyewitness Dakmat A. Lutochin (1885–1942): 'He [Rozanov] was loved and understood [in the editorial office of *Novoe Vremia*] only by the old man Suvorin, who wormed Rozanov [...] as he gave shelter to Chekhov at his time.' D. A. Lutochin, '*Vospominaniia o Rozanove*', *Vestnik literatury*, 4–5 (1921), p. 5.
18 Vasilii Rozanov, '*Pis'ma A. P. Chekhova*', Rozanov, *V chadu voiny* (Moscow: Respublika 2008) p. 207.
19 Cf. E. A. Dinershtein, *A. S. Suvorin: Chelovek, sdelavshii kar'eru* (Moscow: ROSSPEN 1998). L. Azarina, *Chekhov v kritike Suvorina*. *Molodye issledovateli Chekhova*, Vol. 5, Moscow 2005, pp. 25–34.
20 Chekhov, *Polnoe sobranie*, 1: pp. 201–02.
21 See on the relations beween Rozanov and Suvorin: N. Iu. Kazakova, *Filosofiia igry. V.V. Rozanov – zhurnalist i literaturnyi kritik* (Moscow: Nauka 2001), pp. 8–61.
22 Cf. Vasilii Rozanov, *Pis'ma A. S. Suvorina k V. V. Rozanovu. S potretom umiraiushchego A. S. Suvorina, St Petersburg (A. S. Suvorin – Novoe Vremia)* 1913. See on Suvorin's view of Chekhov: *L. Azarina, Chekhov v kritike Suvorina*. In: *Molodye issledovateli Chekhova* (Moscow MGU) Vol. 5, 2005, pp. 25–34.
23 Vasilii Rozanov, *Iz pripominanii i myslei ob A. S. Suvorine* (Moscow: Patriot 1992), p. 14.
24 In an article of 1910, Rozanov himself expresses his envy of the beautiful covers of the volumes of Turgenev and Chekhov: "They should be around my works', I thought with the idea of an egoist.' V. V. Rozanov, 'Vecherkom', *Zagadki russkoi provokacii* (Moscow: Respublika 2005) pp. 449–55, at p. 450.
25 The coffin with Chekhov's corpse was brought from Badenweiler via St Petersburg to Moscow, where he was buried.
26 Vasilii Rozanov, *Iz pripominanii i myslei ob A. S. Suvorine* (Moscow: Patriot 1992) p. 14.
27 Rozanov, *Mysli o literature*, p. 505.
28 Ibid., p. 572.
29 It is remarkable that in his voluminous books *Religion and Culture* (*Religiia i kul'tura*, 1902), *Nature and History* (*Priroda i istoriia*, 1903) and *The Family Question in Russia* (*Semeinyi vopros v Rossii* (1903), Rozanov did not mention Chekhov at all, though in the plays and stories of the latter there is much material referring to the matter at hand.
30 Vasilii Rozanov, *Apokalipsis nashego vremeni* (*Sergiev Possad: Elov* 1917–18), Nos. 1–10.
31 Vasilii Rozanov, *Chernyi ogon'* (Paris: YMCY Press 1991). Rozanov specified this book as part of his projected collected writings, but did not complete it before his death.
32 The same complaints over the insignificance of his own contemporaries can be observed in Rozanov's obituary on Chekhov.
33 An article which Rozanov possibly published in the Journal *Blagovest'*. *Obshchestvennaia, literaturnaia i tserkovno-narodnaia gazeta* (Lubna 1909 or 1910) under the title 'Until Chekhov and After Chekhov' (*Do Chekhova i posle Chekhova*) cannot be traced.
34 Heinrich Stammler, '*Wesensmerkmale und Stil des proteischen Menschen*',Vasilii Rozanov, *Izbrannoe* (Munic: Neimanis 1970), pp. I–XXXVII.

35 Rainer Grübel, '*Melancholische Paraphrenie. Im Spannungsfeld psychopoetischer Identität und Alterität*', Grübel, *An den Grenzen der Moderne: Vasilij Rozanovs Denken und Schreiben* (Munich: Wilhelm Fink 2003), pp. 113–220.
36 Vasilii Rozanov, *Poslednie list'ia 1916 god* (Moscow: Respublika 2000), p. 168.
37 Vasilii Rozanov, '*Literaturnye novinki*', *Novoe Vremia*, no. 10161, 16 June 1904. Suvorin himself in his letter of 3 July 1904 draws Rozanov's attention to this anthology. See Rozanov, *Priznaki vremeni*, p. 317.
38 *Sbornik tovarishchestva 'Znanie' na 1903 God*, Vol. 2 (St Petersburg 1904). The play appeared almost simultaneously as a monograph in the Marks editing house: Anton Chekhov, *Vishnevyi sad. Komediia v chetyrekh deistviiakh* (St Petersburg: Marks 1904).
39 Rozanov, '*Literaturnye novinki*', op. cit. p. 166. Cf. on Rozanov's concepts of the theatre: Pavel Rudnev, *Teatral'nye vzgliady Vasiliia Rozanova* (Moscow: Agraf 2003).
40 Rozanov, '*Literaturnye novinki*', op. cit. p. 166.
41 Rozanov, '*Den'gi dlia deneg?*' in '*Literaturnye novinki*', op. cit. p. 166.
42 Rozanov's tendency to read literary texts as allegoric pictures of Russian history of Russia can be observed in his commentary to the Grand Inquisitor in Dostoevskii's *The Brothers Karamazov*. See Vasilii Rozanov, *Legenda o Velikom inkvizitore: Dve stat'i o Gogole* (St Petersburg: Nikolaev 1894). Rozanov's misunderstanding of *The Cherry Orchard* can be seen in the fact that he does not read the play as a comedy.
43 Trofimov complains about the idleness of others but does not do anything himself.
44 Rozanov, '*Literaturnye novinki*', op. cit. p. 167.
45 In an article of 1909 on the status of labour in Russia, Rozanov takes Trofimov as an example of Russian laziness and notes that in this play all the characters are 'lazy, old, wretched and necessary to nobody'. See V. V. Rozanov, '*Voprosy russkogo truda (Opyt otveta preosviashchennomu Nikonu)*', in *Staraia i molodaia Rossiia* (Moscow: Respublika 2004), pp. 100–08, at p. 102.
46 Anton Chekhov, *Polnoe sobranie sochinenii i pisem v 30 tomakh*. Sochineniia v 12 tomach (Moscow: Nauka 1978), 12–13: p. 223. There are reasons to suppose that Chekhov's own opinion was much nearer to that of the young Ania Ranevskaia who is gradually emancipated from the bondage of tradition and property, and promises to do what Trofimov preaches. See Herta Schmid, *Strukturalistische Dramentheorie. Semantische Analysen von Čechows 'Ivanov' und 'Kirschgarten'* (Kronberg: Scriptor 1973), pp. 381–2.
47 Rozanov, '*Literaturnye novinki*', op. cit. p. 167.
48 Ibid., p. 168.
49 Michail Gershenzon (ed.), *Vekhi* (Moscow: Kriticheskoe obozrenie 1907). This book was a deconstruction of the illusions of Russia's revolutionary intellectuals. Rozanov's articles of his 'liberal' period in 1905–06 were published in his book *When Authority Went Away... (Kogda nacha'lstvo ushlo*, 1905–06).
50 Chekhov, *Polnoe sobranie ... Pis'ma* (Moscow: Nauka 1976) 3: p. 271.
51 Vasilii Rozanov, '*Pisatel'-khudozhnik i partiia*', *Novoe Vremia*, no. 10196, 21 July 1904. Suvorin suggested in his letter to Rozanov of 15 July 1904 to change the title into the stricter version 'Writer and Party' or 'Writers and Parties' (he even admitted to changing the title. See Rozanov, *Priznaki vremeni*, p. 319). Rozanov seems to have resisted the temptation, as the article appeared under the title 'The writer as artist and the party'.
52 This genre was at that time much less developed in Russian than in English, French and German literature, and Rozanov belonged to the few authors who wrote in this style. On Rozanov's aesthetic concepts see Sergei Nosov, *V. V. Rozanov: Estetika svobody* (St Petersburg: Logos 1993).
53 Vasilii Rozanov, '*Pisatel'-khudozhnik i partiia*', Rozanov, *O pisatel'stve i pisateliach*, (Moscow: Respublika 1995) p. 176.

54 Ibid.
55 Ibid.
56 Ibid.
57 Rozanov's article was also an implicit defence against attacks by Mikhailovskii ('*O g. Rozanove i o tom, pochemu on otkazyvaetsia ot nasledstviia*', *Literaturnye vospominaniia i sovremennaia smuta* (St Petersburg 1905), pp. 278–417; N. Mikhailovskii, '*O g. Rozanove, ego velikich otkrytiiach, ego nachal'nosti i filosofskoi pornografii*', In: *Russkoe bogatstvo*, no. 2, (1902) pp. 76–99).
58 Rozanov, '*Pisatel'-chudozhnik i partiia*'', op. cit. p. 178.
59 Ibid.
60 In the background we presume here a certain parallel of the rivalry between Gol′tsev and Suvorin to the competition of Chekhov and Rozanov, as Chekhov preferred to publish in the editing house of Gol′tsev, ever since Suvorin's anti-Semitic engagement in the case Alfred Dreyfus.
61 N. [Vladimir I.] Lenin, '*Partiinaia organizatsiia i partiinaia literatura*', *Novaia Zhizn′*, no. 12, 13 November 1905.
62 The stoicism of Chekhov has also been noticed by Michail Zoshchenko. See '*O komicheskom v proivedeniiach Chekhova*', *Voprosy literatury*, 1976, no. 2: pp. 150–5. Nivat also writes on Chekhov's stoicism. (Zhorzh Niva, *Vozvrashchenie v Evropu*. 2001; published on the Internet at *http://nivat.free.fr/livres/retour/04c.htm#bgn*, last accessed 12 February 2008). On the contrary, in 1925 A.L. Volynskii pointed out Chekhov's general rejection of any philosophy (cf. Elena Tolstaia, *Poètika razdrazheniia: Chekhov v kontse 1880-kh – nachale 1890-kh godov* (Moscow: RGGU 1994), p. 362). Cf. also the recent study: A. S. Sobennikov, '*Chekhov i stoiki*', *Filosofiia Chekhova. Materialy mezhdunarodnoi nauchnoi konferentsii*, Irkutsk 2006. (Irkutsk: *Irkutskii gosudarstvennyi universitet* 2008), pp. 167–179.
63 Cf. Sergei Baluchatyi, *Problemy dramaturgicheskogo analiza* (Leningrad: Aademia 1927), p. 105; Petr Bicilli, *Tvorchestvo Chekhova. Opyt stilisticheskogo analiza* (Sofia 1942), footnot 175. Cf. Also: S. G. Bocharov, '*Chekhov i filosofiia*', *Vestnik istorii, filosofii, iskusstva* (2005), pp. 146–59.
64 *Razmyshleniia Marka Avreliia Antonina o tom, chto vazhno dlia samogo sebia*. Trans. by K. Urusov (Tula 1882). Chekhov's copy of the book with his annotations is kept in the Chekhov Museum in Yalta. Online at *www.yalta.chekhov.com.ua/start_r.php4?&menu=8*, last accessed 11 February 2009. See also: A. S. Sobennikov, '*Razmyshleniia Marka Avreliia v chudozhestvennom soznanii A.P. Chekhova*', *Wschod-Zachod. Dialog języków i kultur.* (Słupsk: Akademia pomorska 2007), pp. 83–9.
65 Alla Chanilo (ed.), *Lichnaia biblioteka A. P. Chekhova v Ialte. S prilozheniem, sostavlennom P. Urbanom*. (Frankfurt-am-Main [a.o.]: Lang 1993. Cf. the German edition: Marcus Aurelius Antoninus, Anton Chekhov and Peter Urban, *Wie soll man leben?: Anton Chekhov liest Marc Aurel*. Ed. and trans. from the Russian by Peter Urban (Zürich: Diogenes 1979). This book is also the most intense study of Chekhov's stoicism.
66 With regard to Rozanov's observation of Chekhov's stoicism, it is relevant to mention that he did not note this in his review of the *The Cherry Orchard*, though Ania Ranevskaia's remark 'Now I am calm. I am calm. I am so happy!' can be seen as a reflex of stoicism in Chekhov's comedy.
67 Vasilii Rozanov, *O ponimanii. Opyt issledovaniia prirody, granits i vnutrennego stroeniia nauki kak tsel′nogo znaniia* (Moscow: Lissner i Roman 1886).

68 On 11 April 1889 Chekhov signed a letter to his brother Aleksandr as 'Antonius XIII' (referring to Marcus Aurelius Antonius) and discussed Marcus Aurelius in a letter to Suvorin. See Chekhov, *Polnoe sobranie... Pis'ma* (Moscow: Nauka 1976) 3: pp. 188–9).
69 Marcus Aurelius Antoninus, Anton Chekhov and Peter Urban, *Wie soll man leben?*, p. 28.
70 Anton Chekhov, *Skuchnaia istoriia. Polonoe sobranie... Sochineniia*, (Moscow: Nauka 1977) 7: p. 288.
71 Ibid., p. 122.
72 Marcus Aurelius Antoninus (versio Schulziana) III, 3 : '*Hippocrates postquam multos morbos sustulit, ipse morbo correptus obiit*'.
73 Anton Chekhov, *Palata No 6., Polonoe sobranie... Sochineniia*, (Moscow: Nauka 1977) 8: p. 109.
74 Liza Knapp, 'Feat and Pity in Ward Six', Jackson (ed.), *Chekhov's text*. Illinois: North Western University Press 1993, pp. 145–56.
75 Martin Freise, *Die Prosa Anton Čechovs: Eine Untersuchung in Ausgang aus Einzelanalysen* (Amsterdam: Rodopi 1997) p. 287.
76 Paul Debreczeny, ' "The Black Monk". Chekhov's Version of Symbolism', Jackson (ed.), *Chekhov's Text*. Illinois: North Western University Press 1993, pp. 179–88.
77 R.-D. Kluge, *Zagadka 'Chernogo monacha'*, Sobennikov (ed.), *Filosofija Chekhova...* 99–106. B. T. Udodov, '*Dialogizm avtorskoj pozicii v povesti A. P. Chekhova, "Chernyi monach"*', *Izvestiia VGU* 2004, 2: pp. 34–5.
78 Aleksandr Skaftymov, '*O povestiach Chekhova "Palata No. 6" i 'Moia zhizn'*', Skaftymov, *Nravstvennye iskaniia russkich pisatelei*. Moscow 1972, pp. 381–6.
79 Svetlana Valiulis, *Lev Tolstoi i Artur Šopengauėr* (Vil'nius 2000). As Schopenhauer was one of the main interests of his philosophical rival Vladimir Solov'ev, Rozanov denied any interest in this German philosopher. He claimed to have read only one page of Schopenhauer's principal work *The World as Will and Representation*. (Vasilii Rozanov, *O sebe i o zhizni svoei* (Moscow: *Moskovskii rabochii* 1990) p. 125).
80 Vasilii Rozanov, *Sacharna*. (Moscow: *Respublika* 1998), p. 243.
81 Vasilii Rozanov, 'A. P. Chekhov', *Russkoe Slovo* 1910, no. 48, 31 March 1904. This article was also included in the anthology *Iubileinyi chechovskii sbornik* (Moscow: Zaria 1910), pp. 115–32, which should not be confused with *Chekhovskii iubileinyi sbornik* (Moscow: Tovarishchestvo I. D. Sytina, 1910), in which appeared the second article of Rozanov on Chekhov. Rozanov's contract with *The New Times* officially prohibited from publishing in other organs. However, this did not stop him from writing for other periodicals under various pseudonyms, such as 'Varvarin', taken from the name of his second wife Varvara Rudneva. Suvorin knew about Rozanov's work for rival papers, but appears to have tolerated them under the condition that Rozanov signed them with adopted names.
82 Vasilii Rozanov, '*Nash Antosha Chekhonte*', *Chekhovskii iubileinyi sbornik*, pp. 179–86.
83 An auto-stereotype is a widespread, standardized opinion which an ethic group forms of itself.
84 Vasilii Rozanov, '*Nash Antosha Chekhonte*', *Legenda o Velikom inkvizitore F. M. Dostoevskogo. Literaturnye ocherki. O pissatel'stve i pisateliakh*, (Moscow: *Respublika* 1996), 510–53, at p. 551.
85 *The Everyman* (*Jedermann*, 1911) is not only the main hero of Hugo von Hofmannsthal's play, but also a typified character of a late fifteenth century English morality play. In the case of Chekhov and Rozanov, it is an average type, built up in contrast to the heroism of the 18th and 19th centuries.

86 Rozanov, '*Nash Antosha Chekhonte*', op. cit. p. 551.
87 Though Rozanov vacillated between these two poles, he generally associated himself more with the Slavophiles. Some Russian Nationalists see him as somewhat of a predecessor.
88 An important component of Rozanov's orientalism is his myth of Egypt (see his book *Vozrozhdaiushchiisia Egipet*. It is significant that Chekhov is not even mentioned in this book. On Rozanov and Egypt, see Rainer Grübel, '*Kopfreise zum Nil und Leibsprache der Münzen. Archaisches Ägypten und Kollektion des Berührbaren*', Grübel, *An den Grenzen der Moderne*, pp. 559–96.
89 Victor Brombert, *Gustave Flaubert et le principe d'impassibilité* (Berkeley, Los Angeles 1950). Juliette Frolich, *Flaubert. Voix de masque* (Saint-Denis: Pu Vincennes) 2005).
90 Rozanov, '*Nash Antosha Chekhonte*', op. cit. p. 551.
91 Cf. Rainer Grübel, '*Der Text als Embryo. Ein früher generischer Minimalismus*'. Grübel, *An den Grenzen der Moderne*, 375–402, in particular pp. 377–8, 383, 389.
92 According to N. K. Mikhailovskii Chekhov indifferently 'directs his excellent artistic ability to swallows and suicides, to flies and elephants, to tears and water' [направляет свой превосходный художественный аппарат на ласточку и самоубийцу, на муху и слона, на слезы и на воздух]. See '*Ob otsakh i detiakh i o gospodine Chekhove*', *Literaturno-kriticheskie stat'i* (Moscow: Goslitizdat 1957), 606. On relations between Mikhailovskii and Rozanov, see Kazakova, *Filosofiia igry*, pp. 66–76.
93 Rozanov, '*Nash Antosha Chechonte*', op. cit. p. 552.
94 Ibid, p. 553.
95 Ibid.
96 This is reminiscent of Shestov's famous 'groundlessness' (*bezpochvennost'*); of Russian culture, and Gumil'ev's views of the orientalism of Russian culture. See Lev Šestov, *Apofeoz bezpochvennosti* (St Petersburg 1905) See also Lev Klein, '*Gor'kie mysli "privedlivogo recenzenta" ob uchenii L.N. Gumil'eva*', *Neva* (1992), 4: pp. 228–46.
97 With some irony Rozanov considered his unheroic attitude a trait of the petty bourgeois. Berdiaev called Rozanov an 'genious Philistine' (*genial'nyi obyvatel'*; Nikolai Berdiaev, *Khristos i mir* (Paris: YMCA 1979), p. 332.
98 Two years later, in 1912, Rozanov wrote a special article warning of suicide amongst the young. See Vasilii Rozanov, '*Maksim Gor'kii o samoubiistve*', in *Legenda o Velikom inkvizitore*, pp. 594–6.
99 'Poor writers do not understand their destiny: once a "toothache descends"– and a female reader puts a "likeable Chekhov" away', Rozanov, *Sakharna*, p. 52.
100 Vasilii Rozanov, 'A.P. Chekhov', Rozanov, *O pisatel'stve i pisateliakh*, pp. 473–82, at p. 475.
101 Rozanov, 'A. P. Chekhov', op. cit., p. 474.
102 The parallel of Job and Chekhov can also be traced in Shestov's view on Chekhov (Lev Shestov, '*Tvorchestvo iz nichego (A. P. Chekhov)*', *Voprosy zhizni*. 1905, 3: pp. 101–42).
103 Rozanov, 'A. P. Chekhov', op. cit., p. 475. Rozanov's rhetorical question 'how can one tell the history of a "happy family"?' refers to the first sentence of Tolstoi's *Anna Karenina*.
104 On the aesthetic concept of the compensational function of art in German philosophy, one notes 'Art, especially literature is not a "reflection" but a "compensation" of the social reality of alienation [*Entfremdungsrealität*], namely of lack of meaning [*Sinndefizit*]. Therefore art [literature] always has the form of utopia. But as it is only art and not political praxis, it betrays reality to the present [*verrät sie die Wirklichkeit ans Vorhandene*]'.

Odo Marquard, *Aesthetica and Anaesthetica: Philosophische Überlegungen* (Paderborn: Schöningh 1989) p. 114.

105 Rozanov, 'A.P. Chekhov', op. cit., p. 477. It was not possible to trace this quotation in Chekhov's works, letters or notebooks. It seems to be the model for Maiakovskii's notorious verse 'I love to watch how children die' (*'Liubliu smotret', kak umiraiut deti'*). Vladimir Maiakovskii, 'Neskol'ko slov obo mne samom', *Polnoe sobranie sochinenii v dvenadcati tomakh* (Moscow: Khudozhestvennaia literatura 1939).

106 Rozanov, 'A.P. Chekhov', op. cit., p. 476.

107 Ibid. p. 478. The emphasis is Rozanov's own. In a typical bout of anti-Semitism, Rozanov would have liked to prevent Jewish intellectuals from analyzing Chekhov. He complained about Arkadii Gornfel'd's remarks (on Chekhov's letters. See *O russkikh pisateliakh* (St Petersburg 1912) Gornfel'd, a Jewish pupil of Potebnia, was at that time a member of the redaction of the journal *Russian Wealth (Russkoe Bogatstvo)*, which Rozanov considered a provocation. On the complex question of Rozanov's views of the Jews, see Efim Kurganov, '*Vasilii Rozanov, evrei i russkaia religioznaia filosofiia*', G. Mondri, E. Kurganov (ed.), *Vasilii Rozanov i evrei* (St Petersburg: Akademicheskii proekt 2000), pp. 219–54, and Rainer Grübel, '*Judenfreund, Judenfeind. Strategien imagologischer (Un-)Vereinbarkeit*', Grübel, *An den Grenzen der Moderne*, pp. 511–58.

108 In an article of 1910, Rozanov articulates his fear that the inadequate application of Jesus Christ's quotations to Tolstoi could in a same incorrect manner be soon applied to Chekhov. V. V. Rozanov, '*Rechi v 'Rechi*', *Zagadki russkoi provokacii* (Moscow: *Respublika* 2005), pp. 395–7, at p. 396.

109 Rozanov, 'A. P. Chekhov', op. cit., p. 480. In another place, Rozanov criticizes Chekhov's description of a peasant in love as a 'wild beast'. See V. V. Rozanov, '*Kulachestvo v literature*', *Okolo narodnoi dushi*. (Moscow: *Respublika* 2003), p. 9.

110 Rozanov, 'A. P. Chekhov', op. cit., p. 482.

111 Ibid., 482.

112 Gollerbach met Rozanov in 1915. Erich Gollerbach, *V.V. Rozanov. Zhizn' i tvorchestvo* (St Peterburg: *Poliarnaia zvezda* 1922), 84.

113 On the strong disapproval of Rozanov's gesture, see S. A. Grigor'eva, N.V. Grigor'ev, G. E. Kreidlin, *Slovar' russkich zhestov*. (Moscow, Vienna: *Wiener Slawistischer Almanach* 2001) 127f. It's verbal equivalent is: 'I have had enough!'.

114 Gollerbach, *V.V. Rozanov*, p. 83.

115 Vasilii Rozanov, '*Pis'ma A. P. Chekhova*', Rozanov, *V chadu voiny*, pp. 207–12, at p. 211.

116 *Pis'ma A. P. Chekhova*. Vol. 6 (Moscow: *Knizhnoe izdatel'stvo pisatelei* 1913–16). The critic might have been motivated for this review by Chekhov's positive assessment of Rozanov in his letter from 30 December 1902 to V. S. Miroliubov, which Rozanov could read in the last volume of the reviewed edition.

117 Rozanov, '*Pis'ma A. P. Chekhova*', op. cit., p. 208.

118 Rozanov inserted many letters in his own works with his own comments. In addition to Suvorin's letters, he also published correspondence with Strakhov and Govorucha-Otrok (Vasilii Rozanov, *Literaturnye izgnanniki* (St Petersburg: Suvorin 1913).

119 Rozanov, 'Pis'ma A. P. Chekhova', op. cit., p. 208.

120 Ibid., p. 209. Rozanov does not explain what this restriction means.

121 On Rozanov's 'feminism' see Genrietta Mondri, '*O evreiskich fluidach v tele russkoi literatury. Delo Beilisa*' in *Vasilii Rozanov i evrei*, pp. 219–54. See also Grübel, '*Der Autor als Gegen-Held und Gegen-Bild. Die Metonymie des Schreibens, Vision vom Ende der Kunst*', in *An den Grenzen der Moderne*, pp. 317–52.

122 In 1913 Rozanov published his book *Mortal Things*. See Vasilii Rozanov, *Smertnoe* (St Petersburg: Suvorin 1913). Also see Rainer Grübel, '*Hebelt philosophischer Stupor poetische Finalität aus? Thanatopoetik und (Apo)Kalyptik bei Vasilii Rozanov*', *Thanatopoetik. Der Tod des Dichters. Dichter des Todes. Wiener Slawistischer Almanach*, Vol. 60, (2007), pp. 197–236.
123 Here we see again a correspondence with stoicism. However, Rozanov does not explicitly address the Latin philosopher.
124 Rozanov, '*Pis′ma A. P. Chekhova*', op. cit., p. 212.
125 Ibid.
126 On the opposition of aesthesia and anaesthesia, see Wolfgang Welsch, *Ästhetisches Denken* (Stuttgart: Reclam 1990), pp. 9–40.
127 V. V. Rozanov, *Mimoletnoe* (Moscow: *Respublika* 1994), pp. 134–5. Rozanov insinuates that Viktor Gol′tscev and Vladimir Korolenko forced their political opinion onto Chekhov. In his quarrel with Suvorin, triggered by the anti-Semitism of the latter (a quarrel which also involved differences in the retrospective view on economical relations: Merezhkovskii seems to have asked Suvorin, to lend him a sum of money), Merezhkovskii quoted Suvorin, who should have said about himself 'May I be even a scoundrel' (*Pust' ia i podlets*; Dmitrii Merezhkovskii '*Suvorin i Chekhov*', *Russkoe slovo*, 22 January 1914). Later on, in a new version of this article (D. Merezhkovskii, *Bylo i budet. Dnevnik 1910–14*, Petrograd: *Tovarishchestvo pechatnogo i izdatel′kogo dela 'Trud'* 1910) the symbolist changed the word 'scoundrel' (*podlets*) into 'bad' (*plokh*), a strange (to say the least) formation. Rozanov refers to this quarrel in *Mimoletnoe*, p. 486. Cf. also Rozanov's open letter '*A. S. Suvorin i D.S. Merezhkovskii*', published 25 January 1914 in *Novoe vremia* (Rozanov, *Velikii inkvizitor*, p. 600).

4

'TREE OF LIFE' AND 'DEAD WATERS': WHY WAS ROZANOV AFRAID OF CHEKHOV?

Michal Oklot

Unanswered Letter

'Of Anton Chekhov [*Vasilii Rozanov*] once said: 'Chekhov?—nothing particular in him. He looked at life, and what he saw he wrote down. A very fine writer, people got to like him, and began to like him. But he is a cold one, and there's nothing particular in him. I understand his success but don't enjoy it.'[1] On another occasion, in 1897, Rozanov dryly remarked: 'I do not like Merezhkovskii, Chekhov…Nietzsche.'[2] In 1914 in the article 'Anton Chekhov', Rozanov does not simply dismiss Chekhov; instead, he is rather disturbed by the phenomenon of this 'genius of mediocrity',' as he calls him. We can even see in the author of *The Dark Countenance* some traces of sympathy toward Chekhov, as the author of 'Peasant Women' (*Baby*)—the story that Rozanov interpreted in the spirit of his own polemics with Christianity[3] and reflections on Russian women and family: 'Peasant Women' should be included in its entirety in 'The History of the Russian Family', in 'The History of Russian Life' [*byt*], in 'The History of the Russian Woman', postulates Rozanov.[4] Finally, in his literary 'embryos' from 1916 known under the working title *The Last Leaves* (one of the unrealized sequels to *Solitaria*), Rozanov lists Chekhov together with two other 'significant' writers whom he greatly admired, Konstantin Leont'ev and Lev Tolstoy, under the rubric of unrealized friendships:

> I have lived all my life with utterly useless people. And when I was interested in [someone] — from the distance.
> (on the copy of Chekhov's letter)

> I lived in monastery yards. I was listening to bells ringing. No, not that I was especially interested in that, but they were ringing anyway.

I was picking my nose.

And I was staring at the distance.

What has happened with the friendship with Chekhov? He was clearly (in a letter) inviting me, summoning me. I have not answered his very nice letter. An act of swinery.

Why?

Fate.

I felt that he was significant. And I did not like to get close with the significant ones.

...at that time [1899] I had read only his 'The Duel', which made a repulsive impression on me; an inspired braggart ('*Von-Koren*', the most tasteless reasoner, one can get suffocated by him, and an intellectual show-off. Then that peasant woman (*Baba*) swimming in front of a man passing by on the boat: disgusting. His wonderful things, like 'Peasant Women' [*Baby*], 'The Little Soul' [*Dushechka*]—I did not read [at that time] and did not anticipate'[5] (trans. M.O.).

As we read in the parentheses, Rozanov was jotting down this 'half-thought' while contemplating the only remaining letter (and probably the last one) that he received from Chekhov 17 years earlier. Chekhov indeed wrote to Rozanov from Yalta on March 20, 1899 in response to the latter's inquiry about ancient Greek coins. Although Chekhov did not know how to help Rozanov with this matter, the rest of the letter shows his warm feelings toward Rozanov and his writings: 'The writer Gor'kii visits me', he writes, 'and we are often talking about you [...] last time, we were talking about your feature for *New Times* (*Novoe vremia*) regarding sensual (*plotskaia*) love and marriage (a propos Men'shikov's article). This article is excellent.'[6] The quoted passage refers to Rozanov's article 'Meek Demonism' (*Krotkii demonism*; 1897) in which he responded to Mikhail Men'shikov's article 'About Superstitions and the Truth of Life.' Rozanov's reply, later included in his book *Religion and Culture*,[7] is not so much a critique of Men'shikov, as one of the first expositions of his *cosmic* philosophy of fertility.[8] Vladimir Kataev, establishing the similarities between Rozanov and Chekhov, identified the traces of this polemic even in Chekhov's story 'The Man in a Case'.[9] As we see then, the relationship (and separation) between Rozanov and Chekhov have quite strong foundations, which touch one of the major problems of their art and thought—the question of the foundations and forms of life, and a proper perspective for their investigation. But still, Rozanov has never answered Chekhov, who, by the way, was prepared for correspondence, making an entry in his address book: '*Rozanov, Vas. Vas., Peterburgskaia storona. Pavlovskaia 2, kv. 24.*'[10] Actually, Rozanov, in a way, responded to Chekhov's letter on May 8, 1899, sending him his newest book, the collection of essays *Literary fragments* (*Literaturnye ocherki*) (1899), with a dedication on the front page:

> Thank you for your nice and beautiful letter, God willing you will get better. Forgive me that I have not answered: a thousand causes [...] I would like to send your young friend *Religion and Culture*, where my point of view on sex is explained, but not even one copy has come out. May God help him to become successful; well, one needs to get a grip on oneself. This is the greatest mystery of how to live, work, and succeed. Do not forget about me and your promise to submit something to the literary supplement of *The Trade-Industrial Newspaper*[11] (trans. M.O.).

Although it was not a book about which Chekhov asked on behalf of Maxim Gor'kii, for good or bad, the 'young friend' did succeed anyway, but Rozanov and Chekhov never became friends. In fact, with the years they became more and more repulsive to each other. Two years later, for instance, when Chekhov learned, incidentally from Rozanov's article, that his friend the publicist Viktor Miroliubov participated in the meetings of The Religious–Philosophical Society, he urged him to dissociate himself from these circles, even if he had to take the radical step of leaving St Petersburg:

> I read the article in *New Times* by that policeman Rozanov, which incidentally told me of your new activities. My dear fellow, I wish you knew how upset I was! It seems to me you ought to leave St Petersburg right now—for Nervi or Yalta, it doesn't matter—but leave. What have you, a fine, upstanding man, in common with this Rozanov, or with this egregiously crafty Sergius, or, finally, with super self-satisfied Merezhkovskii? [...] One should believe in God; if one doesn't have faith, though, its place should not be taken by sound and fury but by seeking and more seeking, seeking alone, face-to-face with one's conscience.[12]

Chekhov's attitude toward Rozanov evolved, then, from that courteous remark to indifference and to the distaste for Rozanov's religious and mystical searching that was rather typical of Rozanov's ideological opponents. Rozanov devoted to Chekhov much more attention than Chekhov to him, writing on him four occasional articles and several entries in his intimate prose project initiated with *Solitaria* (*Uedinennoe*, 1912). At first glance these remarks, as in the case of Chekhov's reluctance toward him, do not go far beyond standard criticism – pointing out Chekhov's materialism, poetics of helplessness, and ideological nihilism. One interpretative strategy when approaching these writers would be to catalogue and comment on all of Rozanov's remarks on Chekhov. We should, however be cautious with such an approach, especially writing about Rozanov, who, as one of the first in Russian criticism, next to, among others, Akim Volynskii, started a serious campaign against an 'empirical' approach to literature, calling for exploration of 'the metaphysical essence' of the writer.[13] The other strategy, followed, for instance, by Kataev, would be organizing this peculiar pair through conceptual, poetic, and biographical affinities.[14]

Let's slightly reformulate this comparative exercise, following Rozanov's 'metaphysical' method, and try to answer the question: Why was Rozanov afraid of Chekhov? What was it that repulsed him about Chekhov? Some critics dismissed the seriousness of this problem, like Aleksandr Nikoliukin, who, in the most complete intellectual biography of Rozanov written so far, argued that in general, Chekhov was just not 'Rozanov's writer', not an ideological foe as, for instance, Nikolai Mikhailovskii, but simply an 'otherworldly' writer, with whom he had nothing in common.[15]

Yet the character of Rozanov's *aporetic* remarks on Chekhov leaves the impression that this problem cannot be so easily dismissed, especially taking into consideration the fact that his reservations could have a much stronger foundation then just literary taste. And Chekhov was the ideological foe to whom Rozanov had never refused philosophical depth.[16] As even this scarce correspondence shows, Chekhov's interests are dangerously close to Rozanov's philosophical territory, whose major concepts are formed by Aristotelian 'materialism', and the critique of positivism and Christianity; also what lies at the center of their private anthropologies is the problem with 'life'; they both, in a way, pursue the twentieth-century problem or philosophical question of the forgotten being. But still, let us stay with the problem that Rozanov never did answer Chekhov's letter. That can be our key question for now.

In exploring this question one needs to probe Rozanov's philosophy: 'embracing angels and trade', as he once characterized it, not excluding its eschatological chapter. One of the auxiliary figures that would help to grasp the nature of this reservation or even repulsion could be Rozanov's lifelong wrestling with his Grand Enemy, Nikolai Gogol´, whose pale shadow on Rozanov's literary and philosophical map was precisely Chekhov. Our second figure is Rozanov's mentor and epistolary friend, a physician and a writer, Konstantin Leont´ev.

Chekhov: Pale Shadow of the Platonic Nihilist Gogol´

Looking at Rozanov's literary maps, we see that he was indeed always including Chekhov in Gogolian clusters associated with the literature of 'boredom', 'irritation', and 'satire'. For instance, in the review of *The Cherry Orchard* (1904) published in Alexei Suvorin's *New Time*, Rozanov places Chekhov into two 'Gogolian' clusters in sketching constellations of Russian literature: 'the deep lyricism coming from boredom and inactivity (Lermontov, Gogol´, Turgenev, Chekhov); 'odes' of expectation of some action (old Russian literature); and deep personal works, coming from the private self not necessarily connected with Russian history and society (Tolstoy and Dostoevskii); or, finally the satire, [expressing] irritation (begun with Gogol´ ; and Chekhov is also included in this category).'[17] One month later, in July, in the article commemorating the death of Chekhov, also published in *New Times*, Rozanov discusses him in the context of the more general discussion of the relationship between literature and politics. This time he reluctantly prizes Chekhov as one of the best of the not-so-great Russian and world writers of the turn of the century, placing him right after the 'excellent' Vladimir Korolenko. He observes, yet without any special enthusiasm, that Chekhov is still better than Gabriel D'Annunzio or Henryk Sienkiewicz[18] (what a combination!). In this 'timelessness' and 'wilderness' of the entire epoch and civilization, Rozanov argues, Chekhov stood out not so much as a gigantic figure, a role for which he was tactlessly nominated after his death, but as a noble, thoughtful, and talented person. His talent had been always of the second rate, not of the rank of Gogol´, Tolstoy, or Dostoevskii. But thanks to the subtlety of his nature and reason, he stood above his crude epoch, concludes Rozanov.[19]

Yet Chekhov's letter remained unanswered. What is more, neither Chekhov, nor Gor´kii ever received from Rozanov his book on his philosophy of sex.

In order to understand the place of Chekhov in Rozanov's conception of literature, we need to begin with his early and only philosophical treatise *On Understanding* (1886), following the recommendations of the author himself, who wrote that '[i]t is impossible to understand anything in Rozanov, without studying (for about ½ year) *On Understanding.*'[20] Part of the chapter 'About the Created, or about Forms of Life' (*O tvorimom ili o formakh zhizni*). Rozanov devotes to literature, which he sees as one of the forms of the manifestation of life (next to science, religion, law, and politics). Following the tradition of Russian post-Hegelian criticism and 'organic' aesthetics, he identifies two major critical constructs which structure the literary work: the literary type and the literary character. Literature of types, he explains, represents life as incomplete, inert, collective, generalized, passive, and immune to change. Literature of characters, on the other hand, represents life as an active force, governed by incident, error, singularity, movement, creativity. Usually, according to this schema, a complete work of literature reflects the tension between type and character, which, in turn, could be interpreted as a tension between matter and spirit.[21] The model of representation creating literary type is a triumph of that which is crude in it—the material; when the character triumphs. It is the victory of the spirit (in the Hegelian sense). Although Russian nineteenth-century prose, with a few noble exceptions (Pushkin, Dostoevskii, Tolstoy), is dominated by the first scenario, writes Rozanov, it does not mean that the character ultimately loses; he loses as a body, but in losing, he leaves behind himself the seeds that would eventually expound, and thereby secure for him, a victory as a growing spirit; even losing the character stirs inertia of the type, which, when affected by it, comes to life pulsating with possibilities.

Rozanov's later view of Russian literature is almost always positioned in relation to one author who had left inerasable imprints in the Russian imagination, but who had not transgressed the crude material rendered in the perfect frames of the literary type—namely, Gogol′. Gogol′, he writes, 'was a genius in painting external literary forms and attached some magical liveliness, almost sculptural to their depiction, so that no one noticed that there is no substance beneath these forms, no soul, nobody putting them on.' Thus, for Rozanov, Gogol′ is the hero of his own art, the 'accursed incognito' who produces endless series of words, leaving the reader with nothing: 'If we closely examine the flow of this speech, we see that it is lifeless. It is a waxen language in which nothing stirs, in which not one word pushes or wants to say more than is said by any of the rest. And no matter where we open the book, no matter which humorous scene we hit upon, we everywhere see this same dead tissue of language in which all the figures being portrayed are wrapped as if in their common shroud.'[22] The Gogolian 'types', taking the same position as the figure of Christ in Rozanov's critique of Christianity, appear to be just phantoms behind which there is nothing but dead matter: 'He [Gogol′] took matter as a *necessity* and in a *utilitarian* perspective; he knew and needed only a prose of the body.'[23] Rozanov then—not departing from the vocabulary and concepts used by Gogol′ 's contemporary critics, like Valerian Maikov or Vissarion Belinskii—translates Gogol′ 's alleged typizations into the pure formalism of a peculiar metaphysical nihilism, or, as he puts it, the dualism of pure type (form) and nothing.

This characteristic of Gogolian language has been rephrased later in *Fleeting* (*Mimoletnoe*), an unpublished continuation of *Fallen Leaves* (*Opavshie list'ia*; 1913, 1915), in which Rozanov makes a remark on Gogol's formalism, which, incidentally, is also a variation on Rozanov's understanding of Chekhov's poetics: 'Indeed, Gogol′ is understood: no content, and genius (exceptional) of form/but exceptional genius of form?. We will 'understand him all up to the bones', Rozanov writes in *Fleeting* (1914), 'if we stop searching for soul, for life in him […] [and] stop at the thought that he is precisely an idiot. There is contentlessness and pride in him. All forms—"unlike in anyone else", may be in association with "form + nothing".'[24]

Although Rozanov would value Gogol's lyricism much higher than Chekhov's prose—and certainly did not consider him as proud, but, on the contrary, a very modest and elegant man—his critique of Chekhov is constructed on the same opposition. As he writes in his review of *The Cherry Orchard*: 'The beautiful frame of nature, in which the author put the picture of Russian life,'[25] '[t]he cherries are blossoming, the people are fading away.'[26] Or in his review of Chekhov's letters: there is just '[t]he beauty of impotency—this is what Chekhov gave us, what he, actually, had been drawing for all his life. The beauty without an arrow, without pain, the beauty of the slow process of dying out... it seems that an ember has been extinguished, or that charred sheets of paper, thrown into the stove, have been extinguished: but you have to blow into them, and suddenly the dead has been revived again, and it is permeated with the flame, red and blue in turn. In such a way, Chekhov is drawing 'dead Russia' everywhere, which is still lightening up under his blowing.'[27] In this atmosphere of helplessness, according to Rozanov's schema, there are no characters in Chekhov, but only unchanging types, like in the harlequinade (and in Gogol'): an enlightened doctor, who is reading 'progressive' authors, an acrobat, or a new man, etc.:

> All the characters [in the play]', writes Chekhov, "are moving in their separate ways, nothing holds itself in its own place, tomorrow it will get worse than today for all of them, and even today it is nasty-nasty [...] [In *The Cherry Orchard*] you do not understand why all those people in the play need love, thoughts, life, customs, money. Nothing remains in man. The only solid foundation—is Lopakhin's pursuit for money: but it is not clear at all why he needs money? Money for money's sake. Even Pliushkin already knew it; and although this new man of the new Russia [Lopakhin] is very energetic and intelligent, he is intelligent and energetic in a stupid way, because in the higher instance, he stays without any goal, any content [...] Lopakhin collects money in the same way that Epidokhov reads 'Buckle'[28] [Thomas Buckle][29] (trans. M. O.).

Certainly, Rozanov does not follow the tone of the critical clichés of his generation, which was finding in Chekhov's characters a subtle psychology.[30] Rozanov found instead a peculiar rhetoric of disemblance rendering the experience of the void of being-in-the-world, which had eventually, in his view, lead Chekhov, like Gogol' , to formal nihilism.[31]

In Rozanov's *aporetic* arguments, there is, however, always a venue that would allow us to move against the current of the main line of the argument; thus again, we encounter the possibility of Chekhov's redemption in the Rozanovian cosmos. Chekhov's 'ultra-formalistic poetics,' as seen by Rozanov, gets very close, strangely enough, to Konstantin Leont´ev, whom, Rozanov, in one place in *Fallen Leaves*, unexpectedly strips of Byzantine theology, letting him appear in excessively splendid Byzantine ornament:

> Yet what is Leont´ev?
> Nothing.
> He was an unusually fine Russian, with a pure, sincere soul, whose tongue knew no cunning; and through this quality he was almost a unicum in Russian literature, which is pretty false, artificial and pretentious. In his person the good Russian God gave the good Russian literature a good writer. And only this.
> And his ideas?
> They cancel one another. And his *opera omnia* are series of volumes 'cancelled' with a blue pencil. It is beautiful reading. But there is nothing in them to ponder over.[32]

And on the next 'fallen leaf,' Rozanov registers: 'There is no counsel nor wisdom in them.'[33]

Maybe then formal beauty can save the work of art after all? Not in Rozanov, for whom there is one essential difference between these two physicians and poetic craftsmen: Leont´ev's ornament, as in the case of that of Epifanii Premudrii, was the way of expressing the unspeakable splendor of God and religion. Chekhov's empty beauty, in Rozanov's interpretation, exposed just an 'empty hole' of human helpless existence. Leont´ev separated his art from the medical profession. Chekhov, in his view, carried the medical perspective and methods of observation into art, and this operation would for Rozanov be hard to forgive.

The Gogolian clusters, which include Chekhov—the 'lyrical', 'boredom and inactivity' and 'satirical'—could be renamed then as 'Platonic-Nihilistic.' And indeed this is the set into which Rozanov included Gogol´, whose artistic perspective, as Rozanov writes, stretched 'from Plato to the Nihilists,' limiting 'his vision' to dead matter and pure form. 'He did not see [anything]—yes. But with his prophesying soul, he saw 'the hell of the earth'...He saw how the 'plants grow' 'underground'... And on the surface of the earth, he did not need to see anything,'[34] concludes Rozanov. In his article 'Our '*Antosha Chekhonte*' (1910), Rozanov—heroically continuing already slightly worn-out critical motifs that concentrate on naturalism—identifies in Chekhov similar imagery: 'everything is creeping over the Earth [*vse steletsia po zemle*] [in Chekhov]. Precisely, 'creeping over', not 'going', but 'creeping over'.'[35] The reversed image of the earth, a series of ornaments consisting of meandering roots, or Chekhovian 'creeping over the earth', recalls the instant awareness of 'being-in-the-world', as the natural being, matter in the famous scene at the garden of Bouville in Sartre's *Nausea*. It was also the direction of Rozanov's reading of Chekhov (in a way, continued later by Lev Shestov), who like Gogol´, felt into irredeemable literature without any possibility of the transgression of crude matter.

Sphere of Observation: Between Brothel and Cemetery

And precisely the question of matter and materialism constitutes probably the major axis of Rozanov's problem with Chekhov; it touches not only his cosmogony, but also, as we will see later in the present text, his personal tragedy. This question dominates the last, and perhaps the most important (especially knowing the value Rozanov attached to the private letter as a literary genre),[36] of Rozanov's four texts devoted to Chekhov, a review of the six-volume edition of Chekhov's letters in which Rozanov openly attacks Chekhov's alleged crude materialism and the religious and metaphysical poverty of his thought; this time, he does not leave any room for counter-thought that could redeem Chekhov, like in the question of his formalism. We need to remember, however, that what is always at stake in Rozanov's unending polemics with Gogol´(and his shadow Chekhov) and Christianity is not so much an argument juxtaposing materialism to any metaphysical or spiritual worldview, as the clash between two concepts of matter: passive matter, synonymous for Rozanov with inertia and death, and vital matter understood as potentiality.

What had Rozanov found out about Chekhov from this most reliable, as he claimed, literary source? Not much. Well, actually, nothing—nothing but crude materialism, which confirmed Rozanov's earlier thoughts on Chekhov.

'Who was Chekhov?', he asks, and then answers: 'Chekhov was a doctor by profession and education, i.e., he received this professional–practical education, which is a calling to the 'observation of the sick', and, in particular, to the observation of the sick's body, just body and nothing more – and [also] to selecting and evaluating 'doctorial medicaments' – 'metaphysics, however, does not come to the mind' of the doctor. Biology, the science 'of life,' is a treasury of metaphysics and its eternally flowing spring. And this is why men such as Bishat, Cuvier, Claude Bernard, Pasteur were metaphysicians and philosophers and were religious. But the present applied science that comes from biology – which takes from biology just conclusions in order to apply them in practice—is an irresistibly materialistic science or, more precisely, irresistibly practical profession. And the medical doctors have always been propagators of the crudest and most elementary materialism.'[37] What strikes Rozanov in Chekhov is his 'sensitivity of a medical doctor', or rather, sensitivity of 'a sick medical doctor', the physiological perspective, stripped of metaphysics and theology—the perspective from which one can see just decomposing matter and nothing more. Such crude materialism places Chekhov on the furthest antipode of materialism, a far distance beyond Claude Bernard, Dmitrii Karamazov's synecdoche for the spiritless, dull, positivistic world.

Rozanov had already identified the limited world of the positivists, and, as he would later add, physicians, as dark, passive matter in *On Understanding*. 'Passive matter – the passive and imageless origin', writes Rozanov:

> never becomes the origin of anything, unlike the idea [...] [I]t arrests everything that is active, resisting any force as the origin of action; it inhibits in itself any movement. [...] This is why passive matter is imageless, even though it sometimes is not devoid of form; nevertheless by its nature it is hostile to any form. It is clear, since any form entering passive matter becomes isolated and contaminated by its singular host, and if not supported by the movement of other forms, it dies out turning into nothing[38] (trans. M.O.).

What is interesting is that in Chekhov we find an almost identical description of the matter of the Neo-Platonically and mystically oriented symbolists and decadents. Who does not remember Konstantin Treplev's play, which begins with the image of passive matter—'cold, cold, cold. Empty, empty, empty. Terrible, terrible, terrible'—with negative ethical qualifications (it is the Devil's offspring)? Although, that play is usually considered a parody, Robert Jackson, however, warns us to not be rash in this matter, arguing that it is 'full of Chekhov's art.'[39] We shall go back to Chekhov's more discursive exposition of his materialism, but putting Treplev's decadent mannerisms to the side, this poetico-cosmogonic insertion in *The Seagull* that juxtaposes impotent matter vs potent matter grasps the essence of Rozanov's problem with Chekhov.

As an illustration of this peculiar perspective limiting cognition to empirical methods of investigation of the material world, Rozanov, in a peculiar obituary dedicated to Chekhov, reconstructs and develops the well-known biographical anecdote about Chekhov's visit to Rome, where his first steps led him not to the Colosseum but to a house of ill fame; it is the same as going for a stroll to the cemetery, Rozanov adds, recalling his own stroll with 'a friend', his second wife. What had led Chekhov to that place was not a sudden sexual urge, but the instinct of a 'sick medical doctor', searching for the proper cognitive perspective. This perspective, Rozanaov argues, was in a way similar to that of the 'young and sad' Gogol', who in his '*Nevskii Prospekt*' (1835) confronted a dreamer–idealist with 'that kind of a maiden.' But it is not just a matter of the proper '*sphere of observation*' [*sfera nabliudeniia*; italics—V. V. R.] limited to an isolated experience; it embraces Chekhov's entire field of perception: 'There is death here (the house of ill fame) and there (Rome); here, there is the death of a man, an individual; there is the death of civilization, a phase of culture, history. [...] 'I like to see when a man is dying. Horribly terrifying. But one wants to look inside of it so much' ',[40] Rozanov ends, quoting Chekhov's imaginary cognitive credo.

And what is inside of a man investigated from such a *sphere of observation* is just a 'gaping hole'[41] or the 'formless bundle' [*besformennyi uzel*] to which the narrator of 'On the Road' (*Na puti*), by no means incidentally, compares one of the characters ('the transformation of a live person into a shapeless bundle').[42] Rozanov's fear of the vision emerging from such a *sphere of observation* also explains Rozanov's obsessive reiteration in his other writings—not necessary concerned with Chekhov—of his disgust with Chekhov's story 'Peasants' (*Muzhiki*) (1897), which was being widely discussed at that time. One phrase had been haunting him in particular, '*you are not a breadwinner*' [*ne dobytchik ty*], which was for him another idiom of crude materialistic reduction. '*Ne dobytchik*', writes Rozanov, 'is a stupid, dull phrase, some sort of an anvil standing on the phrase, so not a literary word, so not Turgenevian—which is sucking out— sucking out your soul night after night. At first it scalds you, and then sucks you out.'[43]

Since matter and the question of materialism were also at the center of Chekhov's discursive thoughts, it is possible to engage Chekhov in the dialogue with Rozanov without needing to establish auxiliary esoteric connections. The letter to Alexei Suvorin (one more plane where Rozanov and Chekhov meet) concerning Paul Bourget's book *Disciple* is perhaps the most explicit declaration of Chekhov's materialism. The major flaw in this novel, according to Chekhov, is Bourget's 'pretentious crusade against materialist doctrine'. 'Everything that lies on Earth', Chekhov writes, 'is necessarily materialistic [...] Outside of matter there is no experience or knowledge, and consequently no truth [...] It seems to me that when a corpse is being dissected, even the most inveterate spiritualists must necessarily come up against the question of where the soul is. And if you know how great the similarity is between mental and physical illness and when you know that both one and the other are treated with the same remedies, you can't help but refuse to separate soul from body.'[44]

Rozanov's response to such a materialistic credo, putting his anti-Platonic currents aside, would be most likely consistent with his mentor Nikolai Strakhov's critique of materialism on its own terms. Strakhov writes:

> Materialism... is the lightest form of metaphysics, and empiricism is the lightest form of the theory of cognition; this is the strength of these teachings. Everyone wishes to know, this is how Aristotle begins his *Metaphysics*; in the same way, one can say that everyone wishes to

act, and consequently imagines how he can act. In this way, the crude understanding of cognition and crude conviction about the existence of things become an inescapable need [...] Materialism is a conception that gives us the full freedom to act. Here, the existence of things is, so to speak, in our hands [...] This is the explanation of the great popularity of this teaching for all those who are trying to escape from subordination to that to which they cannot give a full explanation. And they stubbornly hang on to their points of view, being blind to the fact that empiricism leads to true skepticism, to the negation of cognition, even materialism, and finally to absolute indifference, to the negation of any reality[45] (trans. M. O.).

Chekhov's world, in the face of such critique, was bordering precisely this area? of the unreal, like in Gogol´, who was in this sense a realist describing the empirical life and who eventually had to face the horrors revealed by his 'realism' and become a victim of his own art. 'He had not solved the mystery of the Sphinx, and the Sphinx devoured him',[46] Shestov once noted. The Chekhovian subject, extending Rozanov's argument, was gazing into the terrifying abyss of nature, to be finally swallowed by 'being there', and as an artistic account of this operation, we receive some sort of a cold report of the experience of Heideggerian anguish in the face of 'being-in-the-world' and the realization that 'being-in-the-world' is 'being toward death'. What saved Chekhov from the fate of Gogol´ was his original profession – the indifferent perspective of a medical doctor.

Consequently, Rozanov refuses to find any trace of the subjective perspective not only in Chekhov's work, but even in the 'somatic' Chekhov. Chekhov, as a man and a personality, is for Rozanov some sort of a receptacle of the impotent ideas of the Russian middle class and intelligentsia. And this is why, analyzing the portrait of Chekhov, Rozanov sees not a writer but a reader. In all his portraits, writes Rozanov, Chekhov is 'rendered as if he were only listening, not even talking.' And then he continues: 'As a figure, the countenance and posture of Chekhov is the figure of a subtle, unusual man without any private 'corner' in his soul, without any decisive private 'solitary [thing]' [*uedinennogo*]; thus Chekhov's literary image, an image of the average intelligent man, but rounding off toward 'the better', 'the ideal'.'[47] What is interesting for our comparative pursuit, Chekhov's critique of Rozanov was exactly the opposite. In the letter to Suvorin, at one place he notes that Engelhardt 'belongs to the same category as Rozanov, so to speak, as far as timbre of talent is concerned. What these people have is not a definite outlook, but only enormous, immensely diffused self-love, as well as a morbid destination kept concealed deep within some hidden place of the soul, as if under a crushing gravestone grown over with moss.'[48]

These two symmetrically opposed conceptions of the self reflect another core issue in our hypothetical argument between Rozanov and Chekhov, an issue related to the question of materialism – the problem of cognition. Chekhov, a medical doctor and naturalist, unlike Rozanov always tended towards a complete scientific understanding that limits itself to empirical data, while Rozanov persuing understanding in a cosmic, integral sense, over the years became more and more skeptical, even of the very word 'understanding' which is frequently used as a critical label attached to Rozanov's epistemology. In the first bundle of his *Fallen Leaves*, he even explicitly renounces it in a peculiar confession:

> To think, think, think (to philosophize, *On Understanding*)—that I always wanted, that came 'by itself'; but what was happening in the domain of activity or of 'life' generally—was just chaos, torment and damnation.
> […]
> I was surprised. My 'new philosophy', no longer of understanding but of 'life'—had its origin in great surprise …[49]

Sphere of Observation: Camera Obscura

Where is located, then, Rozanov's own *sphere of observation*, or, rather, the *revelation* from which he contemplated Gogolian monsters and Chekhov's 'empty holes'? What is the philosophy of surprise? It is the reflection on 'The world 'as it is' only a particle and moment of the 'potential world', – the proper object of a complete philosophy and a complete science. The study of the transitions from the potential into the real world, the laws of the transitions and the conditions of the transition, generally, of all that emerges in the stage of transition, filled my thought and imagination,' Rozanov writes 'And, in a word, it seemed to me that my philosophy would embrace the angels and trade [*angelov i torgovliu*].'[50]

This all-embracing philosophy of an instant in which potentiality passes into actuality determined not only Rozanov's singular literary genre of half-thoughts, incomplete aphorisms, contradictions, which he initially called 'embryos', but also became the major lens of his literary criticism. Rozanov positioned almost all the authors about whom he wrote against the image of potentiality assembled by him as early as in *On Understanding*. This pole, set in Russian literature by Pushkin, was precisely an antipode of Gogol′ and Chekhov.

In the section devoted to the classification of the 'forms' of 'potential being', Rozanov's implicit commentary on Book Theta of *Metaphysics*, there is an interesting passage introducing such an image, which is later conceptually replicated in various forms in most of his writings; in a way it is also an illustration capturing his understanding of Sections 418b–419c of *De Anima*, where Aristotle writes on the image of potentiality. Rozanov writes:

> [I]n the sense of 'existence,' potential being is as real (empirically at the present moment), as it is real (absolutely) [...] There are many more of these invisible forms of objects and appearances, than those visible, and the later—an insignificant part at a given moment. Their quantitative relationship could be well expressed, comparing the former [invisible forms – the image of potentiality] to invisible particles of dust filling a dark room, and the later to these particles that garishly sparkle in the ray of sunshine penetrating the room, making an image of the luminous pillar; at the same time, the particles, which continuously come from the dark sphere into the sphere of the ray, look as if they were appearing there for the first time, and those which fall out, as if they were perishing forever. Although, we know that there is neither [any movement] of appearing nor perishing [in the room][51] (trans. M.O.).

This descriptive image of potentiality as a peculiar *camera obscura* has its 'verbal' and formal equivalent in Rozanov's letter to Erikh Gollerbakh of 29 August 1918; it is an example of a poetic that is itself the image of potentiality or, to be precise, the ungraspable moment of suspense between potentiality and actuality.

> But the whole of *On Understanding* is saturated with the 'relationship' between the *seed* and the *tree* that grows out of it. And indeed, simply—out of *growth, living growth*. 'Growing' and that's it [...] The Bells, ringing. Easter, 'Eureka, eureka.' The Word—single: POTENCY ('a seed') – REALIZING. A table: one can have dinner—one cannot have dinner. Yes, now, I will drag myself to Heaven (God). Religion, the Kingdom (the system of Russia)—EVERYTHING is here, in the idea of 'potency,' which is growing. But this essence expressed itself more deeply, namely, in Eleusian mysteries, than (I guess, I haven't read) in Schelling. You also remind us—in 'unmasking invisible things,' and perhaps even better: in clothing invisible things. Everything gets CLOTHED in a dress, and history itself is clothing the Divine plans in dresses. In a word, here, in 'one word,' he has 'made a table'—all the prophets are included, the whole Bible.[52]

The key words are placed in quotation marks to indicate the transitiveness of their ontological status. Like the particles of dust in Rozanov's *camera obscura*, these words might or might not pass into actuality to become the names that establish the world. In the quoted passage from *On Understanding*, we can even trace the emergence of a language that attempts to grasp this particular moment: the word 'unveiling' – indicating the negative operation of unveiling the world of appearance or shedding the light of actuality on the darkness of potentiality – transforms into the positive word 'clothing'. In Russian the only difference between these two words in the locative case is their fourth letter: *oblichenii* and *oblechenii*. In Rozanov's dictionary, vesting seems to stand for a peculiar "anti-Christian" [sic!] miracle of all-embracing incarnation, the miracle of the Eleusian mysteries – 'THE SEED and THE TREE', as he writes in *Fleeting*. Thus the proper answer to the location of Rozanov's *sphere of observation* is that dark room penetrated by a thin sunray.

The idea of the world as potential being, as he writes in the aforementioned letter to Gollerbakh, had not left him throughout his entire life, and almost everything he wrote later was one way or another related to his first book. Although he never wrote a continuation of *On Understanding* in the form of a book – which he 'actually' planned to title 'On Potentiality and its Role in the Physical World and the World of Man' ('*O potentsial'nosti i roli ee v mire fizicheskom i chelovecheskom*') – his entire project of *Fallen Leaves*, 'literature without literariness', the program for literature of sheer immediacy or writing as *sui generis generatio*, (which he juxtaposed to the cold formalism of the heretic Gogol′ and of the nihilist–intelligent Chekhov), is a consistent 'realization' of the discourse on potentiality, which in literature opens the problem of creating a text that would 'be' sheer immediacy negating itself before reaching the actuality of the book in its most literal sense; before it is 'clothed' in a cover, print, and layout.

Although the concept of potentiality implicitly organized many of Rozanov's critical remarks, he associated it with a particular writer usually, while explicitly only once, in his short essay on Maeterlinck, an unexpected guest usually overlooked by Rozanov's commentators. What is interesting, Rozanov shared his admiration for the writer of 'The Tragic in Everyday Life' with no one other than Chekhov.

> 'Maeterlinck', he writes, 'has proved, sketched—not in the philosophical way, but in the artistic one – the 'potential world' – the one which is not yet [*etot, chego net eshché*], but will be, that which is already gone – has never been: but he sketched them not as the *future* and the *past* (that everyone knew and could do), but as existing now, *half-touchable, half-visible, immeasurably powerful* [*nesravnenno moguchestvennoe*]—but which does not have a name and visible form [*no chemu net imen i vida*] [...] The innovativeness and discovery and power of Maeterlinck is included in that

fact that he translated the connections of all the 'now' with the past and the future from the ideal construction precisely into the tactile-material (although the foggy-material). There is the zodiacal world: this is – not matter, but, at the same time, not *not* matter'[53] (trans. M. O.).

This singular philosophical 'poem', perhaps unsurpassable in all of Russian twentieth-century literature, summarizing Rozanov's lifetime project of the philosophy of potentiality, gets surprisingly close to Rozanov's view of one aspect of Chekhov's poetics, which he discusses in his article 'Tolstoy and Life' ('*Tolstoy i byt*') published in *Russian Word* (*Russkoe slovo*) (1907). Rozanov, explaining Chekhov's inability to write longer works, like novels, prizes his poetics of the literary etude, 'the great monuments of literary inspiration,' 'the sketch of just one day, one *event*, not *life* or chain of *events*.' 'He [Chekhov] preserves in the story, 'etude', that what he observed, what he liked, what occupied his thoughts. He does not have a 'collection box' in his soul. There is only the material of the passing day.'[54] It sounds almost like a declaration of Rozanov's own philosophy of style, registering and cataloguing passing thoughts and events that have not yet been actualized in the sequence governed by the chronology of the past, the present, and the future: 'The wind blows at midnight and carries away leaves … So also life in fleeting time tears off from our soul exclamations, sighs, half-thoughts, half-feelings …'[55]

Well, after this poetic pause, we need to go back to Rozanov's problem with Chekhov. Although the last remark opens another crack leading to another possible venue for the possible reconciliation of Rozanov and Chekhov, the question of the status of this 'material of a passing day' remains. Judging from his review of Chekhov's letters, it could be easily interpreted as a record from the empirical observation of accessible material facts in their actuality: 'positivism does not possesses the very *possibility*, the promise',[56] he writes in *Fallen Leaves;* the positivist sphere of observation belongs and is located, as we have said, at the cemetery or brothel, never in the Aristotelian *camera obscura*. Thus even this slight affinity does not bridge the gap between these two connoisseurs of the short form.

Juxtaposing his own conception of matter understood as potentiality ('not matter, and not *not* matter'), Rozanov reverses the Gogolian and Chekhovian images, sympathizing, rather, with Doestoevskii's sensibility, and goes back to the scene in which Maria Timofeevna is celebrating the pagan elemental force of Dostoevskii's Christianity. In *Fleeting*, for instance, Rozanov exclaims, paraphrasing words from her conversation with Shatov:

This earth on which we walk – is the second earth. There is the mysterious and primary one, towards which we strive.

This one – once dry, once damp, bears and does not bear. That one eternally bears and is always damp. And they say not about the planet, but about that primary one:

MOTHER-DAMP EARTH

Primordial dampness ... Eternal smell of weeds, fibers, mud, clumps, and bacteria.

This is where man likes to dig above all. Both scientists and children[57] (trans. M. O.).

He explains this passage in the article 'The Topic of Our Time' (*Tema nashego vremeni*), later included in the book *Vo dvore izaychnikov*. Dostoevskii himself, writes Rozanov, often breaks a fairly rational exposition of his thought, presented, for instance in the teachings of the elder Zosima from *The Brothers Karamazov*, into an incoherent, ecstatic exclamation of the holy fool precisely in order to underline the Hellenic pagan roots of Christianity, or more precisely the cult of Demeter whose etymology he traces to the name Ge Meter that means the earth-mother-holy. Such a concept of Christianity, foreign to the asceticism of Gogol´ and the 'positivism' of Chekhov, demands a special understanding of matter and body. And again, he can find at this very moment yet another possibility for the reconciliation of these two 'materialists', Rozanov and Chekhov. It is Rozanov who stretches his hand first in including the story 'The Little Soul' among his favorites, most likely, not just in a tribute to Tolstoy's literary taste.[58] 'The Little Soul,' as read through Rozanov's philosophy of life and matter as potentiality, could be interpreted as a story of sheer receptivity and blind Old Testament faith in the forces of life, or on the contrary, the impotency and passivity of the life force. In either case, it touches the heart of Rozanov's poetics of potentiality.

The mystery of Rozanov's lifetime problem with Gogol´ and his shadow Chekhov, then, does not leave the walls of his dark room constructed in *On Understanding*.

The Antichrist

As we have said, in the discussed review of Chekhov's letters exposing his crudest materialism, Chekhov, a writer, has also been 'materialized' , in a very detailed naturalistic portrait meticulously assembled by Rozanov. Chekhov is standing in front of Rozanov as if he were alive, like the mysterious oriental man in a Persian robe gazing at his creator, an icon painter, who committed a sin of conforming to the aesthetics of the crudest naturalism, of Gogol's story 'The Portrait': 'The portrait of Chekhov, see how he is 'looking at you' through a pince-nez on a little rope.'[59] So, we find ourselves in the field of vision of 'a sick physician—Chekhov', a writer without countenance reduced to just empty, looking eyes situated in the peculiar *sphere of observation*. It is the creation, Rozanov would say, of the materialist epoch; its pale aesthetic claim. Usually, this radical perspective of the spectator, transforming the narrative *I* into the *eye*, and nothing more, is considered in Chekhov as his aesthetic virtue.[60] Unlike in Rozanov, who in this passive eye, capable of telling any story requested by any demand of modern civilization, spotted something terrifying: 'He is looking at you, he is looking ...' (*Gliadit, gliadit ...*).[61]

Chekhov's materialism and naturalistic conception of cognition could be shifted, through Rozanov's correspondence with Leont'ev, into yet another context, the context introducing the eschatological dimension. Thinking about Roznaov's Chekhov, the figure of Leont'ev[62] seems to be inescapable. In one of his letters to Rozanov, Leont'ev addresses the eschatological problems concerning, to use Shestov's words, speculation and revelation, which we can relate to Rozanov's critique of Chekhov's cognitive methods:

> Try to compare the resurrection, the ascension, the birth from the Virgin who has remained a Virgin, etc. with contemporary physiology, cellular anatomy, Darwinism, etc. As you wish, but either one or another part has to be sacrificed. I have sacrificed science, with joy, a long time ago for the sake my personal life [...] I hate with all my soul all technical improvements and selflessly dream that at least in 25 – 50 – 75 years after my death, new findings of social sciences and the necessities of societies themselves will demand if not annihilation, at least the limitation of all these inventions and discoveries. World inventions (telephones, railways, etc.) are 1000 times more harmful than the inventions to assist in combat. The latter killed many separate individuals, the former kills step by step all living, organic life on earth: poetry, religion, isolation of the nations and *existence*.... 'The tree of knowledge' and 'the tree of life.' Accelerating movement just for itself does not necessary imply the strengthening of life. The machine is moving, and the living tree is standing[63] (trans. M. O.).

Although Leont'ev's orthodox solution to the question of science and religion, separating revelation from knowledge, supports Rozanov's conservatism and his resentment toward positivism, embodied, for instance, in Chekhov, Rozanov cannot agree with such a radical separation in the spirit of the early Church Fathers. He comments on this particular letter in *Literary Outcasts* (*Literaturnye izgnanniki*):

> Well, this is what is at stake: the *method* of science is something completely different from 'revelations'... And the *subjects* are different. And here

just one conjecture comes to mind: astronomy, geometry, astrology, and measuring the degree of the meridian were included in the ancient pagan religions and are not included in religion only today, in our era. Our religion—the religion of the gloom of the heart ....[64] (trans. M. O.).

What Rozanov is saying here, as well as in the quoted passage about Chekhov's crude materialism, follows the main argument of the treatise *On Understanding*, concerning the limits and internal construction of science as integral knowledge, as teaching about the cosmos and the human, about the relationship of science with human nature and life. This is how he develops his conception of understanding, combination and speculation, experience and revelation, overcoming the antagonism between science, philosophy, and religion. Neither Leont'ev's separation in the name of preserving Christian aesthetics, ethics, and eschatology, nor Chekhov's separation in the name of the objective and complete knowledge ('two times two') of the only accessible reality, that is, the material world, would satisfy Rozanov's vision of the organically unified cosmos, embracing 'angels and trade'; the vision of matter as damp earth in which both 'children and scientists can play.'

And this theme comes back in the part of the discussed review of Chekhov's letters where Rozanov argues that Chekhov reduced religious matters to the mechanistic memory of matter. Roznaov writes:

> Chekhov had rather ruthless parents of a merchant profession, who dragged 'small Antosha' to the church, to mass, without [inducing in him] any religious reflection. And one surprising, unfortunate thing: just the long standing in the church, i.e., just the memory of tired legs; just [the feeling of] tiredness has been preserved as his only memory of church.
>
> [...]
>
> The huge defect of his letters lies in the fact that they lack the metaphysical, mystical, and religious to such an extent that you see in them some kind of 'gaping hole.' [...] It would be hard for society to understand anything religious in Chekhov; but it appropriated this 'empty hole' very easily, again speaking with solace [to the reader]: 'Well, Chekhov is so subtle, he is thinking about the same thing as I am'[65] (trans. M. O.).

Rozanov, however, getting carried away by his one-sided critique omits the passages from the letters in which Chekhov actually speaks about religion. One of them, written less than two years before Chekhov's death as a response to Sergei Diagilev's remarks about the inseparability of the questions of the religious movement in Russia from the question of the survival of culture, is particularly intriguing and important for Rozanov's critique. Chekhov writes:

> Modern culture ... is the beginning of an effort that will continue for tens of thousands of years to the end that, if only in the distant future, mankind may know the true, real God, i.e. not conjecturing, not seeking for Him in Dostoevsky, but will know Him clearly, know as it knows that two times two is four. Culture today is the beginning of such an effort, but the religious movement about which we talked is a survival, already almost the end of what is dying or dead. This is, however, the long story that cannot be summarized in a letter.[66]

If we read the last sentence, leaving implicit references to The Religio-Philosophical Society aside, in a context contemporary to them, Chekhov's remark about 'the new religious movement', as a 'survival' after 'almost the end of what is dying or dead', seems to be almost an apocalyptic credo, and Chekhov himself appears as the Antichrist from Solovyov's 'A Tale of the Antichrist' (presented by Solovyov just two years before Chekhov's letter). In this context, as well as that of Leont´ev's letter, the words telling that 'in the distant future, mankind may know the true, real God [...] clearly, know as it knows that two times is four' is a message of the Solovyovian and, to a certain extent, the Dostoevskian Antichrist, the embodiment of Hellenic speculation, which announces: let's leave faith and turn to science and, if possible, occupy ourselves with resurrection. As Sergio Quinzi argues in *The Defeat of God* (*La sconfitta di Dio*),[67] the resurrection of the new world—which transforms it into the modern world, and saves us through the progress of history, the development of science and technology, and social revolutions—is just a pseudo-resurrection. Modernity is in a way pseudo-Christ–Antichrist. The mistake of modernity, its evil, is that it does not situate itself in the ethical space, but is just the mimicking of God and his saving power with the help of purely human means, argues Quinzi. As what saves us is technological progress, the faith in technology is the faith of the Antichrist, not because technology cannot save us or is something evil, but because it is precisely the only salvation in which with a little bit of reason one can place hope.[68]

Roznaov – the man who fell from his chair when Vladimir Solovyov was reading his lecture on 'The Antichrist'[69]– could not understand this letter differently. Such a figure of the Antichrist was, however, rather remote from his own, because of one major reason: in Rozanov's critique of Christianity, the very idea of Christ contradicts the idea of incarnation. The remote, abstract Christ, with a dark countenance, negates the possibility of salvation, dividing the universe according to dualist heresies into an evil earth and the unreachable goodness of the divine. Therefore, Rozanov argues, he is 'the Antichrist' himself, contradicting his own idea.[70] Chekhov then, with his alleged positivist *sphere of observation* would be for Rozanov just a fake Antichrist. Who is He then?

Rozanov presents his Apocalyptic vision in two almost identical texts from the period when Chekhov was writing his own in the aforementioned letter to Diagilev: 'About the Apocalyptic Number' (*Ob apokalipsicheskom chisle*) (1899) and 'The Beast Number' (*Zverinoe chislo*) (1903).[71] In these texts Rozanov foresees the coming of the true Antichrist (not Christ himself) who will bring the victory of 'the tree of life', that is, life and creation, over death (and the idea associated with it of the remote Christ). Both of the texts contain an exegesis of the passage on the apocalyptic number, which is, Rozanov writes in 'The Beast Number': 'the Saturday number, and, at the same time, the number of the tree of life, i.e., supplementing its meaning. It should be read not as 666—'six hundred and sixty six,' but as '6' '6' '6'—'six–six–six.' This is a unique human number, since it names 'the sixth day' i.e., the day of 'the creation of man.' The day of *creation*, and, in general, the principle of creativity.'[72] This interpretation supplements and rephrases Rozanov's initial one from his text of three years earlier 'About the Apocalyptic Number': 'Apparently [it] expresses the unification of man with the tree of life, i.e., as it is shown in both Genesis and Revelation, returning man to the tree of life.'[73] In his exegesis Rozanov also underlines the apocalyptic dimension of the word 'explanation' (*ob"iasnenie*), which is juxtaposed to the scientific and speculative 'method', the catchword of positivism: 'Then everything will become explained [*vse ob"iasnitsia*], John says. He knew that 'explanation' [*ob"iasnenie*]. Science and philosophy are searching for it in vein, and actually, they both are just 'telling fortunes' around or aiming at 'the tree of life.''[74] Rozanov's integral unification in revelation, however, differs significantly from Chekhov's apocalyptic 'two times two', which, if judged from Rozanov's perspective, would only advocate the materialist limitation of cognition to the sphere accessible to scientific knowledge, which Rozanov identified as the specific Chekhovian *sphere of observation* located in the brothel or the cemetery.

However, even this eschatological chapter opens the door a crack for the possibility of reconciliation with Chekhov. The apocalyptic unification of scientific, religious, and philosophical planes in the fourth one, which would be creativity and art, could be Chekhov's defense against charges of crude materialism, for in many places in his letters he was rather reluctant to put the ideas of his two professions together. Chekhov's unusual artistic control over the material of the visible and tactile reality could be then, in Rozanov's argument, another possibility of redemption.

But still we stay with the letter, waiting for an answer from the 'policeman Rozanov.'

Epilogue: 'From Tinder to Tinder'

So, why was Rozanov afraid of Chekhov and Gogol´?

The answer came in the tragic years of the Bolshevik Revolution; the years of the personal tragedy of Rozanov and his refutation of his philosophy of life as potentiality and surprise. Let's recall its reformulation from 1913:

> But my new 'philosophy' of life had its origin not in a question, but rather in sight and surprise: how life can be noble and, in dependence on *this alone*, happy; how people may be in need of everything, of 'herring for dinner,' of coal by the 1st of month': and yet live nobly and happily, live with painful, sad, infinitely sad recollections, and yet be happy for this alone that they sin against no one (envy no one) and are not guilty before anyone.[75]

The last word, however, belongs to the Nihilist Gogol´ and to Chekhov, with his alleged materialism and method of naturalistic reduction. Since Rozanov all his life took literature and all his other pursuits deadly seriously, he had to settle all the internal debates with his most important writers before his death. In 1918 the sick and starving Rozanov confessed to Peter Struve that Gogol´ was ultimately 'right': 'All my life', he writes 'I have hated and fought Gogol´: and being 62, I am thinking: you've won, you horrible straw man you.'[76] Although Rozanov never mentioned Chekhov in his late writings, it is hard to resist the feeling that his very last 'text', dictated to his daughter when he was already lying on his death bed, is some sort of an answer to him; it is an affirmation of the materialism of the unreal 'cold, cold, cold' matter, the only 'reality' accessible to man. Rozanov's own conception of the world as potentiality will share the fate of any Cartesianism when confronted with physical pain.

Rozanov then will not ask again 'Who was Chekhov?'[77] He will be concerned only with one question: 'What [sic!] is Rozanov today?' [*Chto takoe segodnia Rozanov?*]. 'A strange matter', he answers:

> ...all these bones, rising one after another under an obtuse angle, indeed they speak about an image of all sorts of dying things [...] All is crooked, nothing is nimble, everything has dried out. There is no brain anymore, obviously, [just] miserable rags of body. Here it is: the body is being covered with some sort of effusion, which could not be compared with anything other than with dead water. It fulfills all the being of man till the last cell. This is, indeed, dead water, not the living one. Mortal with its own deadliness. Convulsions and shivers cannot be subjected to any

sense. Tissues of the body seem to be dipped into cold, terrible water. And there is not any hope of getting warm [...] Tissues of the body, these flinging rags and angles appear in a wholeness, but in some sort of details, repulsive and mixed in the water of infernal coldness.

[...] The condition of the spirit—Ego—nothing. Because there is not any spirit. There is just exhausted matter resembling a rag, thrown on some sort of hooks.

Till tomorrow.

Nothing physiological comes to mind. Although, a strange thing, the body is so exhausted, nor did anything spiritual come to mind. Infernal ordeal—here it is.

In this dead water, in this dissolution of all the tissues of the body in it. These are the dead waters of the Styx, truly I recognize their image[78] (trans. M. O.).

Chekhov's crude materialism has been empirically confirmed. What is more, in a Gogolian way, it turned to be so 'real' that it became inaccessible by any form of sensitivity—neither physiological, nor spiritual. We should know by now why Rozanov had not answered the nice letter that Chekhov was writing under the gaze of Gor´kii looking over his shoulder. However, the letter with the answer has been sent after all, and its addressee was no other than 'the young friend' Gor´kii, to whom Rozanov complained—in almost the same words as those in his peculiar anti-metaphysical testament, 'From Tinder to Tinder' (*Ot luchinki k luchinke*), quoted above—that his body 'has lost its plan' dissolving in the black waters of the Styx.[79] On that day, 20 January, 1919, Rozanov wrote or dictated several letters, to various addressees, including Dmitrii Merezhkovskii. In none of them, however, did he make such a confession; perhaps this letter was indeed addressed to Chekhov, who, by the necessity of the inescapable material laws, had to be represented by Rozanov's epistolary foe, the materialist Gor´kii, 'the young friend' incidentally involved in this un-actualized dialogue initiated in 1899. What is interesting too is that on his death bed Rozanov also accepted the cold, remote idea of Christ (thereby Gogol´ as well). His world felt apart into two incommensurable parts, ironically following Treplev's Gnostic dualist equation.

Post Scriptum: Doctor Sambikin

What happened next, after the Revolution, in the space reduced to the absurd matter of Rozanov's invented Gogol´ and his pale shadow Chekhov, who in his materialist credo expressed in the aforementioned letter to Suvorin postulated inseparability of the soul from body? Well, a certain medical doctor began the search for the soul in the body conforming to the strictest scientific methods:

> Sambikin opened up the fatty envelope of the stomach, and then guided his knife down the intestine, revealing its contents: inside lay an unbroken column of food that had not yet been assimilated, but soon this food came to an end and the intestine was empty. Sambikin went slowly down the section of emptiness and reached the beginning of the excrement, where he came to a stop.
>
> 'You see!' said Sambikin, opening more widely the slit down the empty section between the food and the excrement. 'This emptiness in the intestines sucks all humanity into itself and is the moving force of world history. This is the soul—have a sniff (*Eto dusha – niukhai*)!'[80]

In 1956 an excellent selection of Rozanov's texts, through which he has been rediscovered by Russian emigrants, was published by the NewYork-based, short-lived, but very significant Anton Chekhov Publishing House.

Notes

1 E. F. Gollerbach, 'A Critico-Biographical Study' in V. V. Rozanov, *Solitaria*, trans. S. S. Koteliansky (London: Wishart & Co., 1927), p. 37.
2 Quoted in V. A. Fateev, *S russkoi bezdnoi v dushe. Zhizneopisanie Vasiliia Rozanova* (St Petersburg: Kostroma, 2002), p. 192.
3 See Julie W. de Sherbinin, *Chekhov and Russian Religious Culture: The Poetics of the Marian Paradigm* (Evanston: Northwestern University Press, 1997), pp. 90–1.
4 V. V. Rozanov, *Sobranie sochinenii. O pisatel'stve i pisateliakh* (Moscow: Respublika, 1995), p. 478.
5 V. V. Rozanov, *Sobranie sochinenii. Poslednie list'ia* (Moscow: Respublika, 2000), p. 53.
6 A. P. Chekhov, *Polnoe sobranie sochinenii i pisem*, 30 Vols. (Moscow: Nauka, 1980), Vol. 26, pp. 140–1.
7 See V. V. Rozanov, *Sobranie sochinenii. Religiia i kul'tura* (Moscow: Respublika, 2009), pp. 144–9.
8 Cf. V. Kataev, 'Chekhov i Rozanov,' in *Chekhoviana. Chekhov and 'serebrianyi vek'* (Moscow: Nauka, 1996), p. 70.
9 See Ibid.
10 Chekhov, *Polnoe sobranie sochinenii i pisem*, op. cit., Vol. 17, p. 190.
11 Ibid., Vol. 26, p. 463.
12 *The Selected Letters of Anton Chekhov*, ed., L. Hellman (New York: Farrar, Straus and Giroux, 1984), p. 296.
13 In 1906 in the 'Afterward to the Commentary on 'The Legend of F. M. Dostoevskii's Grand Inquisitor", he noted that '[t]he work of Merezhkovskii [*Gogol' i chert* (Gogol' and the Devil)], which tried to explore the metaphysical essence of Gogol's spiritual life, is one of the most serious origins of an authentic approach to Gogol' in our [Russian] literature. Till that moment, in the works of Kulish, Tikhonravov, Shenrok, we have had

some sort of *Pliushkinism* around Gogol´: collecting rags remaining after the Great Man. 'They were stretching [them] against the light,' as he wrote about Akakii Akakevich's worn-out overcoat, but all could see that 'it was impossible to sew them on—the stuff [was] quite rotten.' Certainly, biography is important: but please, also give something for the soul and about the soul of the great creator of *Mirgorod*, *The Government Inspector*, and *Dead Souls*' (trans. M. O). V. V. Rozanov, *Sobranie sochinenii, Legenda o velikom Inkvizitore* (Moscow: Respublika, 1996), p. 155. This remark was not only an expression of the modernist concern with the condition of literary criticism in general, which urged a break with the nineteenth century museum-type empirical approach, *Pliushkinism* (what a critical term!); it was also another important element of Rozanov's argument about Gogol´.

14 Kataev, '*Chekhov i Rozanov*', op. cit., p. 68–74.
15 See A. N. Nikoliukin, *Rozanov* (Moscow: *Molodaia gvardiia*, 2001), p. 370.
16 In the article 'The Writer-Artist and the Party,' Rozanov underlines the rich philosophical content of Chekhov's works, giving as an example the critique of stoicism in 'Ward No. 6.' See Rozanov, *Sobranie sochinenii. O pisatel'stve i pisateliakh*, op. cit., p. 179.
17 Ibid., p. 167.
18 By the way, to follow the logic of Rozanov's digressive discourse, how accurate is his remark on Henryk Sienkiewicz inserted in Chekov's literary obituary?: 'Recently, I have read Sienkiewicz—also a European name—the letters about Rome, Venice, Paris … Everything – so ordinary! But I am saying that there is no talent: there are simply the eyes of the observer, no brain of the man gifted with imagination. His famous *Quo Vadis* is nothing different than a crude factory-made oleograph, not a work of art. Starting from the twentieth page, it is impossible to read.' Rozanov, *Sobranie sochnenii. O pisatel'stve i pisateliakh*, op. cit., p. 176. So this is the space in which the phenomenon of Chekhov has emerged according to Rozanov. But even in this critique of Sienkiewicz, Rozanov and Chekhov get very close to each other. In the letter to Alexei Suvorin of April 13, 1885, Chekhov, just as Rozanov, refuses Sienkiewicz any talent and characterizes him as a bard of mediocrity: '…I am making my way through Sienkiewicz's *The Polanetskis*. This book is like a Polish cheese pudding flavored with saffron. Add Potapenko to Paul Boerget, sprinkle them with Eau de Cologne from Warsaw, divide in two and you get Sienkiewicz […] A devilish heap of scenes of family happiness and discourses on love have been dragged in, and the hero's wife is so extremely faithful to her husband and understands God and life so thoroughly 'by intuition' that the final result is sickeningly cloying and clumsy, just as though you had gotten a wet, slobbery kiss. Sienkiewicz apparently hasn't read Tolstoy, is not familiar with Nietzsche, discusses hypnotism like a middle-class householder, but still every one on his pages is brightly colored with Rubenses, Borgheses, Corregios, Botticellis—all neatly done to show off his culture to the bourgeois reader and to make faces at materialism. The novel's aim is to lull the bourgeoisie into golden dreams' (*The Selected Letters of Anton Chekhov*, op. cit., p. 188).
19 Rozanov, *Sobranie sochinenii. O pisatel'stve i pisateliakh*, op. cit., pp. 175–6.
20 V. V. Rozanov, *Sobranie sochinenii. Mimoletnoe* (Moscow: Respublika, 1994), p. 117.
21 See V. V. Rozanov, *O ponimanii* (Moscow: Tanais, 1996), p. 455.
22 V. V. Rozanov, 'Pushkin and Gogol´,' in *Essays in Russian Literature. The Conservative View: Leontev, Rozanov, Shestov*, ed. and trans. Spencer E. Roberts (Athens: Ohio University Press, 1968), pp. 362–3.
23 V. V. Rozanov, *Sobranie sochinenii. V temnykh religioznykh luchakh* (Moscow: Respublika, 1994), p. 419.

24 V. V. Rozanov, *Sobranie sochinenii. Mimoletnoe*, op. cit., p. 117–18.
25 Rozanov, *Sobranie sochinenii. O pisatel'stve i pisateliakh*, op. cit., p. 166.
26 Ibid., p. 166.
27 V. V. Rozanov, *Sobranie sochinenii. V chadu voiny (Stat'i i ocherki 1916–18 gg.)* (Moscow: Respublika, 2008), p. 211.
28 The critique of the 'naïve', crude positivism of Thomas Buckle could be one of the possible planes of convergence between Chekhov and Rozanov.
29 Rozanov, *Sobranie sochinenii. O pisatel'stve i pisateliakh*, op. cit., p. 167.
30 See M. O. Gershenzon, *Izbrannoe*, 4 Vols. (Moscow: *Universitetskaia kniga*, 2000), Vol. 4, p. 303.
31 This line of argument is later charmingly developed by Rozanov's disciple and 'worshiper' A. M. Remizov, in whose unusual writings Rozanov's reservation toward Chekhov has been carried forward. In an occasional essay on Chekhov written in the thirties, later included in *Peterburgskii buerak* (whose motto recalls Epiphanii Premudryi and his account of Stephan's invention of the Perm alphabet), Remizov, like Rozanov, sees in Chekhov just an ornament, a nihilistic version of Ephiphanii's 'word weaving.' The only content of Chekhov's prose, Remizov argues, is 'rubbish-rubbish' (*chepukha-chepukha*)—the only refrain beating out the rhythm of life.
'Chekhov looked at the 'rubbishy' (*chepukhnoi*) world not through the fiery eyes of the demon who has been exiled to the earth, not through Gogol' (*Gogolem*), but through the eyes of inquisitive man, and not with sharp, droughty laughter, responded to the weirdness of the Godly creatures. It was rubbish that provoked in him kind-hearted, light laughter' (A. M. Remizov, *Sobranie sochinenii*, 10 Vols. (Moscow: *Russkaia kniga*, 2003), Vol. 10, p. 350). Remizov, as always in his relations with his older friend Rozanov, tries to shake up his seriousness and play with the alleged depth of the problem. Chekhovian 'nothing' would be just transparency through which Chekhov tried to expose his style. To explain the phenomenon of Chekhov after all, Remizov quotes the famous letter of Flaubert to Luisa Colie, in which Flaubert writes about the ideal book—the book in which everything would be transparent—the author, the idea, the plot—except for the style. We need to underline that according to Remizov—whom we connect with Rozanov—the essence of Chekhov's stylistic purity and affinities with Flaubert does not lie in the striving of the former toward greater objectivity in reporting events, as it was implied, for instance, by Leonid Grossman, in the total elimination from the work of art of everything but style—form. From the perspective of Rozanov's normative aesthetic this is sheer nihilism: 'form + nothing.'
32 V. V. Rozanov, *Fallen Leaves. Bundle One*, trans. S. S. Koteliansky (London: The Mandrake Press, 1929), p. 148.
33 Ibid.
34 V.V. Rozanov, *Sobranie sochinenii. Kogda nachal'stvo ushlo...* (Moscow: Respublika, 1997), p. 221.
35 Rozanov. *Sobranie sochinenii. Legenda o Velikom Inkvizitore F. M. Dostoevskogo. Literaturnye ocherki*, op. cit., p. 552.
36 One of the 'half-thoughts' of *Fallen Leaves*, as Rozanov calls his entries, is devoted to this peculiar genre: 'The postmaster who peeped at private letters (in Gogol's *Inspector General*) was a man of good literary taste. Reading sometimes letters for my servants I used to be struck by the colors of simple folks' speech, of the simple folks' soul, of the people's outlook and mode of living. And I thought: 'Indeed, this is literature, the finest literature! Writers' letters are on the whole tedious, colorless. Like misers, they keep the

'bouquets' for print, and their letters are faded, dim, without 'speech.' They ought not to be published. But private people's letters are indeed remarkable. [...] Instead of the 'rubbishy stories,' of the newest fiction in the magazines, which ought to be thrown out, they should publish...Well, let them publish stuff: science, discussions, philosophy. And now and then – still it would be best to publish it in book form – to reproduce a trunkful of old letters. Zvietkov and Gershenzon might fish out a great deal from it. Many readers too, read it with absorbed attention, and so too, would some serious men..." V.V. Rozanov, *Fallen Leaves*, op. cit., p. 64. Rozanov also devoted a separate essay to letters as a literary genre, 'About the Letters of Writers', in which, he noted: 'One day this category [letters] will become the favorite subject of reading. There is less and less interest in the form of literary works [...] With time, literary critique will become united in focusing itself on the investigation of the personality of the author' (Rozanov, *Sobranie sochinenii. O pisatel'stve i pisateliakh*, op. cit., p. 430).
37 Rozanov, *Sobranie sochinenii. V chadu voiny*, op. cit., pp. 209–10.
38 See Rozanov, *O ponimanii*, op. cit., pp. 252–3.
39 Robert Louis Jackson, 'Chekhov's *Seagull*: The Empty Well, the Dry Lake, and the Cold Cave', in *Chekhov: A Collection of Critical Essays*, ed. Robert Louis Jackson (Englewood Cliffs, N.J., 1967), pp. 99–120.
40 Rozanov, *Sobranie sochinenii. O pisatel'stve i pisateliakh*, op. cit., p. 477.
41 Rozanov, *Sobranie sochinenii. V chadu voiny*, op. cit., p. 210.
42 Chekhov, *Polnoe sobranie sochinienii i pisem*, op. cit., Vol. 5, p. 472.
43 Rozanov. *Sobranie sochinenii. O pisatel'stve i pisateliakh*, op. cit., p. 481.
44 *Anton Chekhov's Life and Thought: Selected Letters and Commentary*, ed. Simon Karlinsky (Berkeley: University of California Press, 1975), pp. 143–4.
45 V. V. Rozanov, *Literaturnye izgnanniki: Vospominaniia. Pis'ma* (Moscow: Agraf, 2000), p. 368.
46 L. Shestov, *Umozrenie i otkrovenie* (Paris: YMCA Press, 1964), p. 331.
47 Rozanov, *Sobranie sochnenii. V chadu voiny*, op. cit., p. 209.
48 *Letters of Anton Chekhov*, Ed. Avrahm Yarmolinsky (New York: The Viking Press, 1973), p. 290.
49 Rozanov, *Fallen Leaves*, op. cit., pp. 73–4.
50 Quoted in Rozanov, *Solitaria*, op. cit., p. 9.
51 Rozanov, *O ponimanii*, op. cit., p. 143.
52 E. F. Gollerbakh, *Vstrechi i vpechatleniia* (St Petersburg, 1998), p. 46-7 (For an abridged version of this quote see Rozanov, *Solitaria*, op. cit., 9.)
53 Rozanov, *Sobranie sochinenii. O pisatel'stve i pisateliakh*, op. cit., pp. 241, 242.
54 Ibid., p. 232.
55 Rozanov, *Solitaria*, op. cit., p. 47.
56 Rozanov, *Fallen Leaves*, op. cit., p. 106.
57 V. V. Rozanov, *Sobranie sochinenii. Mimoletnoe*, op. cit., p. 27.
58 L. N. Tolstoy's private list of his favorite works of Chekhov includes Rozanov's favorites, 'Peasant Women' and 'The Little Soul.' See Chekhov, *Polnoe sobranie sochinenii i pisem*, op. cit., Vol. 3, p. 537.
59 Rozanov, *Sobranie sochinenii. V chadu voiny*, op. cit., p. 208.
60 See Stanisław Brzozowski, *Kultura i życie* (Warsaw: PIW, 1973), p. 103–24.
61 N. V. Gogol', 'Portret' in *Polnoe sobranie sochinienii*, 14 Vols. (Leningrad: *Izdatel'stvo Akademii Nauk SSSR*, 1938), Vol. 3, p. 82.
62 And indeed, Leont'ev, who most likely had never read Chekhov, expresses an interest in him precisely because of their two shared professions: 'The say that the contemporary

Chekhov, is a medical doctor. I have not read him at all, but they say that he has talent' (V. V. Rozanov, *Sobranie sochinenii. Literaturnye izgnanniki. N. N. Strakhov. K. N. Leont'ev* (Moscow: Respublika, 2001), p. 371).
63 Ibid., p. 370.
64 Ibid., pp. 370–1.
65 Rozanov, *Sobranie sochinenii. V chadu voiny*, op. cit., p. 210.
66 *Anton Chekhov's Life and Thought: Selected Letters and Commentary*, ed. Simon Karlinsky (Berkeley: University of California Press, 1973), p. 438.
67 Many thanks to Piotr Nowak, who in our own conversation about physicians and antichrists turned my attention to this singular exegete from Pistoia.
68 See Sergio Quinzio, *La sconfitta di Dio* (Adelphi: Milano, 1992).
69 Indeed, in the culmination of Solovev's public reading of his 'A Tale of the Antichrist', the mystical and solemn atmosphere of the lecture was interrupted by the loud crack of Rozanov falling from his chair, either because he was snoozing out of boredom, or, on the contrary, was shocked by the revelation. Rozanov himself was forcing through the first hypothesis in a short note that appeared the next day in *New Times* as an anonymous letter to the editorial section signed 'Allegedly Fallen from the Chair.' In this note, Rozanov explained in detail the fall, for which he blamed the poor state of chairs in the City Hall and the quality of the lecture, which was lacking 'anything fantastic, mystic or simply interesting' (V. V. Rozanov, *Sobranie sochnenii. Vo dvore iazychnikov* (Moscow: Respublika, 1999), p. 99). For an interesting interpretation of Rozanov's 'fall' in this particular moment, see the last chapter of Piotr Nowak's book on Alexandre Kojeve, 'Przyjęcie Antychrysta. Alexandre Kojeve – Władimir Sołowjow' with the digression 'Upadek Wasilija Rozanowa' (Piotr Nowak, *Ontologia sukcesu. Esej przy filozofii Alexandre'a Kojeve'a* (Gdańsk: słowo/obraz terytoria, 2006), pp. 185–228). Also in Fateev, *S russkoi bezdnoi v dushe. Zhizneopisanie Vasiliia Rozanova*, op. cit., pp. 262–3.
70 See V. V. Rozanov, *Sobranie sochinenii. V temnykh religioznykh luchakh* (Moscow: Respublika, 1994), p. 419.
71 The importance of these two texts has been also noted by V. Fateev in his biography of Rozanov. See Feteev, *S russkoi bezdnoi v dushe*, op. cit., pp. 262–3.
72 Rozanov, *Sobranie sochinenii. Vo dvore iazychnikov*, op. cit., p. 240.
73 Ibid., p. 48.
74 Ibid., p. 241.
75 Rozanov, *Fallen Leaves*, op. cit., pp. 73–4.
76 V. V. Rozanov's unpublished letter to P. B. Struve in *Vestnik russkogo khristianskogo dvizheniia*, No. 112/113 (Paris, 1974), p. 142.
77 Rozanov, *Sobranie sochinenii. V chadu voiny*, op. cit., p. 82.
78 Ibid., pp. 548–9.
79 See V. V. Rozanov's letter to M. Gor′kii of 20 January, 1919 in *Vestnik literatury*, No. 8 (Petrograd, 1919), p. 14.
80 A. P. Platonov, *Happy Moscow*, trans. Robert Chandler et al. (London: Harvill Press, 2001), pp. 73–4.

Part Two
DMITRII MEREZHKOVSKII

5

CHEKHOV AND MEREZHKOVSKII: TWO TYPES OF ARTISTIC-PHILOSOPHICAL CONSCIOUSNESS

Aleksandr Chudakov

I

Chekhov took an interest in Merezhkovskii after the latter wrote an extensive article on the writer in the November 1888 issue of *The Northern Herald* (*Severnyi Vestnik*). In his letter to Suvorin of 3 November, Chekhov, providing a detailed analysis of the article (unprecedented in Chekhov's letters), expressed a series of problems he had with the author. The main one was a disagreement on the point that problems of creativity cannot be reduced to the laws of nature:[1]

> Whoever has absorbed the wisdom of the scientific method and who therefore is able to think scientifically experiences many wonderful temptations [...] One wishes to find the physical laws of creativity, to capture the general law and formulae by which an artist, feeling them instinctively, creates musical pieces, landscapes, etc. [...] From this springs the temptation – to write a physiology of the creative act (Boborykin), and in the case of those who are more young and shy – to refer to science and the laws of nature (Merezhkovskii).[2]

There were other charges too – that Merezhkovskii finds 'failures' amongst Chekhov's heroes, and thus follows the well-trodden path: 'It's time to abandon failures, superfluous people and to invent something of one's own'.[3]

However, Chekhov assessed the article on the whole – indeed one of the best in the early *Chekhoviana* – as 'quite a pleasant thing'.[4]

Chekhov also liked the author himself. 'Twice the poet Merezhkovskii visited me', Chekhov wrote to Suvorin on 5 January 1891; 'he is a very clever person'.[5] The expression of such a characteristic is also rare in Chekhov's correspondence. And another remark, almost a year later: 'Merezhkovskii still sits in Muruzi's house and gets mixed up in bombastic quests, and still he is pleasant'.[6] Merezhkovskii's being 'over-bombastic' is noted right from the beginning, but as a whole Chekhov's remarks about Merezhkovskii up until the 1900s are kind. In 1901 Chekhov recommended Merezhkovskii to the honorary academicians.[7]

Eleven letters by Merezhkovskii to Chekhov have been preserved. And we also know that Chekhov visited the Merezhkovskiis' salon in St Petersburg (from a contemporary account).[8]

Their relationship seems to have been at its closest in the years 1891–92.[9] In the spring of 1891 they ran into each other in Italy, where Chekhov was with Suvorin, and spent several days together. It is this time to which famous Chekhov's phrase in his notebooks refers: 'In the evening – a conversation with Merezhkovskii about death'.[10] This topic of conversation suited Merezhkovskii extremely well – already standard in his articles of the late 1880s to the early 1890s (on Montaigne, Marcus Aurelius and Goncharov). There were, however, other conversations too. But what could such different people talk to each other about?

There were points of convergence between them, especially in the 1890s. Chekhov's ideas of literary association are known – both general: such as partnerships of the men of the 1880s (*'artel'' vos'midesiatnikov*), and concrete, concerning everyday existence: such as creating writers' 'climate stations' or setting up 'belletrist lunches'.

Invectives concerning a lack of 'cultural air' in Russia, of an appropriate 'environment', the need for a 'uniting principle' in literary life are some of the most passionate concerns in Merezhkovskii's book *On the Causes of the Decline and on the New Trends in Contemporary Russian Literature* (*O prichinakh upadka i novykh techeniiakh sovremennoi russkoi literatury*), written precisely then, in 1891–92:

> The Russian writer has reconciled himself with his destiny; until now he has lived and died in complete solitude. [...] Side by side, in the same city, among the same external conditions, with almost an identical circle of readers, every literary group lives its own life as if it were on a separate island. [...] Between the islands, from kin to kin, there is a murderous hostility, which goes as far as blood revenge. Woe to the unlucky miserable poet–dreamer if he is washed ashore on the civic island! Our critics have the customs of true cannibals. Russian critics of the Sixties, like savage islanders according to the accounts of travellers, swallowed alive without reason the innocent Fet and Polonskii in the pages of *Homeland Notes* [*Otechestvennye Zapiski*]. However, isn't this the same bloody revenge

with which the carefree inhabitants of the poetic island later repaid the civic poets? Between Nekrasov and Maikov, as well as between the Westernizer Turgenev and Tolstoi, there did not exist the living, tolerant and all-reconciling medium, that cultural air where opposite and original temperaments encountering one another strengthen one another and stimulate activity.[11]

The interlocutors shared the same attitude towards journalistic criticism, and even towards individual critics, to *pisarevshchina*; Chekhov's biting remarks on A. M. Skabichevskii,[12] as well as on M. A. Protopopov,[13] correspond with Merezhkovskii's elaborations in *On the Causes of the Decline*. Here the proximity of an overriding pathos is also characteristic: these critics do not understand anything of the aesthetic side of literature:

> Russian criticism, with the exception of the best articles by Belinskii, Ap. Grigor'ev, Strakhov [...] has always been an anti-scientific and anti-artistic force. [...] Mr Protopopov declares quite openly that critic has to be a publicist and only a publicist. [...] The dream of these people is to turn literature into a comfortable little podium for the sermons of newspapers and magazines. When the living originality of a talent does not submit to them and does not want to serve as a pedestal for a political orator, Mr Protopopov is outraged and destroys it. Instead of explaining the author's personality, he tramples upon it in order to climb onto his podium more comfortably'.[14]

Merezhkovskii had also expressed similar sentiments earlier – in 1888, in his first major critical article: 'Faced with each work where the socialising tendency, which is only an excuse to talk and argue about something, is not laid out decisively enough, "critics" stop in total, helpless bewilderment...'.[15]

Chekhov would also agree with Merezhkovskii's unexpected statement, in the same book, that 'small-calibre press and illustrated journals, given the fast increasing demand for reading material, could become a large benign and cultural force. The arrogant disdain of the critics and readers of thick journals does not prevent skilful literary industrialists (in fact, it helps them) from poisoning for decades 200–300 thousand people, even those "of little strength", with artistic tastelessness and ignorance'.[16]

A common theme could also be Marcus Aurelius – at that time Chekhov contemplated his philosophy, very much reflected in 'Ward Number Six' (*Palata No. 6*).[17] We could even make the cautious assumption that it is precisely the conversations with Merezhkovskii, an ecstatic admirer of the emperor-philosopher, which renewed Chekhov's long-standing interest in the latter.[18]

They also shared similar attitudes towards Tolstoi, Nekrasov and to their contemporaries – Garshin, Korolenko, Fofanov.

Undoubtedly, they also shared an outlook centred on culture, and a culturological and even *Kulturträger*-like pathos.

In their common artistic sensibility – despite all their differences – there was a shared sense of the union of the spiritual with the material. For Chekhov this is the centre of his artistic model of the world; in Merezhkovskii one can see it in his inexhaustible striving for the 'unity of spirit and flesh, heaven and earth, religion and life',[19] a thirst for a synthesis of Christian and pagan elements. Some statements have striking similarities – for example, Chekhov's famous words that 'in a person everything should be beautiful: his face, clothes, soul and thoughts', and the following passage by Merezhkovskii from the book *Gogol' and the Devil* (*Gogol' i chert*): 'In the human's concern over his clothes there is love and respect for one's body. Byron and Pushkin dressed well; for them this was as simple and natural as writing well: their external elegance demonstrated an inadvertent correspondence, a harmony between the external and internal. In the ancient Lateran statue of Sophocles, the folds of his clothes seem as harmonious as the lines of his tragedies'.[20] Gogol''s spiritual disharmony, according to Merezhkovskii, manifested itself in particular in the former's inability 'to dress well'.

Merezhkovskii saw in Chekhov the beginnings of Symbolism,[21] although, of course, not in the same way as A. Belyi.[22] On the other hand, the case of Chekhov's intent artistic attention to the writings of his young contemporary is well known: one of the sources of the inserted play in *The Seagull* is Merezhkovskii's *Julian the Apostate (Death of the Gods)* (*Iulian Otstupnik* (*Smert' bogov*)).

However, right from the very start, the differences between Chekhov and Merezhkovskii were greater than their similarities.

II

For Merezhkovskii, one of the most important themes was the antinomy of civilization and culture.

> 'The accumulation of empirical knowledge, technology – in brief, all external civilization', he writes in an article of 1893, 'is only a bodily membrane [...] which becomes dead without an internal, sacred flame, without the breath of the ideal life. That is why a high level of civilization does not necessarily presuppose an equally high level of culture [...] Culture should be defined as the interaction of entire generations for the achievement of a single, selfless ideal goal, a mystical, religious goal'.[23]

For Chekhov with his love of good roads, spring carriages, hygiene and science, such an opposition was alien – 'in electricity and steam there is more love toward humanity than in chastity and abstaining from meat'.[24]

Treplev's play within *The Seagull* demonstrates the main features of the artistic manner of the author of *The Death of the Gods*. One of the best articles on the critic notes: 'Merezhkovskii is a master of the external-theatrical scenery, massive brushstrokes over a wide area [...]. What he depicts are, as it were, big cinematographic lines, exaggerated operatic sceneries, giant scenic sketches'.[25] The text of Chekhov's play on the universal soul is not a parody, but it is not a positive picture either – it is both and rocks on the edge of a blade; it is not accidental that within a century the play gained in the theatre so many mutually-exclusive interpretations. These are likely only to multiply in future. What Merezhkovskii discusses in a vague and varying manner on hundreds of pages, Chekhov presents on one. And it is this short text, written with all the might of Chekhov's talent, that absorbed, foreshadowed and forestalled a new artistic language, and which was destined to give birth to the Symbolist ('Decadent') drama of the early twentieth century.

Merezhkovskii the critic understood very well the literary lifelessness of arguments saturated with quotes within artistic texts. 'Instead of feeling simply and deeply, Maikov's first Christians coldly intellectualize at length. They are extremely well read and theologically-educated moralizers. Every so often they pour out quotations from the Scriptures'.[26] However, in his own historical novels Merezhkovskii forces his characters to intellectualize at greater length, in a more scholarly fashion and with more quotes, than does A. N. Maikov.

For Chekhov, not only the author's, but also the characters' moralizing was alien. In his writings it is hard to encounter a character's finished and formulated reasoning on the fundamental questions of existence. 'They somehow never have time, they are snowed under by daily chores. Either they have to deliver the post, or serve cutlets in the "Slavianskii Bazar", or feed their children'.[27]

In Chekhov's eyes there was nothing worse than a lack of independence, a lack of originality, or a slavish following of the trends of the time. Merezhkovskii had exactly this reputation amongst his contemporaries: 'His soul lacks an independent, indivisible core. Winds blow from different directions, and Merezhkovskii gives himself up now to this, and then to that. At first he echoed Nadson, was a Populist, and was intoxicated by Gleb Uspenskii. Then he [...] introduced into poetic literature philosophical motifs with a tinge of intellectual decadence [...] On the way he met Nietzsche [...] and the idealistic trends of modernity, and some neo-Christian motifs started to shine through his neo-pagan tendencies.'[28] Another perceptive critic from the start of the twentieth century characterized Merezhkovskii in the same way: 'He was always an imitator: first he was inspired by Nadson, then he worshipped Nietzsche [...]. In his best critical work [...] the author is already a faithful pupil and heir of Dostoevskii [...] Needless to say that this new "religion" is a mixture of the ideas of Ibsen, Dostoevskii and Vladimir Solov´ev'.[29] Even popular publications wrote about this: 'In the late 1880s the writer is overwhelmed with Nietzschianism and Symbolism. [...] However, the writer, easily carried away, soon betrays Symbolism and Nietzsche [...] Now he is taken by Christianity'.[30]

Chekhov depicts a member of Russian intelligentsia of this type in his story 'On the Road' (*Na Puti*, 1886). Likharev used to be an oilman, a hauler, was a 'Slavophile, a Ukrainophile, and an archaeologist, and a gatherer of folklore'. He preached the denial of property, and his 'last [...] faith was non-resistance to evil'. Curiously, in all of Merezhkovskii's 1888 article on Chekhov, the only (and quite biting) reproaches were directed precisely at this hero. Merezhkovskii doubts the hero's sincerity and authenticity, and does not understand the author's sympathy towards him. The young critic's invectives are coloured in personal feeling, as if he is rushing to distance himself from his own premonitions about himself. Merezhkovskii, when he reached the age of Chekhov's hero (42), although he did not become an oilman or a hauler, managed to change several, substantial, landmarks; and continued in the same fashion. As I. A. Il´in wrote in 1934, he stands 'under the sign of the wanderer, of the roamer – both spatially and spiritually'; his ideas and doctrines 'sometimes turn out to be incompatible, and in essence often affirm mutually contradictory things'.[31]

More than any other Russian writer, Chekhov avoided rigorism, preaching, and didacticism. From early on, these were some of the main features of Merezhkovskii's literary and philosophical position. Chekhov stressed this in 1903, in his famous characteristic of Merezhkovskii, 'who believes definitely, believes *scholastically*...'.[32]

Chekhov forever remained outside political parties, and for this reason too he occupies a special place in Russian culture. By contrast, Merezhkovskii had been sharply partisan right from the start. He accuses Chekhov of not belonging in his famous article of 1914, which expressed most fully his attitude to the writer: 'The truth is in the liberation of Russia [...] Chekhov's mistake – the mistake of the 1890s – is the rejection of this liberation, the reconciliation with reality, philistinism and Suvorin-type values [*suvorinoshchina*]'.[33] One could call this a criticism from the Left if such definitions were applicable to Merezhkovskii. Naturally, he understands liberation and struggle in their connection to religious ideas: 'Social nihilism and religious nihilism are united. It is not accidental that Chekhov passes by not only the religious populist movement of the 1880s and 1890s, but also the religious populism of L. Tolstoi and Dostoevskii in the same years (he did not mention Dostoevskii once in his letters, as if Dostoevskii never existed)'.[34] Quoting Chekhov's words, 'We do not believe in liberation, and have no God', Merezhkovskii asserts: 'We lost both beliefs together, and we shall only find them together'.[35] He deems it necessary 'to overcome *chekhovshchina*, philistinism and *suvorinshchina* in Chekhov himself'. He demands a radical and partisan attitude from Chekhov with almost the same persistence as the Soviet literary critics of the 1920–30s.

Merezhkovskii's partisan tendency was distinctly felt by his contemporaries — for example, by such a shrewd Merezhkovskii critic as the famous philosopher S. Frank: 'When a Godly or Christ-like element is fully identified with the revolutionary movement, and when a diabolic and Antichrist-like element is fully identified with the reactionary one; when the whole essence of faith is interpreted as activity alone, and moreover as socio-political activity, then "God and the Devil", "Christ and Antichrist" become simple nicknames for party movements and the party struggle'.[36] In S. Frank's opinion, Merezhkovskii's religious-political reform can be reduced to the following: 'While preserving intact the revolutionary intelligentsia's soul, to remove from it Marx and atheism and to fill that space with the Apostle John and apocalyptic religion'.[37] L. Shestov also thought that Merezhkovskii 'under the guise of religion offered us [...] an ordinary moralizing idealism'.[38] Merezhkovskii was intrinsically unable to exercise any kind of tolerance.

There is no need to say how alien this was to Chekhov's philosophical adogmatism.

For Chekhov, there was a huge gap between 'solving the question and correctly posing the question', and 'only the latter [is] compulsory for the artist'.[39] The worst sin for Chekhov was 'to write, write, and then blame the Gospel for your text',[40] unforgivable even with respect to Tolstoi. Here too Merezhkovskii is located at the opposite pole: for him the question of the 'last answer' is only a question of time. 'A strange impatience', wrote L. Shestov in 1905, 'has lately taken hold of Russian writers. All of them rushed to hunt the "last word". They seem to think that the last word will certainly be caught — the question is only who will be the first to catch it ...'[41]

III

In the sensibility of 'Merezhkovskii the mystic', there was nevertheless considerable space for a rational element. Its genesis, in the young Merezhkovskii's links with positivism, is a separate topic. But by the 1900s Merezhkovskii's rationalism was for some critics the defining feature in his oeuvre. 'If *The Outcast* [*Otverzhennyi*] is dominated by a vague streak, hot and in places mystical, then by the time of *The Resurrected Gods* [*Voskresshie bogi*] it has been replaced, little by little, by the cold study of the scientist; and in *Peter and Alexis* [*Petr i Aleksei*] mysticism has gone, leaving a cold narrative which breathes with the "dust of centuries" [...] Already on numerous occasions, when speaking of Mr Merezhkovskii's creative oeuvre, we have had to note the coldness of his temperament, the dominance in him of rationality over heart, of study over creativity. There is nothing mystical in the author's nature, he is a typical moralizer, and his work resembles solving a chess problem rather than a sermon, or the rapturous striving to the world of the unclear and the indefinite which Mr Merezhkovskii is trying to break into [...] Without being carried away himself, the author cannot carry the reader away to the "abysses beneath and above" which lure him'.[42]

This rational element was manifested particularly distinctly in Merezhkovskii's literary criticism. A contemporary wrote on his book *Tolstoi and Dostoevskii* (*Tolstoi i Dostoevskii*) that, according to Merezhkovskii:

Tolstoi is characterized by excessive physicality, and Dostoevskii by excessive spirituality. Tolstoi is akin to Michelangelo, Dostoevskii to Leonardo. Both of them are the messengers of the second great Russian and global Renaissance, of the new religion. The whole world, the whole of history needs to be covered by the simple net of a formula of a unified process of logic [...] The role of religion is played by naked schoolish logic. An arithmetic scheme, the logical opposition of terms: East/West, *rat'*/*blagodat'* (army/grace), Mangod/Godman, flesh/spirit – how artificial all this is, and how impassionate, cold and abstract in its artificiality'.[43]

For many this cold logical clarity cast a shadow over the merits of *Tolstoi and Dostoevskii*, one of the best books written on these writers in Russian literary criticism. The particularities of the author's thinking process came in useful in conducting the philological analysis. (Perhaps in the history of Russian culture, Merezhkovskii is predominantly important as a critic and author of studies on Russian and Western literature, a pioneer and predecessor of the most important category of twentieth century philology: 'the structure of the writer's artistic world'.)

In Chekhov's world, one cannot know the realm of the vague – that which lies beyond this world – through rational means. Moreover, for him the life of nature, or the mundane existence of people, its meaning and purpose, remain complex, horrifying or beautiful, and full of mystery. 'It terrifies me to watch the peasants,' says the hero of the story which is also entitled 'Terror' (*Strakh*): 'I do not know for what higher purpose they suffer, or what they live for [...] A hopeless love for a woman with whom you already have two children!

Is that intelligible? And is it not terrifying?' 'I watched the rooks, and it seemed strange and terrifying that they were flying', the narrator says in the same story.

'The whole of life seemed to him as dark as this water which reflected the night sky and in which the weeds grew in a tangle' ('Neighbours': *Sosedi*).

'What is the purpose of the centres and convolutions of the brain, what is the purpose of sight, speech, self-consciousness, genius – if all this is destined to go into the ground, and in the end to grow cold along with the Earth's crust, and then for millions of years without meaning and without purpose to fly around the sun with the Earth?' ('Ward No. 6': *Palata No. 6*).

This may sound paradoxical, but Chekhov is a greater irrationalist and mystagogue than Merezhkovskii. Merezhkovskii's colleagues from the Petersburg Religious-Philosophical Gatherings would be very surprised to hear this.[44] However, some of the most perceptive critics had already noted these features in Chekhov's outlook already then: 'Chekhov is the first of our artists who consciously opposed the rational activity of man to that organic thinking which takes its origins in the irrational depths of our spirit, and rejects the validity of any purely rational thought'.[45]

Rationalism is an essential feature of the Symbolist model of literary consciousness, despite all the intuitive and mystical revelations that it declares. This feature was noticed straight away in the leader of the new movement. 'Briusov's method is a rigorously considered and premeditated weighing of all the ingredients'.[46] 'Can one stay further away from the mystical experience? Read Briusov's prose; it strikes us by the tenacity of its logic and its strong hold on common sense'.[47] 'It is not a creative fantasy that takes the upper hand in Briusov, but a sober, clear mind rendered sophisticated by science'.[48] The fin-de-siècle craved irrationalism and mysticism; this was not intrinsically inherent in some of those who answered this call.

A proximity to science, the turn to precise knowledge, is generally a characteristic feature of the Symbolists. Recall for example the mathematical theories of Andrei Belyi's poetic craft, his graphs, calculations and charts in *The Mastery of Gogol'* (*Masterstvo Gogolia*).

Chekhov too was on the side of scientific knowledge; in his famous autobiography he spells out clearly the role which natural sciences played in his life: 'They considerably extended the area of my observations, enriched me with knowledge whose value for me as a writer only the doctor can understand; they also directed me, and it is probably thanks to the proximity to medicine that I managed to avoid many mistakes. The familiarity with natural sciences, with the scientific method, has always kept me alert, and I tried, whenever possible, to take scientific data into consideration, and where this was not possible I preferred to refrain from writing altogether'.[49]

However, this familiarity is felt in Chekhov's writings only as a superficial cover which does not spill into the text, unlike in the case of Merezhkovskii, Andrei Belyi, Viacheslav Ivanov, or with Briusov, all of whom openly demonstrate their scientific education to the point of achieving a total diffusion of the historical-ethnographic and prosaic types of narrative.

IV

The power of logical constructions is clearly visible in the foundations of Merezhkovskii's *Weltanschauung* – his feelings towards Christianity. For him, Christianity is only ascetic ('the black, colourless shadows of monks' on the marble of Ellada in his *Julian the Apostate*). It is precisely for this reason that he poses the problem of the synthesis of spirit and flesh. However, as a connoisseur of the history of Christianity Georgii Florovskii noted in this regard: 'Historical Christianity was not at all as "fleshless" as was required by the artificial schemes of opposition in Merezhkovskii's work'.[50]

For Chekhov, historical Christianity is as real, concrete and tangible as modern Christianity. The night in the garden in 'The Student' (*Student*) is portrayed as physically and emotionally as the Easter Night in 'The Bishop' (*Arkhierei*), or in 'The Night Before Easter' (*Sviatoi noch'iu*).

Here Chekhov merges with I. Bunin, I. Shmelev and B. Zaitsev – also representatives of the 'old' model of literary consciousness.

For Merezhkovskii, the question of Christianity is central. But the Christianity he needs is not the existing orthodox one, but a logical analysis of it, the search for a new embodiment of Christ in life and life in Christ.

For Chekhov, by contrast, the ontological rootedness of Christianity in Russian life is sufficient, as he brilliantly demonstrates in 'The Bishop': 'His love for church services, for the clergy, for the peal of bells, was innate in him, deep, ineradicable'.

Zinaida Gippius disliked the episode with a girl in Bunin's 'Mitia's Love' (*Mitina liubov'*), which takes place at that very moment when the hero confronts the question of life and death. In Chekhov's 'The Bishop', a few lines after the quoted thoughts of the bishop on the love for the church, he is rubbed all over with vodka mixed with vinegar (compare this with the figure of Father Christopher in 'The Steppe' (*Step'*)). A free juxtaposition of similar scenes is typical also for Shmelev. On 'Pure Monday' (*Chistyi ponedel'nik*), portrayed with awe, the father shouts at the steward: 'Drunken mug!' The same can be found in L. Tolstoi, not to mention Leskov.

The unification and inseparable merging of the sacred with the mundane is the most essential feature of the first (the 'old') model. Here we approach the next most important opposition of these two models.

V

Merezhkovskii does not accept Chekhov's perception of the world, which seemed to him too 'unspiritual' in comparison with preceding Russian literature. 'These giants', he says of Tolstoi and Dostoevskii, 'turned out to be greater than us, whereas Chekhov and Gor′kii are only at the same level as the Russian intelligentsia'.[51] Z. Gippius also expressed this idea, albeit casting the contrast in sharper form relief (as was often the case with this married couple):

> Dostoevskii and Chekhov do not have a single feature in common, neither as people, nor as artists, nor as 'prophets' [...] Dostoevskii drags us painfully and tortuously through all the earth to the very lowest, second Heaven; while Chekhov pulls us along a slippery, although pleasantly-sloping, hillside into a shallow and soft hole, where no Heaven is present, not even the first Heaven.[52]

In a different article she acknowledges that 'Chekhov, reluctantly, unconsciously, lays down Divine motifs'. Still he remains the last poet of the 'trivia and atoms' of life.[53] His 'misfortune is in the fact that the grey and the white, the finest atoms of dust and of diamonds are mixed up in him so much, life and death are so terrifying, so finely and densely interwoven'.[54]

Chekhov's unification of 'dust' and 'diamonds', of the sublime and mundane, the spiritual and the tangible, is impossible for the Merezhkovskiis. For them, everyday life (*byt*) is by definition hostile to life, creativity and philosophy: 'It so happened that two words get confused: *byt* and life [...] But these are two mutually-excluding concepts. *Byt* begins at the point where life ends, and vice versa – when life just begins again, *byt* disappears [...]. Life consists of events, while *byt* is an eternal repetition, the strengthening and preservation of these events in a moulded, immovable form. For precisely this reason, life, i.e. movement forwards, the accumulation of new and yet more new events – only that is creativity. And this creativity excludes *byt*'.[55]

> He is great, maybe even the greatest writer of the everyday [*bytopisatel′*] in Russian literature. This, however, conceals not only his strength, but also his weakness. He knows contemporary Russian *byt* as no one else; but apart from this *byt* he does not know anything and does not want to know anything [...] Chekhov's heroes do not have a life, but have only *byt* – *byt* without events, or with a single event – death, the end of *byt*, the end of existence.[56]

Because he is rooted in '*byt*', Chekhov is 'national, but not international'.[57] They were deeply mistaken; but possibly for Merezhkovskii this revealed most lucidly the difference between the two models. For him, even in Tolstoi's writings there was, using the words of G. Adamovich, 'little spirit. Merezhkovskii "suffocated", suffered from the lack of that special, scarce, freezing ether, which belongs to late Romanticism, and which was the only ether which he, as well as many new people of his type, could breath'.[58]

However, the point was not in the lack of 'spirit' in Chekhov, but in that type of latent, hidden spirituality, which the new literary consciousness perceived as non-spirituality.

For justice's sake, one should say that not everyone from the camp of the new literature shared Merezhkovskiis' view. Andrei Belyi also supposed that Chekhov portrays life's little details, but in these details 'a mysterious code is revealed to us – and the details thus stop being details. The banality of their life gets neutralized by something. In the details, something grandiose opens up everywhere. [...] Trivia takes on a different hue, which was previously unseen [...] Chekhov, remaining a realist, pulls apart the crises of life, and what seemed from afar shadowy crises, turns out to be a flight into Eternity'.[59]

However, general contemporary criticism was gravitating towards the idea that 'the highest tasks of artistic creativity, such as the analysis of the fundamental antinomies of the human spirit and the philosophical synthesis of reality, forever remained alien to Chekhov'.[60]

Merezhkovskii and Gippius did not understand and did not accept the unusual type of artistic-philosophical meditation (different from that in the prose of Tolstoi and Dostoevskii), which avoids speculative and theological terms (of whose abundance critics reproached Merezhkovskii more than once), and is interwoven with the mundane and tangible as well as the transient, and which places itself above the latter, coexisting alongside it without opposing it.

VI

Connected to the above is one of the central antinomies (even though it at first appears more particular) of the two models – their opposition exists not only in literature, but also in life, in the very style of life.

In Chekhov's notebook of 1891, amongst the notes made in Italy, we find: '20th. Cathedral of St Mark. The Doge's Palace. Desdemona's House. The Guido Quarters. The shrines of Canova and Titian. 24th. Musicians. In the evening a conversation with Merezhkovskii about death.

26th. Rain. Must try milk mushrooms with sour cream [...] Went to Bologna in the morning: slanting towers, arcades, Rafael's Cecilia'.[61]

For Merezhkovskii, the juxtaposition of a conversation about death, Rafael, and milk mushrooms with sour cream is, of course, unimaginable.

For him, Italy was painted in one colour which excluded all others: 'Oh, the glory of the old days, oh Rome, fallen Rome!' 'Like a quiet sacrificial altar, the bright summit of Vesuvius smokes. The fire burns red under the moon, And white smoke swirls over it... The Land of your blossoming hillsides is infinitely dear to me, Sorrento with the lemon groves, Oh, golden shores!..'[62] After the meeting with Chekhov, Merezhkovskii told everybody (and then also wrote in his Memoirs) that Chekhov remained cold towards Italy.[63] On 27 May 1891 Chekhov wrote to Suvorin with indignation: 'I would very much like to know who tries so hard, who informed the whole universe that I did not like abroad? My good Lord, I didn't say a word to this effect to anyone. I even liked Bologna. What was I supposed to do? Roar with delight? Smash windows? Hug the French?'.[64]

A. L. Volynskii, who frequented Merezhkovskii's literary saloon in the 1890s, described the hosts' reaction to Chekhov's visit in his Memoirs:

A day later the Merezhkovskiis' household amused themselves loudly remembering their provincial guest. Merezhkovskii quoted excerpts from his words: 'It is better and simpler where I live. Bread is filling, milk is poured in scoops, women have big breasts'. Such was Chekhov's reaction to the banquets of Decadent thought which was creating a new epoch in literature.[65]

For his part, Chekhov wrote: 'Enthusiastic and pure in soul, Merezhkovskii would have done better had he replaced his quasi-Goethesque regime, his spouse and "the truth" for a bottle of good wine, a hunting gun, and an attractive woman. His heart would beat better' (To Suvorin, 1 March 1892).[66]

The contrast in their behaviour and words can easily be reconstructed from the reminiscences of their contemporaries. B. Zaitsev wrote of Merezhkovskii: 'He spoke brilliantly, eloquently and semi-prophetically. Some spiritual obsession attracted him [...] No, not a prophet, of course, but a highly gifted and special creature who created around him an unrepeatable ethos'.[67]

And this is what Chekhov's interlocutor of many years wrote about him: 'He seemed like a very ordinary person. [...] In company he was hardly distinguishable from others: no clever phrases, no pretentions to be witty [...] Everything in him was simple and natural. [...] He never strove either to teach or to preach'.[68]

In the circles of representatives of the 'old' literature there was a commonly shared attitude to Merezhkovskii's style of life, thought and speech. A. N. Pleshcheev wrote to Suvorin on 16 February 1891: 'Merezhkovskii is turning into a bore – he cannot go for a walk, or eat, or drink, without philosophizing about the immortality of the soul and other subjects just as lofty. But the main thing is that he is intoxicated by his own voice. The search for God is a very good thing, but it should not be so loud, because then it makes you doubt its sincerity'.[69] He wrote roughly the same thing also to Chekhov on 12 January 1891: 'Merezhkovskii told me that he visited you [...] I suppose that he kept talking to you about aesthetics or God, with whose search (some say, too loudly) he is now preoccupied'.[70] We can find similar statements by V. A. Tikhonov, A. I. Kuprin,[71] and others. A. Gornfel'd found that the 'stately gown of the prophet' prevents Merezhkovskii 'from being great'.[72]

It is clear that Merezhkovskii could not accept Chekhov's irony, the parody of the lofty discourse concerned with 'ideals', 'the struggle', etc. He wrote the following concerning Chekhov's feuilleton 'In Moscow' (*V Moskve*): 'The words, once sacred, and maybe still sacred, "ideals, honesty, convictions", are here trodden into the mud [...]. This is the verdict of Chekhov-Suvorin. With respect to whom? Only to the "Moscow Hamlet", Kisliaev, Uncle Vania who talked himself into suicide, the "living corpse", or also with respect to the living people, the idealists of the 1880s and 1890s, Mikhailovskii, Uspenskii, Garshin and their predecessors – Belinskii, Dobroliubov, Nekrasov?'.[73]

The most famous photograph of Merezhkovskii depicts him in his study with a huge crucifix in the background. Chekhov would rather die than allow his portrait to be published, where he is, say, depicted with a pen in his hand, or with an anti-cholera leaflet in the background, although his medical work with cholera sufferers mattered a lot to him.

The stylistic opposition grew to be a philosophical antinomy.

However, this was not the antinomy of just two personalities. It represented a change of the aesthetic self-consciousness of Russian literature at the turn of the century.

VII

The image of a writer as a secluded wizard – a creator of texts (even in the case of L. Tolstoi, with his active preaching which became teaching) was giving way to a new image – that of the public person who gives talks, participates in debates and lives in the atmosphere of literary scandal, the image of 'the genius'. Scandals were started not by the Futurists, or by the younger Symbolists with Briusov as their leader. The first literary scandal (although still in quite parliamentary forms) arose with Merezhkovskii's lectures, delivered on 7 and 14 December 1892 in the hall of the Solianoi Gorodok complex. These then laid the foundation of the book *On the Causes of the Decline and on the New Trends in Contemporary Russian Literature*. Being a public figure, shocking, spoken about in the press, became part of the character of the modern litterateur.

A revolutionary change of the paradigm across all the humanities, encompassing philosophy, criticism and literary science, was taking place.

Amongst the main features of the new paradigm was the destruction of the past – not evolution, but revolution (so far, only in the spiritual sphere). The necessary 're-evaluation of established values' 'during the turn to new cultural eras [...] cannot begin other than by mercilessly destroying the ideas which are already dead, incorrect, which serve as brakes for the movement of thought. One has to plough anew and dig up the ground on which nothing any longer grows. And no matter which sacred remains might be found under the ploughshare of a wooden plough, one must continue working without loyalty-driven delays – for the sake of the new sowing and future new shoots'.[74]

This new cultural-philosophical and literary-stylistic paradigm opposed the paradigm of Russian classical literature of the nineteenth century.

However, the first manifestation of this paradigm – the opposition between Chekhov and Merezhkovskii – went unnoticed. The reason for this is that it took place in old-fashioned, gentlemen-like forms. These were those, not yet vanished, forms which A. I. Gertsen described in his obituary 'K. S. Aksakov':

> It happened when our disputes came to the point that neither we, nor the Slavophiles wanted to meet any more; I walked along a street; K. Aksakov was driven on a sledge. I bowed to him in a friendly fashion. He sort of went past me, but then stopped the coachman, left the sledge and approached me. 'It was too painful for me', he said, 'to go past you without saying farewell to you. You understand that after what has happened between your friends and mine I will no longer visit you; it is a shame, a shame, but there is nothing to be done. I wanted to shake your hand and say farewell'. He quickly went up to the sledge, but then came back again; I was standing on the same spot, I was sad; he threw himself at me, embraced me and kissed me very strongly. I had tears in my eyes. How I loved him at that moment of quarrel!

For Chekhov and Merezhkovskii, the rudest weapon in their literary battle was an elegant joke at each other's expense.

Regarding the lectures and brochure by Merezhkovskii, the big names of literary criticism at the time made the following remarks: 'What an unimaginable mess', A. M. Skabichevskii wrote, 'reigns on its pages. You read it and only throw up your hands in dismay! [...] You will see in Mr Merezhkovskii ten different points of view on ten pages [...]. And now try to make sense of this mess'.[75] However, N. K. Mikhailovskii even apologized for his tone: 'Forgive me for this vulgar comparison, but Merezhkovskii's thought jumps like a flea: the direction, speed and generally the character of these leaps may have its internal laws, but looking from the side, one is struck by their capricious unexpectedness and ridiculousness'.[76] But other, less prominent, critics were basically no more cutting: 'Mr Merezhkovskii does not see what is concealed in beautiful words; it does not enter his head that no matter how beautiful a word can be, one has to [...] understand its meaning first';[77] 'a lot of vacuous chatter', 'artificial and short theories';[78] 'disconnected childish prattle, the purposeless rapture of a Decadent and Symbolist';[79] 'meaning, which is often, unfortunately, obscured by pretentious phrases'.[80] Even the habitual literary hooligan V. P. Burenin expressed himself in not much ruder terms: 'the pretentious chatter of a literary teenager'.[81]

However, when ten years later, on 13 November 1901, A. L. Volynskii delivered a scandalous lecture, the tone of the newspapers' reactions in the new era was completely different. Let us offer just a few examples from the collection carefully put together in a special book by N. G. Molostvov, Volynskii's adept, the publisher of the newspaper *The Baltic District* (*Pribaltiiskii Krai*): 'The lecture was over and the audience left in a state of surprise with respect to Mr Volynskii's impudence and the insolence of his manner' ([*The Russian Sheet*] *Russkii listok*); 'In his lecture – which was not a lecture really, but rather a universal "muddling": he cursed everybody, as if having poured sluice all over them' ([*The Courier*] *Kur'er*); 'It was stuffy in the hall and an unbearable stench was felt; this stench was produced by the words of a small man, and became ever stronger and more intolerable. It seemed as if instead of the auditorium we found ourselves in a tip of some sort' ([*The Russian Word*] *Russkoe slovo*); 'Something ugly, almost savage, hardly feasible is concealed in the outburst of this non-entity immersed in narcissism who climbed the podium [...] One can say with confidence that ten years ago such a thing would have been unthinkable' ([*The Moscow Sheet*] *Moskovskii listok*).[82] Ten years previously such expressions were unthinkable. Literary battles had acquired a completely different form and intensity.

On the general cultural plane, the opposition of Merezhkovskii and Chekhov is an opposition of two models, of two types of European cultural consciousness: romantic/positivist; ascending-rhetorical-explicit/descending-reserved-implicit. However, we are interested, of course, not in exalting to the general, but, on the contrary, in concretizing, in the historically definite manifestation of these fundamental antinomies – both because of the outstanding personalities of the opponents, and because of our concern with the primary phenomena.

Translated by Olga Tabachnikova

Notes

1 Merezhkovskii for his part wrote: 'Truly artistic works are not invented and made like machines, but grow and develop like living, organic fabrics [...] But as soon as you agree with the suggestion that the creative act is not a mechanical, conscious invention, but an organic, reflexive phenomenon, you must immediately acknowledge that it is impossible and foolish to apply to the creative act such seemingly theoretical formulae which depend on external laws, in the same way that it is impossible to use external mechanical devices to change an organ's internal and morphological structure, or consciously control biological processes or the manner in which matter grows and lives'. D. Merezhkovskii, '*Staryi vopros po povodu novogo talanta*', A. P. Chekhov, *V Sumerkakh. Ocherki i rasskazy* (Moscow: Nauka 1986), pp. 370–1.
2 A. P. Chekhov, *Polnoe sobranie sochinenii i pisem v 30 tomakh* (Moscow: *Nauka*, 1974–82), Letters, Vol. 3, p. 53.
3 Chekhov, PSSP, Letters, Vol. 3, p. 54.
4 Letter to A. N. Pleshcheev, 13 November 1888. Chekhov, PSSP, Letters, Vol. 3, p. 69.
5 Chekhov, PSSP, Letters, Vol. 4, p. 157.
6 Ibid., p. 336.
7 See his letter to A. N. Veselovskii of 5 December. PSSP, Letters, Vol. 10, p. 131.
8 A. L. Volynskii, *Anton Pavlovich Chekhov*, RGALI, F. 95. Ed. khr. 86.
9 The first attempt to draw a picture of the chronology and evolution of the relationship of the writers was made in the recent text by E. Tolstaia-Segal, '*Venetsiia, muzykant, razgovor o smerti: Chekhov i Merezhkovskii (k interpretatsii "Rasskaza neizvestnogo cheloveka")*', in *Anton P. Chekhov. Werk und Wirkung. Vorträge und Diskussionen eines internationalen Symposiums in Badenweiler im Oktober 1985*, ed. by R.-D. Kluge (Wiesbaden: Harrassowitz, 1990), pp. 736–76.
10 Chekhov, PSSP, Works, vol. 17, p. 8.
11 D. S. Merezhkovskii, *Polnoe sobranie sochinenii* (Moscow: Sytin 1914), vol. 18, pp. 182–3.
12 'I never read Skabichevskii. I recently got hold of his *History of Modern Literature* [*Istoriia noveishei literatury*]; I read a line and then threw it away – I did not like it. I do not understand why this was written. Skabichevskii and Co. are martyrs, who have willingly taken on the religious task of walking the streets and shouting: "The cobbler Ivanov makes bad shoes!" and "The carpenter Semenov makes good tables!" Who needs this?' (Letter to F. A. Chervinskii, 2 July 1891, PSSP, Letters, Vol. 3, p. 245). 'What is Skabichevskii cursing everyone for? What is this tone for, as if they were talking of convicts rather than artists and writers'? (Letter to A. S. Suvorin, 24 February 1893, PSSP, Letters, Vol. 4, p. 173).
13 'No one will get warm from Protopopov's criticism, no one will get cold, because all the critics nowadays are not worth a spoonful of honey – a useless people to the highest degree'. (Letter to A. N. Pleshcheev, 26 June 1889, PSSP, Letters, Vol. 3, p. 227).
14 Merezhkovskii, *Polnoe sobranie sochinenii*, Vol. 18, pp. 200–01.
15 Merezhkovskii, '*Staryi vopros po povodu novogo talanta*', in A. P. Chekhov, *V sumerkakh. Ocherki i rasskazy* (Moscow: Nauka (*Literaturnye pamiatniki*), 1986), p. 332.
16 Merezhkovskii, *Polnoe sobranie sochinenii*, Vol. 18, pp. 194–5.
17 See our commentary to this novella (pp. 447–8, Vol. 8, Works in the Complete Collection of Works and Letters (*Polnoe Sobranie Sochinenii i Pisem*) in 30 volumes.
18 Yet, as E. Tolstaia-Segal appropriately reminds us, it was Chekhov who 'opened' Mark Aurelius before Merezhkovskii. See E. Tolstaia-Segal, p. 746.

19 N. Berdiaev, *Dukhovnyi krizis intelligentsii. Stat'i po obshchei i religioznoi psikhologii (1907–1909)* (St Petersburg, 1910), p. 157.
20 D. S. Merezhkovskii, *V tikhom omute. Stat'i i issledovaniia raznykh let* (Moscow: *Sovetskii pisatel'*, 1991), p. 257.
21 Lena Szilard, '*Chekhov i proza russkikh simvolistov*', in *Anton P. Čechov. Werk.*, op. cit., p. 791.
22 See the *Chekhoviana* compilation.
23 D. S. Merezhkovskii, *Estetika i kritika* (Moscow/Kharkov: Iskusstvo, 1994), Vol. 1, p. 124.
24 Chekhov, PSSP, Letters, Vol 5, pp. 283–4.
25 I. A. I'lin, '*Merezhkovskii – khudozhnik*', in *Russkaia literatura v emigratsii*, ed. by N. P. Poltoratskii (Pittsburgh: University of Pittsburgh, 1972), p. 181.
26 Ibid., p. 451.
27 D. V. Filosofov, *Staroe i novoe. Sb. Statei po voprosam iskusstva i literatury* (Moscow, 1912), p. 222.
28 A. Volynskii, '*Sovremennaia russkaia belletristika*', in N. G. Molostvov, *Borets za idealism (A. L. Volynskii)* 2nd edition, (St Petersburg, 1903), pp. 176–7.
29 M. Nevedomskii, *Zachinateli i prodolzhateli* (Petrograd, 1919), pp. 298–9.
30 See *Russkaia kritika sovremennoi literatury. Kharakteristiki, obraztsy, portrety* (St Petersburg: Vestnik znaniia, 1912), pp. 80–1. Cf. R. Pletnev, *Istoriia russkoi literatury XX veka* (New York: Perspektiva, 1987), p. 24.
31 *Russkaia literatura v emigratsii*, pp. 283–4.
32 Chekhov, PSSP, Letters, Vol. 11, p. 234.
33 D. Merezhkovskii, '*Suvorin i Chekhov*', in *Akropol'. izbrannye literaturno-kriticheskie stat'i* (Moscow: *Izdatel'stvo Knizhnaia palata*, 1991), p. 291. A contemporary observer noted that in 1888 Merezhkovskii had already tried 'to make Chekhov's name the slogan for the battle of literary parties'. (*Russkaia mysl'*, No. 1 (1889), p. 36).
34 Merezhkovskii, '*Suvorin i Chekhov*', op. cit., p. 291.
35 Ibid., p. 294.
36 S. L. Frank, *Filosofiia i zhizn'. Etiudy i nabroski po filosofii kul'tury* (St Petersburg, 1910), pp. 343–4.
37 Ibid., p. 345.
38 L. Shestov, *Apofeoz bespochvennosti (Opyt adogmaticheskogo myshleniia)* (St Petersburg, 1905), p. 262.
39 Chekhov, PSSP, Letters, Vol. 3, p. 46.
40 Ibid., Vol. 9, p. 30.
41 L. Shestov, *Apofeoz bespochvennosti (Opyt adogmaticheskogo myshleniia)*, op. cit., p. 56.
42 A. I. Bogdanovich, *Gody pereloma. 1895–1906* (St Petersburg, 1908), pp. 429–30.
43 B. Griftsov, *Tri myslitelia. V. Rozanov. D. Merezhkovskii. L. Shestov* (Moscow, 1911), pp. 120–1.
44 Accusations of a lack of mysticism came from the closest camp too. Berdiaev later accused Merezhkovskii of not being 'mystical enough' when feeling the other's personality. N. Berdiaev, *O russkikh klassikakh* (Moscow: *Vysshaia shkola*, 1993), p. 238.
45 L. Gurevich, *Literatura i estetika* (Moscow, 1912), p. 47.
46 Ellis (A. L. Kobylinskii), *Russkie simvolisty* (Moscow, 1910), p. 127.
47 K. Chukovskii, *Ot Chekhova do nashikh dnei*, 3rd edition (St Petersburg/Moscow 1908), p. 231.
48 Gurevich, op. cit., p. 119.
49 Chekhov, PSSP, Works, Vol. 16, p. 271.
50 G. Florovskii, *Puti russkogo bogosloviia* (Paris: YMCA, 1988), p. 457. Berdiaev also suggested that Merezhkovskii was 'doomed not to understand "the historical aspect" in Christianity', denying 'the materiality and physicality which actually exists in it'. N. Berdiaev, *Sobranie sochinenii* (Paris: YMCA, 1989), Vol. 3, p. 495. Objecting to Merezhkovskii, he even wrote that 'in our church life there is in fact too much flesh,

too much earthliness, too much everyday life, and not too little'. Aleksandr Men' sympathetically quoted these words in his 1989 lecture on Merezhkovskii and Gippius. See *Russkaia mysl'*, Paris, 1994, 8–14 December, No. 4056 (1989), p. 17.
51 D. Merezhkovskii, *Polnoe sobranie sochinenii*, Vol. 14, p. 60. However, there was a different point of view from a critic who had read Chekhov carefully: 'You can re-read tens of books by Goncharov, Turgenev, Pisemskii, and not come across one page on God, faith, immortality. In this sense Chekhov is infinitely closer to Tolstoi and Dostoevskii'. (A. Izmailov, *Literaturnyi Olimp* (Moscow, 1911), p. 136). The issue lies in the very manner of Chekhov's search for God, which was impermissible for Merezhkovskii.
52 Anton Krainii, '*Eshche o poshlosti*', *Novyi put'*, No. 4 (1904), p. 241. Cf. a critic who was spiritually close: 'In Tolstoi and Dostoevskii there is always: 'Height, divine height/Depth, depth of the ocean or sea'; Chekhov has neither heights, nor depths, no Pelions or Ossas' (D. V. Filosofov, *Staroe i novoe*, p. 221).
53 Anton Krainii, '*Chto i kak. Vishnevye sady*', *Novyi put'*, No. 5 (1904), p. 256.
54 Ibid. Berdiaev had already started to depart from Merezhkovskii over the evaluation of these ideas: 'Merezhkovskii mistakenly identifies the spiritualistic, the spiritual with the heavenly and inaccessible world, and the material, the fleshy with this world, the Earth. But this world is also spiritual, and holds many spiritual riches', Berdiaev, *Dukhovnyi krizis intelligentsii*, op. cit., p. 116.
55 Krainii, '*Chto i kak*', op. cit., 256.
56 Merezhkovskii, *Polnoe sobranie sochinenii*, Vol. 14, p. 66.
57 Ibid.
58 G. Adamovich, *Odinochestvo i svoboda. Literaturno-kriticheskie stat'i* (St Petersburg: Logos, 1993), p. 54.
59 A. Belyi, '*Vishnevyi sad*''', *Vesy*, No. 2 (1904), p. 48.
60 M. Gershenzon, '*Literaturnoe obozrenie*', *Nauchnoe slovo* (St Petersburg), No. 3 (1904), p. 164.
61 Chekhov, PSSP, Works, Vol. 17, p. 8.
62 D. S. Merezhkovskii, *Simvoly (pesni i poemy)* (St Petersburg: A. S. Suvorin, 1892), pp. 220, 237.
63 D. S. Merezhkovskii, 'A. P. Chekhov', *Iubileinyi chekhovskii sbornik* (Moscow, 1910), 327. There appear to have been some grounds for such conclusions by Merezhkovskii. See Chekhov's letter to M. V. Kiseleva from Rome, 1 April 1891: 'I saw everything and crept around everywhere, where they showed me [...] But at the moment I feel only exhaustion and the desire to eat some cabbage soup with buckwheat kasha', PSSP, Letters, Vol. 4, p. 208. See also the note in the diary of S. I. Smirnova-Sazonova: 'Suvorin visited late in the evening [...] He told us about his journey abroad with Chekhov and sons [...] In Rome Chekhov said, "Hey, it would be lovely to lie on the grass now!"' *Literaturnoe nasledstvo*, Vol. 78. *Iz istorii russkoi literatury i obshchestvennoi mysli. 1860–90 gg.* (Moscow, 1977), p. 305.
64 Chekhov, PSSP, Letters, Vol. 4, p. 237.
65 A. Volynskii, 'A. P. Chekhov', RGALI. F. 95. Ed. khr. 86.
66 Letter to Suvorin, 1 March 1892. Chekhov, PSSP, Letters, Vol. 5, p. 8.
67 B. K. Zaitsev, *Moi sovremenniki* (London: Esse, 1988), p. 116.
68 A. S. Suvorin, '*Malen'kie pis'ma*', *Novoe Vremia*, No. 10179 (4 June 1904), p. 2.
69 D. I. Abramovich, ed. *Pis'ma russkikh pisatelei k A. S. Suvorinu* (Leningrad: Izdanie Gosudarstvennoi Publichnoi biblioteki im. M. E. Saltykova-Shchedrina, 1927), p. 131.
70 G. G. Elizavetina, ed., *Perepiska A. P. Chekhova v dvukh tomakh* (Moscow: Khudozhestvennaia literatura, 1984) Vol. 1, p. 372.

71 See V. A. Tikhonov's letter to Chekhov of 1 February 1892. *Zapiski otdela rukopisei GBL*, issue 8 (Moscow, 1940), p. 69. See also A. I. Kuprin's letter to Chekhov of February 1902 (Moscow: *Literaturnoe nasledstvo*, 1960), p. 384.
72 A. G. Gornfel'd, *Knigi i liudi. Literaturnye besedy* (St Petersburg, 1908), pp. 281–2.
73 Merezhkovskii, '*Suvorin i Chekhov*'," op. cit., p. 290.
74 A. Volynskii, '*O simvolizme i simvolistakh (Polemicheskie zametki)*', in *Severnyi vestnik*, Nos. 10–12 (St Petersburg, 1898), p. 218.
75 A. Skabichevskii, '*Literaturnaia khronika. D. S. Merezhkovskii. O prichinakh upadka i novykh techeniiakh sovremennoi russkoi literatury.* SPb, 1893', in *Novosti i birzhevaia gazeta*, No. 69 (11 March 1893), p. 2.
76 N. Mikhailovskii, '*Russkoe otrazhenie frantsuzskogo simvolizma*', in *Russkoe bogatstvo*, No. 2, section II (1893), p. 50.
77 Zhurnalist (possibly E. A. Ganeizer), '*Zhurnal'nye zametki*', in *Saratovskii dnevnik*, No. 59 (18 March 1893), p. 2.
78 Peterburzhets (V. S. Lialin), '*Malen'kaia khronika*' in *Novoe Vremia*, No. 6036 (16 December 1892), p. 3.
79 Zhitel' (A. A. D'iakov), '*Naprasnye zhaloby*', in *Novoe Vremia*, No. 6040 (20 December 1892), p. 3.
80 V. Chuiko, '*Russkaia literatura v 1892 godu*', in *Odesskii listok*, No. 1 (1 January 1893), p. 3.
81 V. Burenin, '*Kriticheskie ocherki*', in *Novoe Vremia*, No. 6126 (19 March 1893), p. 2.
82 N. G. Molostvov, '*Borets za idealizm*', pp. 13–25. Cf his later article on Volynskii's lectures, where he says: 'Having read several public lectures, steeped in passionate spitefulness', *Russkaia kritika sovremennoi literatury*, p. 51.

6

NEGATING HIS OWN NEGATION: MEREZHKOVSKII'S UNDERSTANDING OF CHEKHOV'S ROLE IN RUSSIAN CULTURE

Anna Lisa Crone

He [Chekhov] wanted to kill Dostoevskii in us
Innokentii Annenskii

Did Merezhkovskii under-appreciate the art of Anton Chekhov? Was he, indeed, dismissive of it? The few articles and monographs that treat the personal and literary interrelations of these two contemporaries do convey this impression – whether openly or implicitly. Rosenthal in her major book writes: 'Merezhkovsky did not consider Chekhov great'.[1] Bedford mentions Chekhov's name only three times in 200 pages.[2] Chudakov's substantial 1996 article 'Merezhkovskii and Chekhov' strongly suggests a certain unfairness in this critic's evaluation of Chekhov the man and artist.[3]

Chudakov's article is probably the best contribution to the subject. It attempts to explain their differences from the fact that they represent two opposed types of fin-de-siècle Russian intellectual (as his subtitle 'Two Types of Artistic-Philosophical Consciousness' indicates). According to Chudakov, Chekhov represents an 'older' (he was only six years Merezhkovskii's senior) intelligentsia type – atheistic or agnostic, non-religious, not guided by ideology, devoted to progress, humanism, realistic, scientific, tolerant and non-doctrinaire. Merezhkovskii as his almost diametric opposite represents the new Decadent Symbolist type – committed to a Christian religious ideology, a believer, an idealist, doctrinaire and intolerant: 'Merezhkovskii was organically incapable of tolerance'.[4] Chudakov attacks Merezhkovskii, as many have done before him, for his cold, rational schematism, his way of viewing reality in terms of binary polarities – paganism versus Christianity, flesh versus spirit,

Russia versus Europe, etc. By setting up a similar binary opposition of two artistic-intellectual types, Chudakov unwittingly generates more 'differences' (13 pages in the article) than 'convergences' (three-and-a-half pages). A certain antagonism between the two figures is built into the article's very structure.

A great Chekhov scholar, Chudakov reveals much that is valuable about the philosophical divergences of these writers thus casting their long-standing and fairly close personal acquaintance in an interesting light. Chudakov's open and enthusiastic preference for the type of intellectual Chekhov represents and inability to muster much sympathy for the Merezhkovskii 'type' enables him to hurl certain unfair accusations at Merezhkovskii, such as the notion that the latter 'changed philosophical allegiances too often',[5] and causes him to republish without commentary or analysis a negative criticism of Merezhkovskii by hostile contemporaries. There is no negative treatment of Chekhov to balance off his biased critique. Though he admits that Merezhkovskii and Chekhov expressed their mutual antagonism in 'muted and gentleman-like forms, hardly exceeding elegant jokes', the pro-Chekov bias and defensiveness towards Chekhov creeps into Chudakov's article. The resulting characterization of the relationship is, in my view, more helpful to our understanding of two opposing types of intellectuals (that undoubtedly did co-exist at the fin-de-siècle), and of aspects of the writers' personal relations, than it is for understanding Merezhkovskii's actual critical writings on Chekhov. It is to the latter that the present article is dedicated.

Merezhkovskii's main critical texts touching upon Chekhov are, firstly, his debut article as a critic 'An Old Question on a New Talent' (*Staryi vopros po povodu novogo talanta*, 1888),[6] one of the foundation stones of Chekhov criticism in general; secondly, his remarks on Chekhov in *On the Causes of the Decline and on the New Trends in Contemporary Russian Literature* (*O prichinakh upadka i o novykh techeniiakh sovremennoi russkoi literatury*, 1893),[7] and thirdly his most important piece, the essay 'Chekhov and Gor´kii' (*Chekhov i Gor´kii*, 1906).[8] I disagree with Chudakov that Merezhkovskii's 1914 'Chekhov and Suvorin' is an important statement on Merezhkovskii's overall attitude towards Chekhov.[9]

There are at present vastly more Chekhov scholars than Merezhkovskii specialists, and many of the former are personally 'committed' to Chekhov and quick to defend him from detractors or hostile treatment. The few articles treating these two writers in tandem are inspired by an interest in Chekhov and his oeuvre and, like the present piece, are included in volumes devoted to Chekov studies. History has been much less kind to D. S. Merezhkovskii. Unpopular with many of his contemporaries, he was much maligned in Soviet literary criticism, partly for the strong anti-Soviet positions he consistently took when in emigration. Few have devoted their lives to Merezhkovskii studies in Russia or even in the West, a fact much lamented by Levitsky in his

1966 article on the centenary of the author's birth.[10] In the United States and Canada we have C. Harold Bedford's ground-breaking study (1975), Bernice Rosenthal's monograph on his peculiar revolutionary mentality (1981), the voluminous oeuvre of Gippius scholar Temira Pachmuss, which includes a monograph on Merezhkovskii's historical novels after 1918,[11] a slim volume on his historiography by Heinrich Stammler,[12] and articles by specialists in Russian philosophy, such as Vasilii Zen´kovskii, James Scanlan[13] and Nikolai Zernov. Most post-Soviet Russian scholarship on Merezhkovskii, some of it sympathetic to him, is in the form of introductions to various republications of his works in the 1990s and the last decade.[14] There is a relative dearth of scholarly interest in Merezhkovskii, and even of concrete knowledge about him, especially if one compares him to close contemporaries of the same intellectual 'type' such as Vasilii Rozanov, who exerted great influence upon him, and Berdiaev, who was much influenced by him.

The present author is convinced that unfamiliarity with Merezhkovskii's complex, evolving and voluminous oeuvre in general and among Chekhov scholars in particular, makes his critical pronouncements on Chekhov, which are almost always quoted out of the context in which they were written (the context of Merezhkovskii's thought), appear dismissive, hostile or even unfair. This is especially the case with his longest and most important piece 'Chekhov and Gor´kii', which is often cited in excerpts removed from the context of its overall argument. As a result this text appears the most hostile to Chekhov, when in fact it is Merezhkovskii's most serious and positive treatment of Chekhov's significance for Russian literature and cultural history.

In this article I shall focus on Merezhkovskii's critical writings on Chekhov, placing them in the context of his religious and philosophical preoccupations when he wrote 'Chekhov and Gor´kii' in 1906, in the hope that this will bring clarity to Merezhkovskii's essay and mitigate or dispel the notion that it is in strong opposition to Chekhov.

As persons and litterateurs, these men were not hostile to each other by the standards of the period. As Rosenthal points out, Merezhkovskii had a myriad of literary enemies. Chekhov indeed was one of the few who actually valued him, nominated him to the Academy of Sciences, and repeatedly referred to his high intelligence.[15] They travelled together in Italy, and visited each other though they lived in different cities. Some eleven letters of Merezhkovskii to Chekhov are extant and bespeak positive relations.[16] Quite a solitary figure (except for Gippius and their close associate, Dmitrii Filosofov), Merezhkovskii could not but have appreciated Chekhov's attitude. From his own side, admiration of Chekhov's early stories prompted Merezhkovskii to write his first important literary-critical article, a piece Chekhov greeted as 'a very sympathetic phenomenon'.

This early article is very positive, despite the fact that Merezhkovskii preferred large prose forms where character and plot receive full complex development (the novel), in Tolstoi, Dostoevskii and in himself. Here he treats very brief pieces as 'gems', retelling many of his favourites, and generalizing Chekhov's type of protagonist as the unsuccessful dreamer (*mechtatel'-neudachnik*). Chekhov found this too close to the old 'superfluous man' and longed for a fresher view of his characters.[17] Nevertheless, the failed idealist dreamer was a very sympathetic type to Merezhkovskii, who shortly thereafter was to proclaim that Chekhov inaugurated a 'new idealism'. In the early article Merezhkovskii praises Chekhov's treatment of nature as mystical and semi-religious, and points out that Chekhov's characters never solve their life's dilemmas by rationality, but on the basis of emotion, intuition, and feeling. He further remarks upon Chekhov's humane treatment of his heroes' suffering, something almost universally praised by Chekhov's critics.

This article is Chekhov-centred, written on somewhat objective principles which Merezhkovskii articulated within it. It attempts to understand Chekhov's art in terms of the author's goals.[18] This is the last of the Chekhov pieces that is 'objective' in this sense. Merezhkovskii's *On the Causes of the Decline* places Chekhov at the end of a decadent trajectory and the beginning of new directions in Russian prose. After around 1900, Merezhkovskii treats all literary compositions as manifestations of the state of the Russian national spiritual consciousness, and in terms of their effect upon the (future) development of that spiritual consciousness; that is to say, he treats all literature philosophically and metaphysically, taking great note of its aesthetic qualities, but diminishing their importance. This approach is obvious in his major work comparing Tolstoi and Dostoevskii, their biographies, their art and their respective religions.[19]

Bedford characterizes Merezhkovskii's mature criticism thus: 'in his subjective criticism [he] makes use of a writer to put forth his own ideas'.[20] He hastens to add that 'this does not prevent him from demonstrating perspicacious and penetrating insights into the object of his study [the works themselves]'.[21] Thus Bedford parries the views of those who think Merezhkovskii's neo-Christianity, the philosophy he works out between 1900–15, may somehow weaken his literary-aesthetic judgement or blunt his critical acumen, rendering his writings less valuable or obsolete.[22]

Despite his subtle, and at times not so subtle, ambivalence towards Merezhkovskii, Chudakov concedes Bedford's point vociferously as concerns his work on Tolstoi and Dostoevskii: 'his cold clarity has obscured from many the values of *Tolstoi and Dostoevskii*, one of the best works on these writers in all Russian scholarship. Merezhkovskii's mode of thought there, when submitted to close philological analysis [supposedly a more objective, modern analytical strategy, *A.L.C.*] stands up very well'. In parentheses he adds: 'I think that D. S. Merezhkovskii will remain in the history of Russian culture as a critic and a writer, as a pioneer of one of the most important categories of twentieth-century literary analysis, i.e. "the structure of the writer's artistic world"'.[23]

This admission that religiously-ideological writers can author important critical works that remain valuable for scholarship might seem superfluous in 1996 to Western scholars, and is probably directed to Soviet and post-Soviet ones. Indeed, too much great literary criticism has been authored by religious thinkers of Merezhkovskii's 'type' in the last century. One has only to recall the writings on the poetry of Vladimir Solov´ev, Leont´ev's book on Tolstoi, myriad articles by Rozanov, the articles and books of Berdiaev, Shestov, including one on Chekhov,[24] Viacheslav Ivanov, Mochul´skii and a host of others. One must steer around the religious faith of these scholars and distil what is valuable in their criticism, without embracing the underlying ideology, much as Western scholars glean what is of value in orthodox Soviet literary scholarship.

Recent Chekhov criticism focuses little on Merezhkovskii's first positive article and *On the Causes of the Decline*, where Chekhov is seen as ushering in a New Idealism, something which Merezhkovskii welcomes, or is hailed as a forerunner of Symbolism, the movement to which Merezhkovskii belonged. There is more of a tendency to quote from the 'offending' text *Chekhov and Gor´kii*, which I claim is highly positive, however paradoxically argued. A cardinal reason for the sense of offence is the fact that the essay was published together with 'The Coming Ham' (*Griadushchii Kham*), and is a sequel to the title essay of that collection.

Bedford takes great pains to explain that Hamism (*Khamstvo*) in Merezhkovskii is associated with Noah's youngest son, and says the term should be translated as 'flunkyism'. In Genesis, Ham comes upon his father sleeping naked and tells his brothers. The latter cover that nakedness without gazing upon it. When Noah learns what has transpired he curses Ham, and his descendents the Canaanites: 'Cursed be Canaan, a slave of slaves shall he be to his brothers', (Genesis 9:25). Bedford writes that in Merezhkovskii's oeuvre 'the Ham whose coming is feared is a flunky. Merezhkovsky saw the lack of freedom in a social order based on the bourgeoisie, and consequently on Hamism, which he considered to be the worst of all slaveries [...] The Coming Ham would limit personal individual freedom and Merezhkovsky, ever rebellious against any restraint whatsoever, would naturally conclude that Hamism was his [and Russian's society's] personal enemy'.[25]

It is perhaps academic for the present-day reader whether the Hamism in Merezhkovskii's title refers to the boorishness and brutishness implied by *khamstvo* in common Russian parlance, or to a concept abstracted from the traits of Noah's accursed son. However, the coming Ham is extremely negative. It is legitimate to ask why Chekhov should be discussed at greatest length in a book on such a negative subject and phenomenon. To answer this question, we must discuss the context in which the book arose.

Context: Merezhkovskii's Preoccupations in 1905–1910

'The Coming Ham', the essay and the collection of which it is the first part, is a cautionary tale directed at the Russian intelligentsia at a time when the author felt that the end of the world was near, and was concerned that the Russia's intelligentsia was ill-prepared for the Last Judgement. Despite this, in 1906 he was still hopeful that Russia could emerge from her spiritual-moral crisis. The book's sequel *Sick Russia* (*Bol'naia Rossiia*, 1910) traces historically the passivity and slavish mentality of the Russian intelligentsia from Petrine days forward, providing a detailed diagnosis of the national spiritual malaise, which has brought about the contemporary crisis in which Hamism looms on the horizon.

In the signature essay of the book *The Coming Ham*, Merezhkovskii places a stark existential choice before the intelligentsia, the class to which he himself belongs, and onto which, despite its shortcomings, he pins all his hopes for Russia's future: 'Will the Russian intelligentsia comprehend that its strength lies in [its] future Christianity?'. This is code for the 'New Religious Consciousness', and specifically for his and Gippius's brand of renewed Christianity, reinvigorated with paganism, beauty, what Rozanov called 'the fruits of the earth', a strength which can deflect the spirit of petty bourgeois positivist values (in the values of Russian *meshchanstvo*) and Hamism. Merezhkovskii continues: 'if the intelligentsia manages to grasp this, it will become the first martyr of a new world. If it does not, it will be the last warrior of a dying world, a dying gladiator'.[26]

Merezhkovskii adapts the 50-year-old arguments of John Stuart Mill and Gertsen on the causes of the decline of European culture and civilization to the contemporary problems of Russia. Those two thinkers in the mid-nineteenth century feared and decried the rise of bourgeois values and their growing dominance in Europe. It should be recalled that the arch-conservative Russian religious thinker Leont'ev had advanced essentially the same argument in his book *The Average European as the Tool of Destruction of Civilization* (*Srednii evropeets kak orudie vsemirnogo razrusheniia*).

Mill and Hertsen prophesy the ascendancy of a 'conglomerated mediocrity' (Mill's term), often designated in Russian by the word *meshchanstvo*, as we see on the first page of 'The Coming Ham', which represents the Russian petty bourgeoisie's materialist values and non-spiritual lifestyle. Merezhkovskii opens with Gertsen's words from *Endings and Beginnings*: 'Petty bourgeois values can and must triumph [...] Yes, my friend, it is time to face calmly and resignedly that *meshchanstvo* is the final form of Western civilization. Every day they take over more and more, a crowd not ignorant, but not really educated either'.[27] Mill pointed out that this 'gang' renders everything [that once had value] trite and shallow. The levelling of society is associated with 'a narrowing of the intellect, the erasure of strong individuality' (*lichnost'* in the fullest sense), exclusion of the general interests of humanity from one's life, the reduction of life to the interests of the commercial office and bourgeois creature comforts.[28] This threat is tantamount to a retreat from the Pushkinian universal-humanity (*vsechelovechestvo*) in the Russian national consciousness, to a shallowness and destruction of the spirit.

With his usual irony Merezhkovskii points out that Mill and Gertsen were afflicted with the very spiritual illness they diagnosed, and that the coming Hamism threatens all Russians at the time of writing: 'What Gertsen and Mill feared did not lie only in others, but in their very selves, in the unsurpassable nature of the limits of their religious, or rather anti-religious consciousness. The ultimate limit of all European culture is positivism'.[29]

This diverts Russia from her sacred mission as Merezhkovskii conceives it (and European culture from its mission in Gertsen's view): to adopt, and to take to a Europe mired in spiritual crisis, a new reinvigorated form of Christianity which would rekindle and revive the profound Russian spirit first, and then guarantee, foster and preserve the enrichment of both Russian and European culture in perpetuity. He focuses on a future Christian civilization and culture, a new spiritual consciousness.

In view of this mission, Merezhkovskii's dissatisfaction with the pragmatic positivist credo of Mill and the atheist, socialist philosophy of his illustrious countryman Gertsen is considerable. Pointing out that both socialism and revolution are derivative offshoots from Christianity that have ended up supplanting it as 'false religions', he asks: 'Why rather than wallow in these shallow tributaries of European Christianity did Gertsen not return to the true depths of European Christianity and plumb them before passing his sentence on Christianity and Europe as a whole?'[30] Clearly Merezhkovskii feels Gertsen rejected Christianity too easily. Merezhkovskii himself had rejected the flawed, overly ascetic Christianity of the historical Russian and Western churches, but had then delved deeply into the faith in the Godman and attempted to preserve what was vital, valuable and salvific for mankind in religion. This core is what he endeavours to retain and improve upon in his Christianity of the Third Testament. He isolates the three obstacles that are diverting Russia from her sacred mission: the present autocracy with the dead positivism of governmental bureaucracy which separates the people from the (implied true) Russian church; the historical Russian Orthodoxy of the past, which 'rendered unto Caesar what was God's', the church's enslaving of the spirit, shot through with spiritual *meshchanstvo*, a clear counterpart of governmental positivism; and the future face of Hamism rising from below, hooliganism, hoboism (*bosiachestvo*), which Gor´kii depicts so well, the Black Hundred mentality. These three faces of spiritual *meshchanstvo* are united against the forces of spiritual nobility.[31]

Given this ideological framework in part one of 'The Coming Ham', one is correct to assume that part two 'Chekhov and Gor´kii' will show whether these two writers exacerbate spiritual *meshchanstvo* or provide a way out of it, out of Russia's spiritual-moral crisis in 1906–10.

The paradoxical answer is: although they may *seem* to exacerbate it, in fact they do the opposite. This is a paradoxical argument, which, as we shall see, involves a double negation. Hence, the statements that appear negative about Chekhov turn out to be positive. We learn on the first page that Chekhov's and Gor´kii's art is what the Russian intelligentsia will take to the 'Final Judgement of history'. Here is how they are described: 'Chekhov and Gor´kii are palatable to the Russian intelligentsia. They are the intelligentsia's teachers [*vlastiteli dum*]'.[32] Chekhov and Gor´kii, who represent a decline from Russian literature's past true greatness, appear in the second paragraph to be blamed for the decline of the national spiritual consciousness: however we may judge the comparative magnitude of these two writers, 'one thing is beyond doubt, they have obscured from us the last two giants of Russian literature, L. Tolstoi and Dostoevskii. Because there is no reason to make a secret of our sin: these giants have turned out to be too great for us'.[33] This is at once an attack on the intelligentsia that cannot connect with its greatest spiritual figures as well as on Chekhov and Gor´kii, lesser writers who came in their wake and distracted us from the greats. Despite this, Merezhkovskii hangs his hopes on the Russian intelligentsia, counts himself as its member and appeals directly to that intelligentsia in all his philosophical and critical writings. Like Gertsen, he feels the Russian intelligentsia has not yet succumbed to bourgeois values (Hamism), and that is why it is Russia's and Europe's last hope.

He further defines the two: 'Chekhov and Gor´kii are expressers not so much of our national spirit, but rather of [our] class mentality, not of the national cultural milieu, as of the intelligentsia milieu, that of the Russian Middle Class'.[34]

The decline in the spiritual consciousness is emphasized dramatically. 'Through L.N. Tolstoi and Dostoevskii one can judge not the present Russian reality, but the more or less distant possibilities of the Russian spirit. One can judge not about what exists now, but what could exist, what can exist, but probably will not exist any time soon'.[35]

As in his earlier evaluations of Chekhov (1888–93) as a brilliant new talent and bringer of new idealism, here, 18 years later and two years after Chekhov's death, Merezhkovskii is even more full of praise for Chekhov's art: 'Chekhov is the legal heir of the great Russian literature. If he did not receive the whole of his legacy and only a part of it, in that part he knew how to separate the gold from the chaff. Whether one sees that gold as much or little, in Chekhov that gold is purer than in earlier writers who were greater, with the exception of Pushkin. Here the last great artist of the Russian word coincides with the first, the end of Russian literature coincides with its beginning, Chekhov with Pushkin'.[36] Rosenthal's comment that Merezhkovskii did not consider Chekhov 'great', is here flatly refuted – his use of the comparative '*bolee velikikh pisatelei*' in itself qualifies Chekhov as great, as does the expression '*poslednii velikii*', 'the last great [Russian writer]'.

Nothing very laudatory is said about Gor´kii as a master of the Russian word. His value in this essay does not lie in aesthetics at all. Yet, as we have emphasized, the mature critic Merezhkovskii (after 1900) evaluates all writers and verbal art by metaphysical criteria, i.e. 1) as it represents a particular stage in the development of the Russian spiritual consciousness, and, even more importantly, 2) its net effect on the future state of that spiritual consciousness. Is it a factor in the strengthening or betterment of that consciousness, or in its stagnation or future further decline (into so-called Hamism)? What, in effect, is the metaphysical role of the avowed 'non-metaphysician' Chekhov? Whereas Merezhkovskii had spoken of a certain irrationality and even mysticism in Chekhov in 1888, the writer's metaphysical role is finally fleshed out in 'Chekhov and Gor´kii' 18 years later. On its second page he introduces the main idea of this article: 'Their [Chekhov's and Gor´kii's] authentic creativity was directed towards showing the impossibility of that faith [faith in atheistic humanism, the religion of man alone] and the state of the soul of people who had lost the possibility of true religious faith'.[37] This is their role – their double negation. While seeming to negate a Dostoevskian faith, even consciously negating it, in their very art ('*podlinnoe tvorchestvo*') they negate their own anti-religious message, negate their own negation.

In Merezhkovskii's very Hegelian mode of triadic thought, every development proceeds as thesis–antithesis–synthesis, a higher synthesis in which the original opposition is preserved but its antagonism is overcome at a higher level, what in German is known as '*Aufhebung*'. For Solov´ev, whose Hegelian dialectic both inspired and informed Merezhkovskii's, the metaphysical importance of the negation was never underestimated as it sharpened the opposition and was a catalyst to its resolution in a higher synthesis. Since Chekhov stands in negation to Dostoevskii, comments about the representatives of the negative phase of the dialectic may appear or sound deprecatory, but their role is absolutely essential.

Chekhov's apparent rejection of historical Russian Orthodoxy was, as we pointed out, shared and understood by Merezhkovskii. Chekhov's negation of Dostoevskii was such that it, inadvertently perhaps, revealed its own pointlessness and thus pushed man back towards theism.

This dialectic is spelled out in Merezhkovskii's paradoxical formulae: 'Anti-Christianity is the religion of the Mangod (*chelovekobog*); only Man exists and there is no God. [The negation of theism] God equals nothing and hence "Man is God" means "Man equals nothing". The seeming apotheosis of man leads to the actual destruction of man as man'.[38] It is interesting to note that this is the diametric opposite of the formula one would derive from Derzhavin's famous and theistic ode 'God' (*Bog*, 1780–84), where 'Man is Nothing', while 'God is Everything'. Yet, the poet writes 'And I before you am nothing. Nothing! But you in me shine with the greatness of your goods'.[39] Hence, 'Man is not Nothing', i.e. 'Man is something'.

Merezhkovskii's formula of negation is shown by the critic to be inherit everywhere in Chekhov's and Gor'kii's works. Many examples from Chekhov's protagonists and Gor'kii's hoboes are cited in the essay. Ultimately, they re-illustrate Dostoevskii's argument that the logic of mangodhood (*chelovekobozhestvo*) is a dead end. Merezhkovskii sees both authors as carrying on a major exposé of all the holes in the current intelligentsia religion of man. Assaulting Dostoevskii's logic, they reveal the futility of their own.

Merezhkovskii does accuse Chekhov of never really facing intellectually the dilemmas posed by the problem of religious faith, of dismissing faith facilely like Gertsen: 'There was a moment in Chekhov's life when he met Christ face-to-face and could have gone with Christ, but something frightened Chekhov, repelled him. Could it not have been Russian religion's [the Church's] association with the reaction and the suspicion that Christianity would always entail a denial of human freedom and human reason?'[40] He counter-poses two passages in Chekhov, one where a character fully embraces Christ, and another from a letter to Diagilev where Chekhov says 'I lost my faith long ago and gaze with perplexity at any intellectual believer'. Merezhkovskii rebukes Chekhov for not struggling intellectually with the contradiction these passages pose: 'Chekhov said a final "yes" and a final "no" to Christianity in the same rash and facile manner'.[41] Merezhkovskii had always placed much importance on Chekhov's silences, on the unsaid in Chekhov, and on his not knowing, his halting at the limits of reason: 'Chekhov did not only fail to extricate himself from this contradiction, he did not go into it with his full consciousness as he should have done and passed on by'.[42]

Chekhov as thinker is accused of an intellectual passivity, of a not knowing and not wanting to know. He only tried to cope with death, not with the deeper essences of life. Nevertheless in his art Merezhkovskii sees Chekhov everywhere, proving that the anti-faith position is not a philosophy that can sustain meaningful life. Merezhkovskii shows Chekhov's religion of man exposed as bankrupt by Chekhov himself: '[In Chekhov there is] a certain metaphysical boredom, a sense of the meaninglessness of everything, a feeling of endless emptiness, of not being needed'. To read Chekhov strikes existential fear in the reader: 'Chekhov's simplicity is so great that it is sometimes frightening, as if one more step on the path and there will be mere emptiness, non-being; it is so simple, as if there is nothing, and one has to stare into it very hard to discern in that almost nothing–everything'.[43]

One of Merezhkovskii's striking examples of this fear is the character who says: 'I, my dear, don't understand life and I fear it... when I lie in the grass and look at an insect for a long time, an insect that was born only yesterday and does not understand that its life is full of terrors, I see myself in that insect... Everything frightens me. I am afraid because I do not understand what all this is for and who needs it'.[44] In the same vein the critic repeatedly turns to the deathbed confession of the professor in 'A Boring Story' (*Skuchnaia istoriia*) who devoted his life to believing in science and reason, and yet cannot face death with any equanimity. He, when asked by the young Katia how to live, cannot offer her his own philosophy, and displays, Chekhov implies, only an intellectual inertia: 'In my passion for science and self-knowledge in all my thoughts, feelings, conceptions [...] there is no common thread which would bind it all as a whole. Each of my thoughts and feelings stands isolated on its own. In them all the most talented analyst will not find what is called a general idea or the god of a living man. And when this is absent there is nothing. I am defeated'.[45]

This is almost a verbatim repeat of the definition of integral personality by Slavophile Ivan Kireevskii. In his philosophical 'Fragments' we read:

> The consciousness of the relation of the living Divine personality to the human personality is the basis for faith, or more correctly, faith is that very consciousness, more or less clear, more or less unmediated. It does not comprise purely human knowledge [...] but embraces all the wholeness of the man and manifests itself only in those moments when that wholeness is achieved [...] For that reason the main character of believing thought lies in its striving to collect all the disparate parts of the soul into one force, to find that inner concentration of being where reason and will, and feeling, and conscience, and the beautiful, and the true and the marvellous, the desired, and the just, and the merciful, and the whole volume of the mind unite in a living unity and in this way the substantial personality of man is reinstated in its primordial indivisibility.[46]

Elsewhere Kireevskii writes: 'Theological studies are not necessary for everyone [...] but for everyone it is necessary to link the direction of his life with his root convictions of faith, to harmonize with them his main activity and each specific act, so that each act would be the expression of one effort, so that each thought sought one basis, that each step would lead to one goal. Without that the life of a man would have no meaning'.[47] It is patently obvious that what Kireevskii is describing, is what Chekhov's professor lacks. The dying outcry of such a man has much in common with the pre-death anguish of Ivan Il'ich, of the newly married Levin when he contemplates suicide, and, for Merezhkovskii, for Tolstoi himself in his fear of death. All of them call out in the words of Chekhov's hero: 'Oh, if only I could muster some mysticism, just a small piece of some sort of faith!'[48] He observes the same anguish in Chebutykin in *The Three Sisters* who proclaims: 'We don't exist, there is nothing in the world, it just seems we exist. And what does it matter anyway?'[49] The hollowness of Chekhovian characters' non-consoling projections of an earthly paradise in 300 years' time is equated by Merezhkovskii to the similarly unconvincing 'To Moscow, to Moscow!' of the sisters, uttered when they know they will never leave their family estate.

Overall Evaluation of Chekhov's Art

It is indeed paradoxical for Merezhkovskii to draw a metaphysical message from Chekhov, of which the author may well have been unconsciously, or only fleetingly and peripherally aware. But for Merezhkovskii it is an all-important demonstration of the futility of the atheist worldview, and may be the catalyst that pushes the intelligentsia back into a search for the true God. What Chekhov has done is of great value to Russians: 'Chekhov and Gor′kii truly were "prophets", although not of what the intelligentsia thought they were prophesying, or even what they themselves thought they espoused. They were "prophets" because they bless what they wish to curse and curse that which they wanted to bless [atheistic humanism]. Wanting to show that man without God is God himself, they showed that such a man is a beast, no worse than a beast – cattle, worse than cattle, a corpse – worse than a corpse, nothing'.[50]

Merezhkovskii's final assessment of Chekhov's (and Gor′kii's) negation of his own negation of Dostoevskian theistic religion is unequivocally positive:

> But if they did not teach us what they wished to teach, they did teach us something they did not wish to reveal and this is all for the better. The love by which we love Chekhov and Gor′kii is a sincere love; the crown

we place on their heads is an authentic crown. We love them because they suffer for us; we crown them because they perish for us. But we should remember that these are not the crowns of triumphant heroes, but of redeeming sacrifices, and if the knife raised above these martyrs should be lowered, it will not only smite them, but will smite us all. Let us consider how we can stop that knife.[51]

The Russian intelligentsia will 'plunge a knife into Chekhov' by reading only his conscious superficial message and failing to read into the degree to which it is constantly negated within the oeuvre itself.

From our present-day point of view it may seem wrongheaded to evaluate Chekhov in terms (Christian religious terms) that were certainly not his own. But Chekhov was writing in a very ideological age and the leftist, non-religious, progressive intelligentsia had its own bone to pick with Chekhov. Hence, leading Populist critic Mikhailovskii in his article '*Ob ottsakh i detiakh i o g-ne Chekhove*' ('On the Fathers and Sons and Mr Chekhov') is considerably more judgmental of and patronizing towards Chekhov than Merezhkovskii: 'If Chekhov cannot decisively embrace the common ideas of his fathers and forefathers as his own, and will not work out a general idea of his own – something he should work on – then let him at least wax poetic about a general idea and the tormenting need for such an idea. If he does this his life will not pass in vain and he will leave his mark in literature'.[52] Compared with such a dressing-down for a lack of ideological engagement (the old social mandate, *sotsial'nyi zakaz*, of civic criticism), the religious ideologue Merezhkovskii shows far more forbearance: rather than telling Chekhov what he should do in his art, he discovers and reveals to the intelligentsia the positive aspects of what Chekhov has actually done.

It is immaterial whether or not the present-day reader or critic agrees with Mikhailovskii's impatience with Chekhov's ideological non-engagement, or with Merezhkovskii's understanding of Chekhov's importance and role in Russia's cultural mission. Far removed from the social and spiritual problems of Russia in the Silver Age and unlikely to hold a religious worldview, he probably accepts neither of these positions. What is important in the present study is to understand what Merezhkovskii's rather complex view of Chekhov meant, and that Chekhov's contribution was highly positive to him. Chekhov clearly emerges in this text as a Christian martyr, a Christ-sacrifice, something like the righteous Jew Nicodemus in the Bible, who was almost Christian, tending to be Christian before Christianity. In 1906, Merezhkovskii still thought Chekhov's art might help push the intelligentsia back towards faith and prevent 'the coming Hamism'.

Notes

1 Bernice Rosenthal, *D. S. Merezhkovsky and the Silver Age* (The Hague: Martinus Nijhoff, 1981).
2 Harold C. Bedford, *The Seeker: D. S. Merezhkovski* (Lawrence, Kansas: University of Kansas Press, 1975), pp. 41–2, 57.
3 Aleksandr Chudakov, '*Chekhov i Merezhkovskii: Dva tipa khudozhestvenno-filosofskogo soznaniia*', in *Chekoviana: Chekhov i 'serebrianyi vek'*, ed. M. O. Goriacheva and others (Moscow: Nauka, l996) pp. 50–67.
4 Ibid., pp. 56–7.
5 The criticism that Merezhkovskii disliked the character Likharev because he sensed a type of 'intellectual promiscuity' in himself, that he would in future 'change allegiances' too many times, is not convincing with reference to the 22-year-old Merezhkovskii who authored this article. Nor is there anything very reprehensible in changing allegiances in Merezhkovskii's opinion at that time. This is an argument after the fact by Chudakov, who apparently disapproves of the '*smena vekh*' (change of spiritual orientation) that characterized a large number of the leading thinkers of the Silver Age (Sergei Bulgakov, Berdiaev, etc).
6 D. S. Merezhkovskii, '*Staryi vopros po povodu novogo talanta*', in *Severnyi vestnik* (November 1888), pp. 77–98.
7 D. S. Merezhkovskii, '*O prichinakh upadka i o novykh techeniiakh sovremennoi russkoi literatury*', in *Polnoe sobranie sochinenii* (Moscow and St Petersburg, 1893).
8 D. S. Merezhkovskii, '*Chekhov i Gor'kii*', in *Griadushchii kham* (St Petersburg: Izdatel'stvo Pirozhkova, 1903), pp. 43–101.
9 Merezhkovskii, 'Chekhov i Suvorin', in *Akropol': Izbrannye literaturno-kriticheskie stat'i* (Moscow: *Knizhnaia palata*, 1991).
10 Sergei Levitzsky, 'An Unnoticed Anniversary: On Merezhkovsky's Role in Russian Culture', in *Russian Review*, No. 2 (1968).
11 Temira Pachmuss, *D. S. Merezhkovsky in Exile* (New York: Peter Lang, l990).
12 Heinrich Stammler, 'Russian Metapolitics. Merezhkovsky's Understanding of the Historical Process' (Berkeley, California: California Slavic Studies, 1976), vol. 9, pp. 123–38.
13 James Scanlan, 'The New Russian Religious Consciousness, in *Canadian Slavonic Studies*, Vol.4 (1971), No.1.
14 S. N. Savel'ev, '*Predislovie*', pp. 3–11, and '*Posleslovie*', pp. 238–68, in D. S. Merezhkovskii, *Bol'naia Rossiia* (Leningrad: Izdatel'stvo leningradskogo universiteta, 1990). A. N. Lavrov, '*Istoriia kak misteriia*', (St Petersburg: Izdatel'stvo Ivana Limbakha, 1991), pp. 5–27.
15 See Rosenthal and Chudakov, op. cit.
16 Bedford, op. cit., pp. 92.
17 Merezhkovskii, '*Staryi vopros po povodu novogo talanta*', op. cit.
18 Chudakov, op. cit., p. 56.
19 Bedford, op. cit., p. 126.
20 Ibid., p. 92.
21 Ibid.
22 Bedford, op. cit., p. 20.
23 Chudakov, op. cit., p. 57.
24 Lev Shestov, '*Tvorchestvo iz nichego*', in *Nachala i kontsy* (St Petersburg: Stasiulevich, 1908).

25 Bedford, op. cit., p. 126.
26 Merezhkovskii, '*Griadushchii Kham*', op. cit., pp. 20, 24.
27 Ibid., p. 4.
28 Ibid., p. 14.
29 Ibid., p. 6.
30 Ibid., p. 15.
31 Ibid., pp. 37–8.
32 Merezhkovskii, '*Chekhov i Gor'kii*', op. cit., p. 43.
33 Ibid.
34 Ibid., pp. 43–4.
35 Ibid., p. 43.
36 Ibid., p. 47.
37 Ibid.
38 Ibid., p. 66.
39 G.P. Derzhavin, 'Bog', in *Stikhotvoreniia* (Moscow: *Gosudarstvennoe Izdatel'stvo khudozhestvennoi literatury*, 1958), pp. 32–5.
40 Merezhkovskii, '*Chekhov i Gor'kii*', op. cit., pp. 82–3.
41 Ibid., p. 82.
42 Ibid., p. 82.
43 Ibid., p. 47.
44 Ibid, pp. 85–6, the quotation is from Chekhov's story '*Strakh*' ('Terror').
45 Ibid., p. 92.
46 I. V. Kireevskii, 'Otryvki', in *Polnoe sobranie sochinenii v dvukh tomakh* (Moscow, 1911), vol. 1, pp. 274–5.
47 Ibid., p. 276.
48 Merezhkovskii, '*Chekhov i Gor'kii*', op. cit., p. 92.
49 Ibid.
50 Ibid.
51 Ibid., p. 101.
52 N. K. Mikhailovskii, '*Ob ottsakh i detiakh i o g-ne Chekhove*', in *A. P. Chekhov: Pro et Contra. Tvorchestvo A. P. Chekhova v russkoi mysli kontsa XIX – nachala XX v. (1887–1914). Antologiia*, ed. I. N. Sukhih, A. D. Stepanov (St Petersburg: *Izdatel'stvo Russkogo Khristianskogo gumanitarnogo Instituta*, 2002), p. 86.

7

AN ILLUMINATING MISINTERPRETATION? ON MEREZHKOVSKII'S LITERARY CRITICISM OF CHEKHOV

Karoline Thaidigsmann

I. The Literary Critic Mirrored by His Subject

It is one of the well known premises of hermeneutics that interpreting a piece of art not only illuminates the subject of interpretation, but also sheds light on its interpreter. In regard to A. P. Chekhov, this phenomenon is often so strongly pronounced that, given Russian literary criticism at the turn of the nineteenth century, A. D. Stepanov even declares Chekhov's work to be a 'mirror of literary criticism'.[1] Stepanov's observation also proves appropriate for the present collection of essays. The volume shows Chekhov through the eyes of Russian thinkers and portrays these Russian thinkers through the mirror of their literary criticism. A special place in these reflections of Chekhov is held by Dmitrii Merezhkovskii, who in his essays repeatedly discussed Chekhov and his literary work between 1888 and 1914,[2] and whose opinion on Chekhov changed profoundly through this period. The shifting of Merezhkovskii's judgement on Chekhov, – from his early appreciation of Chekhov's literary talent to his later polemics against Chekhov's alleged religious nihilism, do not depend so much on a development of Chekhov's art. From early on, Chekov's literary work shows a relatively constant philosophy of life and poetics.[3] Merezhkovskii's literary criticism of Chekhov should rather be seen as a mirror that reflects Merezhkovskii's own spiritual development.[4] Nevertheless, his criticism remains open to both sides, illuminating the subject of criticism as well as the critic – even where Merezhkovskii obviously misinterprets Chekhov.

Unlike in his early essay 'An Old Question on New Talent' ('*Staryi vopros po povodu novogo talanta*', 1888) and his lecture 'On the Reasons for the

Decline and the New Tendencies of Contemporary Russian Literature' ('*O prichinakh upadka i o novykh techeniiakh sovremennoi russkoi literatury*', 1893), which contributed to a more profound understanding of Chekhov's art by rejecting the positivistic literary criticism of the time, in Merezhkovskii's later criticism, especially in his essay 'Chekhov and Gor′kii' ('*Chekhov i Gor′kii*', 1906), such an immediate and direct contribution to the understanding of Chekhov's art can no longer be found. This later criticism, expressed after Chekhov's death, rather indirectly provides insights into Chekhov's art by the way Merezhkovskii polemicises against Chekhov and by the way he tries to assign to him certain ideological positions.

II. From Poetic to Religiously-Motivated Criticism

The difference between Merezhkovskii's early views of Chekhov and his later opinion is largely determined by his change of perspective regarding Chekhov. If Merezhkovskii's early criticism was mainly determined by his striving for a new art which found its realization in Symbolism, his later Chekhov criticism arises in the context of his striving for a new foundation and reawakening of Christianity. Merezhkovskii's literary works and literary criticism were increasingly subordinated to this religious demand by the end of the 1890s.[5] These two differing perspectives are connected in their sensitivity for a reality that transcends empirical reality. Nevertheless these perspectives lead Merezhkovskii to diverging approaches towards his subject.

In his lecture 'On the Reasons for the Decline and the New Tendencies of Contemporary Russian Literature', an early manifestation of Russian Symbolism, Merezhkovskii formulates his ideal of a subjective literary criticism (*metod sub′ektivno-khudozhestvennyi*).[6] Subjective literary criticism, for Merezhkovskii, requires the sensitivity of a poet. Only in this way can the critic grasp the artistic level of a literary work: 'The poet–critic reflects not the beauty of real objects, but the beauty of poetic images which reflected these objects.'[7] With his concept of the subjective literary critic, Merezhkovskii turns against positivistic literary criticism that evaluates the world as depicted by literature, regardless of its mode of representation, solely judging it according to utility and morality. This positivistic view of literature also dominated the contemporary literary criticism of Chekhov in Russia. What the positivistic critics condemned as a lack of tendency in Chekhov's literary work, Merezhkovskii positively interpreted as a harbinger of Symbolism, the experience of an indefinite and indefinably mystical dimension of reality which the reader could sense through Chekhov's use of impressionistic techniques of representation. Even if Merezhkovskii in his early Chekhov criticism overemphasizes the elements tending towards Symbolism, he does not only draw attention to Chekhov's central narrative devices.[8] First and foremost he points out that Chekhov's literary works can only be understood in their connection of content *and* form.

In his Chekhov criticism after 1900, Merezhkovskii the poet–critic steps behind Merezhkovskii the religious thinker. Now Merezhkovskii's criticism brings to the fore his own, Christian understanding of reality. This change of perspective is accompanied by an abandoning of Merezhkovskii's proclaimed ideal of subjective literary criticism. In 'Chekhov and Gor'kii', Merezhkovskii explicitly separates the critique of literary form from that of content.[9] Merezhkovskii still appreciates the quality of Chekhov's literary technique.[10] However, his main interest now lies in an ideological evaluation of the world depicted by Chekhov without paying attention to the form of its literary representation. By separating content and form, and by strongly identifying the author with his literary figures, Merezhkovskii gets caught in the trap he himself had warned of previously: the danger of considering and judging the artistic representation of reality beyond its aesthetic conditions.

At least some influence on Merezhkovskii's changing interpretation of Chekhov must be ascribed to his wife Zinaida Gippius. Though acknowledging Chekhov's literary talent, she deeply rejected his work for its alleged lack of spirituality and negation of life.[11] Gippius attacked Chekhov much more fiercely than her husband. Although some of Gippius' harsh rhetoric can also be found in Merezhkovskii, his critiques, despite their polemics, always express a certain respect for Chekhov.[12]

III. Indirect Illumination of Chekhov's Poetic Philosophy in 'Chekhov and Gor'kii'

The fact that Merezhkovskii's post-1900 Chekhov criticism does not merely concern literature becomes obvious in a significant change of rhetoric. The language Merezhkovskii uses from that time on is full of religious pathos, as can be seen in the first paragraph of the essay 'Chekhov and Gor'kii'.

> If now, when the Last Judgement of history calls Russia, the Russian intelligentsia would like to know what accompanies it to this judgement, then the best way to answer this would be with the works of Chekhov and Gor'kii [...]. They are its spiritual leaders [...] the 'masters of the thoughts' of the present generation of the Russian intelligentsia.[13]

The essay was written under the influence of the Revolution of 1905, an event which Merezhkovskii saw as a sign foreshadowing the coming of the kingdom of God.[14]

For Merezhkovskii, Chekhov and Gor'kii were not only quite subtle analysts of the spiritual crisis of the contemporary Russian intelligentsia. More than that, he considered them 'teachers' and 'prophets' of the rejection of God.[15] Gor'kii and Chekhov, according to Merezhkovskii, deprived man of any relation to God, and of all questions concerning the existence of God, by preaching the religion of mangodhood (*religiia chelovekobozhestva*)[16] on the grounds of a 'dogmatic positivism'.[17] However, this dogmatic positivism cannot ultimately answer the questions of the aim and meaning of life, and thus leaves man facing nothingness. For Merezhkovskii the only possible way to escape this terrifying state is faith in the Christian God.

Merezhkovskii's thesis of Chekhov's religious nihilism does not provide closer insight into Chekhov by being particularly convincing. On the contrary, Merezhkovskii's argument contributes to an understanding of Chekhov because it lacks such a convincing force. In reading Merezhkovskii's criticism of Chekhov, it becomes obvious that Chekhov and his literary work resist the attempt to pin him down to any ideological position. Exactly this resistance is characteristic for Chekhov's poetic philosophy. Unintended by Merezhkovskii, Chekhov's poetic philosophy proves its strength in the face of Merezhkovskii's argument. Moreover, in opposition to Merezhkovskii's declaring Chekhov a religious nihilist, Chekhov is revealed as an author with a specific sensibility for spiritual and religious questions.[18]

The Cognition of God and Mathematical Evidence

Merezhkovskii's Chekhov criticism is based on an analysis of Chekhov's literary works, as well as his correspondence and personal statements. In a letter Chekhov wrote to *The World of Art* editor S. P. Diagilev in 1902, Merezhkovskii finds proof of Chekhov's religious nihilism. In this letter, Chekhov states the distancing of the Russian intelligentsia from religion. While not commenting on this development, he criticizes the new religious movement within the Russian intelligentsia, which according to Chekhov considered religion a mere game and part of a declining culture. Chekhov envisions the future in a different way:

> Present-day culture is the start of the work in the name of the great future, the work which will go on, perhaps, for tens of thousands of years in order that humanity, even in the distant future, recognized the truth of the real God, that is, did not try to find Him by conjecture, did not search for Him in Dostoevskii, but knew him, in the same way it knows that two times two is four.[19]

It was on Merezhkovskii's initiative that the Religious–Philosophical Meetings Society[20] was established in St Petersburg in 1901 as part of the new religious movement among Russian intellectuals. Chekhov's criticism of this movement therefore affected Merezhkovskii in a direct and personal way. This might have contributed to his reaction to Chekhov's letter.[21] For Merezhkovskii, the demand for mathematical evidence of God's truth shows Chekhov's rationalism at its extreme, for particularly the cognition of God cannot be captured in such a rationalistic manner. Otherwise, God's divinity would not reach beyond man's reality.

When Chekhov contrasts a process of recognizing God's truth that equals basic mathematics with the searching for God 'in Dostoevskii', naming F. M. Dostoevskii, he intentionally refers to a central figure of identification for the new religious movement, who was particularly admired as a prophetic writer by Merezhkovskii and his wife.[22] The formula 'two times two is four', which Chekhov uses for his argument, is taken from Dostoevskiis *Notes from Underground* (*Zapiski iz podpol'ia*, 1864), where it stands for a rationally determined world order, which Dostoevskii's underground man opposes and in which he tries to preserve his autonomy.[23] Merezhkovskii brings the two alternatives expressed by Chekhov to the opposition of 'inner religious experience'[24], which, according to him, is rejected by Chekhov, or 'clear mathematical evidence'.[25] However taking a closer look at Chekhov's letter, it becomes obvious that it is not Chekhov's intention to deny inner religious experience. When Chekhov disapproves of a search for God 'in Dostoevskii', he opposes the individual's attempt to compensate for the lack of his or her own spiritual experience, by adopting the experience of someone else to whom had been ascribed prophetic authority. In the individual's wish to hand over his or her own uncertain search for a meaning and explanation of life to someone else, Chekhov perceives the danger of dogmatism and a loss of the individual's autonomy: 'If one has no faith, one should not try to replace it with much noise, but search, search, search alone, one on one with your conscience'.[26] Chekhov's demand for a path to God's truth which is as clear and easily accessible for every single human being as the basics of arithmetic, must be understood as merging from his concern for the autonomous individual. Thus Chekhov's cultural work does not entail a naïve belief in endless human progress based on positivistic optimism, but the hope of a society of responsible subjects.

Merezhkovskii's religious search was considerably guided by an opposition to the dogmatism of the church. This dogmatism, according to Merezhkovskii, had too often in Russian history lead to a merging of 'religion and reaction'.[27] From this historical perspective Merezhkovskii well understands Chekhov's concern for the autonomy of the individual. But Chekhov's sensibility for the issue reaches beyond this context. Chekhov perceives the dangers of dogmatism and of a loss of autonomy principally as coming from man's search for a meaning of his existence. Chekhov also detects this danger, as shown above by his reference to the prophetic status of Dostoevskii, in the new religious movement.²⁸ Thus Chekhov's letter reveals a critical look at the theoretically antidogmatic pretension of the new religious movement.

When Merezhhkovskii, based on Chekhov's statement in the letter to Diagilev, is enraged by the depiction of a God who has 'nothing else to say than "two times two is four" ',²⁹ whose truth thus does not extend beyond the 'banality' of rationalism and scientific knowledge, he draws a conclusion about the content of God's truth from the very process of gaining this knowledge.³⁰ By noting Merezhkovskii's inadmissible conclusion, the reader of 'Chekhov and Gor´kii' recognizes Chekhov's specific handling of religious questions: Chekhov is interested in the way that people deal with these questions. When it comes to content however, he abstains from giving definite answers or advice.

To do Merezhkovskii's criticism justice, one must not depict it exclusively as an oversimplified reduction of Chekhov from which one can gain insight into Chekhov's poetic philosophy only *ex negativo*. In some respects Merezhkovskii's criticism in 'Chekhov and Gor´kii' takes on a form where the understanding and misunderstanding of Chekhov's art coincide.

The Fragility of the Positivistic Worldview

Whereas Chekhov demands the clarity and distinctiveness of mathematical evidence concerning a possible cognition of God's truth, he remains however vague regarding not only the content of such cognition but also the time of its realization: 'maybe it still takes some ten thousand years'.³¹ Merezhkovskii notes such vague formulations, pointing to a bright but remote future as one of the leitmotifs in Chekhov's literary work.

> 'In two ... three hundred years, in a thousand years maybe – the point is not about When – a new, happy life will dawn...' [...]. This is the sacred proclamation, the new 'faith' which almost all of those Chekhov's heroes, whom he loves, repeat; he himself repeats that too [...]. It seems that one could rest with this peacefully. All is clear, all is simple, no doubts and no mysteries are left. 'In two, three hundred years' a golden age will come to Earth, but meanwhile one has to wait and hope, and walk towards this rising sun of progress. One could think that. However, Chekhov not only doesn't rest with that, but his tragedy only starts at this point: it is here where his most irresolvable doubts and most insoluble riddles begin. This is where an outer, imaginary Chekhov, all-understanding and understood by all, ends – and another Chekhov comes to the forefront: authentic, 'underground', understanding nothing and understood by no-one.³²

Merezhkovskii clearly sees the contradiction within the given time specifications: they seem to be concrete and measurable in human proportions. But as a matter of fact, the seemingly concrete becomes transparent to the indefinable. Thus the positivistic belief in human progress is virtually undercut by Chekhov, who as Merezhkovskii puts it thereby comes to the end of his capability of understanding and being understood. Even though pronounced polemically Merezhkovskii's judgment quite accurately captures the meaning and effect of Chekhov's writing, as intended by Chekhov himself. As Chekhov stated repeatedly, he saw his literary task not in overcoming doubts and questions concerning the meaning of life.[33] Rather he wanted to point out that these matters lie beyond simple understanding and therefore do not have simple explanations. Although Merezhkovskii recognizes the limits of a positivistic worldview in Chekhov's literary work, he nevertheless fails to achieve an adequate understanding of Chekhov by missing the author's intention in depicting these limits. Merezhkovskii accuses Chekhov of deceiving his protagonists and his readers regarding the limits of positivism and therefore the actual uncertainty of human existence by presenting the vague hope of a bright but virtually unreachable future.[34] Merezhkovskii's criticism of this point might be read positively, as a warning against oversimplifying the reception of Chekhov's literary work. Such an oversimplification fails to recognize the fragility and the limits of the positivistic worldview depicted therein, and thus naïvely hopes for human progress in the future while remaining (passive) in the present.[35]

Merezhkovskii considers the vague hopes of a bright future in Chekhov's work as illusion and deception. Thereby he does not recognize that in these indistinct anticipations of a different state of existence a sensitivity of the individual reveals itself, which transcends rationalism. This sensitivity can also be found in the relations of some of Chekhov's protagonists towards nature. Regarding the protagonists' hopes for the future as well as their relations towards nature, Chekhov opens up the seemingly graspable experience of the world to the anticipation of something indefinable, which possibly extends beyond empirical reality. Chekhov does this without succumbing to mystical speculation. One does not have to interpret this sensitivity as the seed of a spiritual rebirth of Chekhov's protagonists, a conclusion that led S. N. Bulgakov to proclaim Chekhov a Christian writer.[36] But by depicting such sensitivity in some of his protagonists, Chekhov evokes an awareness of the dimensions of reality which cannot be captured by rationality, nor can be taken as pure illusion.[37] It was Merezhkovskii who with regard to the perception of nature, pointed out this sensitivity in his early critiques as a special feature of Chekhov's poetic world. Now, in Merezhkovskii's later criticism, it becomes evident how deeply disturbing such an undefined openness is for Merezhkovskii.

The uncertainty of human existence, which becomes visible through the veil of rationalism, for Merezhkovskii can only be overcome in Christian faith. This becomes particularly obvious when he examines Chekhov's literary representation of death.

Existential Uncertainty in the Face of Death

If man cannot come to terms with life entirely by means of rationality and scientific progress, and if he lacks the feeling of security which the believer experiences in religious faith, life becomes frightening and terrifying. Chekhov's protagonists have to experience these feelings in the face of death, when, as Merezhkovskii puts it, the 'veil'[38] of positivistic optimism is ripped, and man is left helpless confronting nothingness: 'Life is terrifying because it is incomprehensible; even more terrifying, because it is even more incomprehensible, is death'.[39] In analyzing the existential situation of man deprived of religious faith, Merezhkovskii and Chekhov show a similar sensitivity. The consequences they draw from their analysis however differ fundamentally. For Merezhkovskii, existential uncertainty and anxiety in the face of death demand a decision in favour of God and the Christian hope of resurrection.[40] Chekhov on the other hand exposes his protagonists to this uncertainty without showing a way out. Merezhkovskii considers the lack of an alternative in Chekhov's stories equivalent to a rejection of the possibility of such an alternative:

> Chekhov first answered it [the question of immortality] with a decision and irrevocable *no*, placing the thought of death as destruction as the central point of the spiritual tragedy of all his heroes.[41]

When Andrei Evymich Ragin, the physician of Chekhov's story 'Ward Number Six' ('*Palata No. 6*', 1892) is asked whether he believes in the immortality of the soul, he answers with a plain 'no', not even changing this answer in the moment before his death.[42] Merezhkovskii is enraged not only by the lack of an alternative to irrevocable death in Chekhov's story. He particularly opposes Ragin's conscious rejection of such an alternative, a position Merezhkovskii inadmissibly identifies with the position of the author Chekhov.

> Death is death not because there is no immortality, but because 'we do not want immortality', we do not need it, or more likely we *need nothing*. And there is no immortality, not because the unbeliever does not believe in immortality; but because there is no immortality for him; he does not believe in it, he does not want it, and even if he knew that it existed,

he would still reject it [...]. This is precisely what a true death is, not only physical death, but also spiritual, eternal death [...] from which there is no resurrection.⁴³

Quite clear-sighted Merezhkovskii perceives the problem of Ragin in his conviction that it lies in his power to decide in favour of or against immortality. However, Merezhkovskii does not realize that Chekhov himself is interested in exactly this problem. Chekhov's depiction of Ragin shows that Ragin's choice does not answer the question whether immortality exists or not. Chekhov's story is not about answering this question, rather it is about revealing man's limits to decide over it. Even if the *power of the belief* in immortality depends on the acceptance of this belief by the human individual, the *reality* of immortality, assuming immortality does exist, cannot be dependent on the needs and decisions of man. Precisely such an understanding of religion, however – solely defined by human needs, reveals itself in Merezhkovskii's above quoted critique of 'Ward No. Six', where Merezhkovskii shows the reality of immortality as being dependent on its acceptance by man.

* * *

Where Merezhkovskii looks for closure of the existential uncertainty of man, Chekhov instead is interested in depicting the situation of man in this existential uncertainty and in man's struggle to deal with this. Merezhkovskii perceives writers as teachers and prophets.⁴⁴ His polemics against what he perceives to be Chekhov's nihilistic doctrine is determined by this perspective as well. Even though Merezhkovskii calls Chekhov a teacher and a prophet in this negative sense, he actually intends to deny Chekhov the position of a real prophetical writer.⁴⁵ However, Merezhkovskii thereby unintentionally brings to the fore Chekhov's concept of himself as a writer. For as a writer Chekhov explicitly rejected any prophetic pretension. Seen this way, Merezhkovsii's misinterpretation serves Chekhov and the understanding of his poetic philosophy quite well.⁴⁶

Notes

1 A. D. Stepanov, '*Anton Chekhov kak zerkalo russkoi kritiki*' in *A. P. Chekhov: Pro et contra. Tvorchestvo A. P. Chekhova v russkoi mysli kontsa XIX – nachala XX v. (1887–1914). Antologiia* (St Petersburg: Izdatel'stvo Russkogo Khristianskogo gumanitarnogo institute 2002) pp. 976–1007.
2 Chekhov is the central subject of the essays 'An Old Question on New Talent' ('*Staryi vopros po povodu novogo talanta*', 1888), 'Chekhov and Gor'kii' ('*Chekhov i Gor'kii*', 1906), 'Asphodels and camomile' ('*Asfodeli i romashka*', 1908), 'The Brother of Man' ('*Brat chelovecheskii*', 1910) and 'Suvorin and Chekhov' ('*Suvorin i Chekhov*', 1914). A paragraph

on Chekhov's art is enclosed in Merezhkovskii's lecture 'On the Reasons for the Decline and the New Tendencies of Contemporary Russian Literature' (*'O prichinakh upadka i o novykh techeniiakh sovremennoi russkoi literatury'*, 1893). Out of Merezhkovskii's correspondence with Chekhov, 11 letters are preserved (A. M. Dolotovoi, ed., *'Pis'ma D. S. Merezhkovskogo k A. P. Chekhovu'*, in *Chekhoviana. Chekhov I 'serebrianyi vek'* (Moscow: Rossijskaja akademia nauk, 1996), pp. 58–268. See also Bibliography.

3 Chekhov's literary oeuvre is usually divided into his early humorous texts, and his serious works which dominate from around 1886 and eventually displace completely the early texts. Certainly different phases of Chekhov's mature work can also be distinguished. But the main principles of Chekhov's poetics and philosophy of life stay constant, and some can even be detected in his literary beginnings (see e.g. Karla Hielscher, *Tschechow. Eine Einführung* (Munich/Zurich: Artemis, 1987)), Thomas Winner, *Chekhov and his Prose* (New York/Chicago/San Francisco: Holt, Rinehart and Winston, 1966).

4 See A. L. Grishunin, *'Merezhkovskii o Chekhove'*, in D. S. Merezhkovskii, *Mysl' i slovo* (Moscow: Izdatel'stvo Nasledie, 1999), pp. 235–42, p. 238 and pp. 241–2.

5 See Merezhkovskii in the preface of his collected works: 'The reader who wishes to pay attention to this current collection will notice that between these books [...] there exists some inseparable bond [...]. What is Christianity for the contemporary man? The answer to this question is the hidden link between the parts of the whole' (in D. S. Merezhkovskii, *Polnoe sobranie sochinenii I*, Vols. 1–4 (Hildesheim/New York: Georg Olms Verlag, 1973), p. v). See also Grishunin, op. cit., pp. 241–2.

6 D. S. Merezhkovskii, *'O prichinakh upadka i o novykh techeniiakh sovremennoi russkoi literatury'* in D. S. Merezhkovskii, *Polnoe sobranie sochinenii V,* Vols. 17–20 (Hildesheim / New York: Georg Olms Verlag, 1973), Works, Vol. 18, p. 198.

7 Ibid., 198.

8 Merezhkovskii e. g cites 'artistic objectivity', 'brevity' and 'simplicity' as the formal characteristics of Chekhov's prose.

9 'But before talking about content, one must say two words about the artistic form of both writers'. (D. S. Merezhkovskii, *'Chekhov i Gor'kii'*, in D. S. Merezhkovskii, *Polnoe sobranie sochinenii IV,* Vols. 13–16 (Hildesheim/New York: Georg Olms Verlag, 1973), Works, Vol. 14, p. 62).

10 'Chekhov is the lawful heir to great Russian literature' (ibid., p. 695).

11 See Gippius' critique of Chekhov, published under the pseudonym Anton Krainii (Anton the Extreme): *'Slovo o teatre'*, *'O poshlosti'* (1904), *'Chto i kak'* (1904), 'Byt i sobytiia' (1904). All essays can be found in A. Krainii [Z. N. Gippius], *Literaturnyi dnevnik (1899–1907)* (Moscow: Izdatel'stvo Agraf, 2000). On Gippius' criticism of Chekhov see Temira Pachmuss, 'Anton Chekhov in the Criticism of Zinaida Gippius', in *Slavic and East-European Studies* (Montreal, Spring–Summer1966), Vol. XI, pp. 35–48.

12 See Merezhkovskii's early appreciation of Chekhov as revealed in his letters (Dolotovoi, op. cit.). Merezhkovskii's later ambivalent attitude towards Chekhov in his essay 'Suvorin i Chekhov' (1914) is particularly interesting. Merezhkovskii seems to defend Chekhov by blaming Suvorin's influence as a determining factor in Chekhov's 'ideological errors'. But in fact Merezhkovskii thereby depicts Chekhov as a child who can easily be manipulated.

13 Merezhkovskii, *'Chekhov i Gor'kii'*, op. cit., p. 60.

14 See Victor Terras, ed., *Handbook of Russian Literature* (New Haven, CT: Yale University Press, 1985), p. 279 and Ute Spengler, *Merežkovskij als Literaturkritiker. Versuch einer religiösen Begründung seiner Kunst*, Slavica Helvetica Vol. 2 (Lucerne/Frankfurt o. M.: Verlag C. J. Bucher, 1972), pp. 77–8.

15 'The religion of mankind without God, the religion [...] only of mankind [...] until this day has been the unconscious religion of the Russian intelligentsia. Chekhov and Gor´kii are the first conscious teachers and prophets of this religion' (Merezhkovskii, 'Chekhov i Gor'kii', op. cit., p. 70).
16 Ibid., p. 71.
17 Ibid., p. 92.
18 For an example of how productive the topic of religion is in Chekhov's work, see the volume V. B. Kataev, Rolf-Dieter Kluge, Regine Nohejl, ed., *Anton P. Čechov – Philosophie und Religion in Leben und Werk. Vorträge des Zweiten Internationalen Čechov – Symposiums Badenweiler, 20–24 Oktober 1994* (München 1997), *Die Welt der Slaven Sammelbände*, Vol. 1.
19 Merezhkovskii, 'Chekhov i Gor'kii', op. cit., p. 95.
20 The Religious–Philosophical meetings took place from 1901 up to 1903 and were supposed to encourage a dialogue of religious questions between the intelligentsia and representatives of the Orthodox Church. For more detailed information see Charles Bedford, *The Seeker. D. S. Merezhkovskiy* (Lawrence/Manhattan/Wichita: University Press of Kansas, 1975), pp. 114–15.
21 A cooling-off between Merezhkovskii and Chekhov around this time can be seen in Merezhkovskii's letters to Chekhov. The letters Merezhkovskii wrote to Chekhov between 1891 and 1896 are full of respect for and emotional frankness towards Chekhov. The only letter preserved afterwards dates from 1902. This letter has the distanced and cool tone of a business letter (see Dolotovoi, op. cit.).
22 See Merezhkovskii's study '*L. Tolstoi i Dostoevskii*' (1901–1902) (in D. S. Merezhkovskii, *Polnoe sobranie sochinenii III*, Vols. 9–12 (Hildesheim/New York: Olms Verlag, 1973), Works, Vol. 9. Gippius' adoration of Dostoevskii reveals itself not at last in her polemics against Chekhov, where she depicts Chekhov as a contrasting figure to Dostoevskii.
23 The use of the formula 'two times two equals four' in Dostoevskii in turn goes back to Spinoza.
24 Merezhkovskii, 'Chekhov i Gor'kii', op. cit., p. 96.
25 Ibid., p. 96.
26 Letter from Chekhov to V. S. Miroliubov dating from the 17th of December 1901 (A. P. Chekhov, *Polnoe sobranie socinenii i pisem A. P. Chekhova. Vol. XIX: Pis'ma VII. 1901–1902* (Moscow 1950), Works, Vol. XIX, p. 195).
27 Merezhkovskii, 'Chekhov i Gor'kii', op. cit., p. 98.
28 See Spengler, op. cit.
29 'A God in whom nothing more has appeared than two times two equals four'. (Merezhkovskii, 'Chekhov i Gor'kii', op. cit., p. 99).
30 Regarding Merezhkovskii's polemics against the inappropriateness of Chekhov's rational approach to religious issues, it is interesting to read Chudakov's convincing argument that Merezhkovskii had a more rational temperament than Chekhov: 'The role of religion [in Merezkovskii] is played by a naked, poor school logic'. (A. P. Chudakov, 'Chekhov i Merezhkovskii: *Dva tipa chudozhestvenno-filosofskogo soznanija*', in *Chekhoviana. Chekhov i 'serebrianyi vek'* (Moscow: Rossiiskaia akademia nauk, 1996), p. 57.
31 Merezhkovskii, 'Chekhov i Gor'kii', op. cit., p. 95.
32 Ibid., p. 100.
33 'Demanding from the artist a conscious attitude towards his work, you are right, but you confuse two issues: *solving the question and the right way of posing the question. Only the second is necessary to the artist*'. (Letter from Chekhov to Suvorin dating from the 27 October 1888 (A. P. Chekhov, *Polnoe sobranie socinenij i pisem A. P. Cechova. Bd. XIV: Pis'ma II.1888–1889* (Moscow 1949), Works, Vol. XIV, p. 208.).

34 Merezhkovskii is not consistent concerning his statements about whether Chekhov intentionally encourages these hopes, while himself being aware of their illusionary character, or whether Chekhov himself is subject to this illusion.
35 The stagnation of Chekhov's protagonists is a central issue in Merezhkovskii's criticism of Chekhov (see in particular 'Brat chelovecheskii', 1910) as well as in his wife's criticism of Chekhov (see e.g. Gippius' essay '*O poshlosti*', 1904).
36 From an unpublished essay by Henrieke Stahl 'Sergei Bulgakov on Chekhov and the modern crisis of spirituality'.
37 Chudakov speaks of Chekhov's 'hidden spirituality' (Chudakov, op. cit., p. 57).
38 Merezhkovskii, 'Chekhov i Gor'kii', op. cit., p. 103.
39 Ibid., p. 102.
40 On existential uncertainty and fear as the central anthropologic categories which determine Merezhkovskii's religious search, see Spengler, op. cit., pp. 45–7 and p. 159.
41 Merezhkovskii, 'Chekhov i Gor'kii', op. cit., p. 102.
42 See 'Ward No. 6': 'Andrei Efimych [...] recalled that millions of people believe in immortality. And what, if it exists? But he did not want it'. (A. P. Chekhov, *Polnoe sobranie socinenii i pisem A. P. Chekhova. Vol. VIII: Povesti, Rasskazy, Stat'i, Zametki.1892–1895* (Moscow 1947), Works, Vol. VIII, p. 160).
43 Merezhkovskii, '*Chekhov i Gor'kii*', op. cit., p. 110.
44 Rhetorically, however, Merezhkovskii denies this pretension in regard to his own writing: 'I do not want followers or pupils, I want only fellow travellers'. (Merezhkovskii, *Polnoe sobranie sochinenii I*, op. cit., p. vi).
45 See also Merezhkovskii's polemics against the stylization of Chekhov as a 'wise man' or 'teacher' after his death (D. S. Merezhkovskii, '*Brat chelovecheskii*', in *Chekhovskii iubileinyi sbornik* (Moscow 1910), pp. 202–9.
46 For assistance in translating this article I thank Katrin Thaidigsmann.

8

CAN MEREZHKOVSKII SEE THE SPIRIT IN THE PROSE OF FLESH?

Vladimir Golstein

Long before their first encounter, Chekhov seems to predict the outcome of his interaction with Merezhkovskii. In his wonderful story *Doma* ('At Home', 1887), Chekhov depicts the confrontation between a father, a well-respected lawyer named Bykovskii, and his six-year-old son Serezha, who was caught smoking by his governess. After Bykovskii fails in his attempts to educate Serezha on the dangers of tobacco, the lawyer tells the boy a fairytale. The boy is so moved by his father's story that he promises his father to leave the tobacco alone.

Bykovskii recounts the tale while embracing his son and looking warmly into the boy's eyes. This story, along with the highly emotional manner in which Bykovskii tells it to Serezha, reveals the father's own fears and insecurities, his own longing for love and affection. The son responds to this revelation with love and sympathy in his turn, thus confirming a beautiful moment of communication, harmony and love.

The lawyer, however, fails to recognize what it was about the tale that made it succeed. When he muses on what has happened, he does not really understand, and reasons away his confusion with a pragmatic, pseudo-scientific explanation, claiming that a factual truth in order to be effective must be dressed in some beautiful artistic form: the magic moment of human interaction is lost, drowned in banal verbiage.[1]

This dialectic between internal communication and external misunderstanding reflects the dynamics of Merezhkovskii's relationship with Chekhov. On some level, Merezhkovskii seems to understand and appreciate Chekhov's art. This is evident in his very first essay on Chekhov, 'An Old Question on New Talent' (*Staryi vopros po povodu novogo talanta*, 1888), or in his later work 'Asphodels and a Chamomile' (*Asfodeli i romashka*, 1908). Even more frequently, however, Merezhkovskii tends to resort to popular discourse, to the clichés of the period, thus losing the very essence of Chekhov.

In the first part of my essay, I will investigate Merezhkovskii's long engagement with Chekhov. I will also attempt to place Merezhkovskii's reaction towards Chekhov within the general intellectual context of the period, as well as within the general trajectory of Merezhkovskii's thought. Writing about the intellectual attitude of Silver Age thinkers towards Chekhov, Jackson observes, 'Merezhkovsky and his fellow intellectuals passed Chekhov by. They did not look deeply enough into Chekhov's texts to see where Christ and Christianity, where Blake's "Great Code of Art," the Bible, could be found'.[2] As a member of the intelligentsia whose political, social or philosophical concerns were growing ever more urgent, Merezhkovskii seems bound to pass Chekhov by. And yet, because he was also a talented and sensitive reader, at certain moments he still seems to have grasped Chekhov's depth and subtlety.

Merezhkovskii's intuitive appreciation of Chekhov, as well as his admiration for several other authors such as Byron, Lermontov or Turgenev, when coupled with Merezhkovskii's frequent failure to articulate the complexities of their poetics, explains why Chekhov was both sympathetic and dismissive of Merezhkovskii. Chekhov called him a sympathetic figure, a person of exaltation and pure soul on the one hand, and the most sated, self-righteous and religious preacher on the other.

Needless to say, the figure of a deluded and self-deluding member of the intelligentsia makes frequent appearances in Chekhov's work, which Chekhov explored before he even became acquainted with Merezhkovskii. Such stories of the late 1880s as 'At Home', 'Enemies' (*Vragi*, 1888), 'The Chorus Girl' (*Khoristka*, 1887), or "The Princess', (*Kniazhna*, 1889) reveal how self-preoccupation and self-centeredness coupled with a penchant for rhetoric tend to prevent many of Chekhov's educated and seemingly intelligent characters from adequately comprehending their circumstances. Several features of Merezhkovskii's personality clearly fit the deluded type, so it is hardly surprising that they make their appearance in Chekhov, and even less surprising that Elena Tolstaia capitalized on what might seem as Merezhkovskii's presence in Chekhov's work, devoting half of her Chekhov study to the subject of artistic dialogue between the two authors.[3]

Since Chekhov was grappling with a synthetic type of Russian *intelligent* before he met Merezhkovskii, a study like Tolstaia's seems to me misdirected. So rather than pondering on how encounters with Merezhkovskii entered Chekhov's artistic world (creative process is a notoriously murky area), I find it more fruitful to explore what light Chekhov's comments on Merezhkovskii shed on Chekhov's own poetics, outlook and system of values. Why did Chekhov say what he said about Merezhkovskii? What did Merezhkovskii do or say to provide such comments? This exploration will constitute the second part of my study.

Merezhkovskii's shortcomings are not necessarily his own. They reveal a certain failure of thought, a failure that was typical of the intellectual atmosphere of the period, a time when all thought was dominated by the concerns and preoccupations of Russian intelligentsia. Chekhov's attacks on that intelligentsia, his suspicion of its ideology and its ideologues, come to the foreground when considered against the backdrop of his critical remarks on Merezhkovskii.

In his early play 'Ivanov' (*Ivanov*, 1888), Chekhov presents two rather sympathetic characters in conflict with each other; these figures are "honest and straightforward", as Chekhov insisted in his 1888 letter to Suvorin.[4] One of them is a weak Russian nobleman, Ivanov, an individual that has high intentions, a good heart and a respectable education, and yet has realized little of his early promise. Another character, L′vov, is an 'honest but narrow and straight-laced person', a self-righteous ideologue who sees only evil designs behind Ivanov's frequently erratic actions, and fails to see the existence of a 'middle way' anywhere in life. Chekhov, of course, is both sympathetic and critical towards these characters, which explains why Merezhkovskii, who personifies both of the types, elicits both sympathy and anger from Chekhov.

Given its complexity, ambivalence and ambiguity, Chekhov's art was bound to be misunderstood by his readers, especially those who seek a concrete political or ideological message in fiction. I view Chekhov's encounter with such misinterpretation as paradigmatic of Russian culture. Pushkin labelled such an encounter as that of a poet and the mob. In Pushkin's poem 'The Mob' (*Chern′*, 1828), the mob insists that certain pragmatic values must be associated with art. A poet's desire to follow the demands of his or her muse becomes the subject of the mob's irritation and anger. In his turn, the poet rejects the crowd's cry for pragmatism, its need to attain tangible results from poetic experience.

As he declares explicitly in another poem on the theme, 'From Pindemonti' (*Iz Pindemonti*, 1836), Pushkin's poet needs a set of rights and freedoms different from that envisioned by political, social or economic strategists. Whether under the guise of a royal court or censorship, constitution or the market, the mob will always find a way to oppress and ignore the poet and his or her concerns. The poet, therefore, dismisses new political theories or proposals as nothing but 'words', as merely a disguise for the mob's inevitably pragmatic values.

The confrontation of poet and ideologue, of the poet and the commissars of all stripes, is well known in Russian literature in general, and in Chekhov in particular. He exposes this hostile relationship in his well-known story 'The House with an Attic' (*Dom s mezaninom*, 1896), as he depicts the cruel treatment that the protagonist of the story, an artist, receives at the hands of his opponent Lida, a self-righteous commissar of the Populism (*narodnichestvo*) Movement, the intellectual trend that dominated the period and which Merezhkovskii among others embraced. In the third and final part of my essay, I would like to consider the interaction between Chekhov and Merezhkovskii from the perspective of precisely this important dimension of Russian culture, that is the clash between the poet and the mob. I will also explain why this conflict took on a paradoxical form, in which Merezhkovskii would frequently reverse Pushkin's paradigm. Merezhkovskii assumed the mantle of the poet while accusing Chekhov of *chekhovshchina* or *suvorinovshchina*, the tendency to be pragmatic, pedestrian and to promote the petty concerns of everyday existence.

I. Merezhkovskii on Chekhov

The development of Merezhkovskii's thought and attitudes is easy to trace when viewed through the prism of his Chekhov criticism, a field of intellectual exploration that has always been secondary to Merezhkhovskii's chief intellectual concerns. Merezhkovskii became notorious for his ability to use other authors as stepping stones for the construction of his own ideological schemes. In 1909, Minskii emerged with a perceptive evaluation of Merezhkovskii and his brand of literary criticism, a brand that Minskii claims uses literature only as a pretext for preaching: 'Every sermon, as is well known, should be wrapped around some text. Merezhkovskii chose all Russian literature as such a text for his "neo-Christian" sermon'.[5] It is not surprising then, that Merezhkovskii frequently resorts to his popular contemporary Chekhov, and that one of his earlier essays made Chekhov's stories the subject of lengthy aesthetic discussion.

In this essay, 'An old Question on New Talent', Merezhkovskii seems to respond to the poetry of Chekhov's prose, and to defend him against the criticisms of the Populist Movement. Yet, while seeming to argue against populist ideology and its demands for clearly articulated progressive messages, Merezhkovskii's essay still shares the ideological presumptions of populism, the movement's expectation that a work of art be justified by its message. The only difference is his claim that ideology can sometimes be organic, coming from within a text, rather than being articulated explicitly. Yet, by calling Chekhov 'a poet', and his texts 'musical compositions', something to which Chekhov strongly objected, Merezhkovskii helps to undermine the import of Chekhov's position: to call a story 'a poem' without further elaboration is to deny the presence of ideas and to give up on the search for them. Even more misleading would be to impose upon such a story external categories and schemes, a tendency that Merezhkovskii could rarely resist.

Merezhkovskii's later essays already deal with Chekhov's legacy. In 'Chekhov and Gorky' (*Chekhov i Gor'kii*, 1906), written two years after Chekhov's death, Merezhkovskii attempts to evaluate the whole of Chekhov's oeuvre and to locate this within the context of post-revolutionary (1905) Russia. For him, Chekhov and Gor'kii are intellectual leaders of the Russian intelligentsia, and as such are to be blamed for its lack of faith and religion.

At first, Merezhkovskii seems to praise Chekhov; the author's talents granted him the ability to see what others do not see: 'People do not see the most important in them and in others, because it is too familiar to the eye, too well-known. Chekhov's eye is constructed in such a way, that everywhere and always he sees this *invisible familiar*, and at the same time he can see the unusual side of the usual'.[6] Having discerned in Chekhov this power of vision, Merezhkovskii immediately qualifies this, and this point becomes the main thrust of his essay. The only thing Chekhov sees is Russian *byt*, the everyday life of common Russians. He does not know anything else, nor does he want to. Because of this, 'Chekhov is national, but not universal, he is current, but not historical. His *byt* embraces only the present, without past or future... it is not connected to world history or culture... He saw Russia more clearly than anybody, but he missed Europe, he missed the world. Chekhov's heroes do not have life, but only *byt* ... *Byt* and death – these are the two poles of Chekhov's world.[7]

Not only is Chekhov transformed into a blind man after being considered a man of keen insights, he is then accused of deliberately blinding himself toward social and religious matters. 'Chekhov passed Christ by, without looking and without even trying to look in the direction of Christ'.[8] Merezhkovskii concludes that Chekhov is the leader of the intelligentsia, primarily because he encourages its blindness regarding religious and other important matters, and avoids confronting the eternal questions of being. 'And in this, as, by the way, in everything else, Chekhov is a true representative of religious consciousness of the Russian intelligentsia'.[9] With his propensity towards uncontrollable rhetoric, Merezhkovskii concludes that Chekhov's characters are corpses who believe in and want nothing. But he pushed this severe point even further: 'Their fear of non-existence becomes a thirst for non-existence, a thirst for destruction and chaos'.[10] And Merezhkovskii concludes with the following *coup de grace*: 'They [Chekhov and Gor'kii] wanted to show that man without God is God, but showed that he is a wild animal, worse than an animal – a beast, worse than a beast – a corpse, worse than a corpse – nothingness'.[11]

Triggered by the fiasco of the first Russian Revolution, this essay is probably Merezhkovskii's weakest. It is harsh and simplistic, and conflates characters with their author. It refuses to engage with Chekhov on his own level, resorting instead to far-fetched cultural associations, analogies and genealogies.

By 1908, Merezhkovskii seems to change his mind, however. In his 'Asphodels and Camomile', he shows an appreciation of Chekhov's reticence and silence, noting that these are as wise, profound and ultimately more religious than those of the Symbolists.

In this loving and penetrating essay, Merezhkovskii expresses his admiration for Chekhov's embrace of everyday existence, for his sober yet loving acceptance of Russia and Russian people, unadorned by myths, dreams or fantasy. He compares Chekhov to more recent writers, such as Viacheslav Ivanov, Bal′mont, Briusov, Gorodetskii and Sologub, authors whom he dismisses as fanciful 'asphodels', exquisite flowers that exist in some dreamland, the world of the dead, and which contrast with the recently deceased Chekhov, an unpretentious wild flower full of life and charm.

Merezhkovskii's switch signifies his decision to revaluate the lessons of the first Russian revolution. He chooses to do so by composing his own version of *Landmarks* (*Vekhi*), the famous collection of essays published in 1909 in which a number of Russian *intelligenti* call for the revaluation and re-direction of their social and political concerns and preoccupations.

Chekhov clearly shared *Landmarks*' attitude toward the *intelligenti*, towards its values and its way of life. Leaning in the same direction, Merezhkovskii seems to have grasped something important about Chekhov's poetics and his system of values. He has acquired an insight.

Those, who like Chekhov or Blok insisted that Merezhkovskii was pure in soul, a sympathetic figure, an artist, were not off the mark. At certain times he would clearly rise to the occasion and see things clearly, even if such clarity required self-criticism or even a complete dismissal of his own position. This is what he accomplished in his 1908 essay. Commenting on his frequent miscommunications with Chekhov, he writes:

> I was upset, almost:– I talk to him about eternity, and he talks to me about soup. I was irritated by his indifference, his almost contempt for earthly matters [...] We had to say as many superfluous things as we did, we had to sin as much as we did, with sacred words, in order to understand that he was right when he remained silent about sacred things [...] What a joy, what a saintly thing to be silent about the sacred.[12]

Merezhkovskii recognizes that 'In Chekhov, the "acceptance" of Russia emerges from the acceptance of the world, and the blessing of the motherland – from the blessing of birth'.[13] According to Merezhkovskii, Chekhov's acceptance makes him different from most of Merezhkovskii's contemporaries, those who curse life, reject the world, and thus reject God. Merezhkovskii recognizes here a profound truth of Dostoevskii who in his *The Brothers Karamazov* (1880) had opposed such cursers of life, as Ivan Karamazov and Smerdiakov, to Zosima and Alesha Karamazov. Zosima, we recall, encouraged Alesha 'to bless life – and make others bless it—which is what matters most" (Dostoevsky: 1976, 264).[14]

Dostoevskii's religious insight, that from the blessing of life one graduates to the Hosanna to God, seems to provide an answer to some of Merezhkovskii's own pressing concerns, hard as he tried to combine the sacred and the material, the pagan and the Christian. Merezhkovskii now detects manifestations of Dostoevskii's insight in Chekhov. While not fully developing his own intuition, Merezhkovskii at least recognizes that 'Chekhov is the last of Russian authors who did not bow down to a dead God. Maybe he did not know the name of the living God, but he intuited [*predchuvstvoval*] Him'. Chekhov is returned from the ranks of 'corpses' and atheists to the ranks of the living.

In this penetrating essay, Merezhkovskii seems to question his own presumptions, while recognizing that behind Chekhov's fascination with the everyday and pedestrian, lurk profound religious concerns. Yet two years later, all that Merezhkovskii so insightfully praised in Chekhov is dismissed in an extremely self-righteous and myopic manner. In March 1910, Merezhkovskii writes to Briusov, a writer whom in 1908 Merezkhovskii compared with Chekhov (as being a dead man as compared to a living person), that he refuses to participate in the celebration of Chekhov's 50th birthday.

> The Russian intelligentsia likes to waste its time on all kinds of dead people [...] Chekhov has grown into a giant, equal to Pushkin, L. Tolstoi [...] As far as Chekhov is concerned, I can only curse now [...] Starting with Chekhov, Russian literature has acquired a foul taste, a foul bad smell, which has resulted in Artsybashev, Kuprin and so on. But I cannot say all this to the public.[15]

Continuing in the same vein, he wrote another piece on Chekhov, 'The Brother of Man' (*Brat chelovecheskii*, 1910). In this essay, Merezhkovskii tries to describe Chekhov as a human being. He starts by prefacing that he could not understand Chekhov when they first met: 'Chekhov and I were completely different people'.[16] Merezhkovskii then recalls the contrast between Chekhov's nonchalance, with Merezhkovskii's own exuberance at their meeting in Italy.

He depicts Chekhov as a person who avoids intellectual argument, who is not curious about things which others find fascinating, but pays attention to various insignificant details of everyday life, and always responds to intellectual discussion with ironic silence. Chekhov is accused of being weak and for seeing and depicting only impotence and resignation. His illness therefore must have been 'a part of his soul, not just of his body'.[17] He can see the uniqueness of any insignificant and weak Russian person, but that is the only thing he can see. For Merezhkovskii, Chekhov's ability to discern something exceptional in inconsequentiality is extremely dangerous, as it encourages Chekhov's readers in their weakness and resignation.[18]

Once again Merezhkovskii asserts Chekhov's inability to move beyond the banal and everyday. 'With his impotent dreams hidden behind a permanent grin – that was Chekhov, today's son of today's Russia'.[19] Merezhkovskii then boldly suggests that he and Chekhov 'were people of different dreams', but adds that he, Merezhkovskii, understood Chekhov's dreams but did not share them.[20]

The death of Chekhov, which was followed by the assassination of the conservative minister Viacheslav Pleve, signals for Merezhkovskii the death of tired, weak, obedient and dreamy Russia.[21] Merezhkovskii explains Chekhov's popularity in the following way:

> All who are silent, forgotten, beaten, small, impotent, sick, incapable, crushed by the greyness of today – all these were drawn to him. They recognized themselves in him. And they are like him, they are his brothers. ... Of course he is not a world genius, not the ruler of thoughts, not a teacher. He is our equal, a regular person standing next to us, a contemporary man... a child of today's Russian history.[22]

Merezkhovskii stresses Chekhov's peculiar vision. Chekhov, he believes sees that which is ordinary, what hides beyond the silence of ordinary people, but he surely cannot see or appreciate anything extraordinary, and therefore it is important to forget him if one wants Russia to move beyond its grey, impotent existence.

This concept of Chekhov's peculiar vision is developed further in Merezhkovskii's final condemnation of Chekhov, his 1914 essay 'Chekhov and Suvorin' (*Chekhov i Suvorin*).

Chekhov is blind when it comes to Suvorin. He fails to see that Suvorin is merely tempting him with his lies about Russia: he is a demon who presents falsehood and emptiness as truth and reality. Suvorin's lies for Merezhkovskii are 'the rejection of liberation' and 'the rejection of religion'.[23] Seduced by Suvorin, Chekhov failed to see the truth of revolutionary Russian populism and its ideals, preferring instead the reality of little deeds. However, Merezhkovskii asserts:

> Suvorin's hospital is worse than a brothel; Suvorin's church is worse than a pub [...] Chekhov is dead. To revive Chekhov means to separate him from Suvorin, to overcome in Chekhov the spirit of chekhovshchina,

suvorinovshchina, philistinism, this 'Russian darkness' in which he perished.[24]

Chekhov surely had plenty of ideas, but Merezhkovskii was clearly looking in the wrong place. In a paradoxical turn of events, the irony of which Chekhov would surely appreciate, Merezhkovskii criticizes Chekhov's blindness (towards Europe, culture, history, radicalism and religion, among other things), while himself remaining blind toward Chekhov, both man and writer.

Merezhkovskii's reversal from his early insights and sophistication, where he saw Chekhov as profound and alive, to the rather hysterical and simplistic accusations of blindness, deadening materialism, reaction and passivity, is rather puzzling. While his earlier comments defended Chekhov against the populist intelligentsia's indictment of his passivity and lack of radical ideology, Merezhkovskii's later work faults Chekhov for failing to see the truth of radical populists and their revolutionary ideals.

The explanation for such a turnaround is rather simple. Merezhkovskii clearly overreacted to the crisis that followed the first Russian Revolution. He viewed it as a fiasco and thus approached the following decade with despair. Living mostly in France, he denounced the passivity of the Russian intelligentsia, criticizing its failure to carry out the revolutionary and religious transformation of Russia. In his collection *It Was and It Will Be* (*Bylo i budet*, 1915), he accused the intelligentsia of forgetting its long-term goals and turning into 'senseless and carefree creatures whose complex ideologies have been replaced by shortish everyday wisdom'.[25]

Provoked by what he perceived as encroaching political reaction and the intelligentsia's surrender to it (most of the essays in his 1910 collection *Sick Russia* (*Bol'naia Rossiia*, 1910) are devoted to the subject), Merezhkovskii began to attack this spirit of passivity and resignation. Anything short of the revolutionary was to become reactionary, and frequently demonic. In his radicalism, Merezhkovskii went so far as to see Pushkin, not just Chekhov, as the embodiment of Russian weakness and humility. In his famous essay, "*M. Iu. Lermontov (Poet sverkhchelovechestva)*" (1909), Merezhkovskii demands that what he perceives as Pushkin's spirit of contemplation and resignation be overcome by the spirit of Lermontov's rebellion and quest for action.

Of course, one cannot blame either Pushkin or Dostoevskii for what happens in our Russian literature and Russian reality. But there still must be some sort of connection between the last half century of our literature and our reality, between the magnitude of our contemplation and the insignificance of our actions [...] We keep on falling asleep under the lullaby of all Russian literature:

> Not for the earthly troubles,
> Not for material gains or battles,
> We are born for inspiration,
> For sweet sounds and prayers. [Pushkin]

Of course, in later times these 'sweet sounds' were somehow transformed into a sad yet playful song of Chekhov's hero, into "tara-bumbia" [the meaningless song hummed by one of the characters in *Three Sisters*]. But the most profound metaphysical essence of Russian literature, of Russian reality, is in that song – and it is still the same: the contemplative inaction which first Gogol' and then Dostoevskii glorified in Pushkin: 'Humble yourself, proud man'.

This Pushkin element, it seems, has now reached its pinnacle, and, having finally prevailed and won, lost all its energy. Pushkin's sun has descended into a bloody storm. And when the storm abated, we were left with slush, with the grey Petersburg twilight [...].

All Russian literature is dedicated to the hidden battle against Lermontov. Should we not brace ourselves for the forthcoming battle with Pushkin? [...] The question is how to beat Pushkin with Lermontov, our salvation or destruction depends on this question.[26]

Merezhkovskii blames not only Chekhov, but also Pushkin and Dostoevskii for the intelligentsia's passivity and resignation. Russia's history and its lesser literary figures are subjected to even more brutal attack. In his essay 'Mother Swine' (*Svinia-Matushka*, 1909), Merezhkovskii singles out a well-known writer and censor, Nikitenko, dismissing his brilliant memoirs as 'slave narrative of slave life'.[27] (in Russian: "*Rab'ia kniga o rab'ei zhizni*"). He asserts that these memoirs prove once and for all that the only truth about Russia is that it remains in the hands of reactionary and tyrannical conservatism.[28]

Living most of the decade abroad and surrounded by political émigrés and radicals, Merezhkovskii became increasingly shrill and simplistic, abandoning his own insights into Chekhov's outlook, along with the main points of the *Landmarks* criticism of intelligentsia, all arguments that he himself raised in his 1908 essay on Chekhov. Merezhkovskii embraces the axiom that what is not revolution is reaction, adding his own proposition that reaction is the same thing as antichrist. Clearly, Merezhkovskii does not have much room for nuanced discussion: he attacks not only Chekhov, but everyone from Pushkin to the authors of *Landmarks*, accusing these writers of being a vehicle for Russia's emerging reaction and conservatism.

Truth be told, Merezhkovskii's writings in this period recall the ramblings of the maniac speaker whom Dostoevskii mocked in *Demons* (*Besy*, 1872). So overwhelmed by anger and indignation, the only thing that this speaker can do when given a chance to speak is to raise his fist and, 'waving it ecstatically and menacingly over his head' dismiss his times as the most corrupt and shameful, and shout, '"but never, in all the thousand witless years of her life, did Russia reach such disgrace …"'.[29]

II. Chekhov on Merezhkovskii

Chekhov always rejected those who look for tendencies, who politicize everything. In a letter to Pleshcheev, he wrote, 'All our thick journals are dominated by cliquey, party-line tedium [*kruzhkovaia, partiinaia skuka*]. It is suffocating! I do not like these journals and they will never tempt me to work for them'.[30] As he wrote to Pleshcheev, 'I fear those who look for an agenda between the lines […] I am not a liberal, not a conservative, not a gradualist, not a monk, not an indifferentist. I should like to be a free artist and – nothing else'.[31] In the same vein he later wrote, 'When I portray such types or talk about them, I do not think about conservatism or liberalism but about their stupidities and their pretences'.[32]

Chekhov was also sceptical of those who pronounce wonderful and noble slogans. He understood better than most that talk is cheap and that the intelligentsia around him thrived off clichéd slogans. As he puts it in one of his letters, '"Welcome the light and cast out the darkness" is the prudish hypocrisy of all those who are backward, and out of touch and impotent'.[33]

Since Merezhkovskii's first essay tried to avoid the usual political agenda of the thick journals, Chekhov was initially impressed and commented on this in a number of his letters. Yet, as much as Chekhov liked the essay, in his letters he accuses Merezhkovskii of being too scientific, too ambitious, and yet too timid. Ambition consists of the desire to develop the scientific, materialistic laws for art and creativity, to establish general laws and formulae that enable artists to create their works.

Chekhov admits that there might be some physiological laws in the foundations of art, but the pursuit of these should be given up immediately, since the result of such a search would only be further confusion.[34] For Chekhov, Merezhkovskii fails to clarify the matter for himself. He adds that because Merezhkovskii is afraid to say certain things, he merely succumbs to the commonplace instead, calling Chekhov's protagonists – failures. But, insists Chekhov, 'one must be God in order to tell failure from success and not be mistaken'.³⁵

> In the November issue of the *Northern Messenger* [*Severnyi Vyestnik*] there is an article by the poet Merezhkovskii on your humble servant. It is a long article. I commend to your attention its ending. It is typical. Merezhkovsky is still very young, a student, I believe of natural sciences. Those who have assimilated the wisdom of the scientific method and have learned to think scientifically experience many alluring temptations [...]Merezhkovskii writes smoothly and youthfully, but at every page he backs down, gives provisos, qualifications and concessions – and this is a sign that he is not clear about the subject at issue ... He praises me as a poet, my stories as novellas, my heroes as failures, that is, he follows the same routine. It is time to give up these failures, superfluous people etc., and to think of something original.³⁶

With amazing perception, Chekhov notices a certain pattern in Merezhkovskii, a failure to see problems clearly and a tendency to follow the beaten track, to replicate all sorts of clichés. For Chekhov, Merezhkovskii is a person who is afraid to go against the grain; he might express opinions with brilliance and erudition, but these are common opinions nonetheless.

The pair soon met in person, and it appears that Merezhkovskii impressed Chekhov. In 1891, Chekov wrote to Suvorin, 'the poet Merezhkovskii visited me twice. A very clever person'.³⁷ Chekhov's fascination grew after he met the newlywed Merezhkovskiis during their travels in Italy. Yet by the end of 1891, Chekhov sounds alarmed in a letter to Pleshcheev: "Merezhkovskii still abides in the Muruzi house and continues to be lost in his celestial explorations, and yet he still cuts a sympathetic figure after all".³⁸

Despite some disappointment, Chekhov continued to view Merezhkovskii without any overt hostility, recommending him in 1901 for honorary membership in the Russian Academy (along with other 'liberal' authors such as Mikhailovskii, Spasovich and Veinberg).³⁹ Yet Chekhov knew Merezhkovskii's limitations only too well, once calling him 'a plant from a greenhouse'.⁴⁰

In another letter he commends Merezhkovskii, calling him 'exuberant and pure in soul' (*vostorzhennyi i chistyi dushoiu*), but also complains that Merezhkovskii talks about literature incessantly, even when visiting a seriously ill acquaintance in Nice: 'But God, how boring it is to go to Nice only to talk incessantly about literature at Alexei Nikolaevich's [Pleshcheev's] death bed'.⁴¹ In short, there is something not quite human about Merezhkovskii, and it is for this reason that Chekhov suggests that 'Merezhkovskii's heart would have done better had he replaced his quasi-Goethesque regime, his wife and "the truth" for a bottle of good wine, a hunting gun, and an attractive woman'.[42]

But the heart, of course, is not simply a physical organ. It also relates to the life of emotions, to a domain not immediately accessible to the intellect. Merezhkovskii might be pure in soul and exuberant, but empathy, emotional involvement with others – in other words, the very substance that makes possible human interaction and more importantly human understanding – are alien to him.

The world of Chekhov's fiction and plays is of course full of characters who are intelligent and pure, who speak of art, God and the Devil, but who still allow evil to thrive under their own noses. Indeed, only that endearing quality of being 'exuberant and pure in soul' can explain Merezhkovskii's fascination with Pilsudski, Mussolini, and even Hitler, whom he once called the Joan of Arc of his day.

Eventually, in Chekhov's imagination Merezhkovskii became a type. This move is very significant. In 1901, Chekhov reprimands his friend Viktor Miroliubov for his association with the newly-established Saint Petersburg Religious-Philosophical Meetings, and with Merezhkovskii in particular. In his letter to Miroliubov, Chekhov insists, 'What do you, a decent straightforward person, have in common with Rozanov, with the pompously sly Sergii, and finally with the most sated (*syteishii*) Merezhkovskii?'[43]

To be *sytyi* is the opposite of being hungry, to never experience any need, and remaining both physically and emotionally sated. Merezhkovskii appears to possess this quality to the fullest measure. The term *sytyi* means not only 'well-fed' and self-satisfied, but also indicates a spiritual self-righteousness, an intellectual feature that has always been rejected by the best representatives of Russian culture.

In fact, the label *syteüshii* is a striking term that calls for further analysis. Chekhov's appellation is both harsh and surprising, since from a distance Merezhkovskii appears so passionate, so pure, so thirsty for truth. In fact, in his never-ending quest for the religious revival of the world, Merezhkovskii tends to see others, including Pushkin, Dostoevsky and certainly Chekhov, as too smug, too resigned and too satisfied with who they are.

For Chekhov, questions of religion and faith should be embraced by an individual who, like Pushkin, is 'tormented by spiritual thirst'. Merezhkovskii however began to embody the very opposite of such thirst. As noted in one of the most frequently cited Russian proverbs: "the one who is sated cannot understand the one who is hungry" (*sytyi golodnogo ne razumeet*). The state of self-satisfaction becomes the very antonym of all enquiry and comprehension, because the self-satisfied person can never entirely grasp the literal and figurative dimension of hunger.

It is hardly surprising then, that in the same letter Chekhov insists that in the religious questions, what is important is "the awareness of one's one purity, that is, the absolute freedom of the soul – from forgotten or non-forgotten words, from idealisms, and so on, so forth. One has to have faith in God, but if this faith is absent, one should not substitute it with verbal bombast (*shumikha*), but keep on searching, searching on one's one, with only one's conscience as a partner."[44]

Thus, Merezhkovskii's spiritual satiety becomes the subject of Chekhov's criticism from that point on. Invited by Sergei Diagilev to be an editor of *The World of Art* (*Mir Iskusstva*), he rejects the proposition, as in this post he would have to work alongside Merezhkhovskii. In July 1903, Chekhov wrote to Diagilev:

> How would I live under the same roof as Merezhkovskii, who believes with certainty, believes like a teacher, when I lost all my faith long ago and only can look with puzzlement at any believer that comes from the ranks of intelligentsia (*intelligentnogo veruischego*). I respect D. S. and value him both as a human being and as a man of letters, but we will pull in different directions.[45]

To be sated implies an existence where an individual holds unshakeable beliefs and convictions. Coupled with enthusiasm and purity of soul, this tenacity becomes rather dangerous, since such a constantly satisfied person tends to be blind to the paradoxes and complexities of this world, let alone to the true scope of human misery. Chekhov knew long before he met Merezhkovskii that the fusion of self-righteousness with enthusiasm is a deadly combination, having discussed it in a number of his stories, such as 'The Chorus Girl' , 'The Princess', and 'Enemies'.

In 'Enemies', the term *sytyi* is used in reference to the story's smug and self-centred protagonist Abogin at least six times. Besides being self-satisfied (*sytyi*), Abogin also exhibits a penchant for melodrama, phrase-mongering, theatricality and exaggeration, and sadly this propensity of Abogin would later be reflected in the trajectory of Merezhkovskii's life. In Chekhov's story, Abogin would 'run away to complain and commit all sort of stupidities', clearly pre-figuring Merezhkovskii and his litany of complaints, denunciations and foolish alignments.

For Chekhov, such characters as Abogin or the 'exuberant' (*vostorzhennaia*) Princess Vera from 'The Princess' might be artistic, elegant or naïve, but also overly verbose, histrionic, self-satisfied and self-centred. Consequently, they remain oblivious to the misery (or hunger) of others, while responding to their own troubles in a highly melodramatic fashion.

Chekhov always remained on the lookout for emotional, intellectual and even religious complacency. He is relentless in its exposure. Slowly, this type of moral satiety was instilled in Chekhov's notion of the intelligentsia. 'In Petersburg the reviews are written only by satisified and neurotic Jews, there is not a single true and pure person'[46], he remarks rather harshly. Yet, if we recall that Chekhov juxtaposed 'good and straightforward' Miroliubov with the sated Merezhkovskii, the opposition acquires less of an anti-Semitic and more of an anti-satiety character.

In another letter to Suvorin, Chekhov comments on a paradoxical reversal, the type of moral reversal that Chekhov often depicts in his stories. 'A state of self-satisfaction (*sytost'*), similar to any other force carries with it a certain degree of insolence, and this insolence expresses itself in the fact that the sated one (*sytyi*) teaches the hungry'.[47]

This paradox is captured beautifully in 'The Princess'. The protagonist of the story visits a monastery and thinks that by doing so, she is accomplishing a noble, magnanimous and beneficial act, though in truth her presence proves extremely disruptive. Without any understanding of religion, she starts to lecture people, whose life she has destroyed, on the benefits of faith and patience. Her opponent, a doctor, verbally attacks her, only to produce tears. Unlike Abogin, the Princess cannot even understand the essence of the doctor's charges. But we also know that she is 'exuberant and pure in soul'; she clearly never intended to wreak the havoc that she did.

It is clear that in Chekhov's world, being sated puts one at the very bottom of moral development. Chekhov's main grievance with the self-satisfied is the very grievance that he has with Abogin and the Princess: in the self-sated there exists a lack of perspective, and consequently a blindness toward the grief of others. In 'Enemies', Chekhov insists that true grief is both silent and beautiful, as was the grief experienced by Kirillov and his wife at the deathbed of their child. Abogin, and to an even greater degree the innocently cruel and destructive Princess, fail to see or register such grief. They are too blinded by their satiety to do so.

Chekhov is well aware of this pattern in human behaviour: 'Man's eyes are opened only at the time of his misery'.[48] He adds, "How intolerable are the people who are happy, who are successful in everything they do" (ibid). Rejecting the ideology produced by self-satisfied and consequently myopic people, Chekhov remarks in his story, "Misfortune" (Neschast'e) , 'There are plenty of points of view in this world, and a good half of them belong to people who have never experienced misery'.[49]

Satiety appears such a corroding force in the world of Chekhov that even the beneficial effects of an early misfortune can be destroyed by it. In his notebooks, Chekhov describes a character who, though he witnessed human misery in childhood, since then ignored it out of his own satiety:

> Twenty … thirty years later when at some social gathering they began to discuss satiety (*sytost'*) and its hypnotic power, he narrates it [the misfortune that he witnessed in childhood] and confesses that since then he had done nothing for the poor, even though he was struck by what he had heard long ago. The conversation at the gathering starts with this sentiment: "Gentlemen! We were all poor a long time ago and felt indignation, but now we are wealthy, and have we done anything for the poor?[50]

Chekhov's 'The Princess' ends on an important note: '"How happy I am!" she murmured, closing her eyes. "How happy!" The princess' sense of contentment, her closed eyes, her exquisite and plentiful dinner, and her tendency to sleep until noon, clearly make her a perfect representation of the effects of satiety; insensitivity and blindness, it seems, are the product of self-satisfaction and self-preoccupation.

The Princess embodies a very powerful type that exists in the world of Chekhov, and to which he returns repeatedly. He writes about another princess-like character, 'A liberal, educated but bored member of the school board visits the school every day, speaks a lot, does not give a penny, the school is falling apart, but he sincerely believes himself to be useful and necessary. The teacher hates him, but he does not notice'.[51] The true heroes of Chekhov's world, teachers, doctors, for example, are bound to be angry and frustrated, because those who have power and means fail to notice the world around them.

In fact, this blindness to poverty, misfortune and struggle appears to infuriate Chekhov. "There is a bad smell in the estate and a bad taste as well. The trees are planted haphazardly, and in the very far corner the female night guard for hours on end washes clothes for the guests, and nobody notices her. And these ladies and gentlemen are allowed for hours on end to discuss their rights, their nobility, and so on'.[52]

In his essay 'Our Poverty', Chekhov asserts: 'Our society is not used to think about village clergy that works practically for free and is undernourished, or that the teachers who get peanuts for their labour are always on the border of poverty'.[53] As a solution, Chekhov suggests: 'One must think about schools, hospitals and prisons all the time. That is the only way to conquer nature'.[54]

Chekhov therefore never tires of bringing to the surface what others do not see or would prefer to gloss over. He captures such ignored realities in his notes: 'The family. Husband, wife, mother of five children. For five days the children ate only soup made from weeds. It is common for them not to eat for two to five days. I witnessed how a peasant and his wife walked eight miles in the snowstorm to ask for famine relief'.[55]

Likewise he comments, 'when one lives at home, in peace, life appears normal; but once you go outside and begin to observe, to inquire, life becomes terrifying. The Patriarch Ponds neighbourhood appears to be quiet and peaceful, but in fact, life there is hell ('it is so hellish, that it does not even protest').[56]

The causality between complacency and blindness and the consequent failure of these notions to respond to life's evils is summarized memorably in the following words from "The Gooseberry":

> Any improvement in one's conditions, anything like satiety [*sytost'*] or idleness, develops the most insolent complacency in a Russian. ... How many happy, satisfied people there are, after all [...] What an overwhelming force...We neither hear nor see those who suffer, and the terrible things in life are played out behind the scenes [...] There ought to be a man with a hammer behind the door of every happy man, to remind him by his constant knocks that there are unhappy people, and that happy as he himself might be [...] life will sooner or later show him its claws [...] and nobody will see it, just as he now neither sees nor hears the misfortunes of others.[57]

Chekhov, therefore, enables us to comprehend the mystery of Merezhkovskii's blindness and insight. Applied to Merezhkovskii, such a strong term of condemnation as *syteishii* suggests the word's concomitant quality, self-centeredness and blindness to other people's misery. None other than Merezhkovskii's wife Zinaida Gippius acknowledges Merezhkovskii's unresponsiveness towards people who asked him for help. She refers to his 'lack of response to people who appealed to him from afar', his 'lack of attention to different, unknown people who turned to him sincerely'.[58]

III. The Intelligentsia's Satiety and Blindness

Melville's insightful novella *Benito Cereno* brilliantly captures failure to recognize evil under one's own nose, as it depicts the naïve captain of a ship who is prevented from seeing reality owing to his own ideological prejudices. Merezhkovskii's predicament is not dissimilar.

Merezhkovskii's failings are not necessarily his own. They indicate a more serious issue, that of the Russian intelligentsia and its failure to read Chekhov correctly. Merezhkovskii's seriousness – if not his fanaticism, his strange enthusiasms, and his failure to appreciate double meanings, complexities, paradoxes or even jokes – all point to a pure soul, but complacent *intelligent*, one who looks for the sources of evil in all the familiar places: autocracy, tyranny, historical Church, atheism and Bolshevism, but fails to inspect places closer to home, such as his own heart.

Merezhkhovskii, a master of oppositions, dilemmas and dichotomies, was rarely aware of paradoxes, especially the paradoxes of human behaviour. It is hardly surprising that he envied Chekhov's ability to see an official as both a 'kind person' and 'a liar, a drunkard and a womanizer'. This failure or refusal to look into one's own heart might explain why Merezhkovskii, along with the majority of Russian intelligentsia, rejected *Landmarks* and its call for self-exploration and self-perfection.

Chekhov's mistrust, even his fully-fledged dislike of the intelligentsia is a well-known and well-documented phenomenon. He was always suspicious of pomp, self-righteousness, pseudo-authority and the tendency to pontificate or preach. 'The most intolerable people are provincial celebrities [...] How easily people deceive themselves, how they love prophets and soothsayers; what a herd it is! [...] Even your lies will be believed if they are pronounced with authority'.[59] His notebooks are full of observations of this nature.

Of course, the tendency to pontificate is not the worst possible outcome of complacency. In Chekhov's world this quality correlates to insensitivity and blindness. Chekhov would compare this pompous insensitivity to that of military generals, and would attack this quality whenever he encountered it, regardless of who is exhibiting it. Thus attacks such as the one on Tolstoi's preaching of abstinence in his 'Afterword to *The Kreutzer Sonata*' were not uncommon for Chekhov.

> The day before yesterday I read his 'Afterword'. Strike me dead, but it is stupider and stuffier than 'Letters to a Governor's Wife', which I despise. The devil take the philosophy of the great people of this world! All the great sages are as despotic as generals, and are as ill-mannered and as indelicate as generals, because they are certain of their immunity. Diogenes spat in people's faces, knowing that he would not suffer for it; Tolstoi abuses doctors as scoundrels, and displays his ignorance in great questions because he is just such a Diogenes who will not be locked up or abused in the newspapers. And so, to the Devil with the philosophy of all the great people of this world! With its fanatical afterwords and letters to a governor's wife [an allusion to Nikolai Gogol's rather pompous text *Selected Passages from the Correspondence with Friends* – VG], it is not worth one little mare in his 'Story of a Horse'.[60]

Merezhkovskii was another general of the type often condemned by Chekhov, a person who would pontificate on various subjects knowing full well that 'he would not suffer for it'.

Chekhov's period clearly saw a conflict between the ethos of 'little deeds' and the rhetoric of the emerging Symbolist movement. The generals of this movement, Merezhkovskii in particular, viewed Chekhov's concerns as too pedestrian, and preferred instead to pontificate and philosophise on major themes of religion and philosophy. As Merezhkovskii would complain, 'I address him with the issue of immortality, and he replies with his advice about soup'.[61]

Needless to say, Chekhov addressed these and many other critical themes but spoke in his own unobtrusive voice. He remained unnoticed therefore by typical *intelligent* readers who had grown accustomed to the rumblings of literary generals.

It is this kind of intelligentsia that seemed to irritate Chekhov so much, the kind that fails to question its own axioms, that approaches Russian literature and history from a dogmatic and external perspective. Dostoevskii, who witnessed the rise of such restricted thinking, called this 'linearity' (*prostota*), and exposed this throughout his writings. His example of linearity is that of a young nihilist lady who works in a library and yet looks with total contempt at Dostoevskii when he requests a Thackeray novel: the reading of novels appears to her unworthy, childish and otherwise unacceptable.[62]

Consequently, one observes a particular paradox that seems to characterize the relationships between Russian writers and the radical intelligentsia in general, and between Chekhov and Merezhkovskii in particular. Where Dostoevsky or Chekhov detect linearity, smugness, melodrama or blindness, their opponents within the intelligentsia see revolutionary or religious fervour, spiritual thirst or idealism. Conversely, the writers' concerns with everyday tragedies and suffering are seen by the intelligentsia as pedestrian, narrow and materialistic. As Blake put it, 'Both read the Bible day and night, but where you see black, I see white'.

Chekhov was acutely aware of such reversals. 'Today when a decent working man takes a critical position towards himself and towards his own job, everyone around him informs him that he is a pessimist, a complainer, a lazy and indifferent person, but when the idle swindler declares at the top of his lungs that one must accomplish things, everyone applauds.'[63]

Even more poignantly, Chekhov imagines the following scenario: 'They were celebrating the birthday of a modest person. They used the opportunity to show off, to praise each other. And only by the end of the dinner they realized that the subject of the celebration was not invited. They forgot'.[64]

In these words, Chekhov foretold the fate that awaited him for the next hundred years, at least among his own countrymen. Russians continue to misread Chekhov, using him as a pretext to show off and praise each other while completely ignoring the author and what he has to say.

Thus it is hardly surprising that Merezhkovskii tends to blame Chekhov for his *intelligentnost'* while remaining the very champion of the intelligentsia's thought. Merezhkovskii, of course, would accuse Chekhov of being normal and pedestrian, of expressing the typical dreams and aspirations of Russian intelligentsia. Paradoxically, Merezhkovskii was viewed as normal and charged with ordinariness by none other than Lev Trotskii. For Trotskii, Merezhkovskii was nothing but a middle-of-the-road realist, a materialist and individualist, a person afraid to acknowledge his own triviality, banality and normality, and who has to hide therefore behind historical schemes, philosophical dichotomies or literary quotations.[65]

Indeed, everything seems to be rather conventional about Merezhkovskii. As a Russian intellectual, he feels he must argue about death and immortality, or fall in love with the ultra-poetic and exquisite Gippius. Once in Italy, he feels he must admire the beauty of Venice. Indeed, regardless of his various intellectual pursuits, Merezhkovskii remains a typical member of the Russian intelligentsia, responding to circumstances in rather conventional ways. He started as a follower of populism, graduated into a Treplev-type Decadent and Symbolist, and later became involved with the rather banal end-of-the-century search for mysticism, religion, sectarianism and synthesis. He also became a rather typical émigré.

Despite his hard work and artistic sensitivity (Blok stressed both of these Merezhkovskian qualities), Merezhkovskii's trajectory became that of a traditional member of the intelligentsia. Similar to the majority of Russian intelligentsia, Merezhkovskii chose to ignore the authors of *Landmarks*, thinkers who called for self-scrutiny, self-criticism and for a reorientation from their grand schemes of changing the world to a more mundane and practical approach to reality. Because Merezhkovskii is so conventional, one can easily find his traces in any of Chekhov's characters from the intelligentsia's ranks, be it the professor from 'A Boring Story', Treplev, Serebriakov with his Elena, or any other self-satisfied character in his fiction. Yet, rather than recognizing Merezhkovskii in these personas, we should recognize in them and in Merezhkovskii the features that Chekhov tirelessly analyzed and attacked.

We can conclude that the Chekhov-Merezhkovskii interaction replays a paradigmatic confrontation, the clash between the eternally alert artist, open to all kinds of experience, and the intellectual, sated on a very basic intellectual level, who already knows what is good and bad, right and wrong, and never aims to broaden that understanding. Pushkin has labelled such a confrontation as that between the poet and the mob.

Chekhov's heroes are always awake; their eyes are consistently open. This attitude makes Chekhov very similar to Dostoevskii, who rejected the accusations of conservatism from the liberal camp by declaring: 'I am liberal because I never sleep'. To those who accused him of conservatism, Chekhov could have answered in a similar manner.

It is thus hardly surprising that Dostoevskii, according to Merezhkovskii's own 'Autobiographical Note' wrote off Merezhkovskii's early poetry and told the young poet, ' "Do not write poetry. To write poetry one has to suffer, to know what suffering is".'[66]

The confrontation between poet and mob takes various forms. Chekhov was not the first instance of a poet whom the mob accused of being petty, banal, rude or materialistic. Lermontov for example was also accused by his critics of being pedestrian, cynical, and lacking ideas and aspiration. Note the recollection of Lermontov's acquaintance, the Decembrist Nazimov: 'We did not understand each other well [...] He would appear frequently as a realist, glued to Earth, without inspiration [...] He mocked government decisions with which we fully sympathized and of which we dreamed in our unfortunate youth."[67]

The abuse of high rhetoric and the need to descend to reality from the heights of solemn pronouncements was a well-known phenomenon in Lermontov's time. This taming of high Romanticism into a more subdued, modest form has been studied thoroughly by Virgil Nemoianu. During this period, which coincided with the Biedermeier movement in art, the poet would frequently appear more cynical or prosaic than his fashionably poetic audience. Heine, Byron and Lermontov are probably the greatest poets from this movement of deflation. Chekhov was also interested in this process, aware as he was of the Russian tendency, exemplified by his character Ivanov, to have elevated aspirations and yet accomplish very little.

Lermontov mocked the confrontation between the ecstatic, which is in fact conventional, and the deliberately prosaic, which is in actuality extraordinary. This is apparent in his depiction of the Grushnitskii–Pechorin conflict.[68] When Princess Mary plays piano, Grushnitskii cannot find any other words except a typical expression of poetic rapture, '*charmant, delicieux*'. Pechorin, on the other hand, asserts: 'I like music from a medical point of view. Music after dinner puts one to sleep, and sleep after dinner is good for one's health'[69]. One can easily imagine Chekhov playing Pechorin in response to Merezhkovskii's conventional excitement during their meeting in Italy.

In his essay on Lermontov (1909), Merezhkovskii seems to appreciate Lermontov's peculiar, shy, if not chaste, muse and defends it against the philistines who accused the poet of being rude and vulgar. (Merezhkovskii's 1913 essay on Byron is equally insightful). Merezhkovskii even attacks Vladimir Solov'ev for siding with the mob in opposition to the poet. With this essay, Merezhkovskii seems to grasp the peculiar poetics of the Biedermeyer period. Lermontov's was a time of 'reaction', when wild romantic expectations failed to realize; a time of sober modification. Hence Lermontov's , and his main protagonist Pechorin's, verbal deflation in the face of the bombastic rhetoric and wild claims of Lermontov's contemporaries, such as Aleksandr Marlinskii in real life, or Grushnitskii in Lermontov's novel.

Tolstoi once received a poem from his friend Afanasii Fet, and discovered that the poem was written on piece of paper that also contained a calculation for home heating. For Tolstoi, this was decisive proof that Fet was a true poet. Merezhkovskii, on the other hand, always found it difficult to grasp this tension between poetry and prose. Merezhkovskii's dialectical schemes and oppositions, be it spirit or flesh, paganism or Christianity, and his quest to combine them, ignores the obvious fact that true artists who express the spiritual through material forms have already accomplished such a synthesis. Heraclitus, for example, was known to indicate to guests who expressed unease at being entertained in the kitchen that 'Here, too, are gods.'"[70] It is such gods that Chekhov would see in Testov's soup and large shot of vodka, items which he would recommend to Merezhkovskii, only to have Merezhkovskii fail to see anything of significance in them at all. This failure is symptomatic, suggesting that it was as inevitable as the confrontation between a poet and an ideologue, or between a poet and the mob.

Merezhkovskii's thought is in truth never dialectical. He first breaks all complete and indivisible things into opposites, into black and white, the Devil and Christ, flesh and spirit, and then promotes some sort of artificial, intellectual integration. In real life however, as Dostoevskii would remind us, the human heart contains both God and the Devil, as they struggle with each other. Dichotomies, uncertainties and tensions are bound to enter the core of any matter.

For Merezhkovskii, as well as for Ivanov-Razumnik, another ideologue of the intelligentsia, the confrontation between the intelligentsia and social and cultural banality (*meshchanstvo*) is the engine of Russian historical development. Pushkin however sees it differently. For him, anyone who begins to impose pragmatic values upon art becomes a member of the mob, regardless of whether these are the primitive materialistic values of the *meshchane*, or the high political, ideological and religious values of the intelligentsia. Given this broad definition of mob values, the confrontation between Chekhov and Merezhkovskii can be seen as a rather standard encounter between an artist and an ideologue.

During the period of the taming of Romanticism, an era in which Chekhov's confrontation with the neo-Romantic aspirations of the Symbolists can be seen as a spiral-like repeat of such a taming, the mob or crowd might be more verbal and articulate, more poetic and inspiring than a poet or an artist. But the essence of the conflict remains the same. Instead of Ivanov-Razumnik's dichotomy of intelligentsia versus *meshchanstvo*, the dichotomy that Merezhkovskii adopted as the governing axiom of his own writing, one can propose the one suggested by Pushkin: the poet versus the mob.

Tsvetaeva, when she said that the poet is the train for which everyone is late, was hardly off the mark. By calling Chekhov a poet, Merezhkovskii prophesied their respective fates: throughout his life, it seems, Merezhkovskii was always late, always missing where Chekhov was going.

Notes

1 For a more detailed analysis of the story, see Vladimir Golstein, '"Doma': At Home and Not at Home', *Reading Chekhov's Text*, ed. by Robert Louis Jackson (Evanston: Northwestern University Press 1993), 74–85.
2 Robert Louis Jackson, 'Introduction', *Reading Chekhov's Text*, 1–19 (9).
3 Elena Tolstaia, *Poetika razdrazheniia. Chekhov v kontse 1880-x – nachale 1890-kh godov* (Moscow: Radiks 1994).
4 A. P. Chekhov, letter to A.S. Suvorin, dated 30 of December, 1888, *Polnoe sobranie sochinenii i pisem v tridtsati tomakh*, 30 vols (Moscow: *Nauka* 1974–87) 3:109–13.
5 N. M. Minskii, 'Absoliutnaia reaktsiia. Leonid Andreev i Merezhkovskii,' *D. S. Merezhkovskii: Pro et contra. Lichnost' i tvorchestvo Dmitriia Merezhkovskogo v otsenke sovremennikov*, ed. by A. N. Nikoliukin (St Petersburg: *Russkii Khristianskii gumanitarnyi institut* 2001), 171–95 (171).
6 D. Merezhkhovskii, "*Chekhov i Gor'kii*," *A. P. Chekhov: Pro et contra*, 699.
7 Ibid., 697.
8 Ibid., 707.
9 Ibid., 709.
10 Ibid., 716.
11 Ibid., 721.
12 Dmitrii Merezhkovskii, '*Asfodeli i romashka*', in *Akropol': Izbrannye literaturno-kriticheskie stat'i* (Moscow: *Knizhnaia palata* 1991), 209–16 (210).
13 Ibid., 214.
14 Fyodor Dostoevsky, *The Brothers Karamazov*, ed. Ralph E. Matlaw (New York: W. W. Norton & Co. 1976), 264.
15 Taken from a letter by Merezhkovskii to Valerii Briusov, dated 7 March 1910, reprinted in *Akropol'*, 324.
16 '*Brat chelovecheskii*', in *Akropol'*, 247–52 (248).
17 Ibid., 249.
18 Ibid., 251.
19 Ibid., 249.
20 Ibid., 250.
21 Ibid., 250–1.
22 Ibid., 251.
23 Merezhkovskii, '*Chekhov i Suvorin*', in *Akropol'*, 286–94 (291).
24 Ibid., 291, 294.
25 Quoted in C. Harold Bedford, *The Seeker: D.S. Merezhkovsky* (Lawrence: University Press of Kansas 1975), 140.
26 D. S. Merezhkovskii, *Polnoe sobranie sochinenii* (Hildesheim: Georg Olms Verlag 1973), 16:203–05.
27 Ibid., 15:147.
28 Ibid. p. 159.
29 Fyodor Dostoevsky, *The Demons*, 488.

30 Chekhov, letter to A. N. Pleshcheev dated 23 January 1888, *Polnoe sobranie sochinenii*, 2:183.
31 Chekhov, letter to Pleshcheev dated 4 October 1888, *Polnoe sobranie sochinenii*, 3:11.
32 Chekhov, letter to Pleshcheev dated 9 October 1888, *Polnoe sobranie sochinenii*, 3:19.
33 Chekhov, letter to O. L. Knipper-Chekhova dated 17 December 1902, *Polnoe sobranie sochinenii*, 11:94.
34 Chekhov, letter to A. S. Suvorin dated 3 November 1888, *Polnoe sobranie sochinenii*, 3:54.
35 Ibid., 55.
36 Ibid., 53–55.
37 Chekhov, letter to Suvorin dated 5 January 1891, *Polnoe sobranie sochinenii*, 4:157.
38 Chekhov, letter to A. N. Plescheev dated 25 December 1891, *Polnoe sobranie sochinenii*, 4:336.
39 Chekhov, letter to A. N. Veselovskii, dated 5 December 1901, *Polnoe sobranie sochinenii*, 10:131.
40 *Iz arkhiva A. P. Chekhova. Publikatsii* (Moscow: *Gosudarstvennaia ordena Lenina biblioteka SSSR) Otdel rukopisei*, 1960, 211.
41 Chekhov, letter to Suvorin, dated 2 March 1892, *Polnoe sobranie sochinenii*, 5:8.
42 Ibid.
43 Chekhov, Letter to V. S. Miroliubov, dated 17 of December 1901. *Polnoe sobranie sochinenii i pisem*, 10, 142.
44 Ibid.
45 Chekhov, letter to S. P. Diagilev, dated 12 July 1903 , *Polnoe sobranie sochinenii*, 11:234.
46 Chekhov, letter to Knipper-Chekhova, dated 16 March 1902, *Polnoe sobranie sochinenii*, 10:214.
47 Chekhov, letter to A. S. Suvorin dated 20 December 1891, PSS, 4: 286.
48 Chekhov, PSS, 17: 93.
49 Chekhov, PSS, 5: 259.
50 Chekhov, PSS, 17: 111.
51 Chekhov, PSS, 17: 68.
52 Chekhov, PSS, 17: 87.
53 Chekhov, PSS, 16:241.
54 Chekhov, PSS, 17: 27.
55 Chekhov, PSS, 17: 11.
56 Chekhov, PSS, 17: 46.
57 Anton Chekhov, *Short Stories*, ed. Ralph E. Matlaw (New York: W.W. Norton & Co. 1979), 191–2.
58 Zinaida Gippius-Merezhkovskaia, *Dmitry Merezhkovsky* (Paris: YMCA-Press 1951), 116–7.
59 Chekhov, PSS, 17:68; 82; 86.
60 Chekhov, letter to Suvorin, dated 8 September 1891, *Polnoe sobranie sochinenii*, 4:270.
61 D. S. Merezhkhovskii, *Akropol': Izbrannye literaturno-kriticheskie stat'i* (Moscow: *Izdatel'stvo Knizhnaia palata* 1991), 210.
62 F. M. Dostoevskii, "Diary of a Writer May-Oct. 1876," *Polnoe sobranie sochinenii v tridtsati tomakh* (Leningrad: Nauka, 1972–90), 23: 141–2.
63 Chekhov, PSS, 17: 102.
64 Chekhov, PSS, 17: 70.
65 L. D. Trotskii, *Literatura i revoliutsiia* (Moscow: Politizdat 1991), 245–58.
66 Merezhkovskii, *Polnoe sobranie sochinenii*, 24: 111.

67 Quoted in P. A. Viskovatov, *Mikhail Iur'evich Lermontov: Zhizn' i tvorchestvo* (Moscow: Kniga 1989), 272.
68 Vladimir Golstein, *Lermontov's Narratives of Heroism* (Evanston: Northwestern University Press 1998), 133-53
69 Mikhail Lermontov, *A Hero of Our Time*, trans. Vladimir Nabokov (New York: Doubleday Anchor Books 1958), 119.
70 "Heraclitus" *In The Presocratics. Edited by Philip Wheelwright* (Indianapolis: Bobbs-Merrill Educational Publishing 1978) 64–90, 75.

Part Three
LEV SHESTOV

9

LEV SHESTOV ON CHEKHOV[1]

Andrei Stepanov

Shestov's work on Chekhov – his substantial article 'Creation from Nothing' (*Tvorchestvo iz nichego*, 1905) – has not been forgotten in modern Chekhov studies, but is referred to only rarely, and even then in negative terms. The following famous lines are most commonly quoted: 'Persistently, dolefully, monotonously, during his almost 25-year literary career, Chekhov was engaged in one single activity: the various ways to kill human hope'.[2] As a rule, researchers point out that what one should discuss here is illusion rather than hope.[3] I contend that there is more to this matter than appears from this single quotation. Shestov himself felt that the quotation did not necessarily carry a negative meaning. Moreover, it did not prevent Shestov from considering Chekhov as practically the only writer among his contemporaries who spoke the truth, not because he was forced by the 'idea', but out of his own free will.[4] The title of Shestov's article on Chekhov is directly related to the principal statement from *The Apotheosis of Groundlessness* (*Apofeoz bespochvennosti*): 'all creation is creation out of nothing'.[5]

In the current chapter, I examine Shestov's paradoxical interpretation of Chekhov's creativity, by comparing aspects of Shestov's philosophy to Chekhov's artistic world.

In my view, Shestov's philosophy can be characterized as irrational.[6] In both his early and later works, his opposition of speculation to revelation is central. Speculation (or reason), i.e. rational thinking, logic, the law of causality, science, or complete philosophical systems (including ethics), is something that Shestov energetically denounces in every piece of his writing. In so doing, he regards the whole apparatus of categories and processes developed by reason as being only a reaction to the power of objective laws of the universe, that is to say necessity (*Ananke*). Divine Revelation, which became the core of Shestov's philosophy in a later period, remains undefined, and perhaps is indefinable. The only known route to revelation involves overcoming the self-evident and the power of necessity. Already in his early works, Shestov realized that this is only possible in extreme, tragic situations, 'situations of despair'.

Insisting on the primacy of the irrational, Shestov strives to annihilate rationalism in the very exposition of his thoughts. He refuses to use the apparatus of hypotheses and corollaries, and instead builds vast castles 'from nothing' – out of paradoxes and stark denial. This led to a situation where not only materialists, for whom the matter of dispute was meaningless, but sometimes even religious philosophers denied that Shestov's philosophy had independent value. Thus S. N. Bulgakov, in an article written immediately after Shestov's death, wrote: 'Shestov's philosophy is in fact pure rationalism, only with a negative coefficient, with a minus […] If not for this critique [of rationalism], it would have had nothing at all to say for itself'.[7] The same idea was expressed by Berdiaev: 'It was clear what he was fighting against. A positive form of exposition, on the other hand, was fraught with difficulty'.[8]

In other words, one can say with a certain inevitable imprecision, that the quintessence of Shestov's philosophy is the simple denial of any rational ideas, and above all of complete worldviews which claim to be universal and necessary. But what is the quintessence of Chekhov's oeuvre from Shestov's point of view? It is in fact that Chekhov '*a priori*, in advance, rejected all possible consolations, metaphysical or positivist'.[9] Chekhov's path is a path of emancipation from ideas, and it is this which, according to Shestov, is most interesting and significant. Thus he locates a watershed between his views on Chekhov, and Chekhov criticism of the time, which saw a great sin in this 'lack of ideas'.

Among Chekhov's characters, Shestov is primarily interested in those who find themselves in desperate situations and had to create 'from nothing': Professor Nikolai Stepanovich, Ivanov, Laevskii, Voinitskii, Kovrin. The concept of 'creation from nothing' assumes the necessity to live, think, feel and act in someone who is totally disillusioned with the rational ideas which hitherto framed his or her existence. This state of mind is, according to Shestov, pathological, but it gives the person a spiritual headstart, and can even turn this person into a genius of sorts. Shestov implies that Chekhov was in this situation himself, but instead of dying like Ivanov, he continued to live, having become a 'treasure hunter', i.e. a seeker of miracles. Thus Shestov's interest in Chekhov is not accidental: in the writer's oeuvre, Shestov finds both fundamental elements of his own philosophy – the rejection of the rational and the search for the miraculous – but in the aesthetic sphere through Chekhov's characters.

A careful reading of Chekhov's texts provides ample justification for Shestov's ideas. For example, the hero of 'A Boring Story' ('*Skuchnaia istoriia*'), after being asked by Katia what she was to do, reflects: 'It is easy to say "work", or "give your possessions to the poor", or "know yourself", and because it is so easy to say that, I don't know what to answer'. Indeed, this is the stance of a person compelled to 'create from nothing': the hero denies all consolations – positivist ('work') and metaphysical ('give your possessions to the poor', from the Gospels, or 'know yourself', from Socratic philosophy).

There are many more examples. It is clear that Shestov noticed and highlighted an important aspect of the epistemological theme in Chekhov's works, reminiscent of the corresponding constructions in Shestov's own philosophy. However, to see in Chekhov's stories an 'aesthetic double' of Shestov's philosophy is hardly possible. Here the very boundaries of the epistemological spheres of investigation are different.

For Shestov, necessity reigns firstly over two of the three main aspects of human existence – social and anthropological. His irrationalism is directed against the absolutization of strict social determinism and against all disasters (the inevitability of ageing, death, human vulnerability in the face of fatal accidents, etc). Secondly, Shestov repudiates the objective laws of the universe, including for example the laws of physics. 'Any natural connection between phenomena which does not allow for a miracle and which denies a sacred text its authenticity' – is inimical to him.[10].

In this way, Shestov turns out to be only superficially close to Chekhov, for the latter managed to stretch the domain of portrayed social contradictions (in the broadest sense), and to deepen them to include those common to all mankind. In Chekhov's works, necessity can be reduced to the concept of the accepted norm, and then Shestov's invariable denial of the rational corresponds to the 'abnormality of the normal',[11] with its various versions. Of course, Chekhov's texts do not include any denial of science, progress or ethics as such.

However, Chekhov does have something that is not found in Shestov: an understanding of the reciprocal relationship between the rational and irrational. Chekhov's characters, when they act rationally from their own point of view, continually perform deeds which are completely irrational from other people's viewpoints. This not only concerns the characters who are obsessed by an idea (Lida Volchaninova, Kovrin and others), but also the 'unthinking' characters. Recall the letter from the story 'At Christmas Time', written by 'banality [*poshlost'*] itself'. In this letter, the military service regulations are retold, and this is mentioned in the text:

> 'What does your son-in-law do in Petersburg?' asked Egor. 'He was a soldier, my good friend', the old man answered in a weak voice. 'He left the service at the same time as you did'. [...] Egor thought a little and began writing rapidly.[12]

The actions of such a character have subjective meaning: obviously, from his point of view, it is sensible to remind another soldier of the military regulations. However, in the context, this becomes senseless to the point of absurdity. Nevertheless the letter fulfils its function: Efim´ia understood everything without words, absurdity did not hinder meaning. Such mutual transitions of the meaningful into meaningless and back again often turn out to be connected with the theme of non-communicability. But this irrational topic in Chekhov's works turns out to be complicated by the fact that initially rational intentions are present in each agent of the failed communication.

As far as the introspective central characters are concerned – those who are trapped in desperate situations – their irrational actions are as a rule inconsequential. This is what happens after the 'sparrow night' of Nikolai Stepanovich, after Voinitskii's shot, and on many other occasions.[13] A desperate urge transforms into depression and indifference. Perhaps this accounts for the epigraph to Shestov's essay on Chekhov: '*Resigne-toi, mon coeur, dors ton someil de brute*'.[14]

Apparently, Shestov felt that Chekhov's texts were broader than his interpretation allowed. This can be proved by the fact that the following lines by Shestov appeared in connection with Chekhov: 'there exists in the world an invincible force, which oppresses and maims a human being – this is tangibly clear. The slightest imprudence, and the most insignificant of people as well as the greatest fall victim to this force. One can fool oneself only if one's knowledge is restricted to hearsay. But who has once found oneself in the iron claws of necessity will forever lose the taste for idealistic self-delusions'.[15] More often, Shestov used another metaphor for necessity, taken from *Notes from Underground*: a wall, a motionless, insurmountable obstacle. Here, however, it is referred to as an 'invincible force, which oppresses and maims a human being', that is to say it is animated and invested with the ability to act. However strange that might seem, in Chekhov's texts – those which Shestov did not address and possibly did not know – one finds precise parallels to this image. Such is, for example, the 'unseen oppressive force' which binds nature in 'The Steppe'. Such is an obvious metaphor of necessity – the 'peaceful green vastness' which tries to swallow the life of Vera Kardina ('At Home'); such is the 'unknown and mysterious force' which created a similar world in the story 'A Doctor's Visit'. Thus in many ways Shestov's inadequate interpretation unexpectedly touches upon the deep layers of Chekhov's creative world.

This is probably not accidental. Shestov sensed Chekhov's preoccupation with the problem of human cognition, and it is precisely this which allowed him to look 'in Chekhov's writings for a criterion of the most unshakable truths and of prerequisites of our cognition'.[16]

There was, however, yet another similarity between the two authors – in the very form of their thinking which can be called 'discrete-paradoxical'. Shestov thought in 'paradoxical fragments'. The denial which permeated this mental process was subjugated to the task 'not to console, but to disturb people'.[17] Denying the self-evident, Shestov addressed various domains of cognition, and invariably posed more questions than he answered. It is difficult to find a better philosophical parallel to the multiplicity of Chekhov's stories. Both authors strive to commentate on as broad a range of material as possible, not so much a rational *Weltanschaung*, as an irrational sensibility that accommodates multiple truths. In the *Apotheosis of Groundlessness* which was written at the same time as 'Creation from Nothing', Shestov proclaimed that mankind's greatest delusion hitherto had been the presumption of the uniqueness of the truth. He asserted the multiplicity of truths – both metaphysical and empirical. And these truths open up only to separate individuals. 'There are as many truths as there are people in the world'.[18]

Here the abstract Shestov converges with the concrete Chekhov. Shestov's philosophy was not accepted by many, but nobody denied his literary gift. Shestov perceived every idea as expressed by someone, he reasoned in images made up of characters without separating in the process the philosopher (as an individual) from his philosophy. His own heroes were invested with certain recital parts which varied from book to book: Plato's 'exercises in death', Plotin's 'most important', Nietzsche's '*amor fati*', Luther's '*sola fide*' and so on. These narratives were assembled into an infinite plot-free drama of cognition – the best analogue in philosophy of Chekhov's plays. On the other hand, in Shestov's later period, in contrast to Chekhov's, a centre appeared, towards which everything gravitated. This centre is God, who renders the impossible possible. But this is a strong-willed God, too reminiscent of a human. 'God, since he cannot determine an individual expression of will or invest it [*the expression of will*] with meaning, cannot then restrict an individual's will either'.[19]. God is seen as a character – a phenomenon which in Chekhov's world would of course be impossible. Yet the functions of Shestov's God are present in Chekhov's works in the form of those very hopes which Shestov accused Chekhov of annihilating. There are harmonious fragments in Chekhov when his desperate heroes hope in spite of everything. As played out in the finales of 'The Lady with the Lapdog', *Uncle Vania, Three Sisters*, and several episodes in other texts. In this desperate hope for the realization of the impossible we can observe a deep kinship between the writer and the philosopher.

Translated by Olga Tabachnikova

Notes

1 This is slightly amended version of the chapter from *Chekhoviana. Chekhov i 'serebrianyi vek'*, ed. M. O. Goriacheva and others (Moscow: Nauka, 1996).
2 L. Shestov, '*Tvorchestvo iz nichego*', in *Nachala i kontsy* (St Petersburg, 1908), p. 3.
3 See V. B. Kataev, *Proza Chekhova: Problemy interpretatsii* (Moscow: Izdatel'stvo Moskovskogo universiteta, 1979), p. 217; I. N. Sukhikh, *Problemy poetiki A. P. Chekhova* (Leningrad: Izdatel'stvo Leningradskogo universiteta, 1987), p. 157.
4 See L. Shestov, *Apofeoz bespochvennosti* (Leningrad: Izdatel'stvo Leningradskogo universiteta, 1991), p. 66.
5 Ibid., p. 72.
6 Here I must restrict myself to a very general synchronic description. An interesting diachronic interpretation of the early works of Shestov can be found in A. A. Danilevskii, 'A. M. Remizov i Lev Shestov (Statia Pervaia)', *Uch. Zap. Tartusk. Un-ta*, No. 883, *Trudy po russkoi i slavianskoi filologii* (Tartu, 1990), pp. 139–57.
7 S. N. Bulgakov, '*Nekotorye cherty religioznogo mirovozzreniia L. Shestova*', in *Sovremennye zapiski* (Paris, 1939), No. 68, p. 322.
8 N. A. Berdiaev, '*Osnovnaia ideia filosofii L'va Shestova*', *Umozrenie i Otkrovenie* (Paris: YMCA, 1964), p. 8.
9 Shestov, '*Tvorchestvo iz nichego*', op. cit., p. 12.
10 Shestov, *Umozrenie i otkrovenie*, op. cit., p. 190.
11 See G. A. Bialyi, *Russkii realizm kontsa XIX veka* (Leningrad: Izdatel'stvo Leningradskogo universiteta, 1973), pp. 19–22.
12 A. P. Chekhov, *Polnoe sobranie sochinenii i pisem v 30 tomakh* (Moscow: Nauka, 1977), Works, vol.10, p. 182.
13 See A. P. Chudakov, *Poetika Chekhova* (Moscow: Nauka, 1971), vol. 213, p. 4.
14 Charles Baudelaire, '*Le Gout de Néant*' in *Les Fleurs du Mal*.
15 Shestov, '*Tvorchestvo iz nichego*', op. cit., p. 50.
16 Ibid., p. 8.
17 Shestov, *Apofeoz bespochvennosti*, op. cit., p. 52.
18 Ibid., p. 165.
19 R. A. Gal'tseva, *Ocherki russkoi utopicheskoi mysli XX veka* (Moscow: Nauka, 1992), p. 109.

10

BETWEEN TRAGEDY AND AESTHETICS: SHESTOV'S READING OF CHEKHOV – A GAZE DIRECTED WITHIN

Olga Tabachnikova

I. 'Shestovizing' Chekhov: Facts, Conjecture and Existential Philosophy

Objectivity pertains to eternity; however, extreme subjectivity defines living beings. As in one of Bidstrup's caricatures, a new hat that has been sat on and crumpled provokes laughter in a sanguine person, and moves a melancholic person to tears. The same blow sounds sharp on glass and muffled on wood, and upon hearing the sound one is able to guess the nature of the material that absorbed the shock. In exactly the same indirect manner, the outside world manifests itself more expressively through indirect rather than direct speech. From this perspective, Lev Shestov's essay on Chekhov, bearing the intriguing title, 'Creation from Nothing', is in my view primarily (although not exclusively) a testimony to Shestov himself.

The principal idea of Shestov's essay, which provocatively conceals his more authentic insights into Chekhov's work, is delivered in the opening pages, in Shestov's laconic style: 'Chekhov was the poet *of hopelessness*. Stubbornly, despondently, monotonously for almost 25 years, over the whole course of his literary production, Chekhov did only one thing: in one way or another he killed human hope. In my opinion, this is the essence of his creative activity'.[1] Throughout his essay, Shestov circles like a vulture gathering strength over the theme of hopelessness. However, the remarkable point here does not lie in the merits of the case that Shestov makes, nor in what he finds (or, indeed, overlooks) in Chekhov's works, but in something entirely different: Shestov is in fact attacking himself rather than Chekhov; he is tearing up his own shadow, and struggling (unsuccessfully) to avoid taking the route down which he feels irresistibly drawn. For, in retrospect, this route turns out to be the trajectory of Shestov's own life and the foundation of his philosophy.

Indeed, for Shestov, whose primary focus has always been the tragic fate of the individual, the starting point in any philosophical search lay in hopelessness and despair, and philosophical truth for him could be attained only through extreme loneliness. Moreover, his favourite quotation was from Plato's *Phaedo*, that philosophy is nothing other than the contemplation of dying and death. Interestingly, Shestov's entry into philosophy was through the gateway of Russian literature, with its distinctly philosophical flavour concealed in its preoccupation with the cursed questions of existence. Shestov turned his study of literary works into a pilgrimage through the souls of writers, striving to unlock their hidden existential experience. These writers, in Shestov's interpretation, invariably went through crises and breaking points, ending in catharses which gave rise to the total transformation of their convictions. Preoccupied by the enigma of human life, tragedy, injustice and the nature of suffering, Shestov, in the spirit of the long-established Russian literary tradition, placed the human being at the centre of his investigations. Thus his approach to philosophical problems was distinctly anthropocentric. But it was also profoundly psychological, for Shestov's insights were based first and foremost on a psychological analysis of the writer, represented, as it were, by his fictional heroes. As Michel Aucouturier wrote:

> Shestov's critical method resembles [...] the Russian tradition of 'real criticism' in which a work of literature is only the excuse rather than the object of study. [...] Moreover, the reality that interests Shestov is not the outside world, but the inner world of the writer. Shestov sees in a work of literature a personal confession by the author, wherein the characters are simply representatives of the latter. He is not trying to explain a literary piece, but seeks in it a confirmation of what the writer has lived through – as the only guarantee of the philosophical value of the work. For true philosophy in his eyes can grow only out of an existential revelation.[2]

Clearly the figure of Chekhov, who also focused on human psychology and tragic dead-ends, must have provided Shestov with fertile ground for his investigations.

The idea of hopelessness lies at the heart of Shestov's analysis of Chekhov's oeuvre and, like a boomerang, comes back to reflect Shestov's own worldview. Shestov looks for the source of what he terms Chekhov's 'hopelessness' in

Chekhov's personal drama, in the shadowy corners of his life hidden from biographers:

> In 'Ivanov', the main hero compares himself to a worker who has overstrained himself. I think we shall not be wrong if we apply this comparison to the author of the drama as well. Chekhov overstrained himself – there can be almost no doubt about it. [...] Along comes this senseless, stupid, practically invisible incident, and the earlier Chekhov, merry and joyful, is no more; there are no more humorous stories for *Budil'nik*. Instead, there is a morose and sullen man, a 'criminal', whose words frighten even experienced and sophisticated people.[3]

Earlier on in the essay, Shestov makes several general statements about Chekhov's stories along the same lines:

> It is as if he was constantly in ambush, spying on and waylaying human hopes. Don't worry: he will not overlook a single one of them; not one of them will escape its fate. Art, science, love, inspiration, ideals, the future – run through all the words with which mankind has been, and still is, accustomed to be consoled or entertained – Chekhov has only to touch them, and they instantly fade, wither, and die. And Chekhov himself faded, withered, and died before our eyes. The only thing about him that did not die was his amazing art of killing, with a single touch, with even a breath or a glance, everything by which men live and of which they are proud.[4]

It is instructive to compare these ideas with some thoughts on Shestov in a paper by Igor Balachovskii (Shestov's great-nephew), entitled 'Proof by Absurdity'. The author mentions certain biographical events from Shestov's youth:

> The horrors of life, which for many are simply statistical averages, are for others a living reality, and what is even more horrifying than that, is the fact that they, these "others", stand out against the general background of relative wellbeing. Endowed with a lively and shrewd mind, the 12-year-old Liolia Shvartsman, the future Lev Isakovich Shestov, came to know these horrors to their full extent when he was kidnapped by an unknown group, apparently of anarchist orientation, in the hope of getting a ransom. His father, a wealthy Kiev merchant, displayed firmness, refused to give the money and three months later the child returned home, alive and well, but having lived through so much! This is the official biography. However, unofficial legend adds that all was not so simple – the boy could

have been just playing at "abduction" like others play Cossack bandits. How after that can one stop looking for a threatening sign of something invincibly horrible, hiding in the corners and ready to jump out at any time from things that are most common and routine?[5]

He further writes about Shestov's first-born and illegitimate son Seriozha, whose mother worked as a maid in the wealthy Shestov household. The boy was taken into the family and brought up by friends of Shestov's parents.

Balachovskii writes: 'I readily admit that for Lev Isakovich [...] the feeling that his son was not his son in the eyes of the community, that this was the reason why the boy was so stressed, that "air is measured for him so lamentably and sparingly" (Tiutchev) was an open wound'.[6]

This crisis, Balachovskii thinks, opened Shestov's eyes to 'the horrible abyss waiting for us all, a glimpse into which will turn a human being into a philosopher, not "from surprise", as Aristotle thought, but "from despair"'.[7]

Doctors well know, Balachovskii continues, that people become depressed not as a result of external factors, but because such is their inner endogenous design. If Shestov invests so much energy in removing thick make-up to reveal that the philosophy of many great people is a philosophy of despair, he does so only because he himself belongs to the same category and even takes pride in it.[8]

Thus the parallel becomes clearer. Describing the gloom of the 'overstrained' Chekhov, Shestov is in fact fighting with his own mirror image, or rather peering beyond the looking glass into that domain of tragedy that (in his own words) 'people enter only when forced to'.[9] This is even more significant given that, as Simon Karlinsky effortlessly exposed, Shestov distorted Chekhov's biography by 'postulating a traumatic event in Chekhov's life between the completion of "The Steppe" and the writing of his next two works *Ivanov* and "A Dreary Story", which Shestov claimed were autobiographical'.[10] Karlinsky elaborates: 'Shestov believed that "Ward No. 6" was Chekhov's temporary concession to the humanistic ideals of the Russian literary tradition before slipping back into his usual despair in his next work, "The Duel"'.[11] Karlinsky comments that 'the chronology is as wrong as the interpretations',[12] and explains that '"The Steppe" (January 1888) was written after *Ivanov* (October 1887), not before it; "A Dreary Story" (July–August 1889) was written simultaneously with one of Chekhov's most affirmative works, the comedy *The Wood Demon*. This makes a shambles of the trauma of 1888–89'.[13] Karlinsky attests that 'The writing of "The Duel" did not follow that of "Ward No. 6", but preceded it by a year'. He concludes that Chekhov wrote 'a number of stories on melancholy themes before *Ivanov*' and that he in fact 'went on writing humorous stories after the publication of that play'.[14] Thus for Karlinsky, Shestov's essay remains 'a derivative piece of writing that deliberately distorted both Chekhov's texts and his biography', and 'combined Mikhailovsky's "On Fathers and Sons and Mr Chekhov" with Zinaida Gippius's "On Trivia"'.[15] Karlinsky traces the former influence in Shestov's treatment of 'A Dreary Story' as 'Chekhov's most self-revealing work', and the latter in the idea that 'Chekhov "assassinated human hope"'.[16]

However, as Viktor Erofeev observed, the question of the authenticity of a writer's image was for Shestov essentially devoid of meaning.[17] The Salvationist nature of his philosophy forced him to reinvent the writers he studied in his search for the universal ways of dealing with tragedy. Thus Chekhov too, it seems, fell victim to the same 'Shestovizing'. Boris de Schloezer, Shestov's translator and friend, who understood him better than many, reached a similar conclusion. In his introduction to Shestov's book, *L'homme Pris au Piège*, which included the essay 'Creation from Nothing', he considers the preoccupation of both Shestov and Chekhov with the idea of the overstrained individual, and supposes that this might be a reflection of their own personal crises – a turning point in their ideologies. For Shestov, de Schloezer knows that this was actually the case. He writes: 'In fact there is nothing in common between the naïve idealism and moral stance of Shestov's "Pushkin" and his passionate interrogation of Tolstoi'. This leads him to question the validity of Shestov's depiction of Chekhov: 'A natural question arises which cannot be ignored – how precise is Shestov's interpretation of Chekhov; isn't this portrait in fact a self-portrait?'[18]

To appreciate Schloezer's point, we must look in more detail at Shestov's interpretation of Chekhov, but first we must understand the evolution and substance of Shestov's philosophical views. The essay 'Creation from Nothing' was written in 1905; and became part of *Beginnings and Ends* (*Nachala i kontsy*, 1908). This book built upon Shestov's previous works, most notably those on Tolstoi, Dostoevskii and Nietzsche, and was marked by Shestov's distinct attack on positivism and idealism. However, as de Schloezer's remark indicates, Shestov had begun his career on a different note. In his first book – *Shakespeare and his Critic Brandes* – he advocated tragedy and assigned deep meaning to it. As Ivanov-Razumnik writes:

> Shestov stopped with horror before the phantom of the Accidental, which removes any meaning from human life. [...] For years Shestov sought an answer to this tormenting question of the senselessness of human life, of its accidental nature. He first thought that this question could be solved by asserting the meaning of existence, and disavowing that ghost-like Accidentality and replacing it with "sensible necessity". He found this answer in the works of Shakespeare.[19]

Indeed, at the time, Shestov wrote: 'where we see the domain of a ridiculous and senseless tragedy, the poet sees a meaningful process of spiritual development. Under the torments visible to all he uncovers the invisible task of life'.[20] In fact, by assigning an idealistic value and meaning to life with all its tragedies, Shestov was at that time essentially advocating the Kantian point of view of a total predetermination of being through an *a priori* law of nature. He denied the accidental nature of life and tragedy by investing them with a deep moral meaning. However, he soon abandoned this position.

In fact, while searching passionately for meaning in life as a way of justifying tragedy, Shestov was striving to overcome his own growing scepticism towards this idealistic system of beliefs. He thus followed in the footsteps of Belinskii, Dostoevskii, Nietzsche and so many others who started off with an idealistic conception, only to experience complete disillusionment and seek different answers. According to Ivanov-Razumnik, there is a dichotomy in the question about the meaning of life: either there is no meaning and our life is accidental, or there is no accident and so there is meaning to life. 'Shestov', Ivanov-Razumnik asserts, 'began with the second answer, only to arrive ultimately at the first one'.[21] Thus by the time he wrote essay 'Creation from Nothing', Shestov had already elaborated his philosophical position. Right from the start, he focused on the idea that there are aspects of human beings that do not lend themselves to scientific analysis – precisely because they are so individual, private and subjective that they escape generalization and hence lie outside the domain of science. However, science in its steady advance and with a depressing self-assurance claims omnipotence over the human world, if not today then tomorrow, and therefore the very foundations of science have to be questioned, Shestov argued. The objective is trying to oppress the subjective, and human reason – instead of standing up for every living soul – actually justifies this oppression. Shestov thus concluded that knowledge and reason must be deeply flawed at their very roots. By what right, Shestov asks, does Greek philosophy and its direct heir, modern European thought, regard man as no more than another link in the evolutionary chain, thus using reason to seal man's tragic destiny? Shestov reacted with a resolute indignation and revolt to the necessity celebrated by reason. He thus did no less than provide a fundamental critique of the whole history of Western philosophy.

The scholar Andrias Valevičius has observed that in Chekhov, Shestov found a kindred spirit who seemed to uphold the same philosophical position: 'In keeping with his interpretation of Dostoevskii, Shestov likewise understands Chekhov to be rebelling against the "idea"'.[22] Similarly Sidney Monas notes that what Shestov 'loved about Chekhov was precisely the absence of any violating idea, any general conception – indeed, the shrinking into absurdity and ironic exposure of all general ideas, especially ideas about society, human behaviour, and morality, the withering away of idealistic self-delusion'.[23] Indeed, as Shestov states in his essay, 'worldviews and ideas, which a great many people treat quite indifferently (actually these innocent things do not deserve any other attitude) become for Chekhov objects of bitter, inexorable, and merciless hatred'.[24] Shestov demonstrates through his characteristically ironic and indirect discourse Chekhov's opposition to scientific speculative philosophy. He quotes Nikolai Stepanovich, the old professor in 'A Dreary Story', contemplating his imminent death, and emphasizes the fact that in the scientist's gloomy and desperate thoughts, the soul suddenly gains the indisputable upper hand over mind or reason. As if identifying the hero with the author – his usual device, which prevented many literary critics from endorsing him as one of their own – Shestov summarizes:

> In contrast to what occurred before, reason is again respectfully pushed out of the door, and its rights are transferred to the "soul", to the dark, vague aspiration which Chekhov, now that he stands before the fatal boundary separating man from the eternal mystery, instinctively trusts more than the bright, clear consciousness, which beforehand determines even views of the afterlife. Will scientific philosophy be outraged? Is Chekhov undermining its firmest foundations?[25]

Shestov argued that 'even in Tolstoi, who also had no great respect for philosophical systems, one does not find such a sharply expressed aversion to all sorts of worldviews and ideas as can be found in Chekhov'.[26] He continues: 'idealism of all kinds, both open and concealed, arouses in him [Chekhov] a feeling of intolerable bitterness'.[27] Furthermore, the following lines by Shestov about Chekhov are applicable to Shestov himself without any alteration, for they express the essence of Shestov's outlook:

> An inescapable force exists in the world, crushing and crippling man – this is palpably clear. Be there the slightest imprudence, and the greatest as well as the most insignificant people fall victim to it. You can deceive yourself about it only as long as you know of it solely by hearsay. But whoever has once been in the iron clutches of necessity loses his taste for idealistic self-delusion forever.[28]

Although Shestov's words may read like an attack on Chekhov and his 'A Dreary Story', they are in fact an attack against 'omnitude' (*vsemstvo*) – conventional public opinion – which in Shestov 's eyes Chekhov rebelled against in this story within the framework of a broader rebellion – against philosophical trends of the positivist and idealistic variety. Reading between the lines of Shestov's ironic, almost sardonic, indirect discourse, it is clear that he approves of what he sees as Chekhov's anti-idealistic stance. Having described the agony of Chekhov's dying hero, the old professor, Shestov asks provocatively:

> What does Chekhov do? Instead of going past indifferently, he takes the side of this ugliest creature, he dedicates tens of pages to descriptions of his suffering, and gradually brings the reader to develop, instead of a natural and lawful feeling of indignation, some unnecessary and dangerous sympathies to this decaying and petrifying existence. Clearly one cannot help the professor [...]. But if it is impossible to help, then one should just forget – that is a simple truth.[29]

Furthermore, Shestov makes (in the impetuosity of his narration, one might say) some claims that are even more anti-humane (when talking about the same hero of Chekhov – the old professor Nikolai Stepanovich); such claims are, in fact, implicitly directed against 'eternal morality', as Shestov calls it, for he considered the latter to be an offshoot of reason, of speculative philosophy and rationalism. And just as he would align writers' views with those of their protagonists, Shestov assigns anti-humane sentiments to 'eternal morality': 'Looking at this ugly creature evokes a cruel thought even in the kindest and most compassionate of people – to finish off this pitiful and disgusting beast as fast as possible'. If it is not possible to kill him off, Shestov continues, one could at least hide him away somewhere: 'These are the fighting skills permitted not only by our legislation, but also, if I am not mistaken, by eternal morality itself'.[30]

Thus in his philosophical attack on 'ideas' and on autonomous ethics in particular, Shestov discerns Freudian undercurrents, according to which the dominant aspect of each person is animal, carefully hidden beneath manners, education and other social but purely cosmetic facades. This core of human behaviour, Shestov implies, is simply a corollary of the utilitarian function which idealism conceals within itself, as Chekhov, according to Shestov, knew only too well. And the disavowal of basic human sympathy as demonstrated above was surely a tool deployed deliberately by Shestov in order to underline how detached from real life, how 'inhumane' and if you like 'immoral', 'eternal morality' actually is.

There are two important implications that follow from Shestov's interpretation of Chekhov. The first is the close proximity between Shestov's philosophy and Freudian theories (which were still emerging at the time), revealing the inner contradictions of Shestov's thought. The second concerns a certain confusion between what Shestov interprets as Chekhov's hatred of the 'idea' or 'conception', and what in my view is Chekhov's disdain for any kind of hypocrisy. Let us address both of these implications.

II. Shestov, Freud and Positivist Philosophy: Proximity to the Enemy

As Viktor Erofeev observes, 'Shestov's Salvationism in its maximalist foundation runs into contradiction with the demands of the cultural tradition, thus bringing the philosopher to a certain cultural nihilism'.[31] Erofeev stresses importantly that 'Mikhail Gershenzon's pathos as an opponent of Viacheslav Ivanov in their "Correspondence From the Two Corners", in considering culture as a "system of most subtle forces" is very close to Shestov, who becomes delighted every time when "the voice of nature takes the upper hand over superficial cultural habits"'.[32] Georgii Adamovich in his essay 'Viacheslav Ivanov and Lev Shestov' goes even further, asserting that in this polemical correspondence with Gershenzon, Ivanov was really addressing Shestov.[33] Thus essentially Shestov seeks to celebrate what, if taken to its logical extreme, in Freudian terms would be a victory of the Id over the Super-ego. Indeed, Freud's concept of the super-ego – the entity which contains internalized norms, morality and taboos, points to the forced nature of cultural and social norms which are only accepted by humans in order to make their co-existence possible. In other words, the corollary of both Freud's theory and Shestov's attacks on rationalism is an assertion of the purely utilitarian nature of human morality. In the same way, Shestov's assertions, most notably in connection with Chekhov, about the flimsiness of human cultural habits that disintegrate fast in the face of a serious crisis such as illness or death, are also evidence of his proximity to Freudian perceptions, to a vision of man as directly descended from the animal kingdom.[34]

In this, Shestov's perception of Chekhov is strikingly similar to that of Veniamin Al'bov in his 1903 critical review of Chekhov. Indeed, Al'bov's central claim concerning Chekhov's early work is his vision of the incredible instability and ephemeral character of the cultural side of human nature. The following words from Al'bov describing Chekhov's perception of mankind exactly mirror the views that Shestov was trying to promote in connection not only with Chekhov, but with every thinker he ever studied (it is also significant that these words from Al'bov refer to Chekhov's 'A Dreary Story', which is the cornerstone of Shestov's analysis of the writer): 'How quickly this cultural coating rubs off man, under the influence of such insignificant circumstances as illness, fear of death, etc., and what a disgusting animal underlining is exposed under even such a flower of life as the old professor. [...] What an animal generally a human being is – a pitiful, helpless animal, lost in the boundless, incomprehensible world'.[35]

Further on, however, Al´bov's views on Chekhov depart drastically from those of Shestov. Indeed, Al´bov sees a substantial evolution of Chekhov's worldview, observing a 'new and very important point of departure'[36] in Chekhov's work. This is a transition from seeing culture as a thin veneer covering the fundamentally animal nature of a human being, to seeing the cultural dimension as constituting the nucleus of personality and the nucleus of life. For Al´bov 'from this moment on, Chekhov's talent gained a more general significance'.[37] Shestov, by contrast, does not acknowledge any evolution, apart from a progression (akin to his own) from idealistic illusion to tragic revelation.

B. M. Eikhenbaum, on the other hand, argues that, rather than perceiving man as essentially wild and forced into cultural norms through practical necessity, Chekhov displays a distinct animosity towards anything primary and spontaneous (phenomena which Shestov labelled the 'voice of nature') as opposed to the cultural, since Chekhov, asserts Eikhenbaum, was in awe of culture.[38] He traces the source of this divide in what he deems to be Chekhov's belief in the transitory and derivative nature of the gulf between prose and poetry, reality and the ideal. '…it is remarkable that this rift between prose and poetry for Chekhov is not fundamental, not metaphysical, not the same as in Dostoevskii. […] For Chekhov this rift is not permanent or substantial, but is temporary and derivative. Hence his awe before culture and his hostility to all things elemental and primary',[39] Eikhenbaum writes.

Chekhov's conception of man as weak and culturally volatile, which to Shestov clearly signified their common ground, in Eikhenbaum's analysis would be their point of drastic departure. Shestov sarcastically rejects the eternal morality of the above perception of man, and uses this to expose its utilitarian roots. However, his own idea of mankind is in fact little different, owing to his insistence on total freedom, which ultimately comes into conflict with culture. This concept of humanity, of course, also points to Darwinism, and as such exposes the usual contradiction of Shestov's philosophy, where his very struggle conceals within it the seeds of revolt, which grow to turn it into its opposite and to bring Shestov into the enemy's camp.

Paradoxically then, the above considerations of Shestov's proximity to Freud link his extremely anti-positivist stance to its opposite – a materialistic position. This rather natural corollary of Shestov's theories becomes particularly evident in his treatment of Chekhov. In some ways, Chekhov, owing to his immensely tolerant and pluralistic discourse, inadvertently facilitates the disclosure of Shestov's rather extreme philosophical position and authoritarian style. In fact, as Simon Karlinsky notes, the general property of Chekhov's writings serves as a kind of litmus paper that reveals the hidden tendencies of those whose worldview suffers from monologism: 'What is surprising is the way Shestov and other sophisticated metaphysicians of the Symbolist era were led by their fear and mistrust of Chekhov's pluralism to form ideological alliances with the materialists and utilitarians of the earlier generation'.[40]

In a similar way to that in which Shestov ends up in the opposite camp, Nietzsche's philosophical constructions that signify the crisis of nihilism bring him very close to Freud – a similarity that did not go unnoticed among critics. In very basic terms, at the core of both Freudian and Nietzschean theories is a perception of the human being as essentially cruel, self-serving and instinct-driven, whatever attitude these thinkers then went on to adopt in relation to this state of affairs. Similarly, Shestov's struggle was against ideologies and ideals as well as against crude materialism, which he saw as being a corollary of positivism. Yet his protest against necessity, understood too broadly, ironically brought him back into close proximity with the very materialism against which he had rebelled.

'Having subjugated "the laws of nature" to an active attack, Shestov then no less decisively attacks "the laws of culture". He sees the essence of culture in its striving towards "finalization", "synthesis", "extremes", which would allow a European to settle in life with a certain comfort, but which have nothing to do with the truth',[41] Erofeev writes. He then points out Shestov's juxtaposition of the European 'lie', with the 'truth' of the lack of cultural tradition in Russia and a subsequent boldness in Russian literature. However, as Erofeev goes on to say:

> Justly noting the complex and contradictory character of Russia's spiritual dialogue with Europe, Shestov ignores the fact that the selfless search for the truth undertaken by Russian art contrasts with the inadvertent "utilitarianism" of his own stance, which strives to liberate itself from both natural and cultural "limitations" in order that one could finally declare: "There is nothing impossible in the world".[42]

Interestingly, Shestov's inadvertent landing in the opposite philosophical camp, revealed by Shestov's treatment of Chekhov, is a result of his very discourse, which is authoritarian by nature. The importance of this becomes apparent when traced from Shestov's style to the content of his ideas in his interpretation of Chekhov. Indeed, as usual Shestov imposes on the writer his own vertical 'author–hero' hierarchy, that is to say that the author 'inhabits' the hero, as it were, from above, taking on both creative and governing functions. Chekhov, on the contrary, displays in his writings a distinctly horizontal arrangement between the author, his heroes and, for that matter, the reader – as all are located on the same plane, at an equal height. Indeed, Chekhov's plays and stories demonstrate a profoundly democratic vision, free from any kind of didacticism or impositions. As Aleksandr Chudakov pointed out, 'the single dogmatic feature in Chekhov is his condemnation of dogmatism'.[43] In Chekhov's literary world the author speaks from a position of equality rather than dominance, and his voice, if and when it is at all audible, is just another one in the chorus of his heroes who essentially appear to be free from any authorial guidance. As James Wood wrote, Chekhov's characters 'act like free consciousnesses, and not as owned literary characters', they 'forget to be Chekhov's characters'.[44]

Forcing Chekhov's pluralism, like Dostoevskii's polyphony, into Shestov's monological world was bound to cause distortion. Therefore it is not surprising that Erofeev talks of Shestov's 'spiritual terrorism' in his propensity to inscribe the process of overcoming the laws of 'humanness' into a symbolic act of approximating the tragic.[45] Similarly, by labelling it extreme, Balachovskii, in a rhetorical sense only, likens Shestov's ideology to Bolshevism'.[46] Furthermore, if one recalls here that, in the words of Joseph Brodsky: 'Both the German and the Russian versions of socialism sprang from the same late nineteenth century philosophical roots, which used the shelves of the British Museum for the fuel and Darwinian thought for a model',[47] we see Shestov's *de facto* return to Darwinism, facilitated by his inadvertent, even metaphysical, proximity to socialism. Consciously he was extremely opposed to both, condemning, along the lines of Dostoevskii, Darwinian teaching for the consequences it had for human spirituality.

III. The Difference Between Ideologies and 'Lofty Rhetoric'

Let us now look more closely at Shestov's claim about Chekhov's hatred of 'the idea' – the implied rejection of all established concepts. Shestov writes: 'The longer Chekhov lives, the more he grows out of the power of lofty words – contrary to his own reason and conscious will. In the end he completely emancipates himself from ideas of every kind and even loses track of connections between the events of life'.[48] Thus Shestov equates 'lofty words' with 'ideas of every kind'. However, rather than being identical, they are complementary, or more precisely, ideas are traditionally accompanied by lofty rhetoric. This confusion lies in the phenomenon of hypocrisy which for Chekhov, of course, was a crucial theme and constantly present in his writings. As James Wood summarizes, 'his father, Pavel, may be seen as the original of all Chekhov's great portraits of hypocrites. Pavel was a grocer, but he failed at everything he touched except religious devotion'.[49] Wood notes also in connection to Pavel's habitual flogging of his children that he was 'exceptionally cruel' and 'horribly pious'.[50] Thus, Wood comments, 'Chekhov would become a writer who did not believe in God, hated physical cruelty, fought every sign of "splendour" on the page, and filled his fiction with hypocrites. The ghost of Pavel can be found everywhere in Chekhov'.[51]

Indeed, Varvara and the priest in 'In the Ravine', the countess in 'The Countess', as well as endless examples of other heroes, are the hidden embodiment and the actuating force of evil in the world. As Al'bov wrote, repeating Chekhov's own phrase: 'Varvara appears perhaps not as an embodiment of evil – this would be too much to say – but as a defense of evil, as a "protective valve in a machine"'.[52] So too do other of Chekhov's hypocrites, who by their very existence and by their preaching seem to validate and seal off the horrible injustice of the world. Chekhov's disdain for hypocrisy is all-pervasive and puts him next to Dostoevskii in their anticipation of the next century. As Andrei Bitov observed, 'he felt with his skin, like that Japanese fish which predicts earthquakes, what the twentieth century would bring to Russia'.[53] Indeed, if in Russian society in Chekhov's day, hypocrisy was intensified in particular by the emerging bourgeois morality, facilitated by rapid urbanization, but was something that could still be felt as alien and shameful, in Soviet Russia it took on a new level, having become effectively the only official way of life. The hypocritical rhetoric which covered the immense schism between thoughts, words and deeds totally discredited the values it proclaimed. Idealistic pathos was no longer trusted, and cynicism penetrated all layers of society. In Chekhov's time this was not yet endorsed on such a massive scale, but Russian social backwardness and its recent history of virtual slavery had precipitated a national inferiority complex which gave rise to all sorts of authoritarian discourses, including in the cultural sphere.

Brodsky in his essay 'On Tyranny' describes the new tyrants associated with the new level of cruelty and hypocrisy: 'Some are more keen on cruelty, others on hypocrisy'.[54] He also mentions that the easiest and fastest route to dictatorship is to become a family tyrant. Whether or not one follows Wood in making a connection with Chekhov's own tyrannical family, Chekhov was particularly sensitive both to cruelty and to the discrepancy between words and actions, and his very poetics consequently resists tyranny in all its forms.[55]

However, what Shestov correctly observed as Chekhov's intolerance of high rhetoric should not be confused with the writer's hatred for ideas *per se*. When Shestov talks of Chekhov's 'emancipation from ideas', in my opinion he falls victim to a confusion between ideas and the lofty discourse that discredits them. In other words, it is not ideals as such that Chekhov despises, but rather the hypocritical emotionalism of idealism and the philistine values that loom behind it. As, for example, Aikhenvald writes, 'philistinism [*poshlost'*] [...]

makes people use phrases and jokes from which concepts have been removed; it forces one to churn over in one's mind all the same stale ideas, and it turns all the flowers of life, all its garden, into something artificial, breathless, made of paper'.[56]

The topic of Chekhov's relationship with ideals has attracted much critical attention and controversy, for the same reason that the authorial voice in Chekhov's writings is so hard to discern. As Wood writes, 'more completely than any writer before him Chekhov became his characters'[57] (but not in the sense that Shestov means – that Chekhov is self-revealing; rather in the sense of a brilliant actor who has the ability to penetrate another's soul and to convey it to the audience). However, many conflicting critical voices broadly agree that Chekhov oscillated between, or existed on the verge of, horrible reality and the unattainable ideal. The difference in these opinions is largely in the discussion of Chekhov's bias towards either of these two entities, and in the attempts to pin down chronologically the dynamics of his longing for the ideal.

The struggle against idealism that Shestov identifies in Chekhov very possibly originates in the distinctly rebellious elements of Chekhov's art. Indeed, Chekhov's principal drive is that for freedom, for liberation of the human spirit from the bonds of the philistine, the mundane mentality of hypocrisy and self-deception. As such it resonates powerfully with Shestov's own drive for human salvation which he likewise perceived as a boundless freedom; only for him the concept of freedom had a different meaning. For Shestov, freedom is much more abstract than for Chekhov, it is a freedom from all conceptions, a freedom to attain the allegedly impossible, it is a leap into faith. In particular, this philosophical striving of Shestov includes liberation from utilitarian morality, which in Chekhov's case turns into an almost equivalent struggle against social and personal hypocrisy. Thus, it is clear that although Chekhov's understanding of freedom in its concreteness and its ethical nature was substantially different from Shestov's abstract and irrational understanding, Shestov easily singled out in Chekhov elements common to them both (or rather he could easily interpret those elements in that light). In other words, it is the very concept of freedom that was crucial for the two writers.

Indeed, as Susan Sontag affirms, Chekhov's whole *oeuvre* is a dream of freedom, and the same, I would add, can be said about Shestov. Bernard Martin observes that at the time of writing the *Apotheosis of Groundlessness* (contemporary with 'Creation from Nothing') 'Shestov was merely beginning his struggle against the ideas dominating European thought which he felt had to be overcome in order to provide room for what was later to be the chief burden of his positive message'. However, Martin places 'the possibility of the restoration of human freedom through religious faith' at the centre of this message together with 'the reality of the living God of the Bible'.[58]

Chekhov's concept of freedom, though, is not specifically religious in nature; it is 'an absolute freedom, [...] the freedom from violence and lies', as Wood writes, quoting Chekhov, and notices the frequency of 'the open fields' at the edge of a village in Chekhov's works. Because for Chekhov, Wood explains, freedom is 'a neutral saturate', it is more than political or material liberty; it is rather 'like air or light'.[59] For abstract Shestov, freedom is understood more metaphysically. It is the state God originally endowed man with, and it is what rationalism destroyed, thereby subjecting man to universal necessity. Absolute freedom for Shestov lies in overcoming the necessity of existential horrors, it is essentially in the domain beyond the rational and beyond the natural. For the concrete Chekhov, on the contrary, it is certainly to be found within the boundaries imposed on human life by natural law, and stems from our individual inner freedoms which have to be restored by humanity itself. Thus, in a way, both Chekhov and Shestov would agree that the source of man's liberation is in 'remembering our divine image' (using Gurov's phrase from Chekhov's 'Lady with the Lapdog'), even though they would differ in their interpretation of this phrase.

Thus Shestov replaces Chekhov's struggle against illusions with a struggle against ideals.[60] It is in Shestov's fundamental interpretation of ideals as shackles, and hence in waging war on them, where the general confusion actually originates. Because if one's philosophy is grounded in a feeling of love for a human being rather than in misanthropy (and considering the Salvationist nature of his philosophy this was certainly the case for Shestov), then it is precisely in the ideal where the highest freedom of the human spirit is concealed. Chekhov was clearly conscious of this in the latter period of his writing career. This explains his constant striving for the unattainable ideal as an act of spiritual liberation, despite his extremely sober stance regarding reality. Shestov, on the contrary, and quite paradoxically, while desperately seeking the universe where all things are possible, denied the ideal any liberating qualities, and strove instead for something much broader than a system of ideals – namely, for a religious faith. Perhaps the grain of this fundamental difference lies again in Chekhov's very concrete, and Shestov's very abstract nature. Indeed, for Chekhov a human ideal embodies as much as there can be to aspire to spiritually in this life (and he knows no other), while for Shestov the ideal is only an impediment which stands as a deceptive consolation on the way to real salvation – to be sought beyond the rational.

IV. 'Aestheticism' Versus 'Creation from Nothing': Revolt, Cruelty, and Aesthetic Myopia

Despite the distorting excesses of his analysis of Chekhov with regard to ideologies, Shestov nevertheless believed that it was the duty of the writer to portray reality as it is, without dressing it up in illusory idealistic consolations. In contrast to the works of Viacheslav Ivanov, whose ideas, in Shestov's view, were radically separated from reality and instilled with their own independent life because they did not feed 'on the juices of real life', Chekhov's writings depicted reality with great precision, in all its tragic hopelessness. No wonder then that Shestov 'found himself in perfect harmony with the writer who, more than any other, both expressed and typified the "violet hour" of Russian culture'.[61] But the roots of this harmony reached deeper. As Victor Erofeev notes, in opposition to Ivanov's aestheticism and 'in a broader sense to "literature" as a whole, Shestov identified in Chekhov the concept of what he termed "creation from nothing"',[62] because this, according to Shestov, was the defining quality of Chekhov's characters. They were tragic, 'underground' people, the 'living dead,' who found themselves in desperate situations and lost their balance as a result of extreme unbearable strain, but continued to exist as if by inertia. Indeed, for Shestov, Chekhov's central focus and main interest resided in the description of these limiting situations, 'from which there is not, and cannot possibly be, any way out'.[63] It is a description of overstrained individuals for whom there is nothing else left to do but 'fall to the floor, or to beat their heads against the wall'.[64] This route is in fact the route of Job (a story of great personal significance to Shestov) and the route of the ancient prophets: to scream and wail, to beat your head against the wall.[65] Karlinsky, however, pointed out with some disdain that this phrase (and variations of it) became the leitmotif of Shestov's entire essay and was presented as 'the only solution Chekhov ever had to offer to life's problems'.[66] Shestov elaborates on the concept of creation from nothing in the following lines:

> A normal man, even if he is a metaphysician of the most extreme transcendental doctrine, always adjusts his theories to the need of the moment; he destroys only to build later from the old material. For this reason, he is never short of material. Obedient to the basic law of human nature, long ago noted and formulated by the sages, he limits himself to and is content with the modest role of a seeker of forms. From iron, which he finds ready in nature, he forges a sword or a plough, a spear or a sickle. The thought of creating from the void hardly occurs to him. But Chekhov's heroes, for the most part abnormal people, are confronted with this unnatural and therefore horrible necessity of creating from nothing.[67]

Sidney Monas adds yet another angle to Shestov's choice of title: 'Steeped as he was in Cabalist and Neoplatonist literature, he could only have meant to attribute something godlike, something akin to divinity, to Chekhov's melancholy poetry'.[68] However, the main reason for this concept resided in Shestov's idea that the real and only hero in Chekhov is a hopeless person who has nothing left to do in life, who carries about him a contagious destruction wherever he goes. Such a hero has nothing; he has to create everything from the void and this creation is the only thing, according to Shestov, that stirs Chekhov's inspiration: 'When he [Chekhov] has stripped his hero of everything', he 'begins to feel something like satisfaction'.[69] But doesn't this task – to create from the void – go beyond the limits of human strength, of human rights?, asks Shestov. He further adds that even Chekhov himself would not be able to answer that question. In fact, Shestov asserts that those who do have a ready answer which they can deliver without hesitation, have never really encompassed the question, or for that matter any 'final questions' of existence. This is because – and this is Shestov's important and recurrent theme – hesitation is a necessary element in the reasoning process of a person brought to face a fatal task. In 'A Dreary Story', the old professor has nothing better to offer the person dearest to him – young Katia – who feels desperately lost, than to utter: 'I don't know'.

Ramona Fotiade argues in her book on Shestov that 'the ambivalent meaning of this answer can be understood in view of Baudelaire's similar remark: "*Resigne-toi mon coeur, dors ton sommeil de brute*"'[70] (the lines with which Shestov both begins and finishes his essay 'Creation from Nothing'). Fotiade affirms that 'what man discovers in his confrontation with death is not mere resignation (in the sense of a passive acknowledgement of "eternal" rational truths), but resignation mixed with revolt'.[71] This again naturally evokes the figure of Job whose 'revolt paradoxically emerges from utter powerlessness and despair', and similarly whose ' "inhuman", one-to-one communication with God is established not through speculative reasoning, but through a revolt that destroys reason and re-discovers faith as the "creation" of meaning and truth "*ex nihilo*" '.[72]

However, Ivanov-Razumnik's interpretation of Shestov's essay does not touch upon this notion of revolt. He only sees in the quoted lines from Baudelaire a call for a humble resignation, for an attempt 'to come to love your poor, ill and ridiculous life'.[73] In other words, he finds in it a confirmation of Shestov's outlook on life at the time when he subscribed to the Nietzschean formula of '*amor fati*'. This appeared to Shestov much more helpful for dealing with the horrors of existence than trying to rationalize them with high morality and ideals. 'But if all this is so, if the last law on earth is loneliness and the last word of the philosophy of tragedy is hopelessness', Ivanov-Razumnik exclaims, 'if all the norms, all the "a priori" judgments and imperatives came tumbling down; if we cannot thus escape the underground, then how can we avoid the next conclusion of the Underground Man: "I need peace of mind. Yes, I want to be left alone; I'll sell the whole world for a song. Should the world go to pot or should I have my cup of tea? I'll say – let the world go to pot, but I demand my cup of tea'".[74] Thus Ivanov-Razumnik sees Shestov's philosophy as being governed first and foremost by absolute egoism.

Similarly, Viktor Erofeev insists that Shestov's tragic outlook for which the adequate form of perception is 'beating your head against the wall', intensifies not only despair, but also egoism. Erofeev explains that the balance between a tragic person and the world is broken, with the tragic hero placing himself above the external world, hence the morality of tragedy is characterized by moving from humanism to cruelty. However, he then notes that the idea of cruelty is in fact alien to Shestov and can be attributed to the excesses of Shestov's struggle against idealism and positivism.[75]

I find that these views miss the point somewhat. In contrast to them, Berdiaev claimed that the meaning of the underground man's demands lies in the problem of individuality – of the opposition between the private and the general domains. Ordinary egoism, according to Berdiaev, can adjust its needs to the world only too easily; it is free from tragedy and even insured against it. Instead Berdiaev found the question 'concerning tea' to be 'philosophical, ethical and religious; it is a "cursed" question, a fall into the underground kingdom ... This is the problem of theodicy, as it is often called, and it is the main problem of human life'.[76]

Nevertheless, Erofeev's idea prompts an interesting observation: the underlying cruelty of Chekhov's hopeless heroes that stems from their extreme solitude, or in other words the mercilessness that the tragic person involuntarily exudes when severed from the world. However, their mercilessness is derived from their very hopelessness and is directed above all against themselves. In fact, Chekhov's characters overwhelmingly lack the egocentric streak and prefer to suffer in silence without making a drama out of their crisis. This is true of the heroes in 'About Love', 'House with an Attic', 'A Name Day', 'Wife', not to mention 'Lady with the Lapdog' (which is exceptionally full of hope), and many others that seem to have completely escaped Shestov's attention.

As to Chekhov's own attitude to his 'lost' heroes, which has been a point of debate among several generations of Chekhov scholars, I side with those who saw it as entirely opposite to cruelty – namely, as deep compassion: his 'almost every line is a sob',[77] as Shestov noticed too. And when Shestov, following Mikhailovskii, talked of 'evil sparks' in Chekhov's eyes, he might have been misled by Chekhov's deliberate detachment that served a very precise purpose. 'When you describe the miserable and unfortunate, and want to make the reader feel pity, try to be somewhat colder; that seems to give a kind of background to another's grief, against which it stands out more clearly [...] The more objective you are, the stronger will be the impression you make',[78] Chekhov wrote. As a result, his works have a sobering effect on the reader by demonstrating that even in this totally tragic and hopeless world it is possible and necessary to live, and, moreover, to remember 'the higher aims of existence and our dignity as human beings'[79] – an effect which is very different from 'killing human hopes'.

Another problem with Shestov's treatment of Chekhov, as Erofeev shrewdly observes, is that realist writers like Chekhov, whose works (unlike that of Viacheslav Ivanov and his spiritual associates) feed on the juices of real life, resist Shestov's assisted creativity, his help in revealing their 'tendencies'. As a result of such 'resistance', Shestov's intentions change, stealthily turning into unmasking the writers, Erofeev claims:

> It is not only literature that turns out to be guilty of concealing tragedy. Shestov suspects the writers themselves of cowardice, hypocrisy, treachery and retreat ... The main meaning of this unmasking is determined by the fact that Shestov profoundly lacks the pathos of distance with respect to the writer he studies, which in turn has to do with a certain dogmatism of his "adogmatic" philosophy.[80]

This, Erofeev explains, emerges again from a certain monism in Shestov's perception of tragedy, despite his disdain for monism. He further argues that the pathos of distance in Shestov's methodology gives way to the 'arbitrariness' that Shestov himself once proclaimed, provocatively, as his critical method. As a result, the image of the writer is often distorted beyond recognition. I see such a distortion in Shestov's perception of Chekhov taking place first of all at the level of aesthetics. Thus, Kornei Chukovskii was outraged by Shestov's essay on Chekhov, and expressed this in the following terms in his letter to his New York correspondent:

> Now a book by Lev Shestov has been published in the States, which contains an essay on Chekhov, 'Creation from Nothing'. I read it with indignation. I cannot tolerate preachers who want to solve questions of art outside aesthetics, without understanding the first thing about art.[81]

It is possible that a deep meaning is concealed in Chukovskii's remark, for all his life Shestov remained first and foremost a philosopher. In the constant inner struggle between the philosopher and the artist, it was the philosopher who invariably won. This meant that ideas were dearer to Shestov than what Chukovskii calls 'aesthetics'.

For an artist, as indeed for any writer or poet, form is inseparable from content, and even, in a certain sense, prevails over it, if by form one understands the dictates of language. For a philosopher, on the other hand, it is the idea or even the concept that carries weight. In the same way, for Shestov, despite the elegance of his style, the most important thing was his philosophical conception. Thus, Shestov was primarily concerned not with Chekhov, the artist, and not with literature as such, but with its philosophical aspect, and especially with the revolt against speculative philosophy. However, since art, in Brodsky's words, is 'a means of conveyance, a landscape flashing in a window – rather than a destination',[82] its origins are distinctly non-utilitarian, and hence any 'conceptual' considerations in it are secondary. Thus, any 'applied' approach to art is bound to be distorting. It is worth adding to this the fact that, as Milosz suspected, Shestov's personal drama was 'that of lacking the talent to become a poet, to approach the mystery of existence more directly than through mere concepts'.[83]

Thus one has to conclude that Shestov's outlook on Chekhov, despite all its undeniable metaphysical penetration, suffers from the poetic myopia of a philosopher.[84] Subjected to this outlook, which in essence is introverted, the topic under study inevitably turns out to be neglected. In most cases, as from a lamp suspended over the threshold, what remains is only its shadow. As a result, this tendentious attitude (where the ethical unnaturally separates itself from and subdues the aesthetic) obstructs Shestov's access to the infinite space of Chekhov's artistic creativity, in which, as in life itself, no evil (as well as no good) is absolute; and what opens up beyond the horizon is nothing more than another horizon.

Notes

1 Lev Shestov, 'Creation From Nothing: On Anton Chekhov', in *A Shestov Anthology*, edited with an introduction by Bernard Martin (Athens, Ohio: Ohio University Press, 1970), p. 94.
2 Michel Aucouturier, 'Le Dostoïevski de Chestov', in *Diagonales Dostoievskiennes* (Paris: Presses de L'Université de Paris-Sorbonne, 2002), p. 79. In what follows, all the translation is mine, unless otherwise stated.
3 Lev Shestov, 'Creation From Nothing: On Anton Chekhov', op. cit., p. 96–7.
4 Ibid., p. 95.
5 Igor Balachovskii, '*Dokazatel'stvo ot absurda*', in *Léon Chestov. Un philosophe pas comme les autres?*, Cahiers de l'émigration russe 3 (Paris: Institut d'Etudes Slaves, 1996), p. 49.
6 Ibid., p. 50
7 Ibid.
8 Ibid.
9 Lev Shestov, '*Filosofiia tragedii. Dostoevskii i Nietzsche*' ('The Philosophy of Tragedy. Dostoevskii and Nietzsche') in *Sochineniia v dvukh tomakh* (*Works in Two Volumes*), vol. I (Tomsk: Vodolei Publishing House, 1996), p. 327.
10 Simon Karlinsky, 'Russian Anti-Chekhovians', *Russian Literature*, (15) 1984, p. 189. The title of Chekhov's 'A Dreary Story', referred to by Karlinsky in this quotation, is also often translated as 'A Boring Story' (O.T.).
11 Ibid.

12 Ibid.
13 Ibid.
14 Ibid.
15 Ibid.
16 Ibid., pp. 188–9.
17 Viktor Erofeev, '"*Ostaiotsa odno: proizvol*" *Filosofiia odinochestva i literaturno-esteticheskoe kredo L'va Shestova*', ["Only one thing remains: arbitrariness" Lev Shestov's philosophical and aesthetic credo'], *Voprosy Literatury*, (10) 1975, p. 172.
18 Boris de Schloezer, 'Préface', in *Léon Chestov, L'homme pris au piège* (Paris: Plon, 1966), pp. 11–2.
19 Ivanov-Razumnik, *On the Meaning of Life* (Letchworth: Bradda Books Ltd, 1971), p. 170.
20 Lev Shestov, *Shakespeare and his critic Brandes* (St Petersburg: Mendelevich's Publishing House, 1898), p. 234.
21 Ivanov-Razumnik, op. cit., p. 188.
22 Andrius Valevičius, *Lev Shestov and His Times: Encounters with Brandes, Tolstoy, Dostoevsky, Chekhov, Ibsen, Nietzsche and Husserl* (New York: Peter Lang, 1993), p. 45.
23 Sidney Monas, 'New Introduction', in Lev Shestov, *Dostoevsky, Tolstoy and Nietzsche* (Ohio: Ohio University Press), 1969, p. XIX.
24 Shestov, 'Creation From Nothing: On Anton Chekhov', op. cit., p. 108.
25 Ibid, p. 109.
26 Ibid., p. 99.
27 Ibid., p. 121.
28 Ibid, p. 121–2.
29 Shestov, '*Tvorchestvo iz nichego*' ('Creation from Nothing') in *Sochineniia v dvukh tomakh (Works in Two Volumes)*, op. cit., vol. II, p. 192.
30 Ibid.
31 Erofeev, op. cit., p. 172.
32 Ibid.
33 See Georgii Adamovich, '*Viacheslav Ivanov i Lev Shestov*' in *Odinchestvo i svoboda* (New York: *Izdatel'stvo imeni Chekhova*, 1955), pp. 253–54.
34 This paragraph features in my other article ('Anticipating Modern Trends: Lev Shestov – Between Literary Criticism and Existential Philosophy', *Australian Slavonic and East European Studies*, vol. 22, Nos. 1–2, 2008, pp. 105–19), although there further elaboration departs from developing this line of argument. It is only here that I follow up these ideas to their logical conclusion.
35 V. P. Al'bov, '*Dva momenta v razvitii tvorchestva Antona Pavlovicha Chekhova*' ('Two stages in the development of A. P. Chekhov's oeuvre') in *A. P. Chekhov: Pro et Contra. Tvorchestvo A. P. Chekhova v russkoi mysli kontsa XIX – nachala XX v. (1887-1914) (A. P. Chekhov: Pro et Contra. Chekhov's creativity in Russian thought of the late XIX – early XX centuries (1887–1914))*, Anthology, ed. I. N. Sukhih, A. D. Stepanov (St Petersburg: *Izdatel'stvo Russkogo Khristianskogo gumanitarnogo Instituta*, 2002), p. 387.
36 Ibid, p. 389.
37 Ibid, p. 402.
38 B. M. Eikhenbaum, '*O Chekhove*' ('On Chekhov') in *A. P. Chekhov: Pro et Contra. Tvorchestvo A. P. Chekhova v russkoi mysli kontsa XIX – nachala XX v. (1887–1914) (A. P. Chekhov: Pro et Contra. Chekhov's creativity in Russian thought of the late XIX – early XX centuries (1887–1914))*, Anthology, ed. I. N. Sukhih, A. D. Stepanov (St Petersburg: *Izdatel'stvo Russkogo Khristianskogo gumanitarnogo Instituta*, 2002), p. 964.
39 Ibid.

40 Karlinsky, op. cit., p. 190.
41 Erofeev, op. cit., p. 176.
42 Ibid. The phrase 'There is nothing impossible in the world' is a quotation from Shestov, '*Apofeoz bespochvennosti*' ('Apotheosis of Groundlessness') in *Sochineniia v dvukh tomakh* (*Works in Two Volumes*), op. cit., vol. II, p. 140.
43 Aleksandr Chudakov, *A. P. Chekhov's Poetics*, transl. Edwina Jannie Cruise and Donald Dragt (Ann Arbor: Ardis, 1983), pp. 204–05.
44 James Wood, *The Broken Estate. Essays on Literature and Belief* (London: Jonathan Cape, 1999), p. 87.
45 Erofeev, op. cit., p. 173.
46 Balachovskii, op. cit., p. 68.
47 Joseph Brodsky, 'Profile of Clio' in *On Grief and Reason. Selected Essays* (England: Penguin Books, 1997), p. 130.
48 Shestov, '*Tvorchestvo iz nichego*' ('Creation from Nothing'), op. cit., p. 189.
49 Wood, op. cit., p. 78.
50 Ibid.
51 Ibid.
52 Al'bov, op. cit., p. 397.
53 Andrei Bitov, '*Moi dedushka Chekhov i pradedushka Pushkin*' ('My grandfather Chekhov and great-grandfather Pushkin') in *Chetyrezhdy Chekhov* (*Four Times Chekhov*) (Moscow: Emergency Exit, 2004), p. 11.
54 Joseph Brodsky, 'On Tyranny' in *Less Than One. Selected Essays* (England: Penguin Books, 1987), p. 114.
55 For a more detailed discussion on Chekhov's poetics's resistance to tyranny see '*Ot Chekhova k Dovlatovu: Proslavlenie bestsel'nosti, Ili Poetika, okazyvaiushchaia soprotivlenie tiranii*' ('From Chekhov to Dovlatov: Praising purposelessness, Or, Poetics that Resists Tyranny'), in *Filosofiia A. P. Chekhova* [*The Philosophy of A. P. Chekhov*], ed. Anatolii Sobennikov (Irkutsk: ISU Publishers, 2008), pp. 238–56.
56 Iulii Aikhenval'd, 'Chekhov' in *A. P. Chekhov: Pro et Contra. Tvorchestvo A. P. Chekhova v russkoi mysli kontsa XIX – nachala XX v. (1887–1914)* (*A. P. Chekhov: Pro et Contra. Chekhov's creativity in Russian thought of the late XIX – early XX centuries (1887–1914)*), Anthology, ed. I. N. Sukhih, A. D. Stepanov (St Petersburg: *Izdatel'stvo Russkogo Khristianskogo gumanitarnogo Instituta*, 2002), p. 735.
57 Wood, op. cit., p. 83.
58 Bernard Martin, 'The Life and Thought of Lev Shestov', Introduction to Lev Shestov, *Athens and Jerusalem*, transl. Bernard Martin (Athens: Ohio University Press, 1966), pp. 19–20.
59 Wood, op. cit., p. 86.
60 This confusion was pointed out by various scholars. See for example Vladimir Kataev, *Proza Chekhova: Problemy interpretatsii* (*Chekhov's prose. Problems of interpretation*) (Moscow, 1979), p. 217; Igor' Sukhikh, *Problemy poetiki Chekhova* (*Problems of Chekhov's poetics*) (Leningrad, 1987), p. 157.
61 Monas, 'New Introduction', op. cit., p. XIX.
62 Erofeev, op. cit., p. 170.
63 Shestov, 'Creation from Nothing: On Anton Chekhov', op. cit., p. 99.
64 Ibid, p. 100.
65 Shestov, '*Tvorchestvo iz nichego*' ('Creation from Nothing'), op. cit., p. 210.
66 Karlinsky, op. cit., p. 189.

67 Shestov, 'Creation from Nothing: On Anton Chekhov', op. cit., p. 110.
68 Monas, 'New Introduction', op. cit., p. XIX.
69 Shestov, 'Creation from Nothing: On Anton Chekhov', op. cit., p. 115.
70 Ramona Fotiade, *Conceptions of the Absurd. From Surrealism to the Existential Thought of Chestov and Fondane* (Oxford: EHRC/Legenda, 2001), p. 77.
71 Ibid, p. 77.
72 Ibid, p. 79.
73 Ivanov-Razumnik, op. cit., p. 221.
74 Ibid.
75 Erofeev, op. cit., pp. 172–3.
76 Nikolai Berdiaev, '*Tragediia i Obydennost'*' ['The tragic and the Ordinary'], in Lev Shestov, *Sochineniia v dvukh tomakh* (*Works in Two Volumes*) (Tomsk: Vodolei Publishing House, 1996), vol. I, p. 476.
77 Shestov, 'Creation from Nothing', op. cit., p. 96.
78 Anton Chekhov, from letters to Lydia Avilova of March 19 and April 29, 1892 in *Anton Chekhov's Short Stories*, selected and ed. by Ralph E. Matlaw (New-York/London: W. W. Norton & Company, 1979), p. 273.
79 Anton Chekhov, *Lady with Lapdog and Other Stories*, transl. by David Magarshack (London: Penguin Classics, 1964), p. 270.
80 Erofeev, op. cit., p. 171.
81 Kornei Chukovskii, from a letter to his American correspondent, given in L. Rzhevskii, '*Zagadochnaia korrespondentka Korneiia Chukovskogo*' ('A mysterious correspondent of Kornei Chukovskii'), *Novyi zhurnal*, No. 123, June 1976. Cited in Natalie Baranova-Shestova, *Zhizn' L'va Shestova* [*Lev Shestov's Life*] (Paris: Russkaia Mysl', 1981), vol. I, p. 98.
82 Joseph Brodsky, 'Footnote to a Poem', transl. by Barry Rubin, in *Less Than One. Selected Essays* (England: Penguin Books, 1987), p. 202.
83 Czeslaw Milosz , 'Shestov, or The Purity of Despair', in *Emperor of the Earth: Modes of Eccentric Vision* (Berkeley: University of California Press, 1977), p. 101.
84 For a more general discussion of Shestov's attitude to aesthetics see Olga Tabachnikova, 'The Treatment of Aesthetics in Lev Shestov's Search for God' in *Aesthetics as a Religious Factor in Eastern and Western Christianity*, eds. Wil van den Bercken and Jonathan Sutton; *Eastern Christian Studies 6* (Leuven, Belgium: Peeters Publishers, 2005), 179–95. Here I have only cited the summary and main conclusions of that argument in as far as it is relevant to Shestov's treatment of Chekhov.

11

SHESTOV–CHEKHOV, CHEKHOV–SHESTOV[1]

Savely Senderovich

How did the philosopher Shestov interpret the work of the artist Chekhov? What was Chekhov's response to Shestov's philosophical work? These are the themes of the present chapter. What is at stake here is not a dialogue, but two independent episodes, linked by the cast of characters. The philosopher suggested an interpretation of the artist, while the artist used motifs from the philosopher's book. The former episode is exposed to everybody, but requires interpretation. The latter has been hitherto unexamined, and here is discussed for the first time.[2] Such a symbiosis perhaps is telling of the character of the relationship between philosophy and art. As we shall see, Shestov's and Chekhov's turning to each other is no accident: they were united by a deeply-rooted desire to understand the world and life.

***

During his own lifetime, Lev Shestov (1866–1938) became one of the brightest stars on the world philosophical stage. This fact is much better known than the significance he had for the history of the Russian Silver Age. Only one historian of Russian culture, Avril Pyman (in her history of Russian Symbolism) would seem to have granted Shestov his due place.[3] In general, his significance for Russian literature of the first half of the twentieth century, and especially for the Silver Age, otherwise remains ignored. And yet because Shestov's books constitute a substantial part of the intellectual context of that epoch, not taking into account his thought would leave many important texts unread.

Shestov's very early works had attracted the attention of Tolstoi and Chekhov. His first book 'Shakespeare and his Critic Brandes' (St Petersburg, 1898) demonstrated his focus (which never really changed) on the extreme problems of human existence. These problems do not lend themselves to abstract considerations because our experience and knowledge end there (at the stage of ascertaining the problems) and general laws become doubtful. Shestov approached these problems not in order to resolve them once and for all, but distinctly to pose and clarify their difficulties and limitations, and, no less importantly, their tormenting insistence. His strategy in this regard was to consider the experience of the great tragic writers, the relationship between the writer's oeuvre and his personality, and the mystery of this personality concealed in the depth of his fictional texts. This was done in contrast to the pervading intellectual climate, which was dominated by an interest in socio-historical circumstances as the condition of creativity. Furthermore, the background of Shestov's philosophizing, which set high demands for future thought, was his incessant pondering over Biblical texts.

Shestov's second book *Good in the Teaching of Count Tolstoi and Friedrich Nietzsche* (St Petersburg, 1900) attracted the attention of Sergei Diagilev, whose taste and activity were among the most vital formative forces in the culture of the Silver Age. Diagilev suggested that Shestov collaborate with him in his journal *The World of Art (Mir Iskusstva)*, which he founded in 1898 when he was still quite young. The journal's issues 4 to 8 from 1902 inlcuded Shestov's next book, *Dostoevskii and Nietzsche (The Philosophy of Tragedy)*. Schopenhauer and Nietzsche had educated Russian thought of the early twentieth century to accept the sense of one's mortality as a trigger which activates one's dissatisfaction with rational knowledge and enables one to see the individual and tragic aspect of life. They also wrote of how to accept the concept of tragedy as a key motif of cultural history. Whence it was possible to go in two different directions. Viacheslav Ivanov, who, following Nietzsche, focused on the origin of tragedy in the cult of a dying and resurrected god, preferred mystical–metaphysical constructions, which he joined with the the Slavofile idea of the native ground *(pochvennichestvo)* and communality *(sobornost')*. He created an impressive synthesis of the history of ancient tragedy with the history of Christianity, in order to give a new perspective on cultural history, where society and the individual merge in harmonious accord, and cultural history can be seen as universal history. Shestov chose a different route: instead of the traditional grand idealistic constructions, he focused *on tragedy as an existential category*. He defined tragedy as a loss of the ground under one's feet in one's personal world, and accepted *groundlessness (bespochvennost')*, in a paradoxical way, as the only genuine *ground* for human existence, thus creating an ontology of crisis. This was not a reaction to Ivanov's constructions – Shestov's views were formed earlier. His values are not the common and necessary, but the personal and uniquely individual – precisely that which allows man to take off from the common and necessary. He showed that a genuine consciousness, not trimmed for the Procrustean bed of rationalism, together with the profound thought that awakens in it, lives on the territory of tragedy. This understanding is very close to Chekhov's, who, in his own intuitive fashion, moved in the same direction.

I

In the last year of Chekhov's life (1904), Shestov wrote an article on the writer. It was published after the writer's death, in 1905, in the journal *Questions of Life* (*Voprosy zhizni*), and later became part of his book *Nachala i kontsy* (*Beginnings and Ends*, 1908). The philosopher approached the writer from a point of view fully developed by that time. First of all, it was important for Shestov to see the face of the author behind his text, for art and philosophy (as he was shortly to demonstrate) are areas of profound human expression. This stance contradicted the ideological and sociological approaches to literature which were prevalent at the time. Secondly, Shestov was convinced that the motivation for creativity is in suffering, that an artist must experience tragedy and find himself over an abyss in order for his talent to be awakened. The talent of an artist (who is a kind of philosopher) and of a philosopher (who is a kind of artist) is in his ability to create without having ground under his feet, in a state of despair and inability to live, in other words, to create from nothing. 'Creation from Nothing' is the title of Shestov's article on Chekhov. This meant that the writer was considered within an existential framework. Shestov had already approached other writers from this point of view – first of all Shakespeare, and then Tolstoi and Dostoevskii. However, according to Shestov, Tolstoi lived through happy years when young and had his own version of Christianity, while Dostoevskii embraced Russian Orthodoxy and nationalism. Both had illusions with respect to their calling as prophets. Chekhov had nothing of the sort: neither joyous reminiscences, nor illusions. In this sense Chekhov is unique. He disavows all illusions, poses the most difficult questions and does not give answers, does not leave any hope, creates from nothing. Chekhov hates all the standards according to which people and their lives are judged. Above all he hates ideas as stereotyping devices and exposes them as superstitions. In contrast to the usual attacks, in the writings of ideologically-driven critics, on Chekhov's lack of ideology, Shestov values highly all of these characteristics in Chekhov, as these are the features of a true artist-philosopher. Creation out of nothing is the most authentic kind of creativity and a dignified response, truthful and courageous, to the real challenges of human existence. Chekhov is not afraid of the most profound and most final questions of life (this resonates with the title of Shestov's book *Beginnings and Ends*, of which the article on Chekhov became a part).

Shestov's was the first perspicacious response to Chekhov, a writer who was deeply respected and most misunderstood by the Russian reader. And yet Shestov allowed himself to be carried away and somewhat simplified Chekhov's portrait. The face that he saw behind the texts he identified with that of Chekhov's heroes: 'The real and only Chekhov's hero is a hopeless person',[4] and the author, in his view, is the same: 'Chekhov scourges, torments and tortures himself, but cannot change circumstances'.[5] Already at the very beginning of the article, Shestov gives a distinct definition of his vision of Chekhov: 'To define his tendency in two words, I shall say: Chekhov was the singer of hopelessness. Stubbornly, despondently, monotonously during almost 25 years of his literary work, Chekhov only did one thing: in one way or another he killed human hope. And here, in my view, lies the essence of his work'.[6] This is not a reproach, for Shestov highly values this feature of Chekhov, and so he challenges the reader: 'Maybe you will go further and try to find in Chekhov's complaints the criterion of sturdier truths and preconditions of our understanding'.[7]

Shestov made an important discovery: Chekhov was a lyrical poet, and not someone who unmasks the vices of society (as he was often, and still is, understood). He did not depict life, but looked intensely into its non-obvious paradoxes, explained existential problems, which may be cured if the self-evident is submitted to doubt, and, most crucially, only in reflection, in introspection. However, having got carried away by his discovery, Shestov overlooked some aspects of Chekhov's oeuvre which substantially modify the portrait of the 'singer of hopelessness'. We shall point out some of them, but only to the extent necessary to make principal corrections to the portrait drawn by Shestov.

Firstly, neither pessimism, nor singing praises to hopelessness, nor killing hopes, belong to the list of Chekhov's intentions. Chekhov's task is a precise analysis of the profound phenomena of human life, irrespectively of whether his tone is playful or reserved. His analytical examination brings meaningful light, not the kind which answers a question but rather makes the question more acute. Chekhov is not issuing verdicts and prescriptions à la Tolstoi. Shestov is wrong when he asserts that Chekhov follows Tolstoi; as a rule Chekhov disagrees with the Great Teacher. For example, when Tolstoi's Ivan Iliich, at the end of his meaningless life sees a light; this is not a light of truth, but a symbol of a possibility of salvation – a moralizing gesture on the author's part. When the old professor in Chekhov's 'A Boring Story' (*Skuchnaia istoriia*) approaches the threshold of death with a feeling of reaching dead end, this is the price he is to pay for having been able mercilessly to evaluate his own life.

The completed life transcends both tragedy and fortune. When Doctor Ragin dies in 'Ward No. 6' in a fit of rage, in a condition sanctioned throughout the philistine course of his life, he is pitiful, but also makes, albeit for a split second and of no avail, a breakthrough to some kind of understanding of which he had been deprived all his life. There is no promise ahead, in either case, but there is no heroization or stoicism either.

Secondly, Chekhov is highly ironic. His irony is addressed above all to his reader who, as Chekhov knows, is inclined to look at his heroes through the prism of current clichés without paying attention to the subtleties of the language in which these heroes are presented. His irony is situated where it is least expected: just under the surface of the narrative of a failed life, which a reader is used to view compassionately. He allows the reader to see in Likharev in 'On the Road' (*Na puti*) a major and heroic personality, while a detailed plan of his narrative exposes mockingly his pettiness and the falsity of his life. He palms on the reader Laievskii's (*Duel*) description of himself as a 'superfluous person', which served as a standard badge of honour for the reader brought up on Russian literature of the nineteenth century – thus is incapable of seeing the falsity of this label. Moreover, Chekhov shows that a person cannot in principle be assigned to a type (and this during an era when the public educated by criticism looks for types in literature), but is instead an individuality whose ways are unpredictable. In short, one of the most important aspects of Chekhov's literary work is the creation of an independent discourse opposing the commonplaces of culture.

Thirdly, Shestov is mistaken when he separates the young and humorous Chekhov from the mature, tragic one. Chekhov never lost the ability to laugh. Apart from the aforementioned mocking attitude towards the reader, he, in his ever vigilant self-observation, when turning to his own persona, treated it in the language of comedy. This happened in his dramatic work. From 'Ivanov' (or even the prototypical 'Fatherless', *Bezottsovshchina*) on to *The Cherry Orchard*, he projected his own self onto the stage in the style of travesty and even burlesque.[8] If one takes into account that his last dramatic work was his farewell piece, then one can say that Chekhov died with a mocking grin on his lips – ambiguous, full of bitterness, but still a grin.

My correction of Shestov's portrait of Chekhov aims not to reproach the philosopher, but instead to warn against the usual misunderstanding of the path which he in fact opened up.

II

Probably the most admirable thing about Shestov is that he did not assume the pose of a tragic hero, and did not take upon himself the mission of a tragic poet. Over time, having immersed himself in the history of philosophy, he came to share the view of the philosopher of late Antiquity, Plotinus, on the necessity of 'soaring above knowledge', over the despotic will of the common and the obvious. And he favours laughter as the means of this ascent. 'One must plough up the dead and trodden field of contemporary thought. Toward this end, whenever there is an occasion or without occasion, at every step, one must fundamentally and without foundation ridicule the most accepted judgements and express paradoxes. And the chips may fall as they will'.[9] In his books he cheerfully takes on the giants of thought, using mockery as a weapon. He insists, in contrast to Spinoza, who forbade philosophers to cry, laugh, or curse, that it is appropriate for man to express himself precisely in those ways. He himself prefers to laugh; he refuses to acknowledge the finality of the immutable general laws, and poses insoluble questions, missing no occasion to use irony at his own expense. He performs unthinkable mental somersaults without a safety net, and even without the ground below. He is able to see the funny side in the strictly rational thinking of the major philosophers in the European tradition about things which are not amenable to rational thought. He can discern the cracks in their monumental self-confidence, through which their real, concealed, living faces become visible, as well as their doubts and suffering. His main subject is the tragic human predicament, and yet it is pleasant to read him. He is provocatively paradoxical, witty, brilliant and breathtaking. However, much of these characteristics come later – in the earlier period during Chekhov's lifetime, Shestov was only just beginning to form an existential view of tragedy.

Shestov, not understood by his philosopher friends, was perfectly understood and absorbed by the major contemporary artists of the twentieth century.[10] As is usually the case with poets, they reacted not only to Shestov's ideas, but first of all to their concrete verbal realizations – to *motifs*. It is proper to say that Shestov's style of thinking relies not on logical constructions, but on the development of favourite motifs. He coins a phrase or picks up an expression, and circles around it, going away and then returning again, in order to bring out fresh nuances of meaning. A motif rather than an abstract idea is the main unit of Shestov's philosophy.[11] The first of the artists who turned to Shestov's motifs was Chekhov, who did so in a comical context. It is noteworthy that this happened on the eve of Shestov's arrival at a kind of philosophical circus – so Chekhov beat him to it on their common ground. But he managed to listen in to Shestov's paradoxical word, which was already laden with farce.

Chekhov was interested in many things and reacted to many, including philosophy, predominantly contemporary philosophy. One can find on his pages reactions to Schopenhauer, Nietzsche, Spenser, Buckle, Kierkegaard and

Nordau, and therefore it should not come as a surprise that he also managed to respond to Shestov. It is worth noting that a writer at the end of his career was reacting to a philosopher who had only just began his. The meeting point was *The Cherry Orchard*.

* * *

So, in 1904 (the year of Chekhov's death), Shestov dedicated to Chekhov's work the article 'Creation out of Nothing' ('*Tvorchestvo iz nichego*') which was published in March 1905 in the journal *Voprosy zhizni*. (*Mir Iskusstva*, where he had been a regular contributor, had by that time ceased to exist). I shall highlight here something which has not previously been noted: Chekhov's reaction to Shestov, which happened before Shestov managed to react to Chekhov.

Shestov conceived his article on Chekhov when the writer was still alive. At the end of 1901, Diagilev twice sent Chekhov Shestov's request for the chronology of his writings, which was necessary for Shestov's work in progress. Diagilev added to this his assurances of the seriousness of the work planned by Shestov.[12] Chekhov, in the letter to Diagilev of 20 December 1901, gave him a chronological list of his (Chekhov's) published works in the volumes of the first *Collected Works* published by Adolf Marx. One is inclined to think that after that Chekhov did not overlook Shestov's book on Dostoevskii and Nietzsche in *The World of Art*. Seventeen of Diagilev's letters to Chekhov are extant,[13] in some of which the former invites the latter to write for *The World of Art*. He also invites Chekhov to co-edit the journal, but to no avail.[14] In one of his letters Diagilev regrets that Chekhov gave *The Cherry Orchard* not to *The World of Art*, but to Gor'kii's almanac *Knowledge* (*Znanie*).[15] In Diagilev's letters to Chekhov, the former mentions sending to the latter some back issues of *The World of Art*,[16] and Chekhov's praise in response with respect to the journal: 'I feel tempted by your saying in every letter that *The World of Art* is a good journal and should not be closed down'.[17] In sum, there can be no doubt that Chekhov read *The World of Art* at the time when Shestov's writings were being published in the journal. It appears that we find the traces of this reading in Chekhov's *The Cherry Orchard*, written in 1903.

Maxim Gor'kii left evidence of the fact that Chekhov read Shestov's previous book, *Good in the Teaching of Count Tolstoi and Fr. Nietzsche* (*Dobro i zlo v uchenii gr. Tolstogo i Fr. Nitshe*, 1900). In his memoirs on Tolstoi (1919), Gor'kii reports that Tolstoi started speaking about this book by Shestov in Gaspra 'in response to A. P. Chekhov's remark that 'he did not like this book''.[18] Chekhov had apparently changed his attitude to Shestov by the time of reading his book on Dostoevskii and Nietzsche.

(1)

In the 3rd action of *The Cherry Orchard* there is the following episode:

> *Pishchik*: Nietzsche... A philosopher... A very great, most famous ... a man of huge wisdom, he says in his work that it is possible for one to forge banknotes.
> *Trofimov*: And have you read Nietzsche?
> *Pishchik*: Well ... Dashen´ka told me this. And I am now in such a situation that the only thing left is to forge banknotes ...[19]

What is this? Is it one of the comic flourishes that lighten up sad scenes dedicated to the demise of the poetic cherry orchard? But what is Nietzsche doing here? Is he mentioned just for the sake of it, to make things more absurd and funny? If so, then this exchange can be replaced by another one. However, bearing in mind the laconic nature of Chekhov's style, it is appropriate to contemplate a specific function of this episode in the adventures of ideas in this whimsical text.

Nietzsche indeed spoke about fabrication of the *forged coins* in his late book *Twilight of Idols*. Only he did so figuratively – when talking about the philosopher Schopenhauer: 'He explained things, one after the other, *art*, heroism, genius, beauty, great compassion, science, will for the truth, tragedy – as consequences of the "denial of will" or of the need of the will in denial – all this is the greatest psychological fabrication of false coins in history, with the exception of Christianity'.[20]

Chekhov was interested in both Nietzsche and Schopenhauer, whose names were held in great esteem at the beginning of the twentieth century. Judging by Chekhov's letters, he was only slightly acquainted with Nietzsche. He read his early work on Wagner,[21] and extracts from *Thus Spoke Zaratustra*.[22] However, *Twilight of Idols* was not translated into Russian during Chekhov's lifetime, and he did not read the philosopher in the original. So, if it was not Dashen´ka who told him about this book, it must have been Shestov.

In that very book by Shestov, published in *The World of Art* in 1902, there is the following passage on Nietzsche: 'We can see that appreciation and gratitude did not deter him from subsequently writing a biting article on Wagner, did not deter him from calling Schopenhauer 'an old counterfeiter', but this was towards the end of his literary activity, in 1886–88'.[23]

For us not only is the source significant, but also the context. Shestov reconstructs and elucidates that trend of thought which gave rise to Nietzsche's statement. The Russian philosopher Shestov is preoccupied with reconstructing the history of existential thought (without as yet using the term), which is fundamentally inseparable from the condition of life that generated it; thought which, when encountering the extreme problems of existence, not theoretically, but in personal human experience, in the state of despair, is unable to find consolation in the truths sanctioned by rational knowledge and by what seems to be obvious. Shestov, by his own admission, is interested in the truth about human beings rather than human truths, i.e. what people regard as truth in their lack of self-knowledge. Rooted in real life and alien to abstraction, existential thought was being developed not only in philosophy, but in literature, too; so Shestov turns not only to Nietzsche, but also to Dostoevskii. The lyrical hero of the former and the characters of the latter express what is difficult to understand in a human being, and what he himself is unable to understand; their human being talks with anger, hysterics, laughter. There is a region where reason cannot help – it is the domain of tragedy, understood not as a literary genre, but as an existential category pertaining to the living life. On the territory of tragedy there is nothing left to do but weep and laugh – these are the authentic reactions of one who is on the edge, over an abyss. It is in them, these reactions rather than in reasoned conclusion that the truth about man opens up. Shestov traces how Nietzsche becomes convinced that the rational ethics of Schopenhauer, whom he previously considered his teacher, can no longer help him in his state of mind, and the rational values he promoted turn out to be false. Hence the metaphor: the forging of false coins.

However, Shestov goes yet further. Observing Nietzsche, he sees something that escaped the German philosopher (not his truth, but the truth about him). Shestov discovers that, when on the territory of tragedy, where no moral norms are applicable and the compassion of goodwilled people does not help, Nietzsche was still unable to avoid the temptation to give up solitude and addressing an assumed sympathetic reader: 'Like almost any writer, that is a person who speaks to the people, he involuntarily conformed to his auditorium and presented in his judgements to the public a not only consultative, but also deciding voice. Dostoevskii, who felt more attached to the "spirit of the time" than Nietzsche, did the same.'[24]

This observation of the inevitable falsity of the writer who attempts to present to the public his desperate solitude, while being aware of the futility of compassion, must have meant a lot to Chekhov. For him, who experienced a state akin to that in Nietzsche and Dostoevskii, Shestov's analysis opened a different, new, and possibly unique route, which allowed freedom from falsity, into which even these giants fell. This route lay in acquiring a distance with respect to one's own state of mind: instead of turning a hero into a moralizer, a mouthpiece of one's *Weltanschauung*, as Dostoevskii and Nietzsche did, one can imagine himself as a personage, and look at himself from outside, with estrangement and laughter. In this case, turning to the public excludes any attempts to find compassion, and in fact provokes the reader to a lack of pity. If the Dostoevsky's Underground Man, cursing everything, still evokes a sentimental response, then Chekhov's Lopakhin does not evoke any compassion. This is not a surmise, this happens on stage: the characters of the play do not understand him. If the spectators were more perceptive they could feel pity with respect to Lopakhin. Then the author's strategy would have revealed its ambivalence. But the directors who staged the play turned out to be no more perceptive than the characters, they joined the attitude of Lopakhin's detractors in *The Cherry Orchard*, and the stage history of the play only deepened the misunderstanding. The author of the play is by definition a 'man speaking to the people'. And if he turns to the public, presenting his vision of life, and at the same time concealing the fact that he speaks of his own despair, his own state of solitude, and of not being understood, that is to say if he behaves in a contradictory fashion – and *The Cherry Orchard* does just that[25] – then one should expect that he must have found in the aforementioned passage by Shestov an inspiration, a strong impulse which helped to shape his own quest when developing the idea of *The Cherry Orchard*. Therefore the episode with Pishchik deserves careful consideration.

Pishchik translates the philosopher's words into his own language: if Nietzsche says that Schopenhauer makes *false coins*, then in the lips of Chekhov's character this statement is turned inside out: 'it is possible for one to forge banknotes'. A reproach of one philosopher by the other is presented as the authoritative permission to do what he in fact condemns. Pishchik speaks of *notes* (in Russian, it is precisely *notes, papers [bumazhki], banknotes* being implied): and if a *false coin* is a clichéd figure of speech, then a *false note* in Pishchik's lips has a direct meaning, he is talking about forged banknotes. But in this play everything is based on charades and figures of speech, and *false notes* better than *coins* remind us of the literature which goes through the play as a looming subtext. Literature can be termed a forged note rather than false coins. The examination of literature and one's position in it is the target of Chekhov's farce in *The Cherry Orchard*.

In Chekhov's play everything occurs in a special light: both Nietzsche and false money are *stage objects of the intellectual farce*. It is not fortuitously that the phrase under consideration is given to a personage named Pishchik: the name comes from the Russian word for 'to squeak', and a *pishchik* is a kind of squeaking device traditionally used in the Russian Petrushka street show, reminiscent of Punch. Petrushka performers used the *pishchik* to produce the voice of their hero, a peculiar squeaky sound which was soon echoed in Stravinsky's music (and became a cornerstone of the celebrated eponymous ballet), and was memorably described in Andrei Belyi's *Kotik Letaev*.[26] An obvious farcical game in a play, where otherwise farce has an indirect, concealed character, deserves full attention. At the same time, one should not forget that Chekhov's farce is intellectual. The author himself speaks with a *pishchik* in his mouth.

The motif of false notes emerges twice in a row in Pishchik's speech, and this is not mere repetition: firstly: 'Nietzsche ... A philosopher ... A very great, most famous man... a man of huge wisdom, he says in his work that it is possible for one to forge banknotes', and secondly 'And I am now in such a situation that the only thing left is to forge banknotes'. In the first instance the distorted idea of the philosopher is used as a general kind of moral license, as a caricatured transmission of the original idea; in the second – as an expression of a personal state of mind by a man driven to the edge. This is how the two poles of orientation of Chekhov's playing with allusion manifest themselves: the allusion presents its source in the form of a caricature, but this is not the target; the target is something else, something truly Chekhov's. Playing with the allusion presents a caricature of the original source, and at the same time it is a travesty of Chekhov's own serious matter.

A more detailed exposition of the functions of Chekhov's farce with respect to the Nietzschean motif looks as follows: the philosopher's metaphor is translated into the low language of the mundane – the result is funny, but the funny side acquires a specific character of Chekhovian farce, not at this moment, but at the next. As a norm, a comic distortion serves either as a mockery of the original, or as a satire of the ignorance which cannot comprehend the original, or as laughter for laughter's sake. However, Chekhov's caricatured allusion has a different function; it is not a mockery of the philosopher, but a reaction to something else, very personal, which, however, presents itself for a moment as a mockery of ignorance or as laughter for laughter's sake, but only to conceal the fact that it is aimed at a different target. The play presents one thing, but speaks of something else, and immediately mocks the falsity of this concealment. Farce hardly ever reached a higher intensity than when used as an instrument of Chekhov's artistic reflection and his figure of concealment.

It is hard to miss a caricatured translation of the original source into a language alien to it: even if one does not know or remember why Nietzsche was talking about false money, it is still clear that the philosopher meant something different from how it turned out in Pishchik's words. Pishchik's words are a caricature with respect to Nietzsche, for as long as the undeclared target and purpose remain unnoticed. But *the original source is so chosen that its caricature will turn out to be at the same time a distorted shadow of a still different meaning – something of Chekhov's own which is very serious for him and which is the real target of the manoeuvre.* This is akin to the experiment of Gestalt psychologists where one picture be recognized in two ways: looking at the picture as oriented to the right will produce an image of a duck with an open beak, and to the left a rabbit with long ears. However, the two images in Chekhov are not symmetric. In Nietzsche he finds a foothold from which he leaps to laugh at a matter of his own. Chekhov's farcical allusion is a letter sent by the author to someone else while it is addressed to himself.

Pishchik is a secondary character. The farcical element of Chekhov's plays is traditionally seen as their periphery, as wittily spotted details of life, as moments of comic relief. In this case, the comedy of Chekhov's comedy is lost, the play turns into a social drama with vignettes of everyday-life comedy. But *The Cherry Orchard* is not a drama inlaid with comic episodes. Pishchik's Petrushka-type performance as a vignette in *The Cherry Orchard* has a meta-poetic meaning and distinctly emblematizes the umbrose, farcical character of this play as a whole, where Chekhov presented some very personal, profound motifs, including the question of his place in literature, in the language of metaphors, taken from the mundane sphere, most amusingly from the language of economics.

(2)

No sooner is the supposition about Chekhov's turning to Shestov confirmed, than it is carried further by the fact that the case considered above is not unique in the play. Shestov's reflections on Nietzsche are interwoven in the aforementioned book with those on Dostoevskii. Shestov develops his own, specifically Shestovian interpretation of Dostoevskii, which the philosopher often revisits in his later books, as an ally of the Underground Man. He finds that the desperate irrationalism of the Underground Man is not eccentricity, or bravado, or *epatage*, as it may seem from outside, but the tormenting and inevitable state of mind of a person who happens to find himself on the territory of tragedy, in a state of groundlessness. In this state, a man attempts to say something which exceeds the capacity of human language and thus is provoked into incoherence intended to express the rationally inexpressible.

According to Shestov's analysis, an individual enters the territory of tragedy against his will – he did not strive to acquire this new knowledge of life, which is different from commonly-accepted truths. He even resists this new knowledge which brings suffering. That is what happened to Nietzsche. 'The reader recalls the horror that overcame Nietzsche, by his own admission, every time circumstance forced him to accept this new 'knowledge'. He wanted to live in the old style, and only when the new knowledge stabbed him like a knife...' etc.[27] And later on: 'And Faust had suffered a lot before he summoned the devil. In a word, all these "unordinary" people who rose up against the inexorable fetters of the natural laws and human morality, did not rise up voluntarily: they *like serfs, who grew old in bondage, were forced into freedom*. This was not "an uprising of slaves in morality", as Nietzsche professed, but something for which the human language has no words'.[28] A few pages later Shestov summarizes his thoughts on this phenomenon: 'The reader now sees where Nietzsche's task lies: he takes on himself the case of the man who has been *abandoned*, forgotten by the human good, science and philosophy'.[29] He is talking about the *'abandoned'* as the people of tragedy',[30] he means the tragedy discovered by Dostoevskii and Nietzsche. These are the people whom neither morality, nor rational philosophy want to know, because they are oriented towards the general, whereas tragedy does not have a general character; tragedy is personal and exclusive, it is, in this sense, not typical. Note that, starting with his preceding book, Shestov also considers Tolstoi among those who live on the territory of tragedy, thus linking the phenomenon with a certain period of literature and thought. This period can be demarcated as the epoch of Nietzsche and the great Russian novel.

A serf who grew old in bondage, who was forced to become free, and ended up forgotten and left behind – this is such a familiar motif, is it not? And it acquired the image and name in *The Cherry Orchard*, only a year after Shestov created it. The figure of Firs, a servant and former serf who scorns freedom and recalls how it was 'before the disaster', that is before the liberation of the serfs (Act II), and who is left behind in the empty house at the end of the play – is this indeed related to the Shestov's abandoned person? This doubt should be eliminated by its counterpart: could it have been a simple coincidence, given that Chekhov had just read Shestov's book? Having posed such a question, we are prepared to understand the meaning of this connection: a philosophical motif is once again translated into the language of the mundane. *Firs* comes across as a *farcical* presentation of the man of tragedy described by Shestov. I stress – as a *farce on a tragic theme*! In other words, Firs is a farce to the ultimate, paradoxical degree. There is something here which is worth thinking through.

According to the traditions of socially-oriented literature and criticism, Firs is understood as a relic of Russian social history, of serfdom. This is indeed so, but it should now be clear that he is more than that. The question of the functions of the figure of Firs in the play does probably not have an unambiguous answer as it suits a work of art. Chekhov wrote not an allegory (a logical construct), but a farce playing out motifs of deep personal significance. The play-off of motifs cannot be squeezed into the Procrustean bed of normal logic, its sense being whimsical. As an attempt at interpretation, I suggest considering the figure of Firs in the framework of a subtext that runs through the entire play; it can be defined as *literary sociology*.

As was shown in my previous article, in *The Cherry Orchard*, Chekhov makes a travesty of himself and his transitional cultural epoch. In the same way as the spacious gentry seats pass into history, the great Russian novel becomes a thing of the past. Firs is a distinct metonymy of both of these worlds – the gentry estate and the novel – on their way out. On top of that, he is a superfluous man, but not in the sense in which this concept was used in Russian literature and criticism – Chekhov avoided commonplaces at all costs or undermined them when invoking them. Firs is not a *type of a superfluous man*, a famous hero of the Russian novel, he is just a *man who is superfluous*, abandoned, forgotten. He is thus a parody of a cherished commonplace, of a *superfluous man*. Our understanding of this apparently tragic figure in this comedy can be assisted if we bear in mind Chekhov's strategy, dominant in *The Cherry Orchard*, of translating lofty concepts into the mundane. We have already seen that the farce of Chekhov's allusion, apart from the return address, its original source, has one more – direct – address to which it is being sent. Indeed, Chekhov's literary sociology is not a self-sufficient aspect referring to the historical reality, but a context of an intimate expressive significance. What is, then, the expressive meaning of the figure of Firs?

Chekhov lived with a firm understanding that the demise of the great novel meant the advent of a new literary epoch; and he was in the avant-garde of those who carried out this change. As usual he speaks of it in a deflated manner: he only claims to have paved the road to thick journals for second- and third-rate belletrists.[31] In the same deflated and jocular form, in his short stories as well as in *The Cherry Orchard*, Chekhov plays out his cherished motifs. Instead of a *superfluous man*, this emblematic hero of the lofty and tragic Russian novel of the nineteenth century, he populates his stage with diverse people with individual destinies who are not amenable to any generalizing formulae. A new writer is free from the epic tasks and with it – from a *type*. But public opinion and the ideological criticism which expresses it stick to routine: when they encounter something non-typical, they regard it either as an aberration, something second-rate, or in the case of a popular author, prefer not to notice it. The shift which happened in the 1880s from the literature of the typical to the literature of the individual is still little understood. However, Chekhov was distinctly aware of his own novelty: on numerous occasions he objected to typecasting his heroes. Such was Chekhov's social stance, as well as his stance as a writer, in as much as a writer thinks about man and society. Thus, looking at social events depicted in *The Cherry Orchard*, one must remember the peculiar inseparability of the social and the literary in Chekhov.

In his article 'An Old Question on New Talent' (*Severnyi Vestnik*, 1888, 11), Dmitrii Merezhkovskii classified the hero of Chekhov's story 'On the Road' (*Na puti*) as a well-known type of superfluous man. The notion of superfluous man is a badge of honor in the eyes of the liberal public. The article evoked Chekhov's response in his letter to A. S. Suvorin: 'Merezhkovskii [...] praises me as a poet, my stories as novellas, my heroes as failures, that is he follows the same routine. It is time to give up these failures, superfluous people etc., and to think of something original'.[32] Note that Chekhov objects not only to portraying his heroes as types, but even to defining his story in terms of the traditional genre of novella – he is acutely conscious of saying things different from the commonly expected, of using a new language; and he feels misunderstood and left behind in the old, already empty house.

A peripheral figure of Firs at the finale of the play comes to the forefront and attracts – in fact steals – all the compassion of the spectator. Watching Chekhov playing out the comic scenes in *The Cherry Orchard* on the themes of his own literary life, one can recognize in the figure of Firs who nurtured the family of Gaevs-Ranevskiis one more expressive capability: one more distorted shadow, a projection by the author of himself on the literary stage. In this respect its function is auto-irony: *superfluous people* have become merely superfluous, a writer of today is free from the chains of civic duty, while, in the eyes of his readers, he will remain a bard of massive social shifts, who cries over shallow Gaevs and Ranevskiis, and the forthcoming generations will leave him in their emptied house. (Did Chekhov not foreshadow the whole century of his posthumous life?) The eye of the author looking from behind the curtain meets the eye of the spectator in front of the stage and reads in it the distorted image of what is presented. The distance between them is introduced on one side by the tragic Firs, on the other – by farce.

What is being suggested here, then? Well, let us assume that the figure of Firs in Chekhov's play strikingly resembles a Shestov's passage; let us recall that Chekhov read Shestov's book just several months before he started working on *The Cherry Orchard*. Still, for strict, rational, formal, thinking, the connection between such distant objects as Shestov's forsaken person, *a serf who grew old in bondage and who was forced to become free*, and a superfluous person from a Russian novel, with Chekhov's Firs, and finally with Chekhov's own idea of himself, should seem doubtful. This is precisely how it should be: it is precisely against the strict, rational thinking, which can accept only the obvious, the regular and logical, that Shestov fought all his life, following Dostoevskii and Nietzsche, while Chekhov demonstrated in many ways the deficiency of such thinking. The motifs under consideration, indeed, cannot be reduced to a common denominator; an invariant, so beloved by the theory of the passed day, is absent here. But the translation back into the original never coincides with the initial text; it is in this gap that Chekhov's vision is situated.

In the course of our observations we established one amazing feature of Chekhov's comedy, which prevented his contemporaries from understanding it as comedy. The comic in the literature of the new age (as opposed to antiquity), in contrast to the tragic, deals with the typical, general, mass phenomena.

This for us, the people of today, is so obvious that even in those cases when the comedy author implies the absurd (as, for instance, in Beckett's *Waiting for Godot*), we unfailingly tend to uncover a general idea. However, Chekhov's comic is exclusive – exclusive in such a way as befits the tragic. It introduces a unique, unrepeatable, individual case, but presents it in forms of the typical which don't do it justice. A grotesque, ridiculous presentation of the individual as the social, is a favourite Chekhovian device.

(3)

However, this is not all. In all probability there is one more Shestov's reflex in the play: 'Go away, dear, you smell of chicken', says Gaev to the servant Yasha who has just returned with Ranevskaia from Paris (Act I). It would, of course, be natural to understand this as a landlord's eccentricity, amusing snobbery. There is no mistake: Chekhov's travesty uses the clothes of the mundane.

A deeper comment on this arabesque is contained in the last chapter of the same book by Shestov, where there is the following passage: 'Henry IV dreamed that every countryman would have chicken on Sunday. If his countryman saw his ideal in chicken and strove only for a peaceful and quiet life, sacrificing, as Schopenhauer and various adages teach us, "pleasure", only so as not to suffer, maybe the history of mankind would be less terrible [...] But in fact man is as nature made him, ready to accept years of suffering and deep unhappiness for a moment of joy, for a phantom of joy'.[33]

Let us remember this passage as a link with the philosopher Schopenhauer, and follow Shestov further. His thought develops as follows: he speaks of the intelligentsia's cry over the poor common people, its demand for a new order and its placing hopes on progress and science, until Nietzsche and Dostoevskii interpreted the common people differently. They pointed to the doubtful nature of the attempts to bring an individual as well as the people to a state of common satisfaction. These two knew that in a human being the readiness for suffering is always alive. In the face of this inextricable human feature, this readiness for suffering, the notion of the rational character of history's progress falls through. The rational project to create a state of wellbeing for the people thus exposes its absurdity. At this point, an unexpected and very Shestovian turn emerges: 'Our hopes have not been justified. The countrymen will not have chicken for Sunday dinner, and all our material and spiritual goods, which science has given us, will be taken from us'.[34] As we can see, Shestov's philosophical thought does not recoil from topical social problematics – as far as he examines this too in the existential context.

A chicken for a peasant thus turns out to be a symbol from the context of social philosophy, which is distant enough however from *social sciences*. A sort of *existential sociology* can be discerned in Chekhov – let us recall his 'Peasants', 'Women, 'In the Ravine', and other stories on peasant themes which turned out to be so unexpected in view of the ideological traditions of Russian intelligentsia and which baffled his contemporaries. In them the irrational side of the anguished life of peasants is brought to life – maybe not in such a naked anthropological understanding as in Nietzsche and even in Shestov, who both refer to human nature, but rather with an eye on the traditional mentality. And yet Chekhov also speaks of phenomena of irrational order and their place in social life.

The Cherry Orchard too turns to the language of existential sociology: the play depicts a real, historically verifiable social conflict between an old ruling class on its way out, and the new one which has come to replace it. However, the play does not reduce this conflict to that of social forces – here it is, first of all, a conflict of mentalities, sensibilities, human abilities for communication and understanding. But even this is only a matter of which Chekhov's art is made. In *The Cherry Orchard*, his last work, Chekhov eccentrically allowed himself to employ material of existential sociology as a language of farce, in which the figure of the author shines through like a water sign.

Let us return, however, to the motif of the *chicken for a peasant*. The well-fed and impudent servant Yasha belongs to those who, in contrast to 'the people' (*narod*) as understood by the intelligentsia, has his everyday chicken. Using Shestov's favourite expression – 'hence comes the question': what is this – Chekhov's arguing against the radical intelligentsia's sentimental and compassionate view of the people, or his opposition to the radical understanding of the human being as a willing sufferer by Dostoevskii, which erases any sentimentality and belief in social progress? More probably it is a sharpening of Shestov's theme by the means of farce: instead of the face of a peasant subjected to suffering, a different face emerges here: well-fed, impudent, self-satisfied and degenerate. But even this is not Chekhov's last word in the sociological discourse. The central character of *The Cherry Orchard*, 'the little peasant' Lopakhin who is breaking new economic ground, a cartoon of the author who paved new roads in literature, neither did degenerate, nor does fit into the frame of mind of the anti-progressist pessimism of Nitzsche or Dostoevskii. But Lopakhin remains misunderstood on stage as his author in his literary life.

Yet, Shestov's prophecy of the destiny of intelligentsia did come true, and it looks as though Chekhov did not miss it.

* * *

Thus, Chekhov turns to Shestov not for a dialogue (as is expected when discussing inter-textuality), but for the sake of his own artistic goals. The shadows cast by Shestov's motifs are fruitfully projected onto the field of

Chekhov's own concerns and engage each other in an amusing charade. This happens because Chekhov and Shestov share a certain special frame of mind. This can be defined as *existential sociology*, the area where the two terms comprising this notion correlate in a rather grotesque manner: social problems reveal their unnatural and forced association with the roots of individual existence, while the uniqueness of the individual existence presents itself as a farce on social themes.

Notes

1. I express profound gratitude to Yelena Mikhailovna Shvarts who participated in developing this theme.
2. This is an amended form of an article published previously in *Voprosy Literatury*, 2007, no. 1, pp. 290–317.
3. Avril Pyman, *A History of Russian Symbolism*, (Cambridge: Cambridge UP 1994). In *Histoire de la littérature Russe. Le XXe siècle. L'âge d'argent*, ed. by E. Etkind et al. (Paris: Fayard 1987), Russian edition: *Istorii russkoi literatury. XX vek. Serebrianyi vek*, ed. by V. Strad, Zh. Niv and E. Etkind) there is a rather superficial article on Shestov, which does not include a single reference to his links with Silver Age literature.
4. L. Shestov, *Nachala i kontsy* (St Petersburg, printing house of M. M. Stasiulevich, 1908), p. 39.
5. Ibid., p. 27.
6. Ibid., p. 3.
7. Ibid., p. 8.
8. Elena Tolstaia argued that *Ivanov* shows Chekhov's internal experience concerning his romance with Evdokiia Efros and the prospect of marriage to her which never took place. See Helena Tolstoy, 'From Susanna to Sara: Chekhov in 1886–1887', *Slavic Review*, 50/3 (1991), 590–600. As Richard Peace shows, both Trigorin and Treplev in *The Seagull* represent comic lopsided mirrors, in which Chekhov saw himself, therefore the artistic duel between Trigorin and Treplev is a reflection of Chekhov's internal polemics. Richard Peace, *Chekhov. A Study of the Four Major Plays* (New Haven: Yale University Press 1983), p. 29. Finally, I should point out that in *The Cherry Orchard* Chekhov projected his own self in the figure of Lopakhin and did that in the mode of buffoonery. S. Senderovich, "*The Cherry Orchard*: Chekhov's Last Testament," *Anton Chekhov. Bloom's BioCritiques*, eds. E. Silverthorne et al. (New York: Chelsea House, 2010), pp. 9–28.
9. Lev Shestov, *Apofeoz bespochvennosti. Opyt adogmaticheskogo myshleniia*, 2nd edition (St Petersburg: Shipovnik 1911), pp. 40–1 (1st edition 1905).
10. The examination of this theme is S. Senderovich and Ye. Shvarts, "*Kto Kanta na golovu b'et* (K teme: *Lev Shestov i literatura 20-go veka*)," *Quadrivium: Festschrift in Honor of Professor Wolf Moskovich* (Jerusalem: The Hebrew University of Jerusalem 2006), pp. 311–20; and also in *Toronto Slavic Quaterly* 12 (2005).
11. In this regard, Shestov belongs to the category of philosophers such as Schopenhauer and Nietzsche, to mention only those close to him in time.
12. Letters of 24 November 1901 and 12 December 1901, *Iz arkhiva A. P. Chekhova* (Moscow: Gosudarstvennaia Biblioteka SSSR. *Otdel rukopisei* 1960).
13. Letter of 22 November 1903. Ibid. This collection of archive material holds 14 letters.

14 Letters of 2 October 1900 and 23 December 1902. Ibid.
15 Letter from 12 August 1903. Ibid.
16 Letter from 2 October 1900 and 23 December 1902. Ibid.
17 Letter from 12 August1903. Ibid.
18 M. Gor′kii, *Vospominaniia o L′ ve Nikolaeviche Tolstom* (Petrograd: Izd. Z. I. Grzhebin 1919) 58.
19 A. P. Chekhov, *Polnoe sobranie sochinenii v tridtsati tomakh* (Moscow: Nauka 1974), vol 13, p. 230.
20 F. Nitshe, *Sochineniia v 2-kh tomah* (Moscow: Mysl′ 1990), vol. 2, p. 604.
21 Chekhov, *Polnoe sobranie sochinenii*, vol. 6, pp. 29, 54, 395 fn.
22 Ibid. vol. 8, p. 27, fn 377; vol. 11, p. 435.
23 Lev Shestov, *Dostoevskii i Nitshe (Filosofiia tragedii)* (St Petersburg: Shipovnik, 1911), p. 142.
24 Ibid., pp. 226–7.
25 For more details see: Senderovich, "The Cherry Orchard: Chekhov's Last Testament," pp. 9–28. The paper shows that Lopakhin's situation is Chekhov's jocular reflection on his own account.
26 On the *pishchik* in the Petrushka puppet show, see. N. Simonovič-Efimova, *Zapiski petrushechnika* (Leningrad: Iskusstvo 1980), pp. 115–16. In the present context, it is interesting that while considering the transfer of the techniques of the street show from the popular culture into the literary, the author notes: 'One cannot play literary things with a *pishchk* at the roots of the tongue, even more so for the crowd! No one will understand anything [...] We used the *pishchik* only for buffoonery pieces and only at the start of the performance, as a two-minute overture'. Ibid. It is a slight analogy, but this demonstrates the role of Pishchik in the Chekhov's play (as the key to the farcical context).
27 Lev Shestov, *Dostoevskii i Nitshe*, p. 217.
28 Ibid.
29 Ibid., p. 228.
30 Ibid., p. 229.
31 Chekhov, *Polnoe sobranie sochinenii*. Letter to A. S. Suvorin of 10 October 1888.
32 Letter to A. S. Suvorin of 10 October 1888. Ibid. Chekhov uses the notion of the superfluous man, but for him this is not a *type*, but a *literary* type, or even a cliché of cultural mentality. The hero of his 'Duel', Laevskii, considers himself a superfluous man, as he was brought up on this cliché. This is a false role for him, a task beyond his strength. Only by rejecting this can he attain his modest but genuine self.
33 Shestov, *Dostoevskiŭ i Nitshe*, pp. 236–7.
34 Ibid., p. 241.

12

PHILOSOPHY'S ENEMIES: CHEKHOV AND SHESTOV

Svetlana Evdokimova

> Birds of passage, cranes, for instance, fly on and on, and whatever thought, lofty or petty, may drift in their heads, they will keep on flying and will never know what for or where to. They fly and will keep on flying, whatever philosopher may emerge among them; and let them philosophize as they wish, so long as they keep on flying ...
>
> Chekhov, *The Three Sisters*

Compared to such Russian classics as Pushkin, Tolstoi and Dostoevskii who are perceived not only as great writers but as thinkers and philosophers, Chekhov appears to be strangely 'unphilosophical'. This perception is partially shaped by Chekhov himself. At times he appears to be distinctly militant in his attack on philosophers and philosophizing and in his attempt to dissociate himself from every ideological and philosophical movement of his time. This refusal to choose sides and adhere to an ideology is why Chekhov stands out as a lonely figure in the context of Russian culture. Reacting against Tolstoi's 'Afterword to the *Kreutzer Sonata*' ('*Posleslovie k "Kreitserovoi sonate"*', 1891), Chekhov writes to Suvorin (8 September 1891):

> The Devil take the philosophy of the great ones of this world! All the great sages are as despotic as generals, and as impolite and as indelicate as generals, because they are convinced they are safe from punishment. Diogenes spat into people's beards, knowing that he won't suffer for it. Tolstoi abuses doctors as scoundrels, and displays his ignorance in great questions because he is just such a Diogenes who cannot be taken to the police station or scolded in the newspapers. And so, to hell with the philosophy of the great ones of this world![1]

It is hardly surprising then that Chekhov is rarely considered a philosopher. Although several conferences have been dedicated to Chekhov's philosophical and religious outlook and a few publications too, it is hard to speak about the philosophy of Chekhov and about Chekhov the thinker, not only because he left no systematic philosophical account of his views and rejected any kind of philosophizing, teaching or preaching, but also because his writings resist what Chekhov himself calls a 'unifying idea'. Trying to reassert the notion that Chekhov may be considered a philosopher, V. B. Kataev uses terms that carefully avoid any direct reference to Chekhov's 'philosophy' but rather focuses on the 'philosophical basis' (*filosofskoe nachalo*) or 'philosophical density'(*filosofskaia napolnennost*') of his writings. He concludes: 'Chekhov did not offer new ideas, but rather new ways of considering ideas and opinions'.[2] Indeed, Chekhov seems not to have discovered new philosophical truths as perhaps Dostoevskii did; an he was also much less flamboyant than Tolstoi in his attacks on authorities, but he expresses a new sensibility of the modern man undergoing a crisis of traditional religious worldview that signifies a turn to a skeptical philosophy and a new cultural paradigm. It is for this reason that his 'philosophy' is better understood by twentieth century thinkers than by his contemporaries, who admired his art, but objected to his 'ideas' or the lack thereof. Chekhov's oeuvre as a whole reflects the agony of modernization as culture changes from sacred paradigms to a new secular humanism. Moreover, one could say that if there is any philosophy in Chekhov it is to be found precisely in his un-philosophical stance.

Much of the same can be said about the writings of Shestov. Chekhov's status among Russian writers is in many ways similar to Lev Shestov's status among Russian philosophers, whose philosophy also offers no systematic unity and no coherent set of propositions. Shestov refuses to provide theoretical explanations of philosophical problems and engages instead in an exercise in paradoxes and self-contradictions. Regardless of the fact that he later turned out to be an influential figure in the French existentialist movement and was viewed by some as one of the founding fathers of twentieth century religious existentialism, he did not articulate a philosophy of his own until late in his life, but rather launched a powerful and passionate attack on the entire Western philosophical tradition. Both men were iconoclasts who rejected theoretical and dogmatic thought, boldly questioned all accepted norms and 'herd morality'; were skeptical and critical about philosophical and artistic traditions, but refused to openly formulate their own programmatic philosophical or artistic positions. Both were outsiders to some extent and separated themselves from their own 'soil'. Neither of them belonged to any current or movement and refused to accommodate themselves to anything or anyone. Suffice it to recall

Chekhov's famous artistic 'credo', formulated in his letter to A. N. Pleshcheev of 4 October 1888:

> I am not a liberal and not a conservative, nor a gradualist, nor a monk, nor an indifferentist. I would like to be a free artist and nothing else ... Pharisaism, dull-wittedness and tyranny reign not only in merchants' houses and police stations; I see them in science, in literature, among the younger generation ... I consider trademarks and labels to be prejudices. My holy of holies is the human body, health, intelligence, talent, inspiration, love, and the most absolute freedom –freedom from violence and lies, no matter what form the latter two take.[3]

Chekhov persistently refused to present himself under any label and avoided the seductiveness of any metaphysical, Nietzschean, or Marxist beliefs. Likewise, Shestov made it his life's task to debunk all systematic philosophy. N. A. Berdiaev was undoubtedly right that Shestov's was, for the most part, only negative philosophy.[4] Nevertheless, both exerted profound influence on the development of their respective areas of creativity—on the development of Russian and Western prose and drama in the case of Chekhov, and, in the case of Shestov, on the development of Russian and, to some extent, Western philosophy.

It is not surprising then that Shestov finds in Chekhov a kindred spirit and is one of the first readers of Chekhov, along with V. V. Rozanov and S. N. Bulgakov, who sees in Chekhov not only a great artist, but also a philosopher, although a philosopher of a peculiar kind. Somewhat irritated by the prophetic pathos of Dostoevskii and Tolstoi, Shestov recognizes in Chekhov a bold and original thinker, a man who completely breaks with Russian prophetic or didactic tradition. Of all Russian writers he distinguishes Chekhov because, according to him, he is the only one among Russian classics who does not have a 'worldview' and who looks suspiciously at any kind of ideology or unified vision. Shestov senses that which distinguishes Chekhov from his predecessors and makes him express a new philosophical outlook, based on a movement that is gradually taking shape in Russia and Europe, a kind of *Weltanschauung* that is theorized and articulated somewhat later and which lays the foundation of the philosophical movements of existentionalism and phenomenology.

In this essay, I will focus not so much on the similarity of Chekhov's and Shestov's 'ideas'—all the more since both Chekhov and Shestov struggle with 'ideas'; not on their similar 'worldviews' (both rejected readymade worldviews); not on a coherent philosophical system (neither of them created a coherent philosophical system); but rather on that which unites the writer and the philosopher with various philosophical movements of their time.[5] Looking at

Chekhov through the prism of Shestov and existentialist philosophy, helps us to identify some important aspects of Chekhov's modern sensibility; Shestov enables us to see Chekhov's basic philosophical premises better. Conversely, Chekhov's oeuvre throws some of Shestov's propositions into relief.

Shestov's Existential Chekhov

Chekhov's and Shestov's was a one-way encounter. The conditions for true dialogue between the two never existed. While Shestov wrote extensively on Chekhov and was fascinated with him as a writer, the two men never met, and Chekhov never mentioned directly his contemporary philosopher. Given Shestov's somewhat confrontational nature, always ripe for a fight and ready to argue his point and his overall predilection for overstatement, and Chekhov's dislike of any kind of verbal fight and confrontation and his love of understatement, it is unlikely that Chekhov would ever have recognized Shestov as kindred spirit nor would have wished to engage him in a sustained dialogue. There is no question about any kind of mutual 'influence': either conscious or subconscious. It is also obvious that Shestov read and interpreted Chekhov selectively, that is, identified only those elements of Chekhov's oeuvre that corresponded with his own beliefs, or, to put it in Berdiaev's terms, he 'shestovized' Chekhov. To Czeslaw Milosz's list of names in his observation that 'Shestov was often reproached for finding in Shakespeare, in Dostoevskii, and in Nietzsche much that is not there at all', one could definitely add Chekhov.[6] Much of what contradicted his own views, Shestov either did not see or refused to see in Chekhov. When he realized that one or another of Chekhov's texts did not correspond to his conclusion or even contradicted it, as in the case of 'Ward Six' (*Palata No. 6*, 1892), he considered it as Chekhov's temporary 'concession' to 'ideas'.[7] As with most other of his favorite writers and philosophers he picks and greatly exaggerates some feature or other of a writer's views and then proceeds to either omit or explain away any views that are inconsistent with his interpretation.

Being, in Berdiaev's definition, a 'man with one idea, and one unique theme, which entirely dominated and pervaded everything he wrote', Shestov also attempts to reduce Chekhov to one idea.[8] While he himself was exemplifying 'wonderful monotony' (Albert Camus), he also attempts to turn Chekhov into a 'wonderfully monotonous' writer. As reductionist and idiosyncratic as this interpretation of Chekhov is, however, it still elucidates some important aspects of Chekhov the thinker. Probably even more, it shows how Shestov idiosyncratically interprets Chekhov's oeuvre to distill his own philosophy of 'groundlessness'.

In his provocative essay on Chekhov, 'Creation Out of the Void' (*'Tvorchestvo iz nichego'*, 1908) Shestov seemingly makes a number of grave accusations against Chekhov, calling him notoriously 'the poet of hopelessness' and even a criminal:

> To define his tendency in two words, I would say that Chekhov was the poet of hopelessness. Stubbornly, sadly, monotonously, in the course of his almost 25-year long literary activity, Chekhov was doing one thing alone: by one means or another he was killing human hope. ... in ordinary language what Chekhov was doing is called a crime, and is subject to severe punishment.[9]

But this is only on the surface. In the context of Shestov's iconoclastic attitude toward all authorities and his overall 'negative' approach to both philosophy and literary criticism, his accusatory rhetoric should not confuse the reader. His style of writing clearly bears the mark of Nietzsche: he delights in polemic and aphorisms and he often is so extreme in his positions that it becomes obvious that he means them only half-seriously and frequently uses them as rhetorical foil. I. A. Bunin recognizes right away that with all his seemingly negative evaluation of Chekhov's oeuvre, Shestov points to something very important in Chekhov and believes Shestov's essay to be the best that had been written about Chekhov.[10] Chekhov's 'crime' is a crime only 'in the ordinary language', as Shestov himself points out. What is the essence of this 'crime' then?

First and foremost, Chekhov's 'crime', according to Shestov, consists in his absolute honesty and courage in dealing with all the authoritative ideas and accepted worldviews, generated by 'the artificial habits of civilization'. Chekhov does not bow to compromise, violates all ideological taboos (that is why Shestov figuratively compares him to a man who 'would prevent corpses from being buried, and would dig decaying bodies from the grave'); is not afraid to speak about that which most writers and even philosophers are trying to hide, that is, man's complete disorientation in the world and his lack of any 'idea' that could keep him grounded. He claims: 'More and more Chekhov emancipates himself from old prejudices and goes—where? He himself could hardly answer, were he asked. But he prefers to remain without an answer, rather than to accept any of the traditional answers'.[11] Individuals in Chekhov's writings, according to Shestov, are always placed in situations of extreme despair, and their desperate state is precisely what should be hidden from ordinary human eyes, for in a 'normal and healthy mind' Chekhov's 'ghastly occupation' of laying bare all human illusions should rouse 'nothing but disgust and terror'.

It is obvious, therefore, that what Shestov calls a 'crime' is a crime only for philistines, including intellectual philistines and men of letters. He explains how Chekhov 'offended very many literary men', because 'the most conspicuous representatives of literature have been hitherto convinced that ideas have a magical power': 'What are the majority of writers doing? They are constructing conceptions of the world—and believing that they are engaged in a work of extraordinary importance and sanctity!'[12] In Shestov's own terms, however, Chekhov's refusal to participate in constructing conceptions of the world represents rather an extreme audacity of his spirit. (Audacity [*derznoveniie*], it should be noted, is a recurrent term in Shestov's thinking and signifies man's rebellion against necessity.) Likewise, when he claims that Chekhov 'was killing human hope' he, in fact, means not so much hope or hopes, but illusions: 'Art, science, love, inspiration, ideals, the future—select all the words with which humanity is, or has been in the past, consoling or amusing itself—Chekhov has only to touch them and they instantly fade, wither, and die'.[13] In other words, it is not that Chekhov demolishes 'art, science, love, inspiration' per se. Neither does he destroy human hopes per se. He rather questions the hopes that man places *in* art, science, love, and inspiration and demonstrates that viewing them as final truths is merely an illusion.[14]

Shestov is clearly attracted by the supreme liberty of Chekhov's spirit and undoubtedly shares Chekhov's distrust of the way of thinking that subordinates life to ideas, abstractions, and generalizations and thereby kills it. He also relates to Chekhov's high esteem of the unique and unrepeatable individual and his tragic solitude in the face of death and apparent incomprehensibility of the world. Chekhov for Shestov is a 'brother in arms' who struggles against the tyranny of the power exercised over human life by all kinds of ideology. According to Shestov, Chekhov is 'the irreconcilable enemy of all kinds of philosophy': 'Not one of his heroes philosophies, or if he does, his philosophizing is unsuccessful, ridiculous, weak and unconvincing'.[15]

However, it would be a great simplification of Chekhov's thought, as well as of Shestov's, to claim that they struggled with 'ideas'. They both struggled only with totalitarian ideas, the ideas-usurpers which pretend to contain the final truth, the utilitarian kind of ideas that men adjust to the requirements of the moment. In his essay on Chekhov, Shestov views these ideas as 'splinters' that are 'stuck into a living body' and argues that Chekhov is doing precisely this, that is, liberating himself from these false ideas, or hopes, or 'splinters': 'As a splinter stuck in the live body, alien and hostile to human organism, the idea mercilessly performs its high mission, until the man firmly resolves to draw it out of his flesh, however painful that difficult operation may be'.[16] Once the man finds himself in this extreme situation, once 'he stands before the fatal boundary which divides man from the eternal mystery', once he is forced to experience the profound existential despair, he is bound 'creating out of a void'.[17] Chekhov's heroes, concludes Shestov, 'are faced with this abnormal and dreadful necessity. Before them always lies hopelessness, helplessness, the utter impossibility of any action whatsoever'.[18]

Yet it is obvious that this despair is not really a 'crime' for Shestov but rather the greatest virtue, it is the first step toward authentic existence. Shestov sees angst, or despair, as the most genuine human predicament and he is overall hostile to tranquility. Anxiety, he insists, is a creative force that motivates human beings to discover new possibilities of existence and experience. Only through despair can modern man experience revelation. God for him can be reached only by first passing through the experience of despair and a sense of utter abandonment. Here we see that Shestov assigns to Chekhov one of his most cherished ideas, that is, of 'creation out of the void', an idea articulated most clearly and eloquently in his later work, *In Job's Balances* (*Na vesakh Iova*, 1923–9). According to Shestov, man must create all things out of nothing, when he fully experiences the abyss that opens before him when all his laws, his eternal truths, and his self-evident certainties are taken away. This is precisely the state in which the Chekhov hero finds himself, according to Shestov: 'He has nothing, he must create everything himself. And this 'creation out of the void', or more truly the possibility of the creation out of the void, is the only problem which can occupy and inspire Chekhov'.[19] Shestov is one of the first readers to point out that Chekhov's characters experience existential crises, that they are alienated characters who struggle with hopelessness and absurdity, and he senses that Chekhov, along with Dostoevskii, developed positions which were existentialists in all but name.

Shestov may be mistaken about reducing Chekhov to the philosophy of despair or of 'creation out of the void'. My task here, however, is not to dispute this view and find support to the contrary. I prefer to focus on those elements of Chekhov's *Weltanschauung* that both annoyed and attracted Shestov. They attracted Shestov, because he sensed the novelty of Chekhov's positions and ideas, and annoyed him, as well as most of his contemporaries, because these ideas became more comprehensible only in the context of twentieth-century philosophy. Although Chekhov cannot be labeled existentialist and most likely would have rejected the existentialist label if attached to him, the human subject and the individual's conditions of existence is his central concern. Human existence and what it means to be human was indeed a key topic and the focus of his work, and in his representation of existential anxiety of the modern man, of the perpetual state of uncertainty in which he lives, and of his radical freedom he anticipated many of Shestov's own philosophical positions, as well as those of other existential thinkers. It is also obvious that what Chekhov shares with Shestov, he shares with other representatives of existential thought, that is, the sense of alienation, disorientation, and confusion in the face of an apparently meaningless world, the impossibility of rationally understanding the world, the exceptional value of individual human existence, the tragic sense of finality of human existence, and a special interest in the problem of freedom of choice. As most other existential thinkers and phenomenologists, Chekhov regarded traditional systematic or academic philosophy as too abstract and remote from concrete human experience. The point of departure for him was not a theory, nor an idea, but an experience. This is why Chekhov's 'gospel' or 'holy of holies', as he puts it, is 'the human body, health, intelligence, talent, inspiration, love, and the most absolute freedom'. He focused on the question of concrete human existence and the conditions of this existence rather than hypothesizing a human essence. Shortly before his death, Chekhov writes in one of his letters to his wife (20 April 1904): 'You are asking what is life? This is the same as to ask: what is a carrot? The carrot is a carrot, we know nothing else'.[20] In other words, similar to the phenomenologists of Husserlian tradition, he is interested only in how things present themselves in actual experience, rather than the dictates of some theory or system as to how they must be. There is no such thing as the 'carrot's essence apart from its concrete existence and apart from our perception of its existence. We cannot say what is life apart from the personal experience of life. The meaning is to be found only in existence and in personal experience. This is a rather consistent position taken by Chekhov the writer, one that is reflected in his prose, drama, and letters.

Many of the same ideas were formulated by various existential thinkers who also raised the question of knowledge and its limits. Thus, for example, Camus, in a book that was perhaps most typical of the period of emerging existentialist philosophy, wrote about the confrontation between the human need to know and the 'unreasonable silence of the world':[21]

> This heart within me I can feel, and I judge that it exists. This world I can touch, and I likewise judge that it exists. There ends all my knowledge, and the rest is construction .... Aspects cannot be added up. This very head which is mine will forever remain indefinable to me. Between the certainty I have of my existence and the content I try to give to that assurance, the gap will never be filled.[22]

A carrot is a carrot, according to Chekhov. We know nothing else, or, in Camus's terms 'the rest is construction'.

Chekhov's thought rejected systematic philosophy in favor of the individual personal experience, the individual's quest for truth, and emphasized the life of 'flesh and bone', to use Miguel de Unamuno's term, as opposed to that of abstract rationalism. In this sense, Chekhov is as much a 'brother in arms' with Shestov, as he is with predecessors of existentionalism, such as Søren Kierkegaard, Nietzsche, Unamuno, on the one hand, and later anti-rationalist philosophers, whom Camus in his 'The Myth of Sisyphus' mentions as part of the same 'family of minds' as Karl Jaspers, Martin Heidegger, the phenomenologist, and Max Scheler, on the other hand. It is no coincidence that Camus also includes Shestov in the group and believes they had a lot in common regardless of their opposed methods and aims, that is, the notion of indescribable universe 'where contradiction, antinomy, anguish, or impotence reigns'. Camus writes about Shestov:

> Chestov, for his part, through a wonderfully monotonous work, constantly straining toward the same truths, tirelessly demonstrates that the tightest system, the most universal rationalism always stumbles eventually on the irrational of human thought. None of the ironic facts or ridiculous contradictions that depreciate the reason escapes him. One thing only interests him, and that is the exception, whether in the domain of the heart or of the mind. Through the Dostoevskian experiences of the condemned man, the exacerbated adventures of the Nietzschean mind, Hamlet's imprecations, or the bitter aristocracy of an Ibsen, he tracks down, illuminates, and magnifies the human revolt against the irremediable. He refuses the reason its reasons and begins to advance with some decision only in the middle of that colorless desert where all certainties have become stones'.[23]

In his discussion of various authors who deal with the new 'man of the absurd', Camus does not mention Chekhov, nor does he mention Chekhov among those who may have shaped Shestov's anti-rationalist thought, along with Dostoevskii, Nietzsche, and Ibsen. He acknowledges, however, Shestov's pivotal role in the development of the existentialist movement and existential line of thought, a line of thought that undoubtedly also includes Chekhov.

Confronting 'Absurd Walls'

The impossibility of knowledge is a problem that concerned most existential thinkers. What distinguished them is the kind of conclusions they drew from their discovery that the world is incomprehensible. Shestov ends his essay on Chekhov with the description of man's desperate beating his head 'against the wall' as his final predicament. Curiously, Camus starts his 'The Myth of Sisyphus' precisely with an image of the wall, the concept of 'absurd wall': 'All man has is his lucidity and his definite knowledge of the walls surrounding him'.[24] Camus uses the analogy of the Greek myth to demonstrate the futility of existence, but ultimately Sisyphus finds meaning and purpose in his task, simply by continually applying himself to it. Camus concludes his essay with the assertion that 'one must imagine Sisyphus happy'.[25] Where does Chekhov stand in respect to these 'absurd walls'?

In Shestov's interpretation, Chekhov's man reaches the state of complete existential despair. He finds himself in an indifferent, ambiguous, and absurd universe in which meaning is not provided by the natural order. His only response to this absurd, incomprehensible world is 'to beat his head against the floor'. He refers to the 'Boring Story' ('*Skuchnaia istoriia*'):

> 'A man cannot reconcile himself to the accomplished fact; neither can he refuse so to reconcile himself, and there is no third course either'. Under such conditions 'action' is impossible. Therefore, one can only 'fall down, cry, and beat one's head against the floor'. So Chekhov speaks of one of his heroes; but he might say the same of them all, without exception.[26]

Shestov interprets the professor's rebellion as Chekhov's 'method' of the struggle with materialism. He maintains: 'Perhaps Chekhov's method may seem strange to the reader, nevertheless it is clear that he came to the conclusion that there was only one way to struggle, to which the prophets of old turned themselves: to beat one's head against the wall ... in loneliness and silence ... to gather all the forces of despair for an absurd attempt long-since condemned by science and by common sense'.[27] He views most of Chekhov's characters as those who know no better strategy than beating one's head against the wall. Shestov concludes: 'One must spoil, devour, destroy, ruin. To think out things quietly, to anticipate the future—that is impossible. One must beat one's head, beat one's head incessantly against the wall. Where would it lead to? And would it lead anywhere? Is it a beginning or an end? It is possible to see in it the pledge of a new and inhuman creation, a creation out of the void?'[28] Shestov's concept of the 'creation out of the void, 'generated by the extreme state of despair, anticipates the situation traditionally described by the existential thinkers variably as angst, dread, anxiety, nausea, arising from the confrontation with the absurd. Although Shestov seems to deny Chekhov the ability to see anything behind this wall, he himself perceives this beating of the head against the floor or the wall as a potentially creative act. In fact, it is no coincidence that he finds an immense nobility and heroism in Dostoevskii's Underground Man's senseless beating of the head against a stone wall. In *Job's Balances* he thus eulogizes the Underground Man's rebellion against necessity:

> "Those gentlemen always humble themselves before the necessity. Necessity means a stone wall! What kind of stone wall? Well, most certainly, the laws of nature, conclusions of natural sciences, mathematics ... Just try to object!—Goodness sake, they will cry, you must not object: this is twice two is four! ... But, good Lord, what do I care about the laws of nature and arithmetic if I have my reasons for disliking them? Of

course, I won't be able to breach this wall with my head if indeed I am not indeed strong enough to do it, but I don't have to accept a stone wall just because it is a stone wall and I don't have the strength to breach it. ... It is much better to understand and recognize all the necessities and all the stone walls and to refuse to accept any of these walls if surrendering makes you sick ... " Perhaps you already tired to follow Dostoevskii and his desperate attempts to overcome the insurmountable self-evident truth? Dostoevskii was not the first man who happened to experience this incredibly terrifying feeling of crossing over to a different type of existence, a state of a man who must reject all foundations that are given to us by 'principles'.[29]

For Shestov, this resistance to the self-evident truths of science, of laws of nature, and philosophy is the first and most essential step in becoming reconciled with God and regaining freedom. Camus is right when he concludes that Shestovian philosophy may be summed up in his concept of God as rationally impossible: 'For when, at the conclusion of his passionate analyses, Chestov discovers the fundamental absurdity of all existence, he does not say: "This is the absurd", but rather: "This is God: we must rely on him even if he does not correspond to any of our rational categories" '.[30] Camus then astutely observes: 'To Chestov reason is useless but there is something beyond reason. To an absurd mind reason is useless and there is nothing beyond reason'.[31]

Interestingly, the notion that 'there is nothing beyond reason' brings Chekhov closer to Camus than to the irrationalism of the Russian philosopher. When faced with 'absurd walls', Chekhov ultimately chooses the path of Sisyphus so eloquently outlined by Camus and despondently lamented by one of Chekhov's characters, the writer Trigorin.[32] A successful writer, Trigorin, formulates essentially a Sisyphian dilemma:

> Day and night I am obsessed with one idea: 'I must write, I must write, I must'. I have hardly finished one story that, for some reason or another, I must write a second, then a third, and after the third, a fourth. I write incessantly, as if in a post-haste, and cannot do otherwise. What's then, I ask you, so beautiful and bright about this? Oh, what a monstrous life it is!'[33]

As opposed to Shestov and similar to Camus, Chekhov values reason and wants the world to be rationally penetrable, but he finds that it is not. Chekhov laments the clash between the human need for understanding and the world's unintelligibility, what Camus calls 'the unreasonable silence of the world'. 'There is no happiness if I cannot know', says Camus. Chekhov's characters seem to complain much about the same. 'If only I could know' (*'esli by znat'*) or 'I do not know' (*'ne znaiu'*) is a recurrent leitmotif in Chekhov's oeuvre, as has been observed by some Chekhov's scholars.[34] Chekhov's position, however, is more radical than merely lamenting the lack of understanding. In fact, 'those who know' are always portrayed in Chekhov in a more negative light than those who do not know and do not understand the world. His most cherished thought is precisely the utter impenetrability of the world; not the exaltation of folly, as in the case of Shestov, but a sober acknowledgment of our inability to know the truth and yet at the same time the realization that 'there is nothing beyond reason', to use Camus' words. In his letter to Suvorin (30 May 1888), he explains his view of the epistemology and of the task of the writers, referring to his story 'The Lights' (*'Ogni'*):

> Shcheglov-Leontiev blames me for finishing the story with the words, 'There's no making out anything in this world'. He thinks a writer who is a good psychologist ought to be able to make it out—that is what he is a psychologist for. But I don't agree with him. It is time that writers, especially those who are artists, recognize that there is no making anything out in this world, as once Socrates recognized it, and Voltaire, too. The mob thinks it knows and understands everything; and the more stupid it is the wider it imagines its horizons to be. And if a writer whom the mob believes in has the courage to declare that he does not understand anything of what he sees, that alone will constitute good knowledge in the realm of thought and a great step forward.[35]

Chekhov declines to explain the world and wants merely to give a description of actual experiences:

> It seems to me it is not for writers of fiction to solve such questions as that of God or of pessimism, etc. The writer's business is simply to describe who has been speaking about God or about pessimism, how, and in what circumstances. The artist must be not the judge of his characters and of what they say, but merely an impartial witness. I have heard a confused conversation of two Russians about pessimism—a conversation which settles nothing—and I must convey that conversation as I heard it; it is up to the jury, that is, to the readers, to give it an evaluation. My business is merely to be talented, i.e., to know how to distinguish important statements from unimportant, how to throw light on the characters, and to speak their language.[36]

Moreover, if we take the words of some of Chekhov's characters as expressing, in part, his own beliefs (definitely a questionable method, but occasionally a justifiable one if confirmed by non-fictional texts), then Chekhov appears to both question the possibility of human knowledge and rebel against the limits of reason. In *The Three Sisters*, where the phrase 'if only we could know' becomes a refrain – a refrain that also concludes the play, Masha articulates what may be viewed as Chekhov's challenge to traditional theodicy:

> It seems to me, man ought to have faith or search for faith; otherwise his life is empty, empty... To live and not to know why cranes fly, why children are born, why stars are in the sky ... Either you know why you live, or else nothing matters, all the same.[37]

Masha's words, spoken in response to Tuzenbach's acquiescent attitude toward the mystery of life, seem to be an obvious reference to the Book of Job. For God questions Job precisely about his knowledge of the mystery of the creation of the universe. In response to Job's rebellion, God reminds him that he has no knowledge about the creation of the world and cannot, therefore, comprehend the meaning of the universe. This is why man must accept suffering and death. Tuzenbach essentially embraces the traditional wisdom of the devout believer. Similar to Job's friends, he accepts life as it is, with its immutable laws, with its mystery and unjustifiability of suffering and death:

> Not just in two or three hundred years from now, but even in a million years, life will be the same as it has always been; it does not change, it remains constant, governed by its own laws, which are none of your business or, at least, which we will never know. Birds of passage, cranes, for instance, fly on and on, and whatever thought, lofty or petty, may drift in their heads, they will keep on flying and will never know what for or where to. They fly and will keep on flying, whatever philosopher may emerge among them; and let them philosophize as they wish, so long as they keep on flying ...[38].

Masha's conclusion, however, that if one does not know why one lives, then 'nothing matters' ('*vsio pustiaki, tryn-trava*') seems to be a curious modification of Ivan Karamazov's 'if there is no God, then everything is permitted'. While Dostoevskii places the questions of ethics in the ontological context, Chekov is more interested in considering the ethical questions in the context of epistemology. As opposed to Dostoevskii and other thinkers who focus on the existence of evil in the world as central question of theodicy, Chekhov fully accepts suffering, death, and the evil as necessity. As he puts it humorously in his letter to his sister Masha (13 November 1898), 'every summer is followed by winter, as youth is followed by old age, and unhappiness is followed by happiness or vice versa; man cannot always be healthy and happy, he must be prepared for losses and cannot protect himself from death, even if he is an Alexander the Great; and so, one ought to be ready for anything, accept anything as ineluctable necessity, as sad as it may be. One ought only to carry on ones' duty as well as one can – and nothing else'.[39] Yet the awareness of the laws of nature and of necessity does not liberate man from despair. In his story 'Terror' ('*Strakh*') one of his characters, Silin, complains:

> Our life and the other world are equally incomprehensible and terrifying. I don't understand life, my friend, and I am afraid of it ... When I lie on the grass and watch continuously an insect which was born just yesterday and which understands nothing, it seems to me that its life consists of nothing else but terror, and in it I see myself.[40]

It is not suffering *per se* that Chekhov considers a challenge to religion, but rather lack of knowledge. The tragedy of man in Chekhov consists in the fact that he actually never really tasted from the tree of knowledge; that is why he suffers and his life is deprived of meaning. In his story 'Terror', he directly links lack of knowledge and understanding of the meaning of life to the terror of being. For Shestov, who interprets the biblical story of the Fall as the tragic displacement of faith by reason, it is completely the opposite. His goal, he confesses, is to demonstrate the inseparability of 'knowledge, as it was understood in philosophy, and the terror of being'.[41] As Adam ate from the tree of knowledge, man became doomed to the futile pursuit of knowledge that has not led to ultimate truth but to the destruction of man's primordial freedom. As he puts it in his essay on Husserl, 'the tree of knowledge, which brings in death, is juxtaposed to the tree of life. The truths that are brought by knowledge, are overcome by human suffering'.[42] Chekhov recognizes that Truth and God are inaccessible to thought. Yet the tragedy of man is precisely in his striving to transcend the limits of our knowledge and penetrate the inaccessible realm of Truth.

If Ivan Karamazov rebels because there is suffering in the world, Chekhov's heroes rebel because they do not know the meaning of the world. In one of his notes (in connection with *The Three Sisters*), Chekhov writes: 'Until he finds his own God, man will be disoriented, will search for an aim, and will remain dissatisfied. One cannot live for the sake of children or mankind. And if there is no God, there is nothing to live for, one must die. Man must either have faith or search for faith, otherwise he is a shallow person'.[43] Chekhov dismisses all human goals, higher aims, philosophies, and even the sense of duty as inadequate for the task of life. They are merely substitutes for the truth. He makes, however, an important qualification: man won't find peace until he finds 'his own God'. Thus, in a way he seems to echo Kierkegaard's search for a highly personal God, for what is true for him, and anticipates Shestov's desperate, impossible faith.[44] As agnostic as Chekhov may seem to most of his contemporaries, including Shestov, his reflections on faith are consonant with Shestov's own. Shestov insists that one can and must sacrifice everything to find God and that 'one can and must put God above truths, one can look for God and find him in our universe'. In *Athens and Jerusalem* (*Afiny i Ierusalim*) he emphasizes the idea that the kind of God one must sacrifice everything to is also a uniquely personal, unimaginable God: ' the idea of total unity [*ideia vseedinstva*] is an absolutely false idea... It is not forbidden for reason to speak of unity and even of unities, but it must renounce total unity. And then renounce some other things too. And what a sigh of relief men will breath when they suddenly realize that the living God, the true God, in no way resembles Him whom reason has shown them until now!'[45]

Both Dostoevskii and Shestov find reconciliation with God in the book of Job which affirms the irrational, absurd faith in opposition to knowledge. Shestov loves Job precisely for his folly, for his struggle with 'self-evident truths'. Polemicising with Kierkegaard about the meaning of the biblical story of the Fall, Shestov adamantly dismisses the value of knowledge and claims that knowledge is responsible for all human misfortunes:

> The Bible says, on the contrary, that all human misfortunes come from knowledge. This is precisely the meaning of the words of St Paul quoted by Kierkegaard: 'all that does not come of faith is sin'. In its very essence knowledge, according to the Bible, excludes faith and is the sin par excellence or the original sin. Contrary to Kierkegaard, one must say that it was precisely the fruits of the tree of knowledge which lulled the human spirit to slumber. This is why God forbade Adam to eat of them. The words that God addressed to Adam, 'As for the tree of knowledge of good and of evil, you shall not eat of it, for on the day that you eat thereof you shall surely die', are in complete disagreement with our conception of knowledge as well as our conception of good and evil, but their meaning is perfectly clear and allows no other interpretation. I repeat once more: these words alone in the whole history of humankind constitute that which deserves the name of true critique of pure reason.[46]

As opposed to Chekhov, Shestov delights in what he takes to be reason's impotence and views despair only as a point of departure. He claims that 'within the "limits of reason" one may create science, high ethics, even religion, but in order to find God one must tear oneself away from the seductions of reason, with all its physical and moral constraints, and go to another source. In Scripture this source bears the enigmatic name 'faith', which is that dimension of thought where truth abandons itself joyously and painlessly to the eternal and limitless disposition of the Creator'.[47] To him the method of beating one's head against the wall, the method of folly, is the only way to achieve faith and find a conception of God, of the universe, and of himself in a way that lends meaning to such resistance. He juxtaposes, therefore, reason and science to faith, to biblical religion for which knowledge is not the supreme goal of human life:

> In other words, scientific methodology is defined by the character of the problems which science puts to itself. Indeed, not one of its problems can be solved by beating one's head against the wall. But this method, although not a new one (I repeat, it was known to the prophets and used by them) promised more to Chekhov and his heroes than all inductions and deductions (which, by the way, were not invented by science, but have existed since the beginning of the world).[48]

It is no coincidence that Shestov refers here to the old prophets, and undoubtedly to his favorite figure of Job, for he juxtaposes the biblical tradition of 'Jerusalem' to the western heritage of 'Athens', that is, faith versus reason, revelation versus speculation. The biblical revelation, according to him, cannot be harmonized with rationalist metaphysics; it resists logical argument or factual knowledge. According to Shestov, speculative philosophy that seeks to understand the phenomena of the universe brings man to a deadend where he cannot see the ultimate truth, because it maintains that there is nothing in the world that is essentially mysterious and rationally inexplicable. He rejects empirical science as a valid means for revealing truths concerning human existence and views reason as a 'restraint' on freedom.

It is clear that regardless of their many points of agreement, Shestov's worldview cannot fully accommodate the real Chekhov because Chekhov sees no inconsistency between scientific activity and the acceptance of mystery. When confronted with 'absurd walls', Chekhov and Shestov take different paths. Shestov accepted science and scientific method, but only 'within the limits of reason'. Chekhov was fully aware of the limitations of the so-called scientific method and was very skeptical about those who want to 'embrace that which cannot be embraced scientifically',[49] but he preferred to stay 'within the limits of reason'.[50] He was a 'materialist' only in the sense that he believed that the phenomenal realm is scientifically cognizable.[51] Moreover, as opposed to Shestov who placed faith above knowledge and who believed that only faith may allow one to breach 'the stone walls' of natural necessity ('only on the wings of faith may one fly over all the "stone walls" and "twice two is four", erected and deified by reason and rational knowledge'[52]) – Chekhov aspired to reconcile faith to knowledge and even to search for the kind of faith that becomes knowledge. In his letter to S. P. Diagilev of 30 December 1902, a letter that has been much misunderstood and misinterpreted by various critics, including D. S. Merezhkovskii, he raises the issue of the relationship between faith (religion) and culture and seems to polemically refer to the Underground Man's rebellion against the certainty of 'twice two is four':

> The intellectuals so far are only playing at religion, and for the most part from having nothing to do. One may say of the cultured part of our public that it has moved away from religion, and is moving further and further away from it, whatever people may say and whatever philosophical and religious societies may be formed. Whether it is a good or a bad thing I cannot undertake to decide; I will only say that the religious movement of which you write is one thing, and the whole of modern culture is another, and one cannot place the second in any causal connection with the first. Modern culture is a beginning of work for the sake of a great future, a work which will perhaps go on for tens of thousands of years, in order that man may if only in the remote future come to know the truth of the real God, that is, would not conjecture it, would not seek it in Dostoevskii, but would know it clearly, as one knows that twice two is four.[53]

While the Underground Man's scream, 'No!' to 'twice two is four' occupies a central place for Shestov, Chekhov seems to turn religion into a 'compelling certainty', to use Jaspers' term for his characterization of the truth of natural science. Merezhkovskii, by contrast, interprets these words as a death sentence to 'the religious life of humankind':

> To the religious truth that presumably is insufficiently clear and in which Dostoevskii believed, but which was not revealed to humanity by Dostoevskii, but by Christ, Chekhov juxtaposes another one, still unknown truth of the 'real God', which will be discovered, perhaps, in tens of thousands of years and will reduce all the mysteries of God, that people have viewed as terrifying and inscrutable, to the universally accessible clarity of the table of multiplication. By doing so, Chekhov signs a death sentence not only to the current religious movement in Russia, but also the whole of Christianity and the whole religious life of humankind presenting it as a dying out 'prejudice', as a remnant of archaic and unnecessary superstitions.[54]

Shestov too resents any kind of identification of faith with knowledge:

> Today many people—not just little boys, but adult serious people, and not in jest, but sincerely – identify faith and credit. It seems to them that

faith is the same thing as knowledge – with this single difference that he who has faith takes proof on credit under the verbal promise that it will be presented in time. You cannot convince anyone that the essence of faith and its greatest, its most miraculous, prerogative consists precisely in that it does need proof, that it lives 'beyond' proof.[55]

Chekhov's thought, however, is much more complex than either Merezhkovskii or, in indeed, most of the Silver Age religious thinkers, including Rozanov and Shestov, were able or willing to grant him: he speaks about the 'twice two is four' of the truth of the real God. In other words, he is far from denying faith, but merely describes a kind of faith that we encounter in the Apostle Thomas who will refuse to believe something without direct, physical, personal evidence. St Augustine explains this tension between belief and knowledge in Thomas' faith: Thomas 'saw and touched the man, and acknowledged the God whom he neither saw nor touched; but by the means of what he saw and touched, he now put far away from him every doubt, and believed the other'.[56] The knowledge of 'the truth of the real God' is not the rejection of religion and not the reduction of the mystery of God to the 'table of multiplication' as Merezhkovskii infers, but rather just the opposite, a belief in the possibility of revelation, for only in revelation does knowledge merge with faith. Moreover, Chekhov clearly opposes not faith and not even the faith of Dostoevskii, but those who find faith *in* Dostoevskii or in any other speculative philosophy. In other words, he objects to those who replace Truth, which is perhaps inaccessible (and that is why he envisions it only in some kind of indefinite remote future—in the tens of thousands of years) with false temporary truths of human religions and ideologies. The mystery of God, however, is not reducible for Chekhov to any accepted truth. In a letter to V. S. Miroliubov (17 December 1901), Chekhov explains his attitude toward faith in even greater detail and with biting irony and sarcasm tries to dissociate himself from any religious movement and religious philosophers of his time (including Rozanov and Merezhkovskii), referring to Merezhkovskii's 'complete satiety' and calling Rozanov a 'policeman':

> In regard to the questions that concern you, I will also say only that what is important are not the worn-out words, not idealism, but a consciousness of your own purity, that is, an absolute freedom of your soul from all kind of forgotten and unforgotten words, from all kinds of idealism and other incomprehensible words. One must have faith in God, but if you have no faith, one must not replace it with fussiness (*shumikha*), but search, and search for it in loneliness, one-on-one with one's conscience.[57]

As opposed to Kierkegaard, Shestov, Camus and many other existential thinkers Chekhov does not strive to find the truth in the absurd. Instead he confronts 'absurd walls' in his own 'quiet' way, without 'fussiness' and in loneliness. Chekhov was an existential thinker par excellence, and this is a reason why his philosophical or rather un-philosophical positions were not fully understood by his contemporaries and why the twentieth and twenty-first centuries found him more congenial. Shestov probably came closer than others to understanding Chekhov the thinker. Yet he too was somewhat irritated with Chekhov, because to his taste Chekhov never sufficiently embraced folly and madness. He was slightly annoyed with Chekhov perhaps for the same reason he disagreed with Husserl, who was too rationalistic for Shestov, for he intended Reason to be an instrument for discovering absolute and eternal truths, truth valid for 'men, monsters, angels, and gods'. In his essay on Husserl, Shestov interprets the philosopher's ideas using his favorite metaphor of 'twice two is four', against which, as we remember, the Underground Man rebels so passionately:

> Husserl distinguishes between truth and an individual's acts of true judgments. I assert the judgment that $2 \times 2 = 4$. This judgment is, of course, a purely psychological act and as such may be the subject of study in psychology. But, no matter how much the psychologist may find out about the laws of actual thinking, he can never deduce from these laws a principle which will distinguish truth from falsehood. On the contrary, all of his judgments presuppose that he is in possession of a criterion for distinguishing truth from falsehood. The philosopher is not in the least concerned with individual judgments of John or Peter that $2 \times 2 = 4$. There are thousands of individual judgments about a given object, but there is only one truth.[58]

What Chekhov means by 'knowing the truth of the real God' as one knows 'twice two is four' is probably close to Husserl's concept of 'that which is true is true absolutely', that is, an idea that truth is one, identical with itself. Distinguishing between true judgments, which are many and which belong to the realm of transient, and the truth that is fully autonomous and immutable, Husserl posits 'phenomenological reduction' as a method of philosophical inquiry, a method of 'bracketing' empirical data away from consideration. To be sure, Chekhov does not use the terms of philosophy. But he too intuitively distinguishes between the realm of experience and the realm of pure consciousness. His 'truth of the real God', known to us as 'twice to is four' is a kind of 'pure phenomenon', uncontaminated by temporary judgments. It is for this reason that Chekhov objects to any 'conjecture' of truth, or surrogates of faith, be it the faith of Dostoevskii, of the 'policeman' Rozanov, of the 'most satisfied' Merezhkovskii or of any other religious thinker. Their faiths are merely 'truths of judgment'.

One could find multiple examples in Chekhov's texts that align him with philosophers of previous centuries, of his own time, or of our age. Yet his own 'philosophy' remains elusive, indeterminate, and irreducible to the 'judgments' of any of his characters or even his own. Ultimately, Chekhov's struggle with philosophy and his mockery of philosophers is even more radical than Shestov's. Trying to debunk all the foundations of Western philosophy, Shestov not only uses the terms of philosophy and relies on rationalistic language (a contradiction observed by Berdiaev[59]), but also, in the final analysis, pertains to the Western philosophical tradition he so passionately wants to reject, a tradition which is characterized precisely by the continuous reconsideration of all the previous philosophical schools of thought. While Shestov indirectly constructs what I would call a 'misosophy', Chekhov consistently avoids systematic and even non-systematic philosophy and recoils from all philosophy as 'philosophizing' of the 'birds of passage': 'They fly and will keep on flying, whatever philosopher may emerge among them; and let them philosophize as they wish, so long as they keep on flying...' He juxtaposes philosophy not to another kind of philosophy or anti-philosophy, but to life itself, the 'meaning' of which is incomprehensible, but which may be described through a kind of 'artistic reduction', if I may use this term. Chekhov believes that 'psychologists' and 'artists' should not try to deal with the true 'meaning' of reality, because, as he puts it, 'there is no making out anything in this world', but rather refrain from making judgment upon the described universe. The task of the writer is only to describe actual experiences, but to suspend judgment regarding the true nature of reality. I refer again to his letter to Suvorin (30 May, 1888): 'The writer's business is simply to describe who has been speaking about God or about pessimism, how, and in what circumstances. The artist must be not the judge of his characters and of what they say, but merely an impartial witness ... My business is merely to be talented, i.e., to know how to distinguish important statements from unimportant, how to throw light on the characters, and to speak their language'.[60] This method of 'artistic reduction' is best conveyed in Masha's and Tuzenbach's exchange on the tension between the desire to know and the impossibility of complete knowledge:

Tuzenbach ... They [the birds of passage—SE] fly and will keep on flying, whatever philosopher may emerge among them; and let them philosophize as they wish, so long as they keep on flying ...

Masha. But what's the meaning of it?

Tuzenbach. Meaning ... Here, there's snow falling. What's the meaning of that? [*Pause*][61]

What is the meaning of snow? What is the meaning of life? What is a carrot? A carrot is a carrot, snow is snow, life is life. Our experience tells us only about what is, but does not explain the meaning of what is. What we think or feel about snow, a carrot, and life could be rendered, however, through art. Artistic description, to be sure, may not be used as a method of resolving philosophical problems, but it may be used as a way of making us think about these problems, to struggle with the incomprehensible, and to search for truth 'in loneliness and one on one with one's conscience'.

Chekhov is also aware that the kind of art that emerges from the modern man's state of disbelief and his confrontation with the absurd must be different from that which comes to us from centuries of literary and artistic traditions. The lack of any kind of definite 'outlook' or 'conception of the world', which is a 'disease' of the modern man, according to Chekhov, must inevitably lead to a more fragmented, amorphous, and open-ended artistic production, one that is not goal- or end-oriented and that lacks a 'unity' and 'unified vision' characteristic of the great artists of previous centuries:

> Keep in mind that the writers we consider eternal or simply good, who intoxicate us, have one very important trait in common: they are going in a certain direction and they induce you to follow, and you feel not only with your mind, but with your entire being that they have a certain goal ... Depending on their caliber, some have immediate goals – the abolition of serfdom, liberation of the motherland, politics, beauty or simply vodka, as in the case of Denis Davydov; the others have more remote goals – God, the afterlife, the happiness of humankind and so on. The best of them are realistic and describe life as it is, but because each line is saturated with the consciousness of their goal, as with juice, you feel life not only as it is, but also as it should be, and this captivates you. And what about us? Us! We describe life at it is and stop dead right there. ... We have neither immediate nor remote goals, and our souls are completely empty. We have no politics, we don't believe in revolution, there is no God, we're not afraid of ghosts, and I personally am not even afraid of death and blindness. One who wants nothing, hopes for nothing, and fears nothing cannot be an artist (Letter to Suvorin, 25 November 1892).[62]

* * *

Experiencing a profound existential crisis, the modern man, according to Chekhov, must admit that he has no knowledge of life, must feel himself empty and alienated, and therefore cannot be an artist of a traditional sort.

He must seek not only 'new forms', but new modes of expression. Chekhov's dislike of any kind of definitive 'outlook' and his lack of 'unified vision' and 'unified idea' (or 'juice' saturating each line, in Chekhov's own terminology), the state of uncertainty in which he as a modern man finds himself, makes him search for new literary paths. Chekhov's originality was immediately acknowledged by his most sensitive contemporaries, such as Tolstoi, who insisted that Chekhov created 'new, absolutely new forms of writing' and had 'his own unique manner of writing' that distinguished him from all previous writers.[63] Referring to Chekhov, Shestov perceptively observes that the man who rejects all accepted conceptions of the world, must also reject the devices of routine. Indeed, Chekhov himself is fully aware that he is breaking new ground, creating new genres and new forms of artistic expression: 'I am happy that I paved the way to the thick journals for many writers, and I am no less happy that thanks to me those same writers may now count on academic laurels. Everything written by me will be forgotten in five to ten years; but the paths I pioneered will remain intact – in this I see my only merit'.[64] To a large extent, then, Chekhov's innovations in prose and drama are the result of his existentialist outlook, one that becomes distinct when we consider Chekhov in the context of the philosophical thought of his time.[65] He was not a philosopher. He was an intelligent man and an artist who belonged to his time.

Notes

1 A.P. Chekhov, *Polnoe sobranie sochinenii i pisem v tridtsati tomakh. Shochineniia v 18 tomakh, Pis'ma v 12 tomakh* (Moscow: *Nauka*, 1974–83), Works, vol. 4, p. 270.
2 V. B. Kataev, 'Istinnyi mudrets', in *Philosofiia A.P. Chekhova* (Irkutsk, 2008), pp. 69–70.
3 Chekhov, op.cit. *Pis'ma* (Letters), vol. 3, p.11.
4 See N.A. Berdiaev, 'Lev Shestov i Kirkegaard', in *Sovremennye zapiski* (Paris, 1936), No.62, p. 376. See also Berdiaev, '*Osnovnaia ideia filosofii Shestova.*' Preface to Shestov, *Umozrenie i Otkrovenie* (Paris, 1964), p. 8.
5 Among the very few articles dedicated to Chekhov and Shestov, A. D. Stepanov's stands out as an intelligent preliminary account of some points of similarity between the 'dominant aspects of Shestov's philosophy' and Chekhov's 'artistic universe'. See Stepanov, '*Lev Shestov o Chekhove*', in *Chekhoviana. Chekhov i 'serebrianyi vek'*, ed. M. O. Goriacheva (Moscow: Nauka, 1996), pp. 75–9.
See also Savelii Senderovich's essay on Chekhov and Shestov in which he asserts that Chekhov and Shestov share a 'certain common semantic field', which Senderovich defines as 'the context of a peculiar existentialist sociology'. (Senderovich, '*A. P. Chekhov i L.I. Shestov. A takzhe koe-chto ob ekzistentsional'noi sotsiologii*', in *Voposy literatury* (Moscow, 2007), No. 6.
6 Czeslaw Milosz, 'Shestov, or the Purity of Despair', in *Emperor of the Earth: Modes of Eccentric Vision* (Berkeley: University of California Press, 1977), p. 102.
7 Lev Shestov, '*Tvorchestvo iż nichego*', in *Nachala i kontsy. Sbornik statei* (St Petersburg, 1908), p. 47.

8 N.A. Berdiaev, '*Osnovnaia ideia filosofii Shestova*'. Preface to Shestov, *Umozrenie i Otkrovenie* (Paris, 1964), p. 6. (Originally published in *Put'*, No. 58, 1938, pp. 44–8).
9 Shestov, '*Tvorchestvo iz nichego*', op. cit., p. 3.
10 See I. A. Bunin, *About Chekhov: The Unfinished Symphony*, ed. and trans. Thomas Gaiton Marullo (Evanston: Northwestern University Press, 2007), p. 65.
11 Shestov, '*Tvorchestvo iz nichego*', op. cit., p. 29.
12 Ibid, pp. 27–8.
13 Ibid, p. 5.
14 Cf. V. B. Kataev, *Proza Chekhova: Problemy interpretatsii* (Moscow: *Izdatel'stvo Moskovskogo universiteta*, 1979), p. 217.
15 Ibid, p. 50.
16 Ibid, p. 29.
17 Ibid, pp. 30–1.
18 Ibid, p. 31.
19 Ibid, p. 39.
20 Chekhov, op.cit., *Pis'ma*, vol.12, p. 93.
21 Albert Camus, *The Myth of Sisyphus and Other Essays*, translated by Justin O'Brien (New York, 1991), p. 28.
22 Ibid, p. 19.
23 Ibid, pp. 23, 25.
24 Ibid, p. 27.
25 Ibid, p. 123.
26 Shestov, '*Tvorchestvo iz nichego*', op. cit., p. 14.
27 Ibid, p. 58–9.
28 Ibid, p. 67–8.
29 Shestov, *Na vesakh Iova*, in Shestov, *Sochineniia v 2-kh tomakh* (Moscow, 1993), vol. 2, pp. 47–8. In *Afina and Jerusalem* (*Afina i Ierusalim*, 1930–7), referring to the same passage in Dostoevsky, Shestov concludes: 'If we translate to the language of philosophy these astonishing words of Dostoevskii, we will have to admit that he is making decisive and unique in its audacity rebuff to the universal and necessary judgments, our reason is striving to so avidly, according to Kant ... Dostoevskii raises the question which must be the central question of the critique of pure reason and which Kant, similar to his predecessors, has avoided: the question about the provable power of proofs, about the sources of the compulsory nature of self-evident truths. Where did this compulsion come from?' (Shestov, *Afiny i Ierusalim*, in *Sochineniia v 2-kh tomakh*, op. cit, vol. 1, pp. 564–5).
30 Camus, *The Myth of Sisyphus*, p. 34.
31 Ibid, p. 35.
32 In fact, the myth of Sisyphus and the theme of the 'Sisyphus labor' is a recurrent leitmotif in Chekhov's prose and drama. Chekhov's *Uncle Vania* in particular could be fruitfully interpreted in light of the myth of Sisyphus. At the end of the play, Vania and Sonia fully realize that their work is futile. Professor Serebirakov's visit serves specifically to reveal the meaninglessness of their work. They can no longer deceive themselves with lofty ideals, 'progressive thinking', 'certain convictions', and the rhetoric of self-sacrifice. Vania's revolt is the result of his realization that he has lived in the state of perpetual illusion: 'The past does not exist. It's been stupidly wasted on trifles, while the present is terrifying in its absurdity' (Chekhov, op. cit., Works, vol.13, p. 79). Serebirakov only lifts these illusions. Both Sonia and Vania are profoundly unhappy and are on the verge

of despair, yet, ultimately, similar to Camus' Sisyphus, they find meaning in their work by applying themselves to it. Sonia thus admonishes Vania, trying to save him from suicide: 'I may be just as unhappy as you are, but I don't give in to despair. I endure and will keep enduring until my life comes to an end on its own...You must endure too' (Ibid., p. 109). The play's concluding scene creates the sense of utter absurdity:

> Voinitskii. (*Writes*) 'February second vegetable oil twenty pounds... February sixteenth another twenty pounds vegetable oil...Buckwheat groats...'
> [*Pause. The sound of harness bells.*]
>   Marina. He's gone!
> [*Pause.*]
>   Sonia (*Returning, puts the candle on the table.*) He's gone...
>   Voinitskii (*Checking over the accounts and making notations.*) Total...fifteen...twenty five... (Ibid., p. 115).

The play's concluding lines, 'We shall rest', are no more probable than the end of Sisyphus' suffering. Yet, in this endless and futile work and in perseverance, they ultimately find meaning and purpose.

Interestingly, in his 'The Myth of Sisyphus', Camus claims 'there is only one truly serious philosophical problem, and that is suicide'. He suggests that the mind, 'when it reaches its limits, must make judgment and choose its conclusions. This is where suicide and the reply stand' (Camus, 'The Myth of Sisyphus', op. cit., p. 27). There are two possible responses to the absurd, according to Camus, either suicide or recovery. In Chekhov's *Uncle Vania*, Vania contemplates suicide precisely for this reason. Yet Chekhov in this play, as well as elsewhere, insists on persevering in spite of the awareness of the void. In a letter to Suvorin he writes about his own way to cope with illusions and with the realization of the void:

> ... Grigorovich and you think I am clever. Yes, I am at least so far clever as not to conceal from myself my disease, not to lie to myself, and not to cover up my emptiness with other people's rags, such as the ideas of the sixties, and so on. I am not going to through myself like Garshin onto a stairwell, but I am not going to flatter myself with hopes of a better future either (Chekhov, op. cit., *Pis'ma*, vol. 5, p. 134).

Although Chekhov acknowledges that modern man's thought reaches its confines, he rejects suicide as a way of dealing with the void (emptiness). For Chekhov, as well as for Camus and many other existentialist thinkers, this recovery may be achieved only through an unceasing struggle. Camus defines this struggle in terms which echo Chekhov: 'I must admit that that struggle implies a total absence of hope (which has nothing to do with despair), a continual rejection (which must not be confused with renunciation), and a conscious dissatisfaction (which must not be compared to immature unrest) ... The absurd has meaning only in so far as it is not agreed to' (Camus, op. cit., p. 31).

33 Chekhov, op. cit., vol. 13, p. 29.
34 In his article on Chekhov and Rozanov, Kataev points out the centrality of the theme of the lack of understanding and comprehension among Chekhov's characters, and of the world that appears to be incomprehensible. He concludes that the 'lack of understanding

(inability or unwillingness to understand the other) and false understanding are the main cause of human unhappiness in Chekhov's universe'. See Kataev, *Chekhov plius ... Predshestvenniki, sovremenniki, preemniki* (Moscow, 2004), p. 283.
35 Chekhov, op.cit., *Pis'ma*, vol. 2, pp. 280–1.
36 Ibid., p. 280.
37 Chekhov, op.cit., Works, vol. 13, p. 147.
38 Ibid.
39 Chekhov, op. cit., *Pis'ma*, vol. 7, p. 327.
40 Chekhov, op. cit., Works, vol. 8, p. 131.
41 Shestov, *Afiny i Ierusalim*, op. cit., p. 332.
42 Shestov, *Umozrenie i otkrovenie* (Paris, 1964), p. 324.
43 Chekhov, op. cit., Works, vol. 17, pp. 215–16.
44 Cf. Kierkegaard's belief in a lonely search and striving for truth and God who is applicable to him: 'The thing is to understand myself, to see what God really wishes me to do: the thing is to find a truth which is true for me, to find the idea for which I can live and die'. See Kierkegaard, Letter to Peter Wilhelm Lund dated 31 August 1835, in *The Essential Kierkegaard*, edited by Howard and Edna Hong (Princeton: Princeton University Press, 2000).
45 Shestov, *Afiny i Ierusalim*, op. cit., pp. 654–5.
46 Ibid, pp. 500–01
47 Ibid, pp. 332–4.
48 Shestov, "*Tvorchestvo iz nichego*', op. cit., p. 59.
49 See Chekhov's letter to A.S. Suvorin (3 November 1888) in which he gently mocks Merezhkovskii, who 'has mastered the wisdom of the scientific method' and is vulnerable, therefore, to a number of 'delightful temptations'. Interestingly, quite in line with Husserl's famous assertion that 'if we could contemplate clearly the exact laws of psychic processes, they would be seen to be likewise eternal and invariable, like the basic laws of theoretical natural science. Hence they would be valid even if there were no psychic process', Chekhov claims:

> Archimedes wanted to turn the earth upside-down, and present-day hotheads want to embrace that which cannot be embraced scientifically: they want to discover physical laws for creativity, they want to grasp the general law and the formulae by which the artist, who feels them instinctively, creates landscapes, novels, pieces of music and so on. These formulae probably do exist in nature ... Anyone who has a command of the scientific method senses intuitively that a piece of music and a tree have something in common and that both are created in accordance with identically regular and simple laws. Hence the question of what these laws are. Hence the temptation to write a physiology of creativity (Boborykin) and among the younger and more timid to refer to science and to the laws of nature (Merezhkovskii). A physiology of creativity probably does exist in nature, but all dreams of it must be abandoned at the outset ... It's always good to think scientifically, but the trouble is that that scientific thinking about art will inevitably be reduced to a search for the 'cells' or 'centers' in charge of creative ability ... For those who are haunted by the scientific method and whom God granted the rare talent of thinking scientifically, there is in my opinion only one way out – the philosophy of creativity. By gathering together all the best creations of artists through the ages and applying scientific method, we can grasp the common denominator that causes them to resemble one

another and lies at the root of their value. That common denominator will then be law (Chekhov, op. cit., *Pis'ma*, vol. 3, p.53–4).

50 I cannot fully agree with Stepanov's conclusion that Shestov finds in Chekhov's art two 'central aspects of his philosophy: the rejection of the rational and a search for the miraculous'. Not only does Chekhov not reject the rational, but Shestov does not present Chekhov as an irrationalist. See Stepanov, op. cit., p. 76.
51 See Chekhov's autobiography sent in his letter to G.I. Rossalimo (11 October 1899): 'My experience with natural sciences and the scientific method has always kept me on my guard; I have tried wherever possible to take scientific data into account, and where it has not been possible I have preferred not to write at all. Let me note in this connection that the principles of creative art do not always allow full accord with scientific data ... I do not belong to those writers who negate the value of science and would not wish to be one of those who try to figure out everything on their own'. (Chekhov, op. cit., vol. 16, p. 271).
52 Shestov, *Afiny i Ierusalim*, op. cit., p. 570.
53 Chekhov, op.cit., *Pis'ma*, vol. 11, p. 106.
54 D. S. Merezhkovkii, '*Chekhov i Gor'kii*', in *A.P. Chekhov : Pro et Contra* (St Petersburg: Izdatel'stvo Russkogo Khristianskogo gumanitarnogo instituta, 2002), pp. 706–07.
55 Shestov, *Afiny i Ierusalim*, op. cit., p. 628.
56 See Augustin's Tractate CXXI (Jn XX, 10–29) in *A Select Library of the Nicene and Post-Nicene Fathers of the Christian Church*, ed. Philip Schaff, v. VII, *St. Augustin: Homilies on the Gospel of John* (Edinburgh, 1991), p. 438.
57 Chekhov, op. cit., *Pis'ma*, vol., 10, p. 142.
58 Shestov, '*Pamiati velikogo filosofa (Edmund Husserl)*', in *Umozrenie i otkroveniie*, op. cit., pp. 309–10.
59 Berdiaev was right in seeing a contradiction in Shestov's rejection of reason and knowledge while being at the same time a 'man of thought and knowledge': 'His contradiction was in that he was a philosopher, i.e. a man of thought and knowledge, and he was trying to comprehend the tragedy of human existence, while denying comprehension. He struggled against the tyranny of reason, against the tyranny of knowledge which banished man out of paradise, yet he struggled on the territory of that same knowledge, employing the weapons of that same reason'. (Berdiaev, '*Osnovnaia ideia filosofii L'va Shestova*', op. cit., p. 8).
60 Chekhov, op. cit., *Pis'ma*, vol. 2, p. 280.
61 Chekhov, op. cit., Works, vol. 13, p. 147.
62 Chekhov, op. cit., *Pis'ma*, vol. 5, pp. 133–4.
63 'I think, Chekhov created for the whole world new, entirely new forms of creative writing, unlike anything I have ever encountered ... One can no longer compare Chekhov as artist to previous Russian writers—to Turgenev, Dostoevskii or myself. Chekhov has his own unique form of writing, similar to that of the impressionists'. See P. A. Sergeenko, *Tolstoi i ego sovremenniki* (Moscow, 1911), pp. 226, 228.
64 Chekhov, op. cit., *Pis'ma*, vol. 3, p. 39.
65 The relationship between Chekhov's 'philosophy' and his poetics is a topic that goes beyond the scope of this essay. In a somewhat contradictory way, Stepanov makes an attempt to draw some parallels between Chekhov's poetics and Shestov's philosophy. He first correctly observes that 'it is hardly possible to see Chekhov's stories as an 'aesthetic double' of Shestov's philosophy', but then, commenting on Shestov's questioning

self-evident truths and his particular taste for raising questions rather than giving answers, he suggests: 'It is hard to find a better philosophical counterpart to the multiplicity of Chekhov's stories'. He further concludes that in Shestov's philosophy, we may find 'verbal parts that cohered into the infinite plotless drama of cognition – the best analogue to Chekhov's dramaturgy to be find in philosophy'. See Stepanov, op. cit., pp. 76, 78–9.

I do not find it fruitful to make generalizations about the affinities between Shestov's philosophy and Chekhov's poetics, for I do not believe Chekhov's philosophical positions to be uniquely 'shestovian'. There are, to be sure, some aspects of Chekhov's poetics that stem from his 'philosophical' outlook. Among the most important peculiarities of Chekhov's poetics which could be linked to his 'philosophy', may be his struggle with traditional plot (which, as it was believed, required a unified vision), as well as his search for new kinds of beginnings and endings, and the fact that he never managed to write a novel, but preferred instead the genre of the short story, which he modernized and which allowed him to grasp the fragments of existence that could no longer be glued together in a coherent whole. In his 1944 essay on Chekhov, B. M. Eikhenbaum correctly observes that 'the point is not that Chekhov introduced the short story genre to Russian literature, but that this shortness was the matter of principle; as a new and more adequate method of the description of reality it was a counterpart to the traditional genre of the novel and novella'. See Eikhenbaum, *O proze* (Leningrad, 1969), p. 365. The novelistic genre—at least in the way the novel was understood by most of Chekhov's contemporaries, including Tolstoi – required a well-defined 'worldview'. It is no coincidence then that as much as Tolstoi admires Chekhov's talent, he objects to his lack of a 'definite worldview' and of a 'unifying thread' (note the pride Tolstoi took in his own architectonics, inner connection, and 'linking'). Tolstoi thus explains his position in respect to art and to the peculiarities of Chekhov:

> His artistry is of a highest caliber. I greatly enjoyed rereading his stories … But still, this is just a mosaic, you won't find here a truly unifying inner thread … Chekhov, as well as many of our current writers, has developed extraordinary technique of realism. Everything is realistic in Chekhov, to the state of complete illusion; his works make an impression of a stereoscope. He throws words apparently without any order, but, similar to artists–impressionists, he achieves great results with his brush strokes. (A.B. Goldenveizer, *Vblizi Tolstogo* (Moscow, 1959), pp. 68–9.

NOTES ON CONTRIBUTORS

Chudakov, Aleksandr (1938–2005)
Aleksandr Chudakov was Professor at M. V. Lomonosov's Moscow State University and a leading scientist at A. M. Gor´kii's Institute of World Literature of the Russian Academy of Sciences, and one of world's most celebrated Chekhov scholars. He published over 200 articles on the classical Russian authors of the nineteenth century and the history of Russian philology, and authored five books: *Poetika Chekhova* (Moscow, 1971; translated as *Chekhov's Poetics*, Ann Arbor: Ardis Press, 1983); *Mir Chekhova: Vozniknovenie i utverzhdenie* (*Chekhov's World: Origins and Affirmation*; Moscow, 1986); *Anton Pavlovich Chekhov: Biografiia pisatelia* (Anton Pavlovich Chekhov: A Writer's Life; Moscow, 1987); *Chekhov v Taganroge* (*Chekhov in Taganrog*; Moscow, 1987); and *Slovo – Veshch´ – Mir: Ot Pushkina do Tolstogo* (The Word – The Thing – The World: From Pushkin to Tolstoi; Moscow, 1992).

Crone, Anna Lisa (1946–2009)
A. L. Crone was Professor of Russian Literature and Language at the University of Chicago for 30 years. She authored four books – one on Rozanov, one on Derzhavin, one on the Petersburg poets of the Silver Age and beyond, and one entitled *Eros and Creativity in Russian Religious Renewal. The Philosophers and the Freudians*. Prof Crone is best known as a specialist in Russian Religious Philosophy and in Russian poetry from the eighteenth to the twentieth century. She has published over 70 articles.

Evdokimova, Svetlana
Svetlana Evdokimova is Professor of Slavic Languages and Comparative Literature at Brown University. A specialist in nineteenth and twentieth-century Russian literature, Evdokimova holds a PhD from Yale University. Her main areas of scholarly interest include: Pushkin, Russian and European Romanticism, Tolstoi, Chekhov, relations between fiction and history, and gender and sexuality in Russian and European literature. She is the author of *Pushkin's Historical Imagination* (Yale University Press, 1999) and editor of

Alexander Pushkin's 'Little Tragedies': The Poetics of Brevity (Wisconsin University Press, 2004), which was selected as an Outstanding Academic Title for 2004 by Choice. She has published a wide range of articles on Pushkin, Gogol', Tolstoi, and Chekhov. She is currently completing a book, *A Genius of Culture: The Chekhov Phenomenon*, which examines Chekhov's relationship with the Russian intelligentsia and its impact on the formation of his literary self.

Golstein, Vladimir

Vladimir Golstein is Associate Professor of Slavic Languages and Literatures at Brown University. He studied philosophy at Columbia University and obtained his PhD in Russian literature in 1992 from Yale University. Golstein is the author of *Lermontov's Narratives of Heroism* and of numerous articles on nineteenth and twentieth-century Russian authors. Among his publications on Chekhov are essays on *Uncle Vania*, and on several of Chekhov's short stories, including 'At Home' and 'A Doctor's Visit'. He is currently completing a monograph on generational conflicts in Russian literature and culture.

Grübel, Rainer

Rainer Grübel is Professor at the University of Oldenburg in Germany. He was educated in Germany (Göttingen and Frankfurt (M.)) and in Russia (Leningrad). Since 1976 he has held positions at the Universities of Utrecht and Leiden, and since 1986 has worked at the University of Oldenburg where he twice headed the School of Literatures and Linguistics. His main research interests include literary axiology, the theory of poetic language, Russian literature and philosophy of the nineteenth and twentieth centuries, and specifically Anton Chekhov and Vasilii Rozanov. Professor Grübel is the author of four monographs and more than 180 scholarly articles and reviews published in German, Russian, English, French, Polish, Serbo-Croatian, Dutch and Danish. His books include: *Literaturaxiologie. Zur Theorie und Geschichte des ästhetischen Wertes in slavischen Literaturen (Axiology of Literature. On Aesthetic Theory and History*;Wiesbaden 2001), *An den Grenzen der Moderne. Das Denken und Schreiben Vasilij Rozanovs (At the borderline of Modernism. The Thinking and Writings of Vasiliii Rozanov*; Munich 2003). He also co-edits *Studies in Slavic Literature and Poetics* (Amsterdam, 39 vols) and *Slavica Oldenburgensia* (Oldenburg, 13 vols), and is a member of the Advisory Board to *Die Welt der Slaven* (*The Slavic World*; published since 1955).

Kataev, Vladimir

Vladimir Kataev is Professor and the head of school of the history of Russian literature at M. V. Lomonosov's Moscow State University and chairman of the Chekhov Commission of the Russian Academy of Sciences. He is the author of more than 100 publications on Chekhov which have appeared in Russia and in 15 other countries. His books include: *Proza Chekhova: problemy interpretatsii* (Moscow, 1979) (*Chekhov's Prose: Problems of Interpretation*), *Sputniki Chekhova* (*Chekhov's Companions*; Moscow, 1982), *Literaturnye sviazi Chekhova* (*Chekhov's Literary Connections*; Moscow, 1989), *Slozhnost' prostoty: rasskazy i p'esy Chekhova* (*The Complexity of Simplicity: Chekhov's Plays and Short Stories*; Moscow, 1996, 1998, 2000, 2004); *If only we could know: An interpretation of Chekhov* (Chicago: Ivan Dee, 2002, 2003), *Chekhov plius... Predshestvenniki, sovremenniki, preemniki* (*Chekhov Plus... Predecessors, Contemporaries and Successors*: Moscow, 2004), *Ot smeshnogo do velikogo: lektsii o Chekhove* (*From the Ridiculous to the Sublime: Lectures on Chekhov*; Cairo: Al-Shaim University, 2006). He is the editor of *Chekhovskii vestnik* (since 1997) and of *Chekhov Encyclopedia* (now in print); he is also a member of the editorial board of *Chekhoviana*.

Medvedev, Aleksandr
Aleksandr Medvedev is Associate Professor at the University of Tiumen' in Russia, working at the School of Russian Literature. He holds a doctorate from Moscow State University, 1997, for his dissertation entitled 'Essays by V. V. Rozanov on F. M. Dostoevskii and L. N. Tolstoi (A Problem of Understanding)'. His research interests encompass Russian literature and religious-philosophical thought of the nineteenth and twentieth centuries (V. Rozanov, F. Dostoevskii, A. Chekhov, F. Tituchev, M. Prishvin, A. Tsvetaeva and I. Brodskii) in the historical-cultural context of 'big time'. He is the author of more than 50 scholarly publications, including: 'The principle of "big time" in Rozanov's essays on Russian literature' in *Russian literature of the Twentieth – Twenty-First centuries: problems of theory and methodology of research* (Moscow: MGU, 2008), 'Spiritual landscape of Russian literature of the Nineteenth century in V. V. Rozanov's perception' in *History of Russian literature: Proceedings of the XXXVII International philological conference* (St Petersburg: SPbGU, 2008), 'On Christian paradigm in Rozanov's perception of Russian literature' in *Rozanov's Legacy and Modernity* (Moscow: Russian political encyclopedia, 2009), 'Symbolism of oblique rays in Dostoevskii's oeuvre, and Russian Orthodox liturgical and theological tradition' in *Context-2008: historical-literary and theoretical research* (Moscow: IMLI RAN, 2009). He is the author of the article 'Chekhov' in *Rozanov Encyclopedia* (Moscow: Russian political encyclopedia, 2008), as well as of 30 articles in the same edition ('Culture', 'Morality', 'Utilitarianism', 'Essayistic Genre', 'Painting', 'Levitan', 'Tsvetaeva A.' and others). He is also the author of the article 'Rozanov' in *Chekhov Encyclopedia* (currently going to press) and contributing to the preparation of complete works of V. V. Rozanov.

Oklot, Michal

Michal Oklot is an Assistant Professor of Slavic Languages at Brown University, USA. He qualified with an MA from the University of Warsaw, Poland (where he also taught at the Department of Philosophy and Sociology) and with a PhD in Slavic Languages and Literatures from Northwestern University. Prior to Brown he taught at the University of Wisconsin-Madison and the American University in Cairo. He has taught courses on Russian, Polish, and English literature. His scholarly interests include Nikolai Gogol' and his twentieth-century successors; Russian and Polish modernism; and a comparative study of Slavic history of ideas and literary theory. He wrote *Phantasms of Matter in Gogol' (and Gombrowicz)* (Dalkey Archive Press, 2009) and numerous articles on Russian and Polish literature, studying writers including Schulz, Wittlin, Vincenz and Chekhov. He is currently working on a collection of Rozanov's texts on philosophy, religion and literature including translations, commentaries and interpretative essays; as well as on a work on Rozanov's effect on Russian and Polish modernist literature.

Senderovich, Savely

Savely Senderovich is Professor of Russian Literature and Medieval Studies at Cornell University, Ithaca, New York. He completed his PhD at New York University in 1977. He is the author of studies in Russian literature from the twelfth to the twentieth centuries, on the origin of Russian historiography in the eleventh century, the history of culture, folklore, and the history of German philosophy. His latest book is *Morphology of the Riddle* (Moscow 2008).

Stepanov, Andrei

Andrei Stepanov is Professor of Russian Literature at St Petersburg State University. He holds a doctorate from that university on 'Chekhov's Dramatic Art in the 1880s and the Poetics of Melodrama', awarded in 1996. His dissertation for a higher doctorate, on 'Issues of Communication in Chekhov's Works' was obtained in 2005 at Åbo Akademi, Turku, Finland, and at Moscow State University, Russia. His research interests include Chekhov's poetics, contemporary prose, literary theory and modern directions in literary criticism. He is the author of *Problemy kommunikatsii u Chekhova* ('Issues of Communication in Chekhov's Works', Moscow 2005) and 70 scholarly articles on Russian literature of the nineteenth century, Chekhov, problems of literary theory and contemporary prose. He also works as a book reviewer, translator and creative writer.

Tabachnikova, Olga

Olga Tabachnikova is a Leverhulme Early Career Fellow working on Irrationalism in Russian culture at the Department of Russian Studies of the

University of Bristol. In 2001–2002 she held an Entente Cordiale Scholarship at the Sorbonne and in 2007 completed her doctoral dissertation on Lev Shestov at the University of Bath, where she also taught Russian literature, culture and language, and worked on a Leverhulme Trust sponsored project on 'Russian-Jewish cultural continuity in the Diaspora'. She has published widely in the fields of Russian and Russian-Jewish literature and culture, with a focus on cultural continuity. Her annotated edition of the *Unpublished Correspondence of Lev Shestov and Boris de Schloezer* is now going to press. Together with Rosalind Marsh she has edited the forthcoming title *New Women's Writing in Russia and East Central Europe: Gender, Generation, and Identities* (Cambridge Scholars Press). Those of her publications which are thematically relevant to the present collection include book chapters 'Ot Chekhova k Dovlatovu: Proslavlenie bestsel'nosti, Ili Poetika, okazyvaiushchaiia soprotivlenie tiranii' ('From Chekhov to Dovlatov: Praising purposelessness, Or Poetics that resists tyranny') in *Filosofiia A. P. Chekhova (Philosophy of A. P. Chekhov)* (Irkutsk University Press, 2008, ed. A. Sobennikov), 'The Treatment of Aesthetics in Lev Shestov's Search for God' in *Aesthetics as a Religious Factor in Eastern and Western Christianity* (Leuven, Belgium: Peeters Publishers, 2006, eds. Wil van den Bercken and Jonathan Sutton) and 'Russian Diaspora in the Context of French Culture: Lev Shestov and Boris de Schloezer' in *Other Voices: Three Centuries of Cultural Dialogue between France, Britain and Russia* (forthcoming with Cambridge Scholars Press, ed. Graham Roberts), as well as numerous papers in scholarly journals. Olga has also published a book of her own poetry. Her early research career was in mathematics, with a PhD from the University of Bath, 1995.

Thaidigsmann, Karoline
Karoline Thaidigsmann is a Lecturer of Russian and Polish literature at the University of Heidelberg in Germany. After finishing her studies in Slavistics, Psychology and Theology, she received her PhD from Heidelberg University for her dissertation on the literary testimonies of Soviet prison camp inmates (*Lagererfahrung und Identität. Literarische Spiegelungen sowjetischer Lagerhaft in Texten von Varlam Šalamov, Lev Konson, Naum Nim und Andrej Sinjavskij*). Her research interests include Anton Chekhov, Russian and Polish literature of the twentieth century, especially the literature of atrocity.

Ure, Adam
Adam Ure received his PhD from the School of Slavonic and East European Studies of University College London, in 2009, for his thesis on the religious thought of Vasilii Rozanov. He has written on Russian intellectual and cultural history, and in particular on the shaping of Russian culture by theology. He is currently completing a monograph on Rozanov's religious philosophy.

www.ingramcontent.com/pod-product-compliance
Lightning Source LLC
Chambersburg PA
CBHW021820300426
44114CB00009BA/247